*The Communitarian Third Way*
*Alexandre Marc's Ordre Nouveau, 1930–2000*

Ordre Nouveau's "neither right nor left" movement, based on personalism and revolutionary federalism, helped shape modern Catholic political culture in France, the National Revolution instituted by the Vichy regime, the post-war European movement, and the contemporary European New Right. It influenced European youth exchanges, veterans' organizations, trade unions, religious groups, artists, and architects, even the executives of the French national railway system.

In *The Communitarian Third Way* John Hellman introduces us to the non-conformist Alexandre Marc, a Russian Jew who became a Christian convert and full-time professional revolutionary. Marc helped Le Corbusier launch *Plans*, imported the existential philosophy of Husserl and Heidegger to France, helped Mounier start *Esprit*, and was an important force in revitalizing traditional French Catholic political culture. Hellman uses interviews, unpublished correspondence, and diaries to situate Marc and the Ordre Nouveau group in the context of the French, German, and Belgian political culture of that time and explains the degree to which the ON group succeeded in institutionalizing their new order under Pétain. Hellman also examines their post-war legacy, represented by Alain de Benoist and the contemporary European New Right, shedding new light on the linkages between early national socialism and the political culture of Charles de Gaulle, François Mitterand, and pioneers of the post–World War II European movement.

JOHN HELLMAN, professor of history at McGill University, is the author of *The Knight-Monks of Vichy France: Uriage, 1940–1945*

# The Communitarian Third Way

*Alexandre Marc's Ordre Nouveau,*
*1930–2000*

JOHN HELLMAN

McGill-Queen's University Press
Montreal & Kingston · London · Ithaca

© McGill-Queen's University Press 2002
ISBN 0-7735-2376-6

Legal deposit fourth quarter 2002
Bibliothèque nationale du Québec

Printed in Canada on acid-free paper that is 100%
ancient forest free (100% post-consumer recycled),
processed chlorine free.

This book has been published with the help of a grant
from the Humanities and Social Sciences Federation of
Canada, using funds provided by the Social Sciences
and Humanities Research Council of Canada.

McGill-Queen's University Press acknowledges the
support of the Canada Council for the Arts for our
publishing program. We also acknowledge the financial
support of the Government of Canada through the
Book Publishing Industry Development Program
(BPIDP) for our publishing activities.

**National Library of Canada Cataloguing in Publication**

Hellman, John, 1940–
    The communitarian third way : Alexandre Marc's ordre
nouveau, 1930–2000 / John Hellman
    Includes bibliographical references and index.
    ISBN 0-7735-2376-6
    1. Marc, Alexandre.   2. Ordre nouveau.   3. Personal-
ism.   4. France—Politics and government—1914–1940.
5. Conservatism—France—History—20th century.
6. Youth movement—France—History—20th century.
I. Title.

DC389.H44 2002     320.944'09'043     C2002-901551-0

Typeset in 10/12 Baskerville by True to Type

*To Thomas*
*Franco-Texan poet and singer-songwriter*

# Contents

Acknowledgments   ix

Illustrations   xiii

Introduction: The Non-Conformist Third Way   3

1  The Invention of a French Conservative Revolution: Alexandre Marc, Non-Conformism, Young Germany, and Ordre Nouveau   13

2  The Sohlberg Spirit (January 1931–May 1932)   29

3  Left-Wing Nazis, Revolutionary Conservatives, and Otto Neumann   51

4  Hitler: German Adversaries, French Converts, and a Letter to the Chancellor   71

5  The Sohlbergkreis Heritage, the Paris Riots, and the French Popular Front (6 February 1934–June 1936)   97

6  Otto Neumann in Belgium, Networking for the New Order (January 1933–September 1938)   125

7  The Munich Agreements, the *Fédérés*, Defeat and Occupation (29 September 1938 to the Liberation)   159

8  Alexandre Marc's Memories and the European New Right   185

Notes   201

Index   281

# Acknowledgments

For thoughtful reading of part or all of the manuscript, particular gratitude is due to Oz Arnal, Michel Dobry, Bill Irvine, Christian Roy, Josef Schmidt, Bob Soucy, Zeev Sternhell, and Bob Zaretsky. Judy Williams, editor, and Joan McGilvray, coordinating editor, of McGill-Queen's University Press, were outstandingly helpful and supportive. For an opportunity to present some of the material here for informed criticism special gratitude is owed to the Arriba courses (Lisbon), the colloquium in honour of Jacob Talmon (Israeli Academy of Arts and Sciences), the Columbia University colloquium in honour of Robert Paxton, and the Society for French Historical Studies. Among the individuals with whom the subject of this book was discussed particular gratitude is due, above all, to Alexandre and Suzanne Marc, but also to Mireille Marc-Lipiansky, Jean-Louis Onimus, and Christian Roy, and to the members of the community Les Murs Blancs at Chatenay-Malabry for their hospitality over the years. And, in alphabetical order:

Bruno Ackerman
Maurice Agulhon
Donald Baker
François-George Barbier
Gregory and Shirley Baum
François and Renée Bedarida
Albrecht Betz
Hubert Beuve-Méry
Pierre Birnbaum

Anne-Marie Bourdhouxe
Jon Braun
William Bush
M.-D. Chenu, OP
Martin J. Corbin
Rita Corbin
Aline Coutrot
Jackie Clarke
Joe Cunneen

Cardinal Jean Daniélou
Charles Davis
Antoine Delestre
Esther Delisle
Ray Dennehy
Michel Dobry
Jean-Marie Domenach
René-Jean Dupuy
Henry W. Ehrmann
Marc Ferro
Catherine Fieschi
Paul and Simone Fraisse
Jocelyn George
Bertram Gordon
Frank Guttmann
Bernard and Elizabeth Guyon
Robert Hellman
Patrice Higonnet
Peter C. Hoffmann
Stanley Hoffmann
Georges Hourdin
Dick Howard
Guy Hoyon
Deal Hudson
H. Stuart Hughes
Patrick Hutton
Tony Judt
M. and Mme Jean Lacroix
Alain Lemee
Jean-Louis Loubet del Bayle
Cardinal Henri de Lubac
Alexandre and Suzanne Marc
Edmond Marc-Lipiansky

Mireille Marc-Lipiansky
Henri-Irenée Marrou
Bill Miller
Fr. Joe Moody
André Moosmann
Francis J. Murphy
Max and Monique Nemni
Emile Noel
Jean Onimus
John W. Padberg, SJ
Denis Pechanski
Gerard Pelletier
Simone Pétrement
Antonio Costa Pinto
Miranda Pollard
Emile Poulat
Antoine Prost
Jean-Pierre Rioux
Henri Rousso
Bernard Plongeron
R. William Rauch, Jr
Denis de Rougemont
David Schalk
Maurice Schumann
Pierre de Senarclens
Anthony O. Simon
Alain-Gérard Slama
Zeev Sternhell
Charles and Alba Taylor
René Thoreval
M and Mme Michel Trebitsch
Rt. Hon. Pierre Elliott Trudeau
Bob Zaretsky

Among those kind enough to provide information by correspondence, particular gratitude is due to:

Michel Bergès
Albrecht Betz
Etienne Borne
Philippe Burrin
Bernard Charbonneau
Bernard Comte
Dominican Fathers (La Tour
   Maubourg)

Yves Congar, OP
Jacques Ellul
Gaston Fessard, SJ
Etienne Gilson
Laurent Greilsamer

For help with the illustrations:

Christian Roy (Faculty of Theology, Université Laval), Etienne Hellman (Christie's, Paris), Frédéric Lepine (CIFE, Nice), the staff of the Bibliothèque Forney, Paris, and of the library of the Fogg Art Museum, Harvard University, Marilyn Berger (Blackader-Lauterman Library, McGill), and, above all, the late Alexandre and Suzanne Marc.

Arnaud Dandieu (1897–1933). Librarian, writer, inventor of "personalism," and
founder of the review *L'Ordre Nouveau*

Arnaud Dandieu's study, 11 rue Spontini in Paris, where the review *L'Ordre
Nouveau* (1933–38) was born.

Robert Aron (1898–1975) Coauthor, with
Dandieu, of *Décadence de la nation française*
(1931), *Le Cancer américain* (1931), and
*La Révolution necessaire* (1933) and director of the review *L'Ordre Nouveau.* First historian of the Vichy regime, he was elected
to the Académie française.

"*L'Atelier*": the 1931 portrait painted by artist Jean Dries (b.
1905) of his Parisian studio, where the meetings of the Ordre
Nouveau movement were held from 1930 (the year in which
he toured Spain, painting landscapes, with Alexandre Marc).

This 1932 portrait by Jean Dries is of Henri Daniel-Rops
(Henri Petiot) (b. 1901), generational spokesman, popularizer of Ordre Nouveau ideas, and historian of Christianity,
who became a member of the Académie française. A copy
graced Alexandre Marc's living room.

Alexandre Marc (Marc-Lipiansky) (b. Odessa 1904, d. Vence 2000) in 1934. Founder of the Ordre Nouveau movement, of "personalism," and of the European federalist movement.

Alexandre Marc as leader of the European Federalist Movement (c. 1947)

Alexandre Marc in his nineties: the commemorative portrait published by his organization.

Harro Schulze-Boysen (1909–1942). This is a copy of the photo which held a place of honour in Alexandre Marc's living room in Vence. Descendant of Admiral Tirpitz, founder of the Imperial Navy, Berlin representative of the Amis de *Plans* and Ordre Nouveau, leader of Gegner, officer in the Luftwaffe, he was named a member of his friend Reichsmarschall Herman Goering's Institute of Research before becoming a leader of the Stalinist Red Orchestra Resistance group and being hanged as a traitor in 1942.

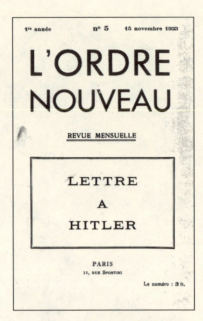

A controversial issue of *L'Ordre Nouveau*

A subscription flyer advertising *L'Ordre Nouveau*

Emmanuel Mounier visiting Denis de Rougement in Frankfurt in June 1936. Otto Abetz had arranged a semester's teaching position for de Rougement at the university.

Swiss existential theologian Karl Barth (right), Barth's young disciple Denis de Rougemont (left), and Alexandre Marc in 1934 in the Dominican convent of Juvisy. Marc and Suzanne Jean of the New Britain movement had been married there the previous November.

The Château Bayard at St Martin d'Uriage,
above Grenoble, seat of the Pétain regime's
Ecole Nationale Supérieure des Cadres.

"Dominican Life. The taking of the habit. Chanting the Te Deum, the choir
greet their new brother." On this postcard (10 October 1933, just days after
Marc's baptism), theologian Yves Congar, OP, wrote from the Dominican convent of Le Saulchoir, Kain, Belgium, to Marc of his entry into "the City of
which the Lamb is the Light": "More than ever I think of you with affection
and the great desire to see you joyful in the truth. That will not settle all questions, I know, as there are still some anguishing ones to resolve. Stay brave!"

The "Voisin Plan" by Le Corbusier (Charles-Edouard Jeanneret)
(1887–1965) graced his memorable Pavillon de l'Esprit Nouveau at the Arts
Décoratifs Exhibition in Paris (1925). On 20 May 1927 he gave a slide presentation of his plans for the renewal of Paris for the rank-and-file fascists of
George Valois's *Le Faisceau* attending the inauguration of their new headquarters. An illustration from, and article on, the "Voisin Plan" had been
published on the title page of Valois's *Nouveau siècle* (1 May 1927) and during the following months Valois published a series of essays in which he
aligned his conception of the fascist "New Order" with Le Corbusier's "New
City." Le Corbusier would develop his ideas on architectural renewal in *L'E-
sprit nouveau* and *Plans* (1931–32). During his eighteen months at Vichy
(1941–42) he was enthusiastic about the Pétain regime's Order of Architects, comparing them to the master builders of medieval Europe and envisaging them carrying out a massive reconstruction program under the direction of an official to be called *l'ordonnateur* (presumably himself).

Le Corbusier, three years after completing the pilgrimage church at Ronchamps with the Dominican Father Couturier, constructing the monastery of La Tourette, at l'Abresle, near Lyon.

This main church of La Tourette is considered, with Ronchamps, to be one of the most important churches, architecturally, of the twentieth century.

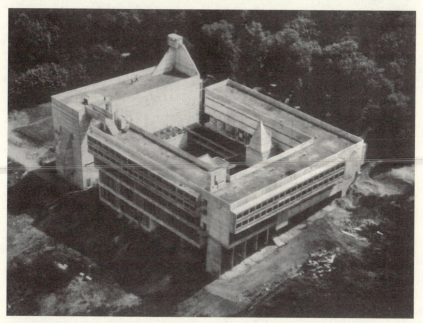

This aerial view of La Tourette shows the church on the left. The small pyramid within the cloister is the roof of the oratory for private prayer.

Alexandre Marc and the author at the Institut Universitaire Européen, the European community's graduate school for advanced study, housed in a former Franciscan monastery at San Domenico di Fiesole (Florence), 14 December 1992. This was the sixth annual meeting of the Réseau d'historiens et de chercheurs sur le personnalisme et le fédéralisme founded by Marc.

*The Communitarian Third Way*

# Introduction
# The Non-Conformist Third Way

During the 1930s and World War II, the French invented a new "non-conformist" politics: so cleverly packaged, it has seldom been seen for what it really was. Claiming to be non-conformists, a group of young journalists, students, and professors invented an anti-democratic and anti-liberal "personalist" approach to life which, although militantly anti-communist, would claim to be "neither of the Right nor of the Left"; it spawned French and Belgian variants of that German "conservative revolution" which helped carry the national socialists to power. Originally intended to help engender a "New Middle Ages" in which the French and other Europeans could husband aspects of their spiritual heritage in a German-dominated New Order, personalist communitarianism had important, enduring, influence.

The New Middle Ages' authoritarian, elitist educational system was to repudiate the Enlightenment and the French Revolution, and Marxism, and be shaped by natural aristocrats – old-stock Frenchmen, sensitive to those invisible realities of their French Catholic heritage neglected by "secular" Jews, Masons, Marxists, non-Europeans, and Americans. The personalist communitarian movement would be against the dictatorship of the proletariat but for the new "national" socialism which favoured a people's heritage and the native born. Expectations of an eventual national socialist victory would generate clandestine networking and planning among the initiated,[1] who – when faced with the mortal danger of Stalinist insurgents subverting weak republican institutions – would favour a nationalist socialist or fascist Europe as the lesser of two evils.

The new personalist discourse would encourage the young to dismiss communism, the free market economy, and liberal and republican values as out of date ... even after the Germans were defeated. Some pre-war non-conformists, such as the political leaders François Mitterrand and Charles de Gaulle, or intellectuals Jacques Maritain and Emmanuel Mounier, would become respectable and well known in France. Other non-conformists, who would be less known after the war, included the interesting and illustrative figure Alexandre Marc.

Anti-Bolshevik Russian exile, Germanophile Jewish convert to Catholicism, Marc would come to embarrass his old comrades by steadfastly maintaining that the non-conformism which he would be instrumental in creating had ... German origins. This Nietzschean anti-Hitler national socialist would claim that Europe owed far more to the conservative revolution than had been admitted. Evoking "pure," "original," national socialism – a generational experience for a "magnificent youth" in Germany, and a fortunate few in France, tragically betrayed by Hitler – Marc would stick out for revealing a family secret well-known to the initiated: the new, fresh, constructive national-socialism had deeply and permanently influenced a European elite.

The anti-individualist, spiritualist, or personalist attack on liberal democracy, which Marc discovered among young Action Française Christian philosophers in the late 1920s, would be melded by him with German ideas to create the discourse for a spiritualized, communitarian, French national socialism. When Marc's defining experience, which he would treasure to his dying day, became politically incorrect, many of his old comrades, and their friends or sympathizers in the French historical establishment, would try to marginalize, if not forget, what he kept saying and what he represented.

Marc's Nietzschean anti-Judaism, conversion to Catholicism and German philosophy, and bonding with tightly knit bands of fervent young men in a conservative insurrection against modern materialism would prove less unique than his stubborn, unshakeable fidelity to the value of his experiences. As it becomes more acceptable to respect the goals of original national socialism, an exposition of Marc's fraternal elitism, embrace of the European heritage, committed anti-communism, and passion for charismatic leaders reveals the stark realities behind his abstract, often murky or enigmatic, rhetoric.

For Marc, the challenge would be to create a hierarchical, anti-individualistic, ethnically based, communitarian, heritage-sensitive socialism, a spiritualistic "New Order" which husbanded the values of both medieval Europe and the anti-Marxist German conservative revolution. What Marc and his *compagnons* said would contrast with what they did – when their noble rhetoric justified the violence and exclusion employed to create their New Order.

A small elite of highly cerebral anti-intellectuals, whose intense lucubrations have been largely forgotten, Marc and his friends nevertheless would represent a France that might have been, a seductive experience and ideal. Marc came to dream of a federated "Europe of a hundred flags" (in Alain de Benoist's phrase) in which eroding ethnic, regional, and religious values and heritage would be reinvigorated by new economic and political structures of a new peoples-based European socialism, planned and run by a network of enlightened elites.

Interviews, diaries, pocket agenda, and unpublished correspondence would reveal not only what the non-conformists proposed but also how they acted.[2] Public quarrels among the initiated would allow non-conformists to camouflage strategic positioning for an anticipated European civil war: blazoned criticism of Hitler and Mussolini, of French fascists or Nazis, would permit the New Right non-conformists to work with the Old Right Action Française nationalists, to quietly infiltrate veterans' organizations, think tanks of architects and engineers, Franco-German contacts, various publications, the executive of the vital French national railways system, and the French Socialist and Communist parties. When the final struggle against the communists came, networks of trusted and trustworthy allies with a shared agenda in publishing, religious institutions, youth movements and education, and the officer corps of the army would hold pivotal positions.

Defeated post-republican France in summer 1940 saw public quarrels set aside in the effort to confront the real, the Stalinist, threat. The Nazis might be brutes but one could work with them toward the common goal of a sanitized France in a new sort of Europe. Non-conformists provided sophisticated critical analyses of the Nazis or the fascists for important Catholic publications and organizations, large veterans' associations like the Croix de Feu and the Parti social français (PSF), the quasi-Nazi Parti populiare français (PPF) of Doriot, and the clandestine Cagoule organizations, all the while focusing on the *real* enemy: communism. These middle or upper-class Nietzscheans, White Russian exiles, royalists, religious converts, or corporatists, understandably considered the communists their mortal enemies. So the enemies of their enemies became their friends.[3]

When non-conformists and personalists earnestly explained themselves, their critics accused them of "muddying their waters in order to make them seem deep." After philosopher Jacques Maritain's conversion, a matter of great public interest and emulation,[4] Alexandre Marc would describe his own evolution (from Russian literature via Kant and Berdyaev, toward phenomenology) as if he had spent his youth in a great library reading room, instead of in propagandist journalism, travel, conspiratorial meetings, networking, and plotting. While Marc would have a conversion experience in which he was, like Maritain, "turned inside out, like a glove," it would come less from discovering St Augustine's *Confessions* in the Bibliothèque Nationale than from dramatic encounters with the charismatic leaders of the new German youth movements. These would precipitate his interest in Nietzsche and the new German existentialist philosophy, his conversion to communitarian Catholicism, his fraternizing with new style revolutionaries, and his passion to transmit the spirit of those princely "new men," the German youth elite, to others. Soon Alexandre Marc would be taken, as an aspiring leader of European Youth, to visit the "Brown Hall" Nazi headquarters in Munich by flamboyant young Harro Schulze-Boysen, candidate for leadership of the Hitler Youth. From what he would observe there, Marc imagined new men being catapulted to leadership positions in France through a national program of "affirmative action." This top-down corporatist program would allow a fresh meritocracy of old-stock Frenchmen distinguished for their leadership qualities to liquidate the old liberal-democratic and capitalist society's materialism and pseudo-democracy, creating a New Order that was truly French.

The attacks on liberal democracy by Marc and his friends had elaborate philosophical baggage. But the real reason why Marc and company disliked liberal democracy was the way its political and economic system over-represented "others," while under-representing the best and the brightest native Europeans. Thus Marc, Jewish immigrant convert, became more French than the French, more Catholic than the Catholics, in contesting the right of "others" to hold power in France as they did in his native Russia, by forming the cream of young "true Europeans" to lead the counter-attack against the rootless subversives ruining the old continent and to fight to establish a healthy, heritage-based European order.

Given the growing resentment against the "others" living and working among Europe's "ancient peoples," Marc's unique populist, regionalistic, federalist communitarianism was – and is – of special interest to those seeking a Third Way for Europe. He would encourage the frank and forthright abandonment of liberal and democratic values in order to construct revitalized ethnic communities which would be appreciative of their traditions, their historical particularities and roots. Not surprisingly, many of Marc's non-conformist friends were to come from privileged Catholic and/or royalist backgrounds – proudly French and Catholic but too highly educated and civilized to indulge in vulgar racism. The Ordre Nouveau (ON) movement which Marc founded included Jews, Protestants, and agnostics, and Marc was to serve as an important link between the European ON movement and potential allies.

When harsh Nazi and fascist realities shocked Marc and his comrades, they would carefully contextualize their vivid memories of the glorious virility and dynamism, the seductiveness, of the early Nazi leadership and of the European New Order. After World War II, the non-conformists would even be happy to be remembered as a marginal, relatively inconsequential segment of that "rebellion of minorities" which furnished some leaders for both the Vichy regime and the Resistance. But non-conformists should also be remembered as the architects of a clandestine, serious, Third Way political and cultural option – a French national socialism with a sophisticated agenda for the economy, international relations, the arts, education, and popular and high culture. All of this might have shaped Europe for generations if Germany had won World War II. In any case elements of the non-conformist Third Way did endure after the war in the European movement, the legacy of Charles de Gaulle and François Mitterrand, and French Catholic religiousness, as well as in the thinking of the contemporary European New Right.

Hitler's failed invasion of the Soviet Union would scuttle dreams of a national socialist France in a European New Order of self-affirming peoples. Instead there was to be the increasingly brutal exploitation of France by a desperate German war machine. The creative and imaginative intellectual architects of the Vichy regime would gave way to servile collaborationists willing to compromise French interests for the Wehrmacht's agenda. Non-conformists working for the Pétain regime came to aid friendly elements of the Resistance against the Germans, emerging at the liberation with the Resistance credentials required for distinguished post-war careers.

The personalist communitarian French New Order model – whether "pure" national socialist, or "white" fascist – would afford a conversion experience projecting a young French elite simultaneously into a warm past and a bright future. This anti-modern modernism, an honourable, defining, unforgettable bonding experience, came to engender a discreetly cherished memory.[5] Wartime mystical communitarianism would draw people into the Scouts or young Christian workers, the Pétainist youth movements *Chantiers de la jeunesse* and *Compagnons de France*, and the fanatically anti-communist counter-insurgents in the *milice*, as well as into Resistance organizations. Christian traditions and values would serve to justify exclusionary and racist laws formulated and administered by high-profile Christian functionaries. Barbarous and brutal behaviour was to be given highbrow justification: the prospect of a post-Marxist, post-capitalist, post-secular New Middle Ages, a New Order Europe. The new Europe would be ascetic rather than self-indulgent, anti-individualist, anti-liberal, anti-American, anti-democratic ... but it would also be creatively spiritual, cultured, heritage-respecting, chivalrous, inspiring and uplifting, fraternally personalist and communitarian.

After World War II, non-conformists were to be active all across the new political spectrum. With Maurras disgraced for collaborationism, his former secretary Jean de Fabrègues, whose Resistance credentials were certified by his former protégé François Mitterrand, would direct the mainstream magazine *La France Catholique* – while mentoring a classic history of the non-conformist movement. Men like Alexandre Marc, Denis de Rougement, and Thierry Maulnier would all translate their old values into the new discourse of the European federalists promoting a united Europe – a white, Christian, federated Europe, uniting Germany and France against the Stalinist East, Third World immigration, Islamic fundamentalism, and American influence. For example, ON's Albert Ollivier and Xavier de Lignac (Jean Chauveau) would move from the Jeune France national cultural organization at Vichy to work for old ON friend Charles de Gaulle – first as propagandists for his anti-communist, patriotic, and populist RPF party, then for the Fifth Republic's highly centralized French National Radio system. Hubert Beuve-Méry would move from Vichy's National Leadership School at Uriage to found *Le Monde*, taking a number of non-conformist intellectuals (e.g., Jean Lacroix and Pierre-Henri Simon of *Esprit*) to aid him in that enterprise.

Non-conformists would never voice public regrets about their sympathy for original German national socialism or its influence on France. Rather than frankly clarifying, documenting, and assessing their itineraries, they came to pretend that their pre-war political beliefs were either youthful folly, which had never really got anywhere, or else left-wing anti-fascist, and certainly not leading to a distinctive French fascism or national socialism: they presented themselves as anti-individualist and anti-capitalist, revolutionary but traditionalist, progressive but spiritualistic, corporatist but populist, quietly supportive of but independent from Nazi Germany. In fact an enthusiastic experiment in France was soon to be undermined by the shift of fortune in the European civil war, which, had the war turned out differently, might have led to the French personalists having much more influence on France and Europe. For Third Way communitarian personalism would remain alluring for post-war champions of bringing Germany and France closer together in a united, anti-communist, Europe. It was also to be valued, and appear as new, in Alain de Benoist's GRECE and in the European New Right, and particularly in the forms of Roman Catholic religious and political culture to be encouraged by Pope John Paul II.

### THE BRIGHTER SIDE

Non-conformism would be remembered as a fresh, original, invigorating, creative political culture with a proud legacy[6] – producing a selfless, idealistic, high-minded Europeanist generation committed to ending those ethnic animosities (particularly between Germans and French) that had ravaged the continent. A program of exchanges between European youth, a European Army (as endorsed by Mitterrand), a European University (administered in Florence, by Emile Noël), and a European identity over against the USA and the Moslem world (as promoted by *Esprit* faithful Jacques Delors) would result.

Non-conformism would also produce resisters against Hitlerite domination of the old continent: Charles de Gaulle, François Mitterrand, Henri Frenay of *Combat*, Emmanuel Mounier, Pierre Dunoyer de Segonzac, Hubert Beuve-Méry, Jean-Marie Domenach, and a host of others directly nurtured by non-conformism, or closely allied with non-conformists, fought to drive the Germans from France.

Non-conformism was to produce visionary intellectuals: Le Corbusier as architect of the New City, and of a new liturgy at Ronchamps, Maurice Blanchot and Paul de Man as literary critics, Rougemont, Marc, and Delors as builders of a united Europe, Mounier, Henri de Lubac, Yves Congar, and the new theology of the Second Vatican Council,[7] philosophers Jean Lacroix and Paul Ricœur, world-renowned critics of technology Jacques Ellul and Bernard Charbonneau. There was also to be Beuve-Méry and his great Uriage-inspired *Le Monde*, de Gaulle as leader of a new, post–Third Republic, Europe against American hegemony. The brilliant, elusive François Mitterrand – publicly the socialist, privately the mystical, double-lived, memory-cultivating, right-wing non-conformist – would become the architect of a new socialism built upon Franco-German friendship, French regionalism, mollifying the Pétainists, and undermining the PCF. Mitterrand would illustrate how non-conformism could produce leadership, *chefs*, in the ultra-individualistic, allegedly leaderless, France of the Third Republic. Non-conformism – with its strong culture-Catholic vein – came to produce an attractive, anti-liberal and anti-capitalist communitarian alternative to Marxism: the result was to be the kind of "white fascism" which would surface among Vichy's intellectual elites. Subsequently, Mitterrand could become, as a rooted, romantic Europeanist, Pétainist, and socialist – one of the most influential leaders of modern France and post-war Europe.

With François Mitterrand, non-conformism came to engender a new politics, attracting the best and the brightest with a political culture promising to transcend self-interest and demagoguery, as non-conformists would help produce a state culture in which managed memory and tradition gave people roots, purpose, and identity. In Jeune France under Pétain (or in France, or Canada, today), intellectuals nurtured by non-conformism would recognize that cultural hegemony was vitally important and so shape and support high culture with considerable effect.

Non-conformism would encourage a serious and sophisticated Nietzschean critique of the Christian tradition and its effect on the Western sense of self. The non-conformist intelligentsia would produce a critique of Americanization and modernity to help European elites define their heritage, while a mixing of elitist Christianity and anti-modern attitudes came to engender, in Ellul and Charbonneau's non-conformists' circle of southwestern France, that country's first ecological movement.

### THE DARK SIDE

The dark side of the non-conformist movement was to be most evident when Europeanist communitarianism represented German anti-egalitarianism, racism, and legitimation of exclusionary impulses. Non-conformism would spawn French collaborators to second Pétain or to help administer the German occupation. Jean Luchaire, Mitterrand, the Uriage group, Paul Flamand, Jean Jardin, Mounier, and a host of others – at least for a time – would help the effort to establish a refined French fascist ideology for France to find her place in a European New Order.

Non-conformism would be particularly adept at spawning collaborationist intelligentsia, youth leaders, and aesthetics: Jean Luchaire, novelist Pierre Drieu la Rochelle, the golden age of Vichy film, the Vichy state culture promoted by Jeune France, the ideology for the Pétainist *milicien* counter-insurgency force, and even encouragement for some French and Belgian volunteers defending Europe alongside the German army on the Eastern Front. The deference to the born *chef* encouraged by non-conformism would help produce Pétainism, Vichy militia leaders, and a host of lesser figures who led people into a repressive, irrational French fascism, which vociferously attacked the political culture of the Popular Front, and of liberal democracy.

Non-conformist leaders would often patronize the middle classes, peasants, and working people with their elitist and top-down, rather than electoral, politics, as they networked in the corridors of power rather than trying to understand the masses and their expressed needs and good sense.[8] Their subsidized state culture would become manipulative, totalitarian, and exclusionary toward culture or cultures, even races, which were not "correctly" rooted (e.g., purging French film of Hollywood influences).

Unlike Marxism or Nazism, or some forms of fascism, French non-conformist fascism would tolerate Christian spirituality (if purified by a Nietzschean critique). But Simone Weil, a non-conformist herself in the 1930s, would reproach her old comrades for having transmuted Christianity into a selfish personalist communitarian ideology directed by pretentious elites of knight-monks and intellectualist theologians for whom generosity and openness displaced charity and kindness, and for whom americanization, modernity, and liberalism were worse than Nazi, Pétainist, or Stalinist totalitarianism.[9] Non-conformists' ecologism would make wilderness more important than people, engendering a neo-pagan elite of architects, metaphysicians, Alpinists, historians, theologians, worker-priests, pilots, journalists, and engineers who would find the working classes obtuse to the "human," healthy living environment which would have to be provided for them.

CONFLICTUAL MEMORIES

In his late eighties, venerated patriarch of a wing of the European federalist movement, Alexandre Marc was invited to return to his native Russia after seventy years of exile to address the former Soviet Academy of Sciences – despite Soviet officials having considered him a dangerous threat to their anti-nationalist vision.[10] With the Cold War apparently over, Marc opened his archives and gave interviews which revealed the decisive attraction exercised by the pre- Hitlerite German youth revolution. He lived to be hailed as a prophet by certain personalities on the Left, but particularly among the European New Right intelligentsia, for whom he represented a Europe which might have been.

When Alexandre Marc's recollections of French contacts with pre-war German youth movements, as reported in my *Emmanuel Mounier and the New Catholic Left, 1930–1950* (Toronto and London: University of Toronto Press, 1981), were queried, he gave an extensive series of interviews to Christian Roy and me, supported by extensive archival resources. In Vence and Nice, in 1988 and 1989, we recorded that material onto a database. Unless otherwise noted, those letters and diaries are central primary sources for this book. Employing this material and sources discovered in other European countries, Roy wrote his PhD dissertation on the origins of personalism, Alexandre Marc et la Jeune Europe, 1904–1934: L'Ordre Nouveau aux origines du personnalisme (Montreal: McGill University, 1993); it was published with that same title by Alexandre Marc's CIFE (Nice: Presses d'Europe, 1999) with an afterword by Thomas Keller.

Besides the true story of the origins of personalism, the Marc archives also revealed the history of personalist and federalist semi-clandestine organizations in France, Belgium, Germany, and Quebec – the entire anti-liberal counter-culture in the background of the National Revolution of Vichy, and the rise to power of an entire generation after the war. This particularly interested me, for I value the liberal democratic traditions that Marc repudiated. Christian Roy, who is generally sympathetic to Marc's positions, found the earlier period of greater importance. I am very grateful to Christian Roy for having generously contributed editorial suggestions, analyses, and factual additions, particularly to the pre-1934 section of this book; his doctoral dissertation constitutes a very important contribution to scholarship on this subject. Our disagreement over what to make of Marc's career suggests the complexity of the subject.

# 1 The Invention of a French Conservative Revolution: Alexandre Marc, Non-Conformism, Young Germany, and Ordre Nouveau

Alexandre Marc was one of the several young Russian exiles in inter-war Paris who detested communism and was looking for a totally new politics:[1] his family had been despoiled by the Bolshevik revolution, his Moscow comrades mowed down around him by machine-gun fire in a street demonstration, and his closest friends executed by the Cheka. After he had fled to Paris in 1919 to study in the famous Lycée Saint-Louis, and then in "Sciences Po" (the private Institute of Political Studies) in the Latin Quarter, he acquired several French comrades with lifelong interests similar to his own. Then, in Berlin in 1922, he encountered the legendary exiled Russian philosopher-prophet Nicholas Berdyaev, whose prophecies of Europe abandoning communism and liberal capitalism for "a New Middle Ages," inspired by new philosophies of communitarian, fraternal spirituality, profoundly affected Marc, who had discovered something new and exciting which he could bring to his new French friends.

Marc could envisage a New Middle Ages more easily than his French comrades because he had seen new ideas, a new mentality, dramatically transform Russia, and so he went directly to study the new German philosophies of phenomenology and existentialism with their masters – Edmund Husserl and Martin Heidegger, Max Scheler and Karl Jaspers and began to see the flourishing German youth movements as embodying this new German philosophy.

Returning to Paris enthusiastic about his German experiences, Marc began organizing German and French youth for the "spiritual revolution," helping bring out new reviews in early 1930s Paris such as *Plans, Esprit,* and Marc's own *Ordre Nouveau*. Soon alumni of his Franco-German encounters were helping Marc's movement publish a review which attracted people, such as Hitler's experts on France,[2] King Albert I of Belgium,[3] and Spanish Falangist leader José Antonio Primo de Rivera,[4] who were interested in thinking about the meaning of fascism and national socialism in a comparative and world-historical perspective. Young Catholics of *Esprit*, groping toward something like a Catholic or "white" fascism or national socialism, were soon trying to Catholicize *Ordre Nouveau*'s ideas.[5] Through Marc's friendship with Otto Abetz, the young German who would become Foreign Minister Joachim von Ribbentrop's expert on French affairs (before serving as Hitler's ambassador to occupied Paris), Marc organized gatherings for people he called "non-conformists" of neither Right nor Left inspired by a new Franco-German post-individualistic philosophy: "personalism."[6] This distinctive, elusive[7] philosophy would be salvaged from its controversial origins before and during World War II to become a kind of reigning philosophical orthodoxy in the Polish pope's Roman Catholic church. This led a first-hand observer at its birth in 1931–32, Denis de Rougemont,[8] to point out that personalism had in fact been largely invented by a relatively unknown Russian Jew: Alexandre Marc.[9] De Rougemont had advanced controversial historical hypotheses before,[10] but a careful dating of texts substantiated this one.[11]

Alexandre Marc discovered that his personalist jargon attracted all sorts of people disgruntled with "conformist" politics: not only anti-Marxist Russian Jewish converts to Christianity like him, but a whole range of spiritual revolutionaries, German youth movement leaders, Action Française dissidents, left-wing Nazi rivals to Hitler, and "National-Bolsheviks." He found that people scornful of egalitarianism and individualism, alienated from Marxism and liberal democratic political culture, could see their diverging aspirations rooted in a common concern for the human person and a rejection of liberal individualism.[12] Marc's day-to-day itinerary during the 1920s, 1930s and 1940s reveals growing hopes for a communitarian spiritual revolution, a New Middle Ages in Europe, a New Order shaped by new sorts of Nietzschean Christians. Inventing a spurious German theologian to promote his ideas, Marc Christianized the German-inspired personalism of his Ordre Nouveau (ON) affording the French Catholic communitarians of *Esprit* an ideology. His essay describing a "Young Europe" on the verge of revolution was honoured by the Académie française.

But in early 1933 Alexandre Marc would see his German allies smashed by Hitler, and then, the following summer, ON's genius, Arnaud Dandieu, take sick and die just as his call for "la révolution nécessaire" appeared. In September, Marc, unnerved by Dandieu's deathbed mysticism, was baptised a Roman Catholic; in October his immigrant status in France was questioned by the police; in November, he secretly married Suzanne Jean, a French representative of a British spiritual revolution movement. That same month he published a controversial open letter to Hitler which led the *Esprit* Catholics to distance themselves from him and come up with their own variety of "communitarian personalism." We shall see how Marc then gave talks on the ideas of Charles de Gaulle, a new ON sympathizer, and was hired to help run some important, original Catholic publications.

We shall see how difficulties with the police over his visa status led Marc, in April 1934, to move to southwestern France: first to a cabin constructed for him by a priest-admirer on the grounds of a convent near Pau, and then, in August 1937, to a farm near Aix-en-Provence. From there he would try to create regional groupings of bright young men who shared his dream of a total spiritual-communitarian national revolution for France. After the defeat of Belgium and France, a number of Marc's comrades abruptly surfaced in influential positions in both countries.[13]

When, in August 1940, Marc, just demobilized, visited a newly influential Emmanuel Mounier at France's new capital at Vichy, had not the ON movement come into its own? But Marc would refuse offers to work in places like the Mounierist National Leadership School at Uriage, or the cultural associations or propaganda ministries which ON alumni were helping to direct, and by the end of 1942, Marc (a baptized Catholic, but known to be Jewish) will have fled with his family to Switzerland, where – unlike most Jewish refugees, who were turned away – he was given political refugee status for the duration of the war. His ON comrade Jean Jardin, Pierre Laval's chief of staff, had also left France to take up residence there. How did it happen, then, that several of Marc's old comrades moved from administering Vichy organizations to Charles de Gaulle's,[14] notably the post-war Rassemblement du Peuple Français (RPF), described as akin to a French fascist movement?[15]

Just after World War II, ON co-founder Robert Aron wrote the most influential history of the Vichy regime – deftly writing the non-conformists and ON out of its origins and administration – and was elected to the Académie française. We shall see how Marc, more single-minded and less opportunistic than Aron, co-founded movements for a united, federalist Europe (integrating the Germans, valuing ethnic differences) which provided political respectability for a number of ex-fascist and ex-Pétainist anti-communists. We shall see how Marc's European federalism rallied people sceptical about the new spirit of working with Stalinists that had been fostered by the Resistance, and how his movement, Fédération, maintained that ethnicity was a vital historical force and that the peoples of Eastern Europe would eventually reassert themselves.[16]

Why, after World War II, did Marc never become as well known as several of his pre-war comrades, disciples, or acolytes such as Le Corbusier, Gabriel Marcel, Mounier, Henri Daniel-Rops, Robert Aron, or Philip Lamour?[17] For whatever reasons, Marc stayed in the provinces and, in 1954, was named director of the Centre International de Formation Européenne (CIFE) and of the Institut Européen des Hautes Etudes Internationales in Nice. His anti-communism and extensive contacts with the European New Right were appreciated by the local Médecin political dynasty and the *pieds-noirs*. Nicknamed "the Pope of European Federalism" (for his federalist dogma and authoritarian ways), he published federalist tracts,[18] served as ideologue for the review *L'Europe en formation*, and taught at the CIFE's Collège universitaire d'études fédéralistes in Aosta, Italy. At his death on 22 February 2000, his importance as a post-war federalist and Europeanist – not as a vital inter-war networker and middleman of ideas – would be noted by a comrade in a brief *Le Monde* obituary.

## THE "NON-CONFORMISTS OF 1930"

A special issue of the prestigious *Nouvelle Revue Française* in 1932 portrayed the "new generation of intellectuals" in Paris as political mavericks and concluded that they were moving outside of mainstream politics, like the young German "conservative revolutionaries": neo-Catholics and neo-Marxists who did not conform to the ways of the older generation. But the following year Hitler came to power and "German youth, after having awakened immeasurable hopes in the world," generational spokesman Alexandre Marc lamented, "was beginning to betray them."[19]

Religion was more important for Paris-based Marc than for his comrades across the Rhine. His ON movement would soon lead in melding the non-conformists' interest in the "human person" with the "new man" aspirations of his ON circle, and with France's Catholic tradition and the idealistic vein of her revolutionary heritage in a search for elements of that "Necessary Revolution" which would improve on the flawed German effort. Marc's conversion to Catholicism in 1929, like that of others of his generation, was also an immigrant's conversion to France — or to a certain idea of France.

When Alexandre Marc came to work for the French Dominicans – one of the most dynamic and influential orders engaged in the Catholic renewal of the time – he brought experience of the European youth revolution, and new religious discourse that would have great influence right up to the 1960s and the Second Vatican Council. Perhaps because Marc was tainted by his German connections, he has never been given credit for his role in creating what became a world-historical force?

The ON movement – like the Dominican and the Jesuit fathers of that period – sought to change young men through intense, unique communitarian experiences and vigorous group living, thus allowing the "complete" and "appropriate" revolution to finally be effected by "new men." Or, as an ON militant put it at the time: "Rather than sacrificing vital Revolutionary energies to the interests of that purely artificial thing called a party, we are already fabricating the Ordre Nouveau society."[20]

Marc and his comrades imagined the total conversion of France and Belgium by "changing men" because Marc concluded, from the German case, that young people could transform entire countries in a matter of months. His own movement, already forming a sort of government in exile, announced a new generation surfacing across Europe and that "finally united for the one essential task, we will cooperate in founding a New Order on earth."[21]

Marc's ON movement addressed the new chancellor, Adolf Hitler, on a fundamental issue: would the Third Reich be primarily for the benefit of Germany, or for the whole of Europe? Come post-republican France, Hitler would have to choose between working with dull holdovers and encouraging the young French fighting for a revolutionary European New Order. Marc's foremost German comrade, Harro Schulze-Boysen, warned the French that they, too, would have to make a similar choice among the contending forces in a national socialist Germany.[22]

In the non-conformist perspective, German national socialism, like Russian communism and Italian fascism, were part of a twentieth-century struggle to create order beyond the conformist disorders of bourgeois liberal decadence, despiritualization, and capitalist materialism. So Marc's ON denounced Hitler's conservative influence on national socialism and made overtures toward left-wing rivals or critics such as Otto Strasser and the Black Front, the young intellectuals of the *Tat*-Kreis, and especially of Harro Schulze-Boysen's *Gegner*. For Marc's group believed in the basic inspiration of national socialism: an authentic rebellion against the conformist spiritual mediocrity of modern society. So for Marc's circle the early 1930s were a turning point, and they held to that when they played significant roles in French life; particularly after 1940 when Hitler had to choose, in German-occupied France, either to support revolutionary change toward a New Order or to treat with the old establishment.

The French sought new men to ignite a spiritual revolution unsullied by racism or deification of the party or state, one which would be more humane – and religious – transcending nationalism, racism, statism, bourgeois compromises, and crude dictatorial or totalitarian impulses. The French could both "virilize" and "personalize" deformed European experiences and improve on their errors and imperfections.

The Parisian anti-republican rioting through the night of 6 February 1934, just some weeks after Marc's letter to Hitler, fitted ON's prophecies.[23] After it, French communitarian personalism was salvaged, transformed, and widely disseminated by the Catholic intellectuals of *Esprit*, who were also, but in their distinctive way, out to create new men. The ON saw a bankrupt French parliamentary system playing its last card when charismatic Third Force idol Gaston Bergery and his neo-socialist and neo-radical allies made overtures toward creating a broad coalition of non-conformists (who were contemptuous of parliamentary politics, and speaking of the need for an "an anti-fascist fascism").

Marc and his friends regularly claimed to be of neither the Right nor the Left and yet worked with the Nazis. They called themselves "non-conformists" and yet gravitated toward regimes that instituted authoritarian and dictatorial conformity. While the ON, like the twentieth-century New Right in general, claimed to reject the whole capitalist economic system, they were often out to displace targeted "anti-national" groups within that system. As part of an underground network to counter the French Popular Front (while pretending to avoid taking "electoral or partisan positions"),[24] they were shaping a new, larger "national" coalition.[25] With its politicized apoliticism and paradoxical discourse about fascism, Bergery's non-conformist "Common Front against fascism" may itself have been turning into an original form of fascism or French national socialism, all in the name of a newly emergent, broadly based "spiritual revolution."[26] Soon a whole cohort of self-styled leaders appeared preparing a *coup d'état* in the name of true Frenchmen and true

France, bent on excluding the "conformist" communists and socialists, the "secular" Jews, the Masons, the decadent bourgeoisie, and
the Americanophiles who had been undermining France's true
European heritage.

We shall show how, in this climactic period, Nazi intellectuals still
pretended to take French and Belgian non-conformist ideas seriously,[27] subjecting them to critical analyses which were, in turn, duly
reported back to the French.[28] Non-conformists, having learned
from what happened in Germany, did not bother with the day-to-
day activities of traditional French political parties, but rather sent
agents to infiltrate them. These so-called new socialists' efforts to
engage in "entryism" in the Socialist party (SFIO) and the union
movement (CGT) were discreet, coordinated, opposed to negativistic,
pessimistic anti-fascism, and geared toward promoting total national
renovation.[29]

The Belgian non-conformists and personalists, in contrast to the
French, engaged in relatively public interaction with friendly socialist
leaders and German visitors.[30] All the while the French Catholic avant-
garde employed Marc as a professional networker as well as an authority on the new German and Belgian communitarian ideas, facilitated
his marriage as part of an effort to get him immigrant status in
France.[31] For when Marc got devout Catholics to experience some of
the European "youth revolution," they were, like the Frenchman
Mounier and the Belgian Raymond de Becker, dramatically affected.
And all the while Marc was unshakeable in his vision of the role of non-
conformism, of Franco-German youth contacts like the Söhlbergkreis
experience for a Europe threatened by Bolshevism. He worked from
his refuge in southern France to gather all French non-conformist
movements and circles into a coalition of so-called *fédérés*: a network, a
broad counter-culture, of young people inspired by personalist ideas
and linked in a semi-secret way which has hitherto escaped the attention of historians.[32]

Non-conformists established ties between the various groups out
to displace liberal democracy with a revolutionary new order. The
need for an abstract, philosophical review passed: once the theory
and the discourse had been worked out and were generally accepted,
the time for action had come. For his part, Alexandre Marc played
a unique role in promoting links between Catholic activists (e.g.
of the Dominicans and the *Sept/Temps Présent* circle) and non-
conforming *fédérés*, technocrats, and Third Way revolutionaries
such as the Frontists, who were involved in national planning
schemes but not normally interested in working with religious
groups.[33]

Marc's contacts ranged from the extreme Left to the Right, many of them militant anti-communists, as well as sharp adversaries of liberal democracy, unfettered capitalism, and the United States. They tended to be political and economic mavericks, interested in avant-garde art and architecture, supporters of technocratic planning and some sort of European New Order with a greater role for Germany. Although pretending to be ecumenical in his approach, Marc snubbed the old parties in his effort to gather all non-conformist revolutionary elites to surreptitiously plan and coordinate a frontal assault on the old order:[34] communitarian bonding was to render the old religions and politics obsolete.[35] Husbanding the original non-conformist flame, the hard core of the initiated, the alumni of the Sohlberg meetings, kept in contact with Marc.[36]

Technocrat Georges Lamirand's youth ministry would orient the Pétain regime's tone and style, words and symbols, the whole of *maréchaliste* discourse for young people, in a post-liberal and post-individualistic, personalist, and communitarian direction. From the French collaborationist and German Nazi point of view, Lamirand was too much the Catholic spiritualist, but for non-conformists he represented a healthy mixture of religious idealism and technical competence. Catholics and non-conformists agreed that France needed new leaders to help shape the official state culture, the new kind of national community, into a community of communities.[37] Pre-war non-conformists had ranged from royalist authoritarians to neo-socialists before Marc and Emmanuel Mounier brought them together on the eve of the war, and they worked together, under Vichy, in places like the Uriage National Leadership School near Grenoble. After World War II, Mounier and the Uriage group built Resistance credentials from the fact that they had been silenced by Vichy (even if erstwhile non-conformist comrades such as Jean de Fabrègues – not Hitlerites or collaborationists – were behind this silencing).

We shall demonstrate how the broader network provided the new elites to run various French institutions during the Vichy regime. A number of these people held influential positions through a succession of political regimes. This book will suggest how a clandestine pre-war network among determined rebels, as revealed in newly available sources, did much to configure the Vichy National Revolution.[38] German philosophical discoveries like existentialism (called *Existenzphilosophie* then) and phenomenology had helped point the way to the new European sense of self, rooted in defining community experiences.[39] The early Vichy National Revolution partook of a more general communitarian "revolt against individualism and against liberal democracy."[40]

After the German invasion in spring 1940, non-conformists and personalists were named to key propaganda positions in France and Belgium. But given the opposition to "Mounierism," the non-conformists in the French propaganda ministry of Paul Marion came more from the pre-war royalist/Thomist/*Combat* milieu than the old Esprit network. Young Right leader Jean de Fabrègues and the more authoritarian right-wing non-conformists (like young François Mitterrand) particularly prized German "prison camp" communitarianism. Fabrègues and Mitterrand had been prisoners of war in Germany and believed that Pétainist communitarian experience was crucial to the National Revolution. Mitterrand recommended creating a new sort of elite in the chivalric spirit of the Service d'Ordre Légionnaire (SOL) and of the tough, heavily armed anti-communist pre-war Cagoule organization.

This book illustrates the direct continuity between the German conservative revolution's utopian youth movement and Vichy France's right-revolutionary aspirations. It shows how this idealistic current passed, thanks to German agents, through francophone Catholic Belgium – particularly receptive to buoyant, spiritualized national socialist ideology. Some prominent Belgians thought, as did their comrade Alexandre Marc, that original German national socialism embodied a basically healthy reaction against that modern sense of weightlessness and breakdown of community engendered by liberal individualism and free-market capitalism. National socialism was not intrinsically perverse: "a national form of socialism," as the 1940 Bergery declaration put it, was a universal aspiration, as was the search for a "new man." We shall see why it proved important that French non-conformist fascism tolerated Christian spirituality (if revitalized by Nietzschean manliness), and why, after World War II, those who had shared in this hopeful project found it inordinately difficult to explain to succeeding generations.

The non-conformists' new post-liberal, anti-materialist order promised something other than hated individualistic and materialistic self-indulgence, the heedless mixing of peoples and races, the inane parliamentary game, and crude capitalist materialism. They proved that even in liberal democratic France, anti-liberal and anti-democratic elite networks could suddenly appropriate power.

European populist national socialism camouflaged anti–Third World, highbrow racism with lofty culture-chat. The "European Idea" *seemed* democratic, populist, pluralistic, and progressive – self-affirmation of

European heritage and tradition against economic exploitation, capitalism, the robotization of modernity – and so touched a profound chord. As the memories of Hitler fade, it again challenges the old Left and Right, appealing to deep, hidden longings contrary to dominant modern, materialistic values.

Intelligent people, with a populist and altruistic bent, apostles of a united Europe or of ethnic and heritage politics, continued to adopt a basic non-conformist/communitarian personalist approach to politics which was very much in the ON line. A number of the initiated steadfastly maintained their admiration for people like Alexandre Marc – one of the frankest and longest-lived examples of someone who unapologetically believed in a "pure" national socialism or a "white" fascism.[41] In his old age Marc was cheered by the fact that post-war Poland had produced prominent anti-Marxist leaders such as Tadeusz Mazowiecki and Pope John Paul II who were personalist communitarians, with solid ties to members of the old French non-conformists.[42] We shall study how the Franco-German youth movements of the early 1930s invented a language, an approach, or experience that proved useful to prophets and architects of a very different kind of Europe from that in which they lived.

## HOW IT ALL BEGAN: ALEXANDRE MARKOVICH LIPIANSKY IN BERLIN AND PARIS (1919–30)

When the Russian Revolution ruined the Lipianskys in Russia and, in 1919, they fled to Paris, Mark Lipiansky rented a luxurious apartment because, like many of the émigrés, he believed that the Bolsheviks would soon be ousted and his considerable fortune restored.[43] He enrolled his son Alexandre, well trained by his tutors, in the celebrated Lycée Saint-Louis in 1919. For a time Mr Lipiansky moved to Berlin, for business reasons,[44] and it was in the large Russian colony there that, in 1922, after passing the French *baccalauréat*, the eighteen-year-old Alexandre encountered Nicholas Berdyaev, who gave an electrifying public lecture celebrating human spiritual community in anticipation of the imminent publication of his "theology of history" predicting a "New Middle Ages."[45]

Berdyaev's historical prophecy in *A New Middle Ages* envisaged the obsolescence of Renaissance and Reformation humanism, and modern rationalism and scientism: Russian communism, then Italian fascism, were precursors of a new Middle Ages with religion no longer a private and bourgeois affair but, rather, a spiritual force melding the individual and society in a common reverence for invisible realities.

Young Alexandre was moved by Berdyaev's vision of a new post-Bolshevik age – a spiritual New Order of personalist socialism after the aridity of Marxism, with a spiritual elite creating a more humane community.

After Berdyaev kindled intellectual interests, Alexandre Lipiansky heard of phenomenology and transferred from the University of Berlin in 1923 to the University of Freiburg-im-Breisgau to attend the lectures of Edmund Husserl.[46] Although bored by Husserl's lectures, he was taken by the man known as "Husserl's Catholic assistant": Martin Heidegger, called "our new Aristotle" by students. A few lectures by Heidegger were enough: Alexandre heralded the latter's *Sein und Zeit* when it appeared in 1927, tried to translate "Was ist Metaphysik?" in 1930, and regularly cited him through the 1930s.[47]

Years later Alexandre Marc recalled vignettes of his personal rapport with Husserl and Heidegger: "I tried," he remembered, "to discern elements which I could assimilate in one or the other thinker."[48] After Berdyaev, Husserl, and Heidegger, Lipiansky would seek out Max Scheler, Karl Jaspers, and Hendrik de Man in Germany in his quest for an anti-materialist philosophy, taking on the role of a sort of conduit of ideas between Germany and France.[49]

In 1923, when Lipiansky also sought out Max Scheler at the University of Cologne, he discovered the national-revolutionary line which he would encounter elsewhere in Germany: that a revitalized Germany stretching from the Baltic to the Mediterranean could defend the West from the new Russian threat.[50] Lipiansky also discovered that Scheler called himself a "personalist" Christian, holding to a philosophy centred on the supreme Person: God, as each person was fulfilled in the loving union of the *Gesamtperson,* or the plural person.[51] Lipiansky saw the importance of Scheler's thinking which he began to translate into French,[52] despite the fact that back in Paris he ran into a patronizing French philosophical establishment that dismissed the new German philosophy – whether of Scheler, Husserl, or Heidegger – as word games.[53] For young Lipiansky, Scheler, like Heidegger, was a genius.[54]

When young Lipiansky presented the new ideas of Husserl, Scheler, and Heidegger to the young Parisian intelligentsia, he represented a budding youth movement for whom terms like *Personalismus* had great practical import. Once interest was aroused by Lipiansky, Scheler's brightest pupil, Paul-Ludwig Landsberg was welcomed to Paris to further explain the implications of Scheler's ideas.[55]

In this time of effervescent German youth, Lipiansky first encountered Adolf Hitler in a beer hall. Like his Munich hosts, he saw this "Hittel" as a "ridiculous" figure – but he also found him "dangerous," to be taken very seriously, like the German situation in general.[56] Franco-German ties were Lipiansky's highest priority when, after graduation from Sciences Po in 1927, he went to work full time at promoting them with his own Société Pax-Press publishing venture, making repeated trips to Germany between 1931 and 1933. Taking on the truncated version of his Russian patronym – "Alexandre Marc" – as his legal name, he submitted an article in 1929 to the review *Le Correspondant* envisaging the real possibility of Hitler's coming to power. It was rejected as absurd conjecture.[57]

### JEAN DE FABRÈGUES: ROYALIST ANTI-INDIVIDUALIST AND THE YOUNG RIGHT

School comrades of Alexandre Lipiansky at Sciences Po and Lycée St-Louis included several Action Française Catholics who introduced him to Jean de Fabrègues, a bright young Action Française writer known for discussing epistemological issues as a peer with the Thomist sage Jacques Maritain and serving as personal secretary to Charles Maurras – until having enough of the Action Française's leader's Germanophobia, political indecision, and cranky dismissal of the papal reprimand of 1926. In April 1930, Fabrègues and some serious Catholic friends started *Réaction pour l'ordre* as a voice for a young Right respectful of Rome.

Alexandre Marc wrote several articles for Fabrègues's *Revue du Siècle* (successor to *Réaction pour l'ordre*) in 1933 and 1934. Fabrègues's young Right manifesto – which appeared one year before Marc's for an Ordre Nouveau – was one of the first expressions of a new, 1930s, generational language as it melded the old royalist, retro-medievalist summons for a "political reaction against democratic decadence" with a call for a mass movement against "individualism, statism and class struggle, to permit the free maturation of the human person in his natural social contexts ... 'We have experienced human unity, [but] we have lost it,' Maurras said. Harmony can only be restored if a foundation exists from the beginning; only the spirit [*l'esprit*] can provide it, that is the lesson from the Christian XIIIth century."

Fabrègues's new Right "political renaissance," rooted in late medieval philosophical insights, rejected individualism in favour of "the human person" nurtured by "monarchy" (a vague but authoritarian "subordination of economic life to the common good" in an overarching "Christian order").[58] This manifesto's defence of the human person against the individualism – of liberalism, of the whole Western world since the thirteenth century – implied a New Middle Ages like Berdyaev's: a spiritual unity derived from the anti-individualism engendered by Christianity. Subsequently, this new term "person" became, as the historian Henri-Irénée Marrou (who was there) recalled, a "kind of handy label, or rallying cry" in a new discourse about a "new man" which became the rage among French young people, particularly those who had experienced the new Germany.[59] Fabrègues would eventually help lead a communitarian revolution in the name of the human person, as we shall see ... but under a marshall instead of an anointed Christian prince.

Jean de Fabrègues was just one of the young Action Française people encountered by Alexandre Marc who were tired of Maurras's inertia in the face of economic collapse and aggressive, extremist movements. For Marc, the German wing of the ON movement was made up of those revolutionary conservatives who had little in common with the Action Française, yet were confident of transcending capitalism under the leadership of sharp, new, spiritually minded elites. Youth meetings allowed the young Frenchmen to experience the vibrant new Germany first-hand. Marc resigned from a job at Hachette in June 1930, to found his pro-German Europeanist press agency, Pax-Press, with the inheritance of one of his Sciences Po friends, Charles-Edouard Glachant, to fight for a European New Order by encouraging "understanding among peoples through the flow of information"[60] and bring young French and German elites together. Maurras would never favour such a Europeanist initiative, with its assumption that Germany would play a hegemonic role in a New Order in Europe, but Fabrègues and his new Right were more open to the prospect.

## REVOLUTIONARY NUCLEUS: THE SOHLBERGKREIS (1930)

As director of the Germanophile Pax-Press agency, Marc attended the first large German-French youth encounter, from 26 July to 3 August 1930, on the slopes of the pine-covered Sohlberg mountain in the Black Forest. Otto Abetz, the German organizer, was a native of nearby Karlsruhe and head of the city's youth movements' umbrella organization (Arbeitsgemeinschaft Karlsruher Jugendbünde). This young drawing teacher was of a Catholic background, an incurable romantic, and claimed to be a social-democrat: no one there seemed to imagine that he would build upon his extensive contacts with the young

French intelligentsia to become the German foreign minister's chief advisor on France. Jean Luchaire, the leading French sponsor of the encounter, was editor of the weekly *Notre Temps* and already known as an apostle of Franco-German reconciliation. There were long discussions, hikes up to the summit of the mountain from where the ethereal spires of the Cathedral of Strasbourg could be made out in the distance, and singing around campfires in the evenings.

One of the young Frenchmen there, journalist André Moosmann, was struck by Alexandre Lipiansky, who pretended to be something of a socialite – "an amusing, rather dandy-like Russian Jew" who shared his metaphysical anxiety and confided that he was considering converting to the Roman Catholic church.[61] Also in attendance were representatives of the official French organizer, the GUFA (Groupement Universitaire Franco-Allemand), some of whom would soon join Marc's ON movement, and several other journalists and academics. Compared to that of the succeeding Franco-German youth meetings, the atmosphere was subdued, but it did display some exalting *Wandervögel*-like spirit, an ambitious generational politics rallying both countries' youth against the old parties, to create a new Europe.

Alexandre Lipiansky came back from that remarkable meeting yearning for a common front of European youth, and, with his friends, would work as "Alexandre Marc" for this in the review *Ordre Nouveau* from 1933 to 1938, as well as in other publications calling for a spiritual youth revolution. These included the more aesthetic, technological, and pro-Mussolini *Plans* and the Catholic *Esprit*.

A first meeting of the French alumni of the Sohlberg – the Amis du Sohlberg – was held on 27 October 1930 in a private dining room in a restaurant on the rue du Moulin Vert near the Porte d'Orléans in Paris. Jean Luchaire founded the Club du Moulin Vert to husband the Söhlberg spirit. There Alexandre Marc described a Western civilization in crisis and called for a New Order with a movement of that name to bring it about in Europe. When André Moosmann attended the Moulin Vert meetings, Marc had unexpectedly displaced Luchaire as the motive force of the circle, and now "seemed obsessed by his search for new precepts and by religious problems."[62]

In the fall of 1930, Alexandre Marc became much involved with Gabriel Marcel, a well-known philosopher also interested in the new German philosophy and preoccupied by religion. Marcel, whose mother was Jewish, had converted to Catholicism the previous year and met Marc in one of the intense religious discussions for which the intellectual salon of Charles Du Bos was notorious. Marc then brought Marcel along to the religious discussion group he founded alongside the Moulin Vert meetings. Marc had got the Orthodox Nicholas Berdyaev, now settled in a suburb of Paris, involved, while André Moosmann, a student of Slavic languages well connected in Russian *émigré* circles, brought colourful religious non-conformists such as Father Eugraphe Kovalevski (who would eventually found the controversial semi-schismatic Eglise Catholique Orthodoxe de France), the French Orthodox convert Father Lev Gillet (a former Benedictine monk now associated with the Mouvement des étudiants chrétiens russes), and the theologian Father Sergei Bulgakoff (an authority on sophiology) along to join Berdyaev.[63] Moosmann sought out some fellow Protestants – prominent young pastors Charles Westphal, Pierre Maury, and W. Visser t'Hooft (later a world leader of the ecumenical movement), and the Swiss clergymen Max Dominicé and Roland de Pury, who would bring along the Barthian essayist Denis de Rougemont. Marc co-opted the young Catholic elite in the Dominicans from the renowned Juvisy community and the young Jesuit Jean Daniélou (a future celebrated theologian and cardinal), while an exceptional young Dominican, Yves Congar, encouraged Marc from his novitiate at Le Saulchoir, in Belgium. Several of these people would soon have international reputations as theologians or ecumenists.

Ordre Nouveau, as a third, independent, group, came from this. The ecumenical discussion circle continued for another year or two – one of the first of its kind at a non-institutional level[64] – and had a lasting impact. Marc had brought together people who would become world leaders of the ecumenical movement,[65] as common hope for a spiritual revolution eroded confessional barriers, just as it had the ethnic ones on the Sohlberg. New initiatives grew out of the experience – not all of them appreciated by religious people, democrats, or liberals. The original sparks for early ecumenical discussions are largely absent from the participants' post-Hitler memoirs.

As he became more interested in Catholicism, Marc helped the Dominicans of *La Vie Intellectuelle, Sept,* and *Temps Présent* to regroup Catholics after the shipwreck of the Action Française, by promoting communitarianism and spiritual revolution, a new political culture in the Catholic church. This bright, enthusiastic, engaging, and articulate Russian Jew brought together people who might not otherwise have met with his idea of transforming France into vanguard of the New Order. He became convinced that Catholicism would transform the West as it would him, as he moved toward conversion to the New Order in his own life.

Marc was the pioneer, the exemplar, the real generational spokesperson for the non-conformists of 1930: his revealing story sheds much light on that of a remarkable, dramatic, and influential generational experience.

# 2 The Sohlberg Spirit (January 1931–May 1932)

In 1930 Paris, religious, philosophical, and political conversion experiences overlapped with, mutually reinforced, one another. A man like Alexandre Marc could share his intense religious and philosophical concerns with a host of other intellectuals who could understand and sympathize, like the young philosophy professor Gabriel Marcel. Son of a Jewish mother and religiously indifferent father, *agrégé* in philosophy at only twenty, Marcel had been upset by his World War I experiences, and soberly recorded his search for meaning in a formal *Metaphysical Journal*, published in 1927. Like Marc, Marcel was attracted to both Christian religiosity and Nietzsche, and to German philosophers like Karl Jaspers sympathetic to both.[1] Marcel was the first in France to call his new way of doing philosophy "existentialism." Although the term "existential" had been employed thirty years earlier in France[2] to stigmatize Kierkegaard's writings,[3] it was new for a philosopher to identify with it. Marc, Jaspers, and Marcel all thought German phenomenology had important religious implications,[4] and Marcel had converted to Catholicism in 1929. Marcel, like Marc, frequented Charles Du Bos's salon, and was brought along by Marc to Club du Moulin Vert and Ordre Nouveau (ON) meetings, which he found stimulating.[5] This philosopher with a growing reputation helped Marc's early efforts,[6] co-signing Marc's first manifesto ("Appel") for an Ordre Nouveau in March 1931.

Marcel encouraged Marc's interest in Jaspers as someone who (like the German Max Scheler) wanted to reconcile Christian transcendence and spirituality with the Nietzschean critique of the conventional Christian personality, of the alienating characteristics of mass society, liberalism, and of the listless Weimar Republic. Marc also remembered Jaspers as a penetrating critic of liberal democracy who was deferential to Christianity.[7]

Marc admired Jaspers's Nietzschean Christianity along with Péguy's Christian heroism, Sorel's revolutionary mystique, Blondel's philosophy of action, and Scheler's communitarian personalism. Marc interested French Nietzscheans with his novel talk about a new philosophy of action respectful of spirituality, and of communitarian values, a radical alternative both to liberal democracy and to Marxism.

In early 1931, Gabriel Marcel brought Catholic convert Henri Daniel-Rops (pen name of Henri Petiot), beginning his teaching career as the youngest History *agrégé* in France. Son of an army officer, "Rops" was already known for his essay *Notre inquiétude* (1927), which described a troubled post-war generation's spiritual yearnings, irresolution, self-questioning, interest in the absolute, and unfocused religiousness as either fostering a religious revival or swelling the ranks of religious surrogates like Communism. Daniel-Rops's novel *L'âme obscure* (1929) suggested sympathy for the Church, and he quickly became a serious, committed Catholic (he would begin his well-known *Histoire de l'Eglise* in occupied Paris, in 1943, followed by *Jésus en son temps*). Although a conservative and a religionist for Nietzscheans, Daniel-Rops, too, was attracted to a convert milieu which offered the German youth movement experience, experimental theatre, visionary architects, and intense communitarian commitment.

Daniel-Rops wrote for *Notre Temps: La revue des nouvelles générations* (a review founded by Jean Luchaire in 1927 to promote Franco-German *rapprochement*),[8] and shared the ON group's interest in Germans, and their scepticism about liberal democracy, and – explicitly in his book *Le monde sans âme* (1932) – their search for a new order.[9] Like the Nietzschean anti-Americans Arnaud Dandieu and Robert Aron, Daniel-Rops worried that the French were becoming Americanized, embracing "a way of life in which quantity would outstrip quality ... the human spirit ... indulge the craving for comfort,"[10] and materialism would engender "a generalized spiritual decadence ... inducing modern man ... to lose the very sense of being."[11] For convert Rops, only a "spiritual revolution" would "renew man's perception of his true destiny."[12]

Daniel-Rops soon became ON's most prestigious and effective popularizer of the ideas of Nietzscheans like Arnaud Dandieu (acknowledged to be ON's most original thinker);[13] as a reputed generational spokesperson he lent stature to the work of the Marc group. Sohlberg alumni reunions evolved into a movement cultivating a Nietzschean Christian spirituality: new ideas came from Germans like Jaspers, Scheler, Husserl, and Heidegger, and Frenchmen like Marcel, Dandieu, and Daniel-Rops. Behind the scenes there were the facilitators Alexandre Marc, Otto Abetz, and Jean Luchaire.

In March 1931, Alexandre Marc and Gabriel Marcel distributed ON's first manifesto/"Appel"[14] in which they introduced themselves as non-conformists: "TRADITIONALISTS, yet NOT CONSERVATIVE, REALISTS, yet NOT OPPORTUNISTS, REVOLUTIONARIES, yet NOT REBELS, CONSTRUCTIVE, NOT DESTRUCTIVE, Neither WAR-MONGERS nor PACIFISTS, PATRIOTS, yet NOT NATIONALISTS, SOCIALISTS, yet NOT MATERIALISTS, PERSONALISTS, yet NOT ANARCHISTS, HUMAN, yet NOT HUMANITARIAN." Over against Charles Maurras's famous precept "Politique d'abord," the ON movement's motto was: "THE SPIRITUAL FIRST, THEN ECONOMICS, POLITICS AT THEIR SERVICE."

This brash text used the term "personalism" in a political as well as philosophical sense for the first time, in a revolutionary "non-conformist" stand that seemed much in the spirit of the Sohlberg meeting, It delighted Otto Abetz, who asked for thirty more copies to send to his compatriots for the next summer's follow-up gathering in rural France.[15]

The Marc-Marcel manifesto appealed to all sorts of people. In early 1931, Marc had an important encounter with the Nietzschean Arnaud Dandieu, who, with his good friend Georges Bataille, worked as a librarian at the Bibliothèque Nationale[16] and, like the lapsed Catholic Bataille, was interested in new understandings of the human personality. Dandieu liked to pose as an anti-intellectual, even an "enemy of the intelligentsia," despite being, as Emmanuel Mounier remarked when Marc introduced them, "an intellectual to the fingertips."[17] In the introduction to his *Anthologie des philosophes français contemporains* (1929) Dandieu called for a new sort of philosophy fusing action with reflection, from daring thinkers liberated from traditional approaches. Upon learning that this apostle of a new sort of action-philosophy was nearby, Marc rushed out of his Pax-Press office on Place de la Madeleine and, though penniless, hailed a taxi to search out Dandieu at the Nationale.[18]

Dandieu shared Marc's interest in German phenomenology (if not in the spiritualist communitarians like Max Scheler who captivated Marc)[19] and enthusiastically joined ON, bringing his confidant Robert Aron along with him. Dandieu and Aron had met at the Lycée Condorcet where both had been taught by Gabriel Marcel, and then got together at least twice weekly since 1927. When Julien Benda's *La trahison des clercs* denounced a "treasonous" slippage of the intelligentsia toward Bergsonian irrationalism, the two decided to counter Benda's "disembodied," abstract, decadent individualism with what they called "l'homme réel" – rooted in instincts and homeland, action-oriented.[20] This "real man" notion seemed close to Marc's "person," so Dandieu and Aron began to frame their hopes for collective spiritual and moral renewal in the new lexicon of Alexandre Marc's Franco-German experiences, publishing two widely remarked "new generation" books: *Décadence de la nation française* (1931) and *Le cancer américain* (1932).

The metaphysical sufferings of Gabriel Marcel, Daniel-Rops and Marc left these two arrogant Nietzscheans cold. (Marc recalled that, in his first conversation with Aron, the cosmopolitan surrealist muttered: "La religion, c'est de la merde!") Like several other ON militants, they thought that "real, concrete man" could put the spiritual first without religion. But they were offset by others with religious fixations, such as the French Swiss essayist Denis de Rougemont whom Marc encountered at one of Charles Du Bos's soirées in the spring of 1931. An aspirant writer and editor, earnest disciple of the Swiss existentialist theologian Karl Barth, de Rougemont, like Nietzsche, was a pastor's son. This gave him psychological problems and a background in German culture rare for a francophone intellectual. After studies in Switzerland, Vienna, and Wurtemberg, de Rougemont settled in Paris in the fall of 1930 to help Editions Je Sers publish existentialists like Karl Barth, Kierkegaard, Ortega y Gasset, and Berdyaev.[21]

De Rougemont also, like Daniel-Rops, Dandieu, and Aron, warned of "Le Péril Ford," the danger which American culture and economic power represented for traditional Europe.[22] His acerbic, patronizing tract, *Les méfaits de l'instruction publique*, castigated the Neuchâtel educational system that had trained him for destroying creativity and spontaneity in the young. The democratic model – forcing egalitarianism on children, leading to a "bastardization of the race" – engendered the sterilizing, soulless conformity which marked his schooling. A de Rougemont compatriot observed: "This pamphlet was not only an accusation levelled against an educational system, it was also a condemnation of democracy";[23] de Rougemont admitted it showed him to be "allergic to democracy."[24] Patrician, aloof, conscious of his aristocratic lineage, de Rougemont thought his personal spiritual journey a very serious matter. His first published autobiographical journal, appearing the next year, described an evolving *vie intérieure* in settings like the brooding, romantic plains of East Prussia, whose aristocrats were described as historic defenders of the West.[25] Public self-analysis became the favoured mode of expression of an immodest man, who, if not exactly a Nietzschean Christian, displayed the self-conscious intellectuality, the sense of being a man to be reckoned with, and the bridling at repressive Christian sexual doctrines common in Marc's circle.

De Rougemont was, he recalled half a century later, much impressed by Marc – "un personnage d'aspect massif, courtois et souriant" – whose Russian accent enhanced his exhortations to "doctrinal and revolutionary rigour." He was also delighted by Marc's personalist approach: "The formulas in the little manifesto which Marc handed me simply clarified what I was painfully trying to decipher on my own, and what I was already thinking without realizing it."[26]

Alexandre Marc's zeal to bring like-minded people together particularly impressed de Rougemont, as, within two years the energetic Russian was behind a host of publications, and French, German, and Belgian study groups. De Rougemont, in his turn, gathered the articulate elite of the new generation for a special late 1932 issue of the *Nouvelle Revue Française*. "One single thing is sure and certain in all of that," de Rougemont later mused, "it was Alexandre Marc who precipitated almost all of the meetings ... contacts between the emerging groups and their organizers."[27]

At a time when German existentialism was being dismissed as the murky thinking of German youth given to mindless tribalism, Marc and company subjected the German scene to serious intellectual analysis. Marc urged established authorities to make serious study of subjects like phenomenology and the communitarian qualities of Germany's "magnificent youth." Marc, knowledgeable about Husserl, Heidegger, and Scheler, brought de Rougemont and Marcel – experts on Barth and Jaspers and two of France's brightest young Nietzscheans – into a team that came to include several of France's leading new philosophers. Years later, Denis de Rougemont remembered that this "very anti-Marxist" circle was studying German authors and "discovering existential thought fifteen years before M. Sartre."[28]

FRENCH INTELLECTUAL ARCHITECTURE
FOR THE YOUTH REVOLUTION: LE CORBUSIER
AND LAGARDELLE

The non-conformism of the 1930s inspired art, architecture, musical composition, and film, and, in January 1931, an unconventional highbrow review with an international perspective caught Marc's interest as a possible place to air his group's avant-garde ideas. *Plans* was launched by one of France's very few authentic, home-grown, self-conscious, and self-described fascists. Philippe Lamour, a young lawyer

known for his fiery oratory, had started his short-lived Parti fasciste
révolutionnaire after being expelled from Georges Valois's Faisceau
français in March 1928.[29] After writing for the charismatic architect Le
Corbusier's *L'Esprit Nouveau* (to which Marc's friend Robert Aron contributed a regular "Lettre aux jeunes"),[30] Lamour was asked to express
the spirit of the new generation in the "Compagnons de la Grande
Route" collection published by the Editions de la Renaissance du
Livre. Lamour, with his romantic notions of syndicalism and of the
medieval corporation of artisans, began to describe "compagnons" as
the true representatives of a healthy and dynamic new generation:
their special characteristic was being simultaneously free and disciplined – in contrast to the "comrades" of the Bolsheviks and the
"citoyens" of the French Revolution. "Compagnons" subsequently
became a greeting and password among the non-conformists. Marc
seized upon the term, using it to describe the vast federation of non-
conformist groups he would try to create at the end of the decade:
Compagnons would become the principal official youth organization
of Vichy's National Revolution in which a number of non-conformists
would play administrative roles.

Chief compagnon Philippe Lamour's *Entretiens sous la Tour Eiffel*
(1929) – dedicated to the unusual trinity of Le Corbusier, Lenin, and
the car-maker Citroën – reflected new thinking about aesthetics, some
Sorelian ideas, and a strong interest in innovative technology. In 1930,
Lamour, with funds provided by Jeanne Walter, the wealthy wife of a
Parisian architect and the one who seems to have had the original
idea, started *Plans*, which described young people searching for "the
main purposes of a civilization created by machines, institutions suited to a new collective world, ideals appropriate to the new way of
life."[31]

Like Alexandre Marc, Philippe Lamour wanted established
thinkers to provide clarification and legitimacy to the bright ideas of
the enthusiastic young, and so he went down to Toulouse to get
Hubert Lagardelle, long-time disciple of Georges Sorel, to work with
Le Corbusier, with Pierre Winter the homeopathic physician who had
been head of the ephemeral Parti fasciste révolutionnaire, and with
François de Pierrefeu, an unconventional young businessman, to
publish *Plans*. The review was striking for Le Corbusier's plans for *La
Cité radieuse* on special art paper, and for the highbrow essays on art,
cinema, and literature by the likes of composer Arthur Honegger,
painter Fernand Léger, architect Walter Gropius, graphic artist Frans
Masereel, and film-makers Claude Autant-Lara and René Clair,[32] as it
called for a totally new politics and aesthetics. It was adorned with
romantic photographs of young people on the march in the Soviet

Union, Germany – and Italy, where Lagardelle was venerated as a social prophet by the Mussolini Fascists. The review suggested that young people could create a European federation and even a new world, since their unity transcended all the old national and party divisions.[33] Le Corbusier provided *Plans* its flair, but its original conception of "l'homme réel" nurtured by syndicalist (or trade-unionist) and regionalist politics came from Lagardelle, whose ideas Lamour had studied for his thesis on *Le Mouvement socialiste* – the political and social theory publication which Lagardelle had edited with Georges Sorel and Arturo Labriolo, and which Lamour saw as the model for *Plans.*

In fact Hubert Lagardelle was internationally known as a social thinker because, before World War I, *Le Mouvement socialiste* had been, as Lamour thought, "one of the best reviews ever published in Europe," much influencing radical trade-unionism with its revolutionary syndicalist socialism.[34] Disdainful of both liberal democracy and social democracy in its peculiar "extreme left-wing non-conformism," the journal was also anti-Semitic and fiercely hostile to the high-minded, democratic, "bourgeois" parliamentary socialism engendered by the Dreyfus affair.[35]

Lagardelle liked to say that mainstream French syndicalism had been engendered by the proletariat's rejection of "so-called" social democracy, just another example of "bourgeois hegemony."[36] Lagardelle was becoming a "non-conformist Marxist" like the famous anti-militarist Gustave Hervé,[37] and the more his Marxist faith flagged and his opposition to "democratic socialism" hardened, the more he came to reject both Marxism and liberal democracy. Other 1930s "deviationists" (e.g. Marcel Déat, Jacques Doriot, and Hendrik de Man) would evolve along similar lines.[38]

Like his mentor Georges Sorel, Lagardelle saw true socialism characterized by the absolute segregation of social classes and the abandonment of all dreams of political renovation. The utopia of Sorel and Lagardelle can be seen as an ideal type of fascist society, run by "conscious, rebellious" men contemptuous of democracy, universal suffrage, parliamentarianism, and bourgeois life. Lagardelle welcomed proletarian alienation from the liberal democracies, because his and Sorel's syndicalist society would develop a new kind of man, displaying "the boldness, the marvellous discipline" of the "workers' army" on strike. Some revolutionary trade-unionists even imagined themselves a new aristocracy leading the proletarian army into the "social war."[39]

Certain syndicalists shared the ON group's interest in new German thinking: old engineer and social thinker Sorel liked Nietzsche's contempt for the bourgeoisie and wanted to transform his Übermensch into a new sort of revolutionary. A Nietzschean appreciation for heroic elites, for dynamism and self-confidence, and for the purifying effects of violence revolutionized the Marxism of trade-unionists like Lagardelle, who began calling for creative individuals to change the course of history.[40]

In the 1920s Lagardelle quit the Socialist party and moved to Toulouse. Although keeping a low profile there, he did, in 1926, join the local Faisceau organization.[41] When Philippe Lamour, as president of the Faisceau universitaire, was in Toulouse and paid him public homage, Lagardelle responded that he had quit the Socialist party and now wanted "the victory of fascist ideas." Once he had secured Lagardelle's support and collaboration, Lamour proudly situated his own attacks on liberalism and parliamentary democracy as in the direct line of the "admirable turn of the century French syndicalist movement" and of "compagnon" Hubert Lagardelle and his "magnificent *Mouvement socialiste*, with which *Plans* is proud to declare itself in direct continuity."[42] Lagardelle's ideas shaped the early *Plans*: a "modernistic, avant-garde publication, an almost perfect example of a technically oriented fascism that was enamoured of skyscrapers, the work of Walter Gropius and Le Corbusier, and the art of Fernand Léger, and at the same time aspired toward an organic, harmonious society – the society of the 'real man.'"[43]

*Plans* was quick to call attention to Adolf Hitler: in March 1931 Lamour's good friend Aldo Dami warned that those dismissing him as an inconsequential rabble-rouser might have to revise their views dramatically within the year.[44] Dami, a much-travelled Germanophile Swiss, who as a Faisceau had administered Georges Valois's Librairie Nationale publishing house,[45] was close to both Lamour and Lagardelle. His unique geopolitical analyses of the European situation soon encouraged serious respect for Hitler – and eventually a pro-Munich faction – in personalist circles.[46]

After their tête-a-tête on 27 April 1931, Alexandre Marc decided he could use Philippe Lamour in his revolutionary movement, and the ON meeting two days later endorsed the idea. Lamour was delighted to be invited, but told Marc that his older *Plans* associates were less enthusiastic for the ON group: "These people are not of our generation: young people like us must shape the revolution."

Although Hubert Lagardelle was revered as an intellectual architect of the twentieth century in fascist Italy, Marc claimed that the older man was dead weight in the *Plans* offices and that Lamour became impatient with him.[47] Mussolini, however, remained grateful to the veteran trade-unionist for having introduced him to the ideas of Georges

Sorel and, in January 1933, after having endorsed the Duce's "nationalist corporatist" ideas, Lagardelle was named "counsellor for social questions" at the French embassy in Rome by ambassador Henri de Jouvenel. (He would remain there until the fall of France in 1940, when he became one of the several non-conformists to administer the Pétain regime: eventually serving as labour minister.)

Marc, sensitive to Lagardelle's misgivings about ON influence on *Plans*, but determined to get control of the review, got Lamour, in early June 1931, to formally request ON help on that publication. Marc was also trying to get his people to take sides in the dividing German national socialist movement.[48] Hitler's left-wing national socialist rival, Dr Otto Strasser, leader of the "Black Front," published his positions first in *Plans* in late 1931 and then, at more length, in Emmanuel Mounier's *Esprit*.[49]

The follow-up camp to the previous year's Sohlberg meeting was held near the French town of Rethel in the Ardennes from 2 to 9 August. There was much lofty Europeanist rhetoric, soaring far above secret national agendas. But as long as the French idea of "Europe" retained any trace of the French hegemony institutionalized by the Versailles Treaty, it didn't interest Germans.[50]

The appeals to European solidarity seemed most resonant when addressed to a generational common ground which transcended national rivalries. For all these young men "rejected the capitalist economic system, so that when Bertrand de Jouvenel [the son of France's ambassador to Italy] called for a joint capitalist exploitation of the African continent by Germany and France he met little positive reaction. But when Philipp [*sic*] Lamour, the energetic editor of the review *Plans*, in fiery rhetoric, proposed that European youth encourage anti-capitalist thinking, his project, thanks to the fascinating personality of its author, was well received. However it ran up against the meetings' precondition that no decisions be taken, no resolutions adopted."[51]

It was Philippe Lamour's eloquence which persuaded Marc to bring him along as part of the ON delegation to Rethel. Jean Luchaire had been trying to temper the political rhetoric of the gathering, despite Otto Abetz's sympathy for Marc, so Marc was happy to see the fiery Lamour "bring Luchaire down in flames."[52] ON and *Plans* were to form a joint Franco-German committee for a European Union, which was to be militantly anti-capitalist, radically federalist, in orientation.[53]

The Rethel Congress ended with the radicals in the movement for Franco-German youth *rapprochement* lining up behind Philippe Lamour, Marc, and German youth leader Harro Schulze-Boysen (supplanting Abetz as Marc's chief German contact), while the Sohlbergkreis evolved in a public forum for clarifying Germany's foreign policy objectives.[54] Marc remembered that he was soon shocked to learn that his comrade Abetz was working with the Hitlerite national socialists, despite his earlier warnings to Marc about them.[55]

*Plans* summoned young Europeans to a common struggle against capitalism: in October 1931 it excerpted Aron and Dandieu's forthcoming books *Décadence de la nation française* and *Le cancer américain* castigating the "Yankee spirit" for "the hegemony of rational mechanisms over [those] concrete and sentimental realities" which constituted "the profound sources of true progress for man." To counter the "American cancer" there would have to be "the definitive revolution" which would be "spiritual before everything else, or it will not really change anything." Human beings were to put "The spiritual first, then think about economics, and then put politics at their service."

This ON revolutionary line was formally endorsed by *Plans* in November 1931: Lamour warmly saluted "the arrival in our ranks, in perfect order, of the young ON group"[56] and announced the new *Plans*-ON joint operations committee made up of Alexandre Marc, Robert Aron, Arnaud Dandieu, Gabriel Rey, Philippe Lamour, and Jeanne Walter. This elite cohort worked to gather all European youth to fight against the cancerous American capitalist decadence and to bring about the elevating New Order. The conversion experience of Alexandre Marc and his circle was to be projected onto an entire continent.

## THE REVOLUTIONARY ALLIANCE OF EUROPEAN YOUTH, FROM RETHEL TO FRANKFURT (AUGUST 1931–FEBRUARY 1932)

The *Plans*-ON group organized the French branch of the new Front unique de la jeunesse européenne (proclaimed at the Rethel youth congress the previous August by the "radicals" who backed Philippe Lamour). Their *Appel à la jeunesse*, written by Aron and Marc on 16 October as the ON group's German policy,[57] was to be given to German youth leaders whom Marc and Lamour would meet with on their tour to prepare an all-European Front unique congress.

This ON manifesto urged "Radical remedies for a radical Crisis!" Since "THE CAPITALIST WORLD IS FINISHED" alienated youth, "all who, with ardent mind and resolute heart, want to build a new order," should reject "OBSOLETE SOLUTIONS" such as Briand-style pacifism, "whose cowering baseness is equalled only by its total inefficacy," or

"Hitler-style nationalism." Hitlerism mobilized the formidable energies of "a vigorous and healthy patriotism" ... but for the benefit of the possessing classes, the international banking system. So French young people resolutely rejected "nationalist errors," as well as any "French hegemony based on the Yankee-inspired credit system": an economic system constituting a "betrayal of the spiritual traditions of France." They also repudiated the Treaty of Versailles's institutionalization of Germany's subjection, that "tragic misunderstanding which separates Germany and France" and which "thwarted any efficacious attempts at collaboration between German and French young people ... the two main forces which could free the world from the growing *malaise* which threatens all civilization." Europe was at the centre of the human drama, French and German young people were at the centre of Europe.

This manifesto was Europeanist but dismissed conventional efforts at Franco-German reconciliation in favour of a "common revolutionary struggle" joining the "two great spiritual forces of the modern world" – French and German youth – who were to transcend nationalism and internationalism, "capitalist anarchy," "Fordist rationalization", "degenerate rationalism," and even something called "naturalistic sociologism." The "unique heroic and creative vocation" of human beings would manifest itself in "REVOLUTIONARY SPIRITUALITY."

"Revolutionary spirituality?" Marc's old Russian, Socialist Revolutionary rejection of Marxist determinism, his reservations about *völkisch* racism, the spirit of the pre-war trade union movement which Hubert Lagardelle brought to *Plans*, all involved the notion that people could play a heroic role in shaping history. But "revolutionary spirituality," here, was more Nietzsche's notion of life beyond good and evil as "conversion," or the transvaluation of all values. According to Marc and Robert Aron, "we must resolve to effect, amidst the collapse of all which is artificial and misleading, a GENERAL REVISION OF ALL VALUES and a GENERAL CHANGE CHANGE OF PLANE" in a "Retour à l'Homme réel," approaching all problems in a new light, with a radically different focus. The ON manifesto portrayed modern society "suppressing or rationalizing the living, free and active human being ... his psychological and sensual life ... originality," while American hegemony threatened to extinguish Europe's revolutionary energies.

Aron and Marc wanted "a real European federalism/ For an organized economy/ For the European Plan, constitutive and liberating." (This was and is the "global" or "integral federalism" issuing from ON.)[58] The *Appel à la jeunesse* concluded with a call to arms: "TO CONSTITUTE A FREE AND LOGICAL EUROPE, TO ESTABLISH AN ORGANIZED

ECONOMIC SYSTEM/ ELIMINATING SOCIAL INJUSTICE, TO SAVE THE SPIR-
IT,/ LET US FORM THE REVOLUTIONARY SINGLE FRONT OF EUROPEAN
YOUTH."[59] This appeal for generational unity, the Front unique's
manifesto's "AFFIRMATION OF REGIONAL PATRIOTISM," its call for the
"LIQUIDATION OF CAPITALIST ANARCHY" by the "ESTABLISHMENT OF
UNITARY ECONOMIC MANAGEMENT," anticipated the "Précisions sur
l'Ordre Nouveau" that would appear in the December *Plans* – alongside the Black Front manifesto of Hitler's rival Otto Strasser. And
despite certain ideological problems,[60] men on the Nazi Left such as
Strasser represented the possibility of a "socialist" evolution of the German national movement, whose revolutionary energy Hitler might
otherwise divert. Alarmed at Hitler's progress, Lamour and Marc tried
to network Germans sympathetic to their federalist and anti-capitalist
New Order which, alone, claimed to promise a lasting European
peace.

The Marc group's Front unique first had Otto Abetz as its leading
German representative, and then dashing, youthful Harro Schulze-
Boysen, who was closer to ON's revolutionary line. After discovering
*Plans* the previous summer in Paris, Schulze-Boysen had formed one
of those Amis de *Plans* circles which the review encouraged for the
international networking of its sympathizers, in Berlin. Schulze-
Boysen's organization became *Plans* for the German-speaking world
(with the backing of avant-garde Franco-German artistic, trade-union,
and entrepreneurial circles).[61] In November 1931 Marc finally met
the charismatic Schulze-Boysen face to face and he would always
remember him as the resplendent symbol of a Europe which might
have been.[62] No modest teacher like Abetz, Harro Schulze-Boysen
was the well-connected son of a navy officer, and grandnephew of
Admiral von Tirpitz (father of the imperial German Navy) and of Ferdinand Tönnies (the sociologist whose distinction between the
*Gemeinschaft* and *Gesellschaft* was the source of the personalist notion
of community). Although Schulze-Boysen was five years younger than
Marc, the Russian found him a strong and striking personality: trustworthy, and committed to Marc's non-conformist approach to the
fluid political situation.

He began to ask me a lot of questions about our ideas ... and I began to have
confidence in Harro Schulze-Boysen because I saw that he was an extraordi-
narily energetic man ... he counted for something, he was known. ... despite
his youth he was able to obtain extraordinary things for me ...[such as] a free
pass to travel on Lufthansa flights ...
    When I first met Harro Schulze-Boysen he ... was very young ... His main
idea was ... to reconcile the Germans, but beyond parties, independently of

parties. The word "Adversary" [*Gegner*] is his slogan: "Today's adversaries will be tomorrow's allies" ... He worked with dissident Nazis as well as with Communist dissidents, or with utopian socialists, etc. I furnished him with an ideology. He was enthusiastic and said: "These are magnificent ideas, just what we need" ... A man of very quick, but not abstract, intelligence, he supported me completely. I decided to build up stocks of arms in Germany with him ... he wanted all the Germans in a sacred union against Hitler, but also against Weimar, which was decadent, etc.[63]

By the time Marc met him in November, Schulze-Boysen had already become "a picturesque leader of the 'lost generation'... and a familiar Bohemian figure in those days in Berlin, where his black sweater, his thick mane of blond hair and his penchant for revolutionary poetry and politics attracted attention. At the time he rejected both Communism and Nazism, though he considered himself a man of the Left."[64] Schulze-Boysen wanted to use generational solidarity to meld radical elements of Right and Left into a vast coalition; once named director of the review *Gegner*, the next March he also began promoting the ON/*Plans* European revolutionary party, which was supposed to hold a congress and adopt an agenda before the end of the year.[65] The *Gegner* editor soon claimed to have people from all the German parties, from the Nazis to the Communists,[66] along with a Flemish nationalist, a Hungarian, an Italian Fascist, and even a Soviet Komsomol delegation.[67]

Schulze-Boysen soon displaced Otto Abetz as Marc's principal German youth contact, and for the rest of his life Marc vividly recalled the excited, desperately idealistic Harro, convinced that he and his comrades could change the world. For Marc, when he sadly remembered 1931–32, Germany's golden, tragic youth, they were like the French student insurgents of May 1968, or Russian revolutionaries before Lenin and the Bolsheviks: "a magnificent younger generation – completely severed from preconceptions, from the old political parties, from obsolete institutions – looking for something new ... But it was captured by a madman: Adolf Hitler."[68]

Marc returned to Paris at the end of 1931 an emissary of the German youth revolution, recognizing the growing influence of the Hitlerites, but working with prominent German youth leaders to counter them by fostering that "revolutionary spirituality" which would save Europe. The ON circle began as a nucleus of people committed to Franco-German *rapprochement*: colleagues from the Hachette publishing house, comrades from Sciences Po (such as René Dupuis, son of the school's vice-principal, and Jean Jardin, Action Française Catholic, soon private secretary to a succession of powerful administrators).[69]

They were joined by the aforementioned Aron, a surrealist aesthete then producing Antonin Artaud's imaginative plays, and also the soon to be legendary librarian-metaphysician super-brain Dandieu. In December 1931 the band of Catholics led by Mounier came to see Marc. They, too, were part of the spiritual youth revolution, about to start *Esprit*. They, too, thought themselves elites of the impending trans-European youth revolution which would bring about a New Order.

Large excerpts of ON's manifesto appeared in the November 1931 *Plans*, and "Précisions sur l'Ordre Nouveau" followed in December. The ON stance paralleled that of Otto Strasser's Black Front when the review published[70] "an essential document": the Black Front's founding Fourteen Theses, and Strasser's Burg Lauenstein manifesto of 4 October 1931. The introduction[71] described Otto Strasser's program as "at once very close to us in essential inspiration and a cause for abhorrence in certain points ... The main point ... is the specifically national character of a German revolution issuing from a political situation and economic development peculiar to that country ... texts such as these express ... what nearly all of the German people feel." For its part, ON/*Plans* clarified the special national character of the revolution necessary in France:

L'Ordre Nouveau is a group of non-conformists with a revolutionary spirit ... Between liberal capitalism and State capitalism, no conventional liberal or Marxist response bears up under serious, methodical analysis ... The radical change that we are urging is psychological above everything else ... a hierarchy of values which would put the human person in the first rank ... Economic and social mechanisms for the person and not the person for the economic and social mechanisms. The labour-saving achieved by scientific progress ... to the benefit of the creative personality ... This "personalism" implies a break with both the abstract individualism of liberals and with doctrines which take the State ... to be the highest value ... putting the means of production in common and equally redistributing indispensable work ... allows an ever greater liberation of the creative personality; the spiritual first, then economics ... If we concentrate the forces for spiritual revolution ... the means of economic distribution will be subordinated to them ... Breaking national frameworks will promote decentralization liberating the deeply patriotic ... freeing up of the ... fruitful relationship of man with the land, the race ... cultural tradition. The New Order must be built on three bases:
a) Personalism: primacy of man over society
b) Anti-productivist communism: subordination of production to
    consumption
c) Land-based racial and cultural regionalism.[72]

Regionalism was, of course, characteristic of German conservative revolutionaries, and changing men's minds and hearts sounded like the *Wandervögel* hiking from hostel to hostel. Sohlberg people thought of psychological revolution, spiritual transformation, the inevitable revolution of the twentieth century.

French political scientist Jean-Louis Loubet del Bayle took over Alexandre Marc's term and described the whole new generation of intelligentsia in early 1930s Paris as "the non-conformists of 1930," inventing a new, home-grown French political and social thinking. French historians, seldom well read in German sources, have followed this nomenclature.[73] But if the new French initiatives were "non-conforming" to French political culture they were less original when set against the *Wandervögel* and Alexandre Marc's comrades in the various German political movements in the early 1930s.

The notion that regions, races, and peoples follow their own particular genius was essential to the German *völkisch* "spiritual revolution."[74] The French most familiar with Germany – Marc, Lamour and company – thought the French should find their own voice and call for a distinctive spiritual revolution on French soil. Soon the French, uncomfortable with the intensely collectivistic Germans, began using the term "person" for the "new man" whom they wanted to transcend the abstract "individual" of liberal political culture. Alexandre Marc invented this discourse and began to designate his whole effort to liberate the human personality, create a "new man," as "personalism."

But the dark shadow of Adolf Hitler continued to grow over the shining prospects of Germany's radiant youth. As early as December 1931, back from his first tour around Germany with the zealous Marc, Philippe Lamour reported in *Plans*[75] that "La Révolution allemande est commencée": "Hitler is already virtually in power." But Lamour thought that Hitler would soon be swept aside by the "real" revolution. Marc and Lamour were convinced the world was at a decisive moment; their comrades were about to effect world-historical change.

## A EUROPE WHICH MIGHT HAVE BEEN: YOUNG GERMANY AND YOUNG FRANCE IN FRANKFURT

The Frankfurt European Youth Congress, held from 7-9 February 1932, had Belgian, Dutch,[76] Swiss, and Italian delegates, and even a Russian expatriate delegate from Prague's national-revolutionary "Eurasian" party,[77] but the serious talk was mostly between *Plans* people and various German groups whose views Schulze-Boysen would soon reflect in his review *Gegner*.

While preparing the congress, Marc ran into Sohlberg alumnus André Moosmann in Mannheim, who was surprised to discover "a new Marc. The dandy had totally disappeared. He kept talking about 'revolution' and was in a constant state of exhilaration."[78] Denis de Rougemont later recalled the electricity of Europe-wide youth revolution in a special, dramatic setting, combining the ancient and the very new:

I travelled with comrades from several of the new political groups which had surfaced, and slept in the baggage net of a third class train coach. At Frankfurt we were put up in a youth hostel. Philippe Lamour, dramatic forelock ... presided ... There I encountered ... Otto Strasser, uniformed leader of the Black Front, and, closer to our way of thinking, Harro Schulze-Boysen, head of the *Gegner* group ... intransigent and handsome ... Carnival filled the streets ... around the palace in which the Holy Roman Emperors of the German Nation had been elected. I had a sense of living in transitory ... "decadent" times. On my makeshift work table ... I scribbled: "the times are forcing us to choose ... Frankfurt in Carnival ... A cataclysmic reality outside the parameters of ... Cartesian logic is carrying us to new regions of spiritual experience in which action is ... becoming our only measure of coherence ... We must beware of ... fanaticism. More than ever, one has to discern in the midst of this vertiginous experience."[79]

The effervescent new European youth politics captivated this well-travelled observer, who related his confused mystical longings to the fraternal optimism of youth meetings. But, for his part, Marc later claimed to have been disgusted with the homosexuals and the "weak and irresponsible people" in the German delegation.[80] Marc recalled that he had been wandering broodingly through the streets when, in the Old Town, he joined a distinguished-looking gentleman on a bench, telling him that he had come to Frankfurt to avert war by helping France and Germany find common interests. The man dramatically confronted Marc, saying: "But you have come too late. It is already too late. *Zu spät*."[81]

While several German observers, including Schulze-Boysen,[82] were embarrassed by the Germans at Frankfurt, they were impressed by the French new politics. One of those Germans was Franz Mariaux, an essayist with a sensational vision of Germany revolutionizing her inert neighbour in the sort of "great, wild intoxication which always engenders life."[83] Mariaux particularly delighted Harro Schulze-Boysen as a genuine revolutionary conservative after his own heart when they met at Frankfurt: Mariaux's *Der Schutthaufen,* praised in *Gegner* later that year,[84] was to be translated into French for *Plans.* After reading the complete series of *Plans,* neo-nationalist Mariaux sent a five-page laudatory report on the new movement to the Frankfurt Congress. It was published in the *Deutsche Führerbriefe* and then forwarded to Rudolf Pechel, editor of the *Deutsche Rundschau,*[85] the most influential journalist of the late Weimar Republic[86] (along with Hans Zehrer, another major "revolutionary conservative" figure whose review *Die Tat* also had links with *Plans*/ON). Pechel seems to have been fascinated by the piece and asked for an essay on the *Plans* movement for the *Deutsche Rundschau.*[87] Did leading German political observers consider this account of a get-together between young people as signalling important historical developments?

Mariaux conceded that the Frankfurt Congress had lacked direction, apart from the informal leadership of Harro Schulze-Boysen, who had been working with the French for months and seemed an "infinitely likeable facilitator, with many personal contacts if no clear political agenda." The plenary discussions were marked by the German Black Front leaders, the Gray Corps (especially the militant nationalist Fred Schmid),[88] the "Neo-Prussian Struggle League," pro-Trotzky Communists, anarcho-syndicalists, and a host of other younger people claiming to speak for groups or groupuscules. Amid the confusion the Germans did take the common position that there was not just one German delegation with one German point of view. The French, however, with fervent Philippe Lamour as their spokesperson, made a clear distinction between the capitalist system and its so-called democracy on the one hand, and the European New Order on the other. The French position certainly lacked rigour, Mariaux conceded, but the Frenchmen like Lamour were waiting for the great revolution that would overthrow capitalism to happen first in Germany, opening the way for France.

Mariaux conceded that the Frenchmen's ideas often seemed muddled, their knowledge of German revolutionary thinking second-hand (perhaps taken from national socialist or *bündisch* publications.) The key contact person between the French and German groups, Mariaux noted, was "a Polish Jew who lived in Paris" (probably Marc). A leader of the French contingent (also probably Marc) complained to Mariaux that immature German national-revolutionaries were making collaboration difficult. Mariaux portrayed the Franco-Belgian delegation as led by *Plans* with a "band of people who appear to encompass the whole of the national-revolutionary forces of young France." These "young journalists, writers and, especially, lawyers" were clearly "an expression of the revolt of young, modern, open to the world and

activist France against ... an old democratic, literary, artistic, and political regime, [which] monopolizes all the positions, closes itself off to
the outside world ... leaves the French people vulnerable to the world-
wide economic crisis ... and avoids modern transformational revolutionary forces."

Mariaux pointed out that as the Depression got worse, the possibility of these outsiders coming to power in France was growing, and it
was necessary for German nationalist circles "which have gone beyond
puberty" to get to know these French young people, since some of
them were bound eventually to get political and economic power. The
cynical German nationalist recommended that German leaders
"should observe the French, converse, develop personal relationships
with them, help them get to know Germany, and get Germans to lecture and write in France ... Talking with these clever and activist types
has its advantages ... They are keen to translate the new German
nationalist writings, have Germans write for their publications, and,
above all, convince French public opinion *they* are the ones who can
work with the real Germany ... on the level of the European anticapitalist cause."

Francophile culture-Catholic Otto Abetz always dreamed of achieving genuine camaraderie between French nationalists and Germans.
But now it was youthful Harro Schulze-Boysen who embodied Lamour's and Marc's dream of a renewed Germany in a post-Versailles,
post-liberal, "converted" Europe. Young Harro, with his myriad
connections, arranged talks, contacts, and free Lufthansa flights for
Lamour and Marc in Germany, while asking *Plans*-ON to provide the
*Gegner* people with an ideology. But despite Marc's claims[89] that his
German friend totally adopted ON's federalism, Schulze-Boysen was
essentially an activist with a pragmatic view of ideologies, mining rival
texts for gripping rhetoric to meet the immediate situation.

Did Schulze-Boysen's openness to ON ideas represent a Germany
which might have been, as Alexandre Marc strongly believed until the
day he died? In an essay written for the review *Gegner* in May 1932,[90]
the German youth leader analysed the political situation as per the
*Plans*/ON manifesto: "contemporary society is in a state of complete
dissolution. The peoples of Europe have ... failed to adapt their
lifestyles to ... industrialization." Man has become "the slave of his
economic and technological creations." The "trusts," with their insa-
tiable demand for dividends, reduced society to an expendable
labour supply. Schulze-Boysen's essay maintained that "the rebel-
liousness of the masses did not increase with pauperization." The
decisive moment of this "Revolution of the living person" ("Revolu-

tion des lebendigen Menschen"/ "l'homme réel") would happen "in accord with the masses, but not because of their initiative"; it had to be the work of a "resolute minority," a "*community of people prepared to act.*" "*The only true revolutionary is someone who can experience tomorrow, in himself, today.*" The capitalist world could only be up-ended by a "company of fighters whose defining values are from completely outside of the old order."

This Gegner notion of "forming an elite of leaders committed to order" impressed Alexandre Marc as coming from the grass-roots, through revolutionary cells like those of ON, "Voluntary revolutionary associations," an "invisible circle," already constituting the "*New Unity*" of the nation, "the organic life-unity of tomorrow," beyond class divisions. "Only a state made up of councils will have a genuine *Volksgemeinschaft.*" Over against the budding New Order society, liberal democratic institutions were "a lie": "The ... equal weight given to votes within a society divided into classes is folly. Imparting state power, and the formation of political purpose, to parliamentary political parties is tantamount to handing over power to their backers, their benefactors and demagogues. The procession to the holy voting urn ... leads to a dead end. Leadership, responsibility, decision grow from different soil ... the institution of parliament ... constantly demonstrates its impotence. It has exhausted its historical role."

ON trumpeted the autonomy of local communes, self-management in the workplace. Harro Schulze-Boysen's background in the Jungdeutscher Orden engendered a demand for neighbourhoods (*Nachbarschaften*) as the basic units of the national community of a people (*Volksgemeinschaft*), and he referred to "these communities, *Councils or Leagues,*"[91] which would "both in the communes, and in the business world, take over *the new ordering ... of the State, of the political economy.*" The debate was engaged in Germany (especially in the pages of *Gegner*) by the likes of Oswald Spengler, Karl Jaspers, and Ernst Jünger. Schulze-Boysen argued that "the problem posed by the machine can [only] be resolved by ... the will to organize. This presupposes a breakthrough, the liberation of the individual personality."

Expressions of regard for the human person were rare in the hardcore collectivistic rhetoric of German neo-nationalists and revolutionary conservatives, but they were central to *Plans*'s and ON's schemes to organize society. So this is a sign of personalist influence on Schulze-Boysen, who, like Marc, refused the mystical nostalgia engendered by the ugly side of industrial society: he complained that "German 'Fascism' [reduced] the concepts 'Blood and Soil' to *petit-bourgeois* expressions of anguish."

Over against what he saw as the propaganda and myths of the reactionary imperialists, Schulze-Boysen thought Germans should pay attention to ON's idea of rejecting monolithic national borders since: "millions of Germans live outside the borders of the Reich. The *question of minorities* will not be resolved by the annexations, but by *devaluing the old concept of border.*" This was very different from the neo-nationalists' economic self-sufficiency transcending capitalism, and it echoed Alexandre Marc's views.[92] "As a result of this insight the New Unity supports close cooperation, solidarity, with the forces of renewal of all other countries," "the awakened forces of all peoples" coming together "not to eradicate or to fossilize natural differences and cherished singularities, but rather to save peoples from degeneration and barbarism." But Schulze-Boysen admitted that the *Plans*/ON-style International of young non-conformists "angered many nationalists."[93]

Among those troubled by Schulze-Boysen's frequentations was the neo-nationalist extremist Ernst Niekisch, leader of the "National-Bolshevik" movement and editor of the journal *Widerstand* (which he had founded, with supporters from various radically anti-bourgeois nationalist groups, in 1926). Niekisch's ideas, "remarkably close to those of the Italian syndicalists,"[94] involved advocating a military-style "Prussian socialism" to liberate the proletariat from international capitalism by overthrowing the bourgeoisie and creating a strong state, a vibrant national consciousness among workers. Echoing the rhetoric of some pre-war, imperialist forerunners of Italian fascism such as Corradini and Prezzolini, Niekisch portrayed Germany as a proletarian, "have-not" nation about to lead a world-wide class struggle against the Western capitalist powers, thus achieving national liberation in an inexorable historical cataclysm.

Such extravagant geopolitical notions would shape Schulze-Boysen's political commitments.[95] Like Niekisch and other National-Bolsheviks, and like Otto Strasser, he patronized Hitler as a mere fascist, a lackey of capitalists, a corporatist who would only temper, not eliminate, class struggle. Niekisch, for his part, visited a sympathetic Mussolini in 1935 to complain about Hitler. The Duce agreed that their common perspective was left-wing in origin, and that any attack by Hitler on the Soviet Union would be pure folly.[96]

Like the other National-Bolsheviks Marc met through Schulze-Boysen, Niekisch seemed friendly toward the French, but, when Marc managed to get the cordial Bavarian drunk in a restaurant, Niekisch sadly confided that Germany would have to occupy at least half of "negrified" France, to help sift the good Frankish stock from the others.[97] Marc concluded that he had no future with Niekisch – despite their common lament that Nazism was demagogic, polluted by capitalist and liberal values.[98]

Ernst Niekisch did not approve of *Gegner*'s meeting with the Marc group in Frankfurt, and this precipitated the *Widerstand* National-Bolshevik break with the *Gegner* circle. They accused the Schulze-Boysen group of collusion with the French: after Schulze-Boysen's final take-over of *Gegner*, *Plans* had indiscreetly referred to "our German voice."[99] Schulze-Boysen and his friends were suspected of scheming for a Franco-German alliance against both Russia and the United States.[100] Schulze-Boysen retorted: "Clearly the concept of international, revolutionary and socialist solidarity and collaboration is alien to Herr Niekisch. His attachment to [Russia] blinds him to everything West of her."[101]

But in fact Soviet agents, we now know, were secretly supportive of Schulze-Boysen's romantic projects: the Soviet embassy tided over *Gegner* until a new backer, Fred Schmid, a Basle industrialist and *bündisch* leader, was found.[102] *Gegner* now began working with Schmid's Gray Corps, one of the most militantly pro-Soviet, collectivistic, and ultra-nationalist *bündisch* groups in Germany – a group whose position seemed strikingly opposed to the European federalism of *Plans*. The humanistic personalism in *Gegner*'s discourse gave way to a different tone once Ernst Jünger's *Der Arbeiter*, much discussed among activists, appeared.

By late 1932, political crisis and near-dictatorship obliged Schulze-Boysen to use jingoist rhetoric in line with cutting-edge activist thinking. *Gegner* began to say little about *Plans*' European Front of revolutionary youth, or a continent-wide New Order.[103] And the Front unique was not holding together very well in France either: returning from the last of his 1932 visits to Germany, Alexandre Marc told ON about his plans to smuggle weapons from France to help their friends prevent Hitler from taking over, and was reproached by his comrades for what seemed an initiative of "a terrorist cell."[104] Meanwhile Philippe Lamour was annoyed with ON for failing to take immediate practical action in Germany while being mired in Byzantine theoretical discussions; *Plans* would stop publishing, for financial reasons, in 1933.

Philippe Lamour and *Plans* also began distancing themselves from Alexandre Marc because of what they saw as his new soft-headed involvements with Catholics, and his relationship with the Jeune Droite. As Marc's enthusiasm for the German revolution became tempered, his growing piety led him to interact with young Frenchmen of strong religious beliefs fired by his personalist talk of spiritual revolution. Marc moved effortlessly from working with the German youth movements to interaction with French and Belgian communitarian spiritualists. Were these companies of political zealots and religious mystics as different from one another as most people seemed to assume?

# 3 Left-Wing Nazis, Revolutionary Conservatives, and Otto Neumann

"A national socialism which might have been" generated the involvement of Alexandre Marc and his friends with German neo-nationalists and anti-Hitler early Nazis. While Hitler rose in an atmosphere of bullying, raw brutality, and demagoguery, the national socialist movement also represented youth, the outdoors, virility, and fresh approaches to philosophical analysis – new ideas which young people thought could change the course of history. The "progressive" or left-wing Nazis in the national socialist movement, the "social nationalists" like Harro Schulze-Boysen and the Strasser brothers, represent important, if short-lived and relatively forgotten, historical possibilities.

Nazi dissident Otto Strasser was Ordre Nouveau (ON)'s best-known contact among the radical opponents of the beleaguered Weimar regime. Strasser, claiming to have introduced the idea of the "Third Reich" (borrowed from Moeller van den Bruck) into the Party, with his charismatic older brother Gregor (and Josef Goebbels) had created a "Party within the Party," rivalling Hitler's leadership. But the Strasser brothers were too impractical and theoretical for Adolf Hitler. Otto, holder of a doctorate in economics, wanted a neo-feudal conservative socialistic order involving Germany's withdrawal from world markets, the curtailing of private property, decentralization of economic and political structures, and a Russian alliance. Hitler – eager for donations to the Party – rejected the Strassers' "violent anticapitalism and their fanatically revolutionary agenda."

In 1926 Hitler attacked the Strassers' hold on Northern Germany by winning over Goebbels (appointing him *Gauleiter* of Berlin), and reaffirming his own twenty-five national socialist directives against their program. After several infamous heated meetings with Hitler in May 1930, Otto left the Party, and with the slogan "Socialists are leaving the NSDAP" founded his own the "Black Front" (Kampfgemeinschaft revolutionärer Nationalsozialisten/Struggle Community of Revolutionary National Socialists): the colour black, thanks to Moeller van den Bruck, was symbolic of radical conservatism – the black flag of the 1525 peasant uprisings. Gregor Strasser, the second most popular figure, after Hitler, in the Party, the man who had done more than anyone else besides Hitler to build it, continued the struggle, despite promising Hitler to break with his younger brother.[1]

The Black Front sought allies in the circle around the review *Die Tat*, and among Niekisch's "National-Bolsheviks," to counter the NSDAP. The Black Front's hammer and a cross over a swastika symbolized "a good deal of ideological crossbreeding, if not confusion, in Strasser." An aggravated Hitler, in arguments with Otto, called him a Marxist or Bolshevik; a scholar later summed him up as "the Trotsky of the Nazi Party."[2] He was not easily situated on the political spectrum: perhaps because he was original, perhaps because he was confused, or perhaps because he was both. Klemens von Klemperer, in a classic study of Germany's "New Conservatism," dismissed Otto Strasser as "a muddy, mystical thinker" whose ideology came out of the Youth Movement and neo-conservatism, and whose own movement in power "would have incorporated the worst features of both Rightist and Leftist extremism."[3] "In their stand against National-Socialism the neo-conservatives became more and more like their opponents ... They were irresponsibles ... confused and spread confusion. And the advent of National Socialism heightened and sharpened the dilemma. It represented the final test which the conservatives did not pass."[4]

Several "Strasser wing" qualities of the NSDAP appealed particularly to those of Marc's group interested in Catholicism. Imposing Gregor Strasser, with his shaven head and stentorian voice, "when not issuing directives or delivering speeches on behalf of the party, found delight in reading Homer and other classics; a unique, impressive, not unattractive man on the one hand, a dedicated, occasionally brutal National Socialist on the other."[5] "He was an odd sight, this big man in his home-made breeches, black woollen stockings, and heavy shoes, with a little Tyrolean hat perched like a plate atop his head, completely out of harmony with his broad and massive features ... he impressed me with his calm strength, his pithy humour, and robust health, ... something oaken and powerful."[6] As long as he was able, Gregor Strasser represented an effective internal party challenge to Hitler, "a national socialism which might have been."[7]

The Strassers' national socialism reflected devout Bavarian Catholic origins; their brother, and biographer, Bernhard, became a Benedictine monk in Collegeville, Minnesota; their father published a pamphlet advocating a blending of socialism, nationalism, and Christianity into a "German socialism."[8] Gregor, a Jesuit-educated, self-described "*völkisch* Catholic," saw Christianity as essential for human self-fulfilment and refused to admit any irreconcilable conflict between Christian and national socialist principles. More activist and organizer than the more cerebral Otto, Gregor held political views that were always "ill-defined" and "almost certainly of Otto's unacknowledged inspiration."[9] His anti-capitalist, anti-bourgeois, "socialist" rhetoric was laced with attacks on "international Jewish capitalism" and "the materialistic spirit."[10] Like the ON-*Esprit* people, his first priority was a "conversion" to anti-capitalism, a total change in mentality, the surmounting of "the materialistic spirit."[11] Revolutionary anti-capitalism involved transforming life-styles before class structures.

By late 1931, when *Plans* published his manifesto, Gregor Strasser had much annoyed Hitler by claiming authority over the whole national socialist movement and working with other revolutionary groups, particularly with neo-conservatives like those of the *Tat*-Kreis. The review *Die Tat* led the press in debating national and social issues vital to young people. From a circulation of eight hundred in 1929, it had reached thirty thousand under the brilliant editorship of Hans Zehrer, a former journalist at the leading liberal daily *Vossische Zeitung.*[12] Zehrer, at the peak of his influence, unwisely concluded that defeat in the March–April 1932 elections had finished Hitler and so he began working for a new authoritarian ruling elite to effect a "revolution from above" to incorporate a combination of conservative and socially progressive ideals. Zehrer's revolution was to be led by a Third Front made up of the army under General Kurt von Schleicher, the trade unions, and Gregor Strasser (to whom Schleicher had been introduced in Zehrer's Berlin home). In a widely remarked article in the April 1932 *Die Tat*, Gregor Strasser called for a broad political front ("Querfront") as in the *Tat*-Kreis program, and Zehrer subsequently multiplied his dealings with Strasser.[13]

But unexpectedly, in the legislative elections of 31 July 1932, the NSDAP, with 13,745,000 votes, became the largest party in the Reichstag. Since the last elections two years before, the Nazis had increased their vote by over seven million, their parliamentary representation from 107 to 230. While they had won some thirteen million new votes since 1928, they were still far short of a majority in a 608-member house and commanded only 37 per cent of the popular vote. Most Germans were still against them, and, despite their considerable momentum, the Nazis were still divided between Hitler and the rival left wing led by the Strasser brothers.[14]

In 1932 *Mouvements*, an ON-inspired newsletter on the new international non-conformist movement, reported on the various German movements – the second (July) issue containing an interview with Otto Strasser, whom the ON had met in the apartment of *Mouvements* editor Pierre-Olivier Lapie.[15] There seemed in July 1932 a national, even international, convergence of youthful idealism, as was reported in Daniel-Rops's widely remarked essay, "The Aspirations of French Youth." *Plans* and ON efforts would soon be complemented – it announced – by a major review drawing upon "a Christian, if not expressly Catholic, tradition (its directors being Catholic)."[16] This would be Emmanuel Mounier's *Esprit*.

Zehrer's Third Front appealed to the ON group, and in the October 1932 *Revue d'Allemagne*, Marc signalled *Die Tat*'s guidelines for a "national communism" and what he saw as the striking similarities between the pre-revolutionary France of 1789, Russia in 1917, and contemporary Germany. Hitler's electoral successes were perceived as ephemeral in the light of Germany's profound spiritual crisis. No mere "Third Reich," "as imagined by Hitler's acolytes," but a total new destiny for Germany would come out of the crisis. Germany's future was some form of "National-Communism," "not a form of society instantly constituted and crystallized" but rather "a melding of tendencies whose subsequent evolution remained difficult to foresee."[17]

The German situation described in *Die Tat* was a "distinct illustration in line with the Germanic tradition and temperament" of a general spiritual movement gradually spreading to all European youth and "more or less crystallized according to the particular circumstances of each country."[18] Marc heralded the *Die Tat* analysis of bankrupt modern capitalism as reflected in Ferdinand Fried's *Das Ende des Kapitalismus* (Jena, 1931), the first serious nationalist critique of capitalism, soon nearly as influential in France as in Germany.[19]

Marc stressed the common goal which "the French spiritual movement" (especially ON and *Plans*) shared with the *Tat*-Kreis: "that necessary revolution" which would "put an end to the disorders in the economic realm and re-establish that primacy of the spiritual" without which everything would "go off course and end in chaos." The *Tat*-Kreis, Marc argued, stressed the state's role in replacing the priority of the economic with the priority of the spiritual, albeit while putting more emphasis on the political than did ON. But *Die Tat*'s *Volksstaat* was the institutional embodiment of a revolution transcending the political and social order, effecting a "revolution of the soul," a new "incarnation of man," a new civilization. The *Tat*-Kreis revolution would, like the Reformation, give "a new face" to much of humanity, fulfil the hopes of the revolutionary people, the collective will to create an "homme nouveau."[20]

Marc acknowledged that the proletariat were to be the foundation of the new *Tat*-Kreis state, a "Revolution from the Right" which would rebut and even transcend Marxism and communism.[21] The *Tat*-Kreis, rather than neglecting the economic dimension of life, considered it necessary, but secondary, subordinated to the spiritual. Zehrer showed that the "revolution" was first against the liberal mentality – and its political expression in the parliamentary political system.[22] Zehrer rightly condemned the German Catholic Centre party for enlisting religion's support for dying liberalism; but if the Church broke with the doomed modern world it would have new and magnificent "possibilities." Zehrer and *Die Tat* represented a dynamic spiritualism within the German youth movement – more civilized, more promising than what Hitler's group represented. The *Tat*-Kreis could play a significant role "as the [moderate] parties' influence diminishes ... as the burgeoning German revolution gathers form and consistency ... We need pay attention only to the extremes: the national socialist wing on the one hand, the communists on the other ... there have ... been links ... between the *Die Tat* group ... [with] their sporadic sympathy for fascism, and national socialism."

But the *Tat*-Kreis's position was more reserved and critical about national socialism as it turned into "a mass movement." The *Die Tat* circle "resolutely condemned large, clumsy vote-getting organizations" while the Nazis went into "the most demagogic sorts of activities."

Marc approved the *Tat*-Kreis's aloofness in the tense, complex, German situation, citing Fried's dictum: "He who does not have the courage to forego all impulsive action is a spiritual deserter."[23] *Die Tat* people "had to repudiate Adolf Hitler's noisy displays" and "draw up the uncompromising balance-sheet on what it calls the bankruptcy of liberalism and capitalism." Since "both advancing flanks of the revolution had failed in their mission," Zehrer's only hope for communism was in its discarding Marxism and Stalinism and fusing with German national traditions into a "national-communism."[24]

The real significance of *Tat*-Kreis's role was as intellectuals with a distinctive revolutionary vision which intertwined with that of the growing "spiritual party" in France. Hans Zehrer and his group thought "All revolution only ... worthy of the name if it culminates not only in radical change in institutions ... but, above and before all, in a ... 'new man.' The new man can only come from a concentrated spiritual effort of depth and intensity. In the very heart of our present chaos, we must 'reunite' in 'groups for thought and action' – ... 'lodges' ...

organically linked societies of men, preparing the future." And cere-bral, spiritualistic men in that dramatic fall of 1932 had to come to terms with rubbing shoulders with the masses, with "a new attitude toward life and the world; [not as] thinkers in ivory towers ... but rather 'concrete revolutionaries' profoundly linked to the people and ... projecting the paroxysms and maturation of the people onto the spiritual level."[25]

There were several arresting and, in retrospect, interesting assump-tions governing Marc's outlook at this historical turning point. Despite our later assumption that there was an inevitability to Hitler's rise to power, it is clear that, as late as October 1932, the triumph of the Hit-lerites within German national socialism was not self-evident to those involved with the events. French admirers of the German Youth Move-ment, then, still envisioned the victory of the erratic Hitler's national-revolutionary rivals – even of some form of "national-communism." The governing ideal of the "primacy of the spiritual dimension," the "new man" of the *Tat* circle in Germany, was much like that of Marc's milieu in France: although the *Tat* people were, unlike Marc, given to assume that the promotion of the spiritual dimension of life was the role of the national state, they, too, had their spiritual elites, and simi-lar strategies and tactics. Despite the language and cultural differ-ences, and the different political contexts, the French spiritual move-ment around ON, *Plans,* and *Esprit* could feel strong affinity for, even identify with, groups like the *Tat*-Kreis. There were also *Die Tat*'s revo-lutionary elites – carefully trained men of intellect, training, activist bent, and true spirituality – to represent, distil, and focus popular aspi-rations. *Die Tat*'s project to go beyond Marxism in their search for the "new man" resembled that of the non-conformists in France. Because of significant German groups like that, young Frenchmen could sup-port German anti-republican revolutionaries, even certain national socialists ... while loathing Adolf Hitler and his cohorts. The fluidity of this situation and the evidence that things might have turned out dif-ferently oblige us to rethink our understanding of the "inevitabilities" which we too often factor into our understanding of the meaning of Hitler and Nazism and of the Vichy regime in France.

Take the example of Hans Zehrer's intention to reform and purify, not obliterate, the Christian churches. This policy, not unlike Marc's (and in contrast to Harro Schulze-Boysen's dismissal of them as irrelevant vestigia), and his idea of integrating Communism, stripped of its Marxism and Stalinism, into the national tradition, were like the Jacques Maritain/*Esprit* dream of somehow Christianizing these traditions.[26]

Men whose imaginations were stimulated by these fresh ON ideas would, in the next few years, serve as ideologists or propagandists for various French or Belgian right-wing groups, for Colonel de la Rocque's Croix de Feu, Jacques Doriot's PPF, Marshal Pétain, and Pierre Laval ... as well as for General de Gaulle, as we shall see. Though these were very different political leaders and configurations, and not always in a clear ON line, the governing ideal of converts engendering a true revolution, close to *Die Tat*'s,[27] remained.[28] Hans Zehrer's dream of a vast anti-capitalist and anti-liberal coalition for spiritual revolution and the "new man" in Germany, and Alexandre Marc's spiritual party in France, did not seem hopelessly quixotic as late as the fall of 1932, even if the German situation soon dashed their hopes.

While in November 1932 German elections seemed to confirm Gregor Strasser's predictions of a Nazi defeat owing to Hitler's rigid and autocratic style of national socialism, Hitler claimed that Strasser's socialist views alienated middle-class voters. Strasser had to either abandon his leading role in the NSDAP or to fight for the leadership; he now feared a Hitlerite Germany, arguing that Hitlerism and genuine national socialism were very different things.[29] In December, Kurt von Schleicher, now chancellor of the Weimar Republic, offered to make Gregor Strasser premier of Prussia and vice-chancellor of Germany, thus satisfying Hans Zehrer. Failing to persuade Hitler to join the government, Schleicher hoped to split the Nazis, because "among the left-wing element, which really believed in a national socialism, [Strasser] was more popular than Hitler. As leader of the Party Organization he was in direct touch with all the provincial and local leaders, earned their loyalty."[30] Zehrer, in his 11 December editorial in the *Tägliche Rundschau* (the *Tat*-Kreis's short-lived daily newspaper), celebrated Strasser as the exemplar of true National Socialism, and portrayed him as about to take over the NSDAP.[31]

At a 5 December meeting in Berlin, Strasser asked the Nazis to tolerate the Schleicher government, but Hitler – swayed by Goering and Goebbels – refused. In the bitter quarrel between the two Party leaders on the 7th, Strasser heatedly denied trying to displace Hitler but accused him of destroying national socialism; Strasser ended by resigning his positions in the Party. Goebbels thought this the greatest blow to Hitler since the Party's rebuilding in 1925. "Now, on the threshold of power, his principal follower had deserted him and threatened to smash all he had built up in seven years."[32] Hitler spoke of a ruined party and contemplated suicide.

At the crucial moment, as his comrades searched Berlin for Strasser to make peace to save the party, a disgusted Strasser took a train south for a vacation in sunny Italy. "Hitler, always at his best when he detected weakness in an opponent, struck swiftly and hard." The political organization built by Strasser was taken over personally by the Führer, the Strassers' friends were purged, and all Party leaders were summoned to Berlin to pledge fidelity to Adolf Hitler. "Gregor Strasser, whom so many had thought to be a greater man than Hitler, was quickly destroyed."[33] Despite his retirement from politics, Strasser was taken from his family meal and murdered on 30 June 1934 – the infamous "Night of the Long Knives" – as General von Schleicher was also liquidated.

The leaders of heavy industry, banking, and large agriculture, who had been alarmed at the Schleicher-Strasser dialogue, were encouraged at the ruin of the "socialism" in Hitler's movement.[34] Otto Strasser portrayed the December 1932 crisis as the Party's socialists' last stand against a pro-business Hitler.[35] Whether this socialist threat was real or illusory,[36] ex-chancellor Heinrich Brüning said in a letter to Father Bernhard Strasser: "your brother was the only person in the NSDAP who could one day have eliminated Hitler ... and prepared a party evolution which might have spared Germany and Europe all that has occurred."[37] Gregor Strasser might well have rejected a high-profile SS, systematic state racism or anti-Semitism, extensive rearmament, an aggressive foreign policy, terror, repression, and brutality, and fought for "a rather different kind of Germany, strong, respected, proud, but never fanatical, destructive, intolerant."[38]

Did the Strassers represent a national socialism or even a Germany which might have been? Alexandre Marc, years later, allowed for that, whatever his misgivings about those he remembered as "dissident Nazis – but Nazis still." The historian of the *Die Konservative Revolution*, Armin Mohler, considered Hans Zehrer's "Third Front," which assumed the spontaneous decomposition of the mass parties (Nazi and Communist), as a flaccid construct devoid of any possible political impact.[39] Similarly, ON's non-conformism, poised between political divides, had a novel point of view but no solid political base.

The Strasser–*Tat*-Kreis episode bared the harsh realities of the so-called German Revolution for the Marc group. While *Die Tat* had envisaged a radical break to create a "new man," and ridiculed the insincerity of internationalism and pacifism, its writers soon slid back into nationalistic totalitarian politics themselves, and called it "spirituality." Hence *Die Tat*'s ambiguous conciliatory policy toward General von Schleicher, whose attitude toward trade unions hardly promised a new world.[40] *Die Tat*/Schwarze Front/National-Bolshevik projects – such as that economic, "autarchy" which had alienated Hitler from Otto Strasser – Marc concluded to be "popular above all in marginal national socialist political and sociological circles"; "the 'autarchians,' after their war cry against materialism and the priority of the economic, were opting for an organization with a purely materialistic base," even "statist nationalism." ON would hold to "a truly healthy and original conception of a New Order." Marc now tempered his sympathy for his German friends with some overdue critical detachment.[41]

The February 1933 *Esprit* issue on Germany foresaw a confrontation between the Strasser brothers and Hitler, explaining that Otto had founded the Black Front after Hitler rejected the restructuring of German heavy industry. Otto had "quit the National Socialist Party as insufficiently revolutionary," calling Hitler "our revolution's Kerensky"; Strasser wanted to collectivize key industries, and revitalize the *Mittelstand* – the middle classes and small peasantry – to help stabilize the country.[42]

Marc saw German youth's prospects dimmed by the Strasser-*Die Tat* group setback in December. The most politically committed were turning toward communism or toward national socialism, while Marc's non-conformists kept faithfully to their new approach, which would appeal to many of them. Marxists faced "Marxist socialism's spiritual deficiency" and "Moscow's dogmatism" while young Nazis were in a particularly complex, divisive situation:

The National Socialist party is surely *a party of the young* ... the most attractive aspect of that movement which the Führer, Adolf Hitler, is slowly leading to ruin. To become a Nazi was ... to demonstrate independence from the established disorder. It was to condemn a world devoid of grandeur ... liberalism's cowardly compromises and the materialist temptation. ... to nobly affirm the virtues of discipline in a corrupt and degenerate world. The young National Socialists were moved by a sincere need for spiritual grandeur which, moreover, ran directly against the racial primacy doctrine.[43]

But recent developments in Germany had shaken these great hopes, for "While the [Nazi] leaders received subsidies from heavy industry, the young imagined themselves fighting for a national and idealist socialism ... [but] *Today the best of them have lost confidence* ... [So now] the young National Socialists represent an eminently favourable audience for the 'non-conformist' groupings' message."[44]

Otto Strasser's Black Front, Marc said, represented a "pristine national socialism" against Hitler's compromises. The Strasser group's "national idealism" set out "corporative ideas" and "a hierarchical and non-egalitarian organization of the economy" as an anti-capitalist alternative to socialism and Marxism, and Marc noted their healthy interest in "the federal principle" despite the fact that their thinking was "sometimes afflicted by a rather confused *biological mysticism* ... incompatible with our conception of the spiritual." Other groups –

Ernst Niekisch's *Widerstand* among them[45] – were searching for a new way between communism and nationalism, but would only find it in ON's "integral federalism"; the young anti-Stalinist Communists would only find what *they* wanted in a "revolutionary personalism."

Marc's hopes that a *Gegner*-style coalition of non-conformists (prefigured by the Strasser/*Tat*-Kreis initiative) would save the unsullied revolutionary current had been shaken by the December ordeal. Marc thought that Hitler's opportunistic conservatism threatened youth's enthusiasm for revolution, but not that Hitler would take power with an iron hand.

Alexandre Marc (a bit like Martin Heidegger) saw no fatal poison or peril in "young" national socialism, much less that it was – as Pope Pius XI said of communism – "intrinsically perverse." Marc, despite his grisly Russian experience, was not particularly wary of the danger of youthful idealists being coopted by manipulative tyrants. He remained convinced that only the generosity and altruism of the young could produce a generation of converts, create a new man for a new world, as German youth had promised in these exciting, hopeful, yet ominous, months.

### FIRING UP THE CATHOLICS: OTTO NEUMANN

German young people as a whole proved to have special energies which fascinated French young people interested in the religious conversion experience. On returning from his German visit in early December 1931, Alexandre Marc was sought out at *Plans*' offices on rue Geoffroy L'Asnier by three earnest young Catholics – a philosophy graduate student, a lawyer, and an architect – who told Marc they wanted to start "a review like *Plans*, only Catholic" and needed his help. They were led by Emmanuel Mounier, a new *agrégé* from Grenoble, who had the backing of the Catholic philosopher Jacques Maritain, in whose renowned intellectual salon in Meudon the project had germinated. Leading thinkers such as Gabriel Marcel and Berdyaev attended those Sunday afternoon discussions *chez Raissa et Jacques*, as well as those at the Berdyaevs' in nearby Clamart. There were Thomist metaphysicians, expatriate Russians, composers, essayists, artists, theologians, and mystics carrying on high-level spirit talk with the brightest of the young Catholics at their feet. The papal condemnation of the Action Française in 1926 obliged Maritain to distance himself from Charles Maurras's organization and start a new, spiritual review – *Esprit* – to give a voice to new thinking. Alexandre Marc, self-assured expert on the exciting new German philosophers, found Mounier – a literary type sharing Jacques Maritain's interests in religion – weak and malleable, but thought *Esprit* could serve as "a sort of literary supplement to *Plans*."[46]

The three Maritain salon regulars who brought the Catholic *Plans* project to Marc were contrasting personalities. Georges Izard, another one of those converts in the Maritains' orbit who marked the period, was a flamboyant young lawyer who had been secretary to the radical deputy Charles Daniélou and had married his daughter. Izard had adopted the rigorously intellectual approach to religion of his mother-in-law, the celebrated Catholic educator Madeleine Daniélou, and her children. Madeleine Daniélou's son Jean (destined to become a famous theologian and cardinal) shared Mounier's and Izard's interest in the late Charles Péguy's combining of socialist ideals and nationalist fervour in Joan of Arc. Their *La pensée de Charles Péguy* (Paris, 1931) was written with Péguy's son Marcel (replacing Jean Daniélou, become Jesuit seminarian). The third of the *Esprit* founders, Louis-Emile Galey, was a jaunty architect (albeit unemployed for the moment, like many *Esprit* people) who shared Izard's penchant for organizing ardent young men into companies of scrappers – notably a group of street demonstrators called "La Troisième Force." Galey would become a specialist in designing youth groups and films rather than buildings (especially under the Vichy regime). Maritain, Marcel, and Berdyaev were looking for new Christian political thinking to displace the now out of bounds, exclusionary, hyper-nationalism of Maurras: enthusiasm was supposed to be tempered by Thomistic analytical rigour in the Maritains' salon. (Always "to prune, to prune" was described as Jacques Maritain's approach in philosophical discussion.) The Maritains at Meudon and Mounier at *Esprit* were surrounded by bright people looking for direction and so marshalling considerable learning and creative talent to rethink the Catholic conversion experience and hence political culture.[47]

Here the Germans seemed to have something inventive to offer. Like the *Plans* circle, the *Esprit* set was very interested in the "150 groups" of young Germans which the ON movement claimed already represented their common ideas beyond the Rhine.[48] When Mounier caught up with Marc at the *Plans* offices, he seems to have entrusted him with responsibility for *Esprit*'s contacts abroad, and Izard and Mounier took to Marc's suggestion to have the logo "French edition" of an "international" review on their title page (ON was described as the "French section" of an international movement in its manifesto the previous year). Marc was given an office directly across from Mounier's in the Belgian-supported Catholic publishing house Desclée De Brouwer, the base of operations for the new review.

In the first *Esprit*'s lead article (October 1932), Berdyaev predicted the Christianization or spiritualization of the world communist movement.[49] Mounier then seconded Berdyaev's appeal in *A New Middle Ages* to transcend the "communalism" of the East and the "individualism" of the West.[50] Marc's personalist, "anti-individualist" spiritual revolution suggested there was hope of "Christianizing" the revolutionary temper of young people.

Emmanuel Mounier saw hope for the "new Renaissance" of his dreams in that "personalism" to which he kept alluding. On 18 October 1932, Marc took Mounier to meet ON guru Arnaud Dandieu at the Bibliothèque Nationale. Mounier had mixed feelings about Dandieu: discovering an "enemy of the intellectuals, an intellectual to the fingertips, and with the expression of one to boot. Long hair brushed back, cold stare, fixed smile, thick glasses for short-sightedness. Visibly making an effort to be pleasant." In a nearby café opposite the Bourse, Dandieu pontificated on "the very complicated hierarchy of values which constitutes the 'Ordre Nouveau' system," all of which was presented in a tone of "extreme doctrinaire rigour." Mounier, who was expecting "some sort of encounter on the cutting edge of Christianity," found instead a "terminology which ... though neither stupid nor obtuse, was repeated over and over again" by a sort of little exclusionary sect.

Mounier was turned off by Dandieu's personality, and didn't like ON's "opportunistic" cooperation with several new right-wing groups, but he was interested in Dandieu's new philosophy of personalism as "an affirmation of creative powers ... admittedly Nietzschean ... (all creation, being personal, is pure act for Dandieu.) He grants the existence of something irreducibly passive, a 'feminine' element in the world, ... [which] far from fulfilling the person ... [is] the very obstacle that it must overcome ... talk of renunciation, of giving ... [is] to cater to that passivity ... He literally sees in God an adversary to human creation ... who would diminish the person ... because He is always the initial creator, at the very foundation ... of His creation."

For Mounier, Dandieu's Nietzschean personalism was "saved" by Alexandre Marc, who "spiritualized" it "with his Catholic vision of a universe in which God is a person living in Christ and through his mystical body in ourselves. So, as a result, our person is only raised to the level of personality by the divine motion of the Mediator. He believes he can reach both God and Dandieu in this way. Dandieu, who resists, above all, the Protestant God ... admits that the Catholicism of A. Marc can be in line with his thought, but he denies that it can be orthodox. I will grant the orthodoxy of it, but I deny that Marc's interpretation owes allegiance to Dandieu's thought."[51]

Mounier was fascinated by Dandieu's philosophy as found in *Plans*, *Mouvements*, and some widely noted monographs. *Esprit*, too, had its volatile librarian in André Déléage – a Nietzschean street-fighter given to employing what Mounier called "Hitlerite language."[52] Déléage, like Dandieu, like Marc, thought Mounier weak, piously timorous. But Marc wanted ON spiritualized, since he was ever more concerned about religion ... and the direction of the spiritual revolution across the Rhine.

In the November 1932 *Esprit*, Marc described the new generation as recognizing "the bankruptcy of modern civilization," searching for a "New Order" while rejecting Marxism and all "fascisms," including "the Stalinist version."[53] Berdyaev had established *Esprit*'s world-historical perspective on the future of revolution, Marc and ON confidently provided the new doctrine of a 'New Order.' In the second issue of *Esprit*, Marc and René Dupuis, in line with ON essays in *Plans* and *Mouvements*, mentioned "our conception of the personality"[54] – namely that personalism which had been expounded by ON for a year now. It would take Mounier another two years to formulate his own communitarian personalism to distinguish it from that of Marc.[55]

## DE ROUGEMONT AND THE "GENERATION OF 1930"

The ideas of Marc and his friends seemed so popular among the intelligentsia by late 1932 that they provided the material for a special issue of the eminent *Nouvelle Revue Française* presenting a "new generation." And the idea that the young French intelligentsia were becoming like the German conservative revolutionaries alarmed older Catholic intellectuals like Jacques Maritain, as well as French Marxists.

Denis de Rougemont and Daniel-Rops had described the radical "common cause" uniting French and German young people in July.[56] Rougemont described the meeting organized by Marc and his friends: "The Frankfurt Congress organized by *Plans* brought to light a basic unity, created ... by the disconcerting misery of an epoch in which everything a man could love or want is cut off from its living origins, wilted, denatured, inverted, sabotaged. Revolution does not mean hatred, nor destruction ... It means the salvation of man as man." Rougemont saw "the better minds of our generation" working at ON, *Esprit*, and *Plans*: "never, perhaps, had a generation so spontaneously found a commonality of essential attitude." "Neurasthenia depresses the cities, where we are perhaps the only ones to experience strength and *présence*. We know the truth ... we only need to seize it in its imperious self-evidence and in its eternal violence."[57]

It was at the end of the summer that de Rougemont received a letter from Jean Paulhan, director of the *Nouvelle Revue Française*, suggesting that he might gather testimonials of this new generational consensus and draw a conclusion from them: "That might be ... interesting ... perhaps rather serious." The *NRF*'s "Cahier de revendications" presented thirteen spokesmen for self-described "revolutionary" groups. These included Thierry Maulnier, Philippe Lamour, Alexandre Marc, Dandieu, Aron, Dupuis, Mounier, and Izard for *Esprit*, and the young Communists Henri Lefebvre and Paul Nizan of the Association des Artistes et Ecrivains Révolutionnaires.

De Rougemont's conclusion was that "the youth of 1932" shared "a revolutionary 'exigency' to an unprecedented extent," and were looking for a third way "between a deposed bourgeoisie and a false Marxism" because "There is nothing for us on either the Left or the Right. We see ourselves at the beginning of something else ... lost on those who [simply] recite Marx ... The testimonials ... define two revolutionary positions ... one materialist, the other personalist; the first is just being realized in the USSR, the second has hardly left the stage of doctrinal formulation ... Ordre Nouveau, *Esprit* are working in tandem with deep revolutionary forces in France. This revolt of the person represents what is still valuable and dynamic in the revolt of '89 ... [it is] the new French Revolution.[58]

Reactions were mixed: André Gide was "troubled," Daniel Halévy was disturbed by the vagueness of the declaration, but Gabriel Marcel was "enchanted, on the same wavelength as Ordre Nouveau." Pierre Drieu la Rochelle, soon France's foremost fascist intellectual, was "bouleversé: the young are fascist!"[59]

### THE CRITICS:
### CATHOLICS AND COMMUNISTS

Even before de Rougemont's "Cahier" was published, mentor Jacques Maritain worried about ON influence on *Esprit*, blaming a Dandieu essay for its "impossible tone," errors, and "numerous confusions," as the sort of "goose-stepping philosophy" found among the Germans.[60] Maritain also complained to Mounier,[61] after the second issue of *Esprit*, that de Rougemont's essay and the Dupuis-Marc "Revolutionary Federalism" manifesto were "aggressive volubility and insolent dogmatism disguising a poverty of sclerotic thinking," warning that "*excités*" were alienating good people from the review.[62] Mounier, conceding the regrettable "atheism" in Dandieu and the "intellectual *arrivisme* of certain self-styled and pretentious prophets" like Marc, promised to steer *Esprit* on a course independent from them.[63] Mounier claimed to be in "a perfect state of contrition,"[64] but secretly remained captivated by Marc's energizing fusion of ON's personalism with Catholicism, and believed that it had drawn other people to *Esprit*.

The well-known young writer Paul Nizan – Catholic turned Communist after a stint in Georges Valois's Faisceau – claimed to have been tricked into the NRF "Cahier."[65] Philippe Lamour claimed that he had been drawn into a spurious common front with dubious elements, including open counter-revolutionaries.[66] Nizan granted that *Esprit* did not have "a very precise and very clear fascist consciousness," that it was out to "decant, purify, and perfect the thick foreign currents" and invent a "French national socialism": more refined, "more artful than the others."[67]

Nizan thought that "among all the European movements [the Nazis] preferred pre-fascist ideological movements which most resembled *Esprit* or Ordre Nouveau, movements [which could be] rapidly absorbed by national socialism." He mentioned the *Die Tat* and *Gegner* groups, the Black Front of Otto Strasser, and the English movement New Britain as of this kind. The "person," Nizan charged, was similar to a concept of Joseph Goebbels, who had described the Nazi doctrine as "that of the personality."

Nizan mocked young "*petits-bourgeois* pretending to be crushed by 'Big Capital' but attached to private property – to 'their' land, 'their' person, 'their' house, 'their' wife." The ON personalist society reminded Nizan of that "small artisanal universe surrounding man in the thinking of M. Heidegger, official philosopher of national socialism."[68] (Heidegger had been nominated as rector of the University of Freiburg in April 1933 and, at the beginning of May, at the request of the minister of education, had joined the National Socialist party. This was the beginning of his period of open support for the Nazi revolution.)[69]

Nizan saw French "spiritual revolutionary" circles as made up largely of highly educated but unemployed youth: "The proletarian condition seems difficult and unworthy of them ... All their teachers told them that they were the elites. [Their] philosophies are the philosophies of disappointed 'elites.' How could they resist the attraction of social movements in which a few of them might become 'leaders,' 'persons': in which these failures ["déclassés"] would provide fascist cadres? Goebbels was an unsuccessful *littérateur* ... [as is] a Daniel-Rops, a Maxence. The youth mystique expresses their anguish in the face of an uncertain future."[70]

Nizan thought "personalists" sincere revolutionaries and not simply "fascists." While "not considering themselves fascist at all," they were distilling the "thick foreign currents" of German national socialism into a peculiarly "Catholic," and self-consciously "refined," French

variant. But someday, he warned, "the defenders of the Person, in fascist uniforms" would line up behind a Christian prince, in the bourgeoisie's final battle against communism.[71]

Nizan's attacks on the personalist spiritual revolution were dismissed as party propagandizing by de Rougemont and ON at the time.
But in fact Nizan was prophetic in suggesting it was a concept which
could be used by a reactionary regime.[72] The defence of spiritual values could mask the defence of the socio-political status of Catholic
elites threatened by materialists. Both the fascist personality cult and
the personalist call for spiritual leaders envisaged a determined few
changing the course of history.[73]

### THE THIRD FORCE

De Rougemont's "Cahier" claimed that France needed a "Third Way,"
neither Right nor Left. The first issue of *Esprit* in October 1932 included Marc's "Chronicle of the Movement," describing intentions, and
the second, in November, his "Chronicle of the Third Force," showing
progress. By the end of that month, Georges Izard, Louis-Emile Galey,
and Georges Duveau (a young "Proudhonian" historian of trade-
unionism) were setting up an organization to break heads, if necessary, for *Esprit*-ON ideas. They followed Marc's suggestion for a name
(inspired by a *Tat*-Kreis essayist): the "Third Force."[74] This "Troisième
Force" hosted German *émigrés* from the *Gegner*-Kreis, recommended by
Harro Schulze-Boysen, at its meetings.[75]

The French Third Force was convoked in a dramatic and colourful
setting: Catherine Daniélou-Izard secured a cob-walled shed at 110
rue de Sèvres, lit by two oil lamps and charcoal heaters whose red
reflections on the frosted window created a surrealistic, theatrical
impression on the audience of about thirty or so. A "wilfull and direct"
German economist in her mid-forties, "violently daubed in red by a
nearby lamp," set a dramatic, apocalyptic tone (*"Messieurs*, we are in
1788"). The power struggle in Germany arose when a member of the
audience, who had just returned from there, defended the role of his
*Die Tat* friends and the new Right. This French Third Force assumed
that the youth revolution would quickly radiate beyond their circle of
editors, journalists, philosophers, lawyers, seminarians, and architects.
But Mounier mused after the meeting: "German youth has already
gone through the first stages, [is] further along than us."[76]

The Third Force was soon infusing new ideas into French politics –
especially in the milieu of the renegade neo-radical Gaston Bergery.
Izard lauded "young Radicals" such as Bergery as representing a "truly
revolutionary" vanguard of a new politics, and hoped Bergery would
soon have his own coalition.[77]

OTTO NEUMANN:
BAPTISING REVOLUTIONARY PERSONALISM

Marc was fast becoming a *pur et dur* professional revolutionary, but passionate love intervened in the person of an extremely wealthy Argentine romantic poet. Margarita Abella Caprile, in her early thirties, met Marc at a Décades de Pontigny (a yearly thematic gathering of the intelligentsia organized by Paul Desjardins in the famous refurbished Cistercian Pontigny abbey in the Yonne). Her family owned stock in *La Nación* of Buenos Aires, then one of the world's leading newspapers, and she arranged for the publication of a series of articles on the European youth movements by Marc there (they became the core of his *Jeune Europe*, in the fall of 1933). Marc's diary recorded his difficulties as a converted bohemian with his painful unrequited love for the strict Catholic poet.[78] Heart-broken, Alexandre Marc waved from the quai at Le Havre as the beautiful Argentine virgin sailed home in 1931 to continue her literary career.[79]

In early 1933, after his shattering disappointment in love, Marc took on a Catholic spiritual director (as was common in those days), and soon encountered a very different, more marriageable, young woman – Suzanne Jean, a disciple of the Serbian guru Dimitrije Mitrinovic. Jean was of Provençal Protestant background, and had been teaching for four years in an experimental school in Bristol while involved with the New Britain movement. In one of his oracular pronouncements, Mitrinovic – while in a deep meditative state[80] – had told the young woman: "I think Marc, I live Marc, I breathe Marc," and sent her off to the offices of *Esprit* in Paris to find the prophetic young man. Suzanne Jean found Marc via Mounier, told of the message she had received from "notre maitre spirituel," and was taken along, for a first date, not to a romantic café in the Latin Quarter but to the founding meeting of the Third Force. Mlle Jean remembered that she was touched by Marc's idealism and dedication, so close to the spiritual revolution of the New Britain movement. The couple quickly became united for life by their common ideal, as happened relatively often in that generation of converts.[81]

By early 1933, *Esprit* attracted other New Britain people for its self-assured way of representing the younger generation, but Mounier and his *Esprit* comrades were worried about the Nietzschean dimension of ON's personalism. Mounier, embracing Marc's Catholicized version of it, was hounded by Jacques Maritain – *Esprit*'s crucial patron – to distance the review from Arnaud Dandieu's "goose-stepping philosophy." To mollify Maritain, Mounier put together an issue of *Esprit* on Christianity and Revolution, based on an evident "Rupture entre l'ordre chrétien et le désordre établi." (It is a telling detail to this story that "established disorder" was Marc's ironical phrase, coined by him to describe just what the Nazis abhorred; it was in his article on German youth in the February *Esprit*,[82] and used the next month to title a watershed special issue opposing Christianity to the bourgeoisie. "Established disorder" became a new commonplace in the discourse of anti-establishment social critics – always attributed to "clean" Mounier, never to the "murky" Russian Jew Marc.)[83] The essays in the March issue from the elders, Maritain and Berdyaev, seconded by ON "Young Turks" Denis de Rougemont and Alexandre Marc, included Mounier's exposition of new Belgian initiatives such as the Centrale politique de la jeunesse and its publication *L'Esprit Nouveau* (which he described as having become the *enfant terrible* of the Catholic party). Belgian radical Catholicism was celebrated, reflected in Raymond de Becker's fiery pamphlet *Pour un Ordre Nouveau.*

Alexandre Marc's remarkable essay "Le Christianisme et la Révolution Spirituelle"[84] represented a turning point in the ON-*Esprit* movement. Annoyed by Mounier's timorousness about ON philosophy,[85] and though no Catholic himself, Marc showed – citing the new monograph *Revolution des Geistes* by a young German Catholic theologian called Otto Neumann – that a Catholic personalism was possible, viable, and compelling. For according to Otto Neumann, "Christianity alone ... made the individual into a person: that is why the individual is liberal, and the person Catholic ... that is why the individual is reactionary and the person revolutionary."[86]

This was the first appearance of *Esprit* and Mounier's juxtaposition of progressive Catholic personalism against reactionary liberal individualism.[87] On 5 November 1932, Mounier had still been tormented by the thought that "an overtly Catholic stance will discredit us ... until we have shown that one can be both wholly Catholic and sincerely revolutionary."[88] Then this obscure German theologian conveniently provided a respectable alternative to the ON's Nietzschean personalism. Mounier read Marc's exposition of Neumann's "CHRISTIANITY, THE SOURCE OF REVOLUTION" in which Marc wrote: "The order, discipline, Tradition of the Church are thus not incompatible with a frankly revolutionary stance. But Neumann goes much further ... proclaims, against the enemies of the Church and those of Revolution, that 'not only do these two orders not exclude each other,' but 'they form, in fact, a single reality.' Neumann shows, in a striking fashion, that without Christianity, the revolutionary spirit would not exist."

"Otto Neumann" was thus an inventor of "liberation theology," since for him, "Revolution and Christianity are inseparable": what is actually called for is "l'esprit révolutionnaire de rupture et de création," because "revolution unites innovation and tradition in a single act."

But lest one mistake the political orientation of this revolution, "Neumann" cautioned about any "dangerous and deceptive 'drift to the Left'" (while Emmanuel Mounier, for his part, was privately worried over "the right-wing elements of ON, who seem more and more joined in a common front with the new Right").[89] Like Alexandre Marc, "Neumann" embraced the formula "Neither left nor right" as his own, dismissing Marxism as "the supreme and most coherent expression of capitalism" while mere fascism was little more than a "lyrical reformism": "he condemns it as clearly as we do," wrote Marc, adding that he knew people were already calling Marc himself a "fascist."[90]

Mounier was particularly struck by Neumann's restoration of "catholicity" through a "communalism" which prefigured on a worldly plane "the radiating universality of the Church" in a revolutionary "affirmation of integral man."[91] Mounier would subsequently situate the creative portion of the Mystical Body of Christ (an ecclesiological notion of the German theologian Karl Adam, soon popularized in France by the Dominicans) in the great secular collective movements of the twentieth century, now perceived as harbingers of Berdyaev's New Middle Ages.

For Marc, "Otto Neumann constantly reminds us that man is made in the image of God, and called upon to participate in 'the demiurgic vocation,'" and in support of this notion Marc referred to the Catholic philosopher of action Maurice Blondel, and to Charles Péguy, attributing to Neumann the old (Marc) dictum that "man always transcends" ("l'homme dépasse toujours"). Human destiny for the German theologian "is not scattered about in the material, cannot be ... reduced to social necessities: it is, on the contrary, concretized, to transcend all these givens, in the very act of creation."[92]

Many Christian Nietzschean ideas first expressed in *Esprit* by Otto Neumann would later show up in Mounier's writings, at the heart of his personalism. Alexandre Marc's German theologian first presented personalism as an essentially Catholic doctrine, Catholicism accorded with revolution in a philosophically cogent way. This ON notion of revolution, camouflaged, in Catholic language, several themes which had presented problems for *Esprit*. The name "Otto Neumann," "new man" with the initials O.N., hinted that Marc was the author of this text, yet Mounier was excited by the "discovery" of a young German genius. Marc had hoped to show that Mounier bridled at ON revolutionary conceptions, but welcomed them if they were packaged in the words of an *illustre inconnu*.[93] Marc had warned at the beginning of his review of Neumann's *Revolution des Geistes* that "the author, a German Catholic, is not afraid of using tough words to illustrate bold thinking which is bound to shock." The real shock for Mounier would have been to learn that the author was a fabrication.

But Emmanuel Mounier, already fascinated by Belgian efforts to revitalize Catholicism into a revolutionary force, insistently pressed Marc for Neumann's writings and for a French translation of *Revolution des Geistes* for the new *Esprit* monograph series. Mounier's letter to Marc on 21 December 1934 suggests Marc's attention to Mounier's entreaties about Otto Neumann, while producing reasons for excusing Marc for not coming through: "As for Otto Neumann, I would like to have the manuscript of his whole book if possible, with you as intermediary, if it is truly dangerous that I know his address. If this is quite impossible, of course you can always send me fragments."[94]

Thus, many months after *Esprit*'s supposed public break with ON, Mounier still found Neumann's work absolutely vital to his communitarian personalism for Catholic consumption. Marc cited the theologian's need for a low profile under the Nazis. When Mounier enthused about *Esprit*'s publishing the complete works of the German genius in French, Marc announced Otto Neumann's sudden death in a car accident, and a stricken Mounier urged Marc to hunt down all the writings which remained.[95]

Neither Mounier nor the *Esprit* people ever learned how "Otto Neumann" brought "Catholic personalism" to *Esprit*, or ever doubted Neumann's importance. Witness the headings in the 1960s publication *Mounier et sa génération*: for the year 1933, the editors listed Otto Neumann's name first under the "religious events" heading – before Chesterton, the *Commonweal*, Karl Barth and the crisis of German Protestantism, and even the social encyclical *Quadragesimo Anno* of Pope Pius XI.[96]

Otto Neumann had (to use Paul Nizan's phrase) "distilled the thick foreign currents" of new German thought and the German Youth Movement into a coherent anti-liberal, spiritual yet revolutionary ideology. Marc had picked up on the extraordinary complementarity between the counter-cultural zeal of the German Youth Movement and the passion for religious conversion and renewal of a self-styled French Catholic avant-garde. This marriage of *mystiques* was so unexpected that it could, at first, only be presented by subterfuge.

This Otto New-Man gambit allowed Marc to express the religious dimension of his ON commitment without compromising the movement's non-denominational, secular character (in contrast to *Esprit*'s unofficial Catholicism). As Otto Neumann, Alexandre Marc talked like a Catholic without being one; soon he talked himself into membership in the Church.

# 4 Hitler: German Adversaries, French Converts, and a Letter to the Chancellor

In January 1933, Alexandre Marc, who had begun to live for revolution, placed his hopes in the healthier elements among those in revolt against the German political and economic system. But on the Left, Marxist approaches seemed at a dead end, and on the Right, the National Socialists scored electoral victories while conservative nationalists governed. Hitler used anti-capitalist rhetoric, but barons of industry sponsored his party. Marc had reservations about Otto Strasser, but he saw things in a "Strasserite" perspective:

The Führer's coming to power ... marked his victory and the beginning of his decline. His alliances ... revealed the deeply reactionary cast of an ambiguous movement which had been enkindled by the idealism, sacrifices, and faith of many young Germans. Certainly Hitler continued to show a certain adroitness; he has not given up on outsmarting his political allies. But whatever ... the staying power of a National Socialist dictatorship shaped by country squires and captains of industry, bolstered by the Reichswehr and the police, Hitlerite National Socialism is demonstrably incapable of deeply transforming German destinies, of leading the Reich to anything but war.[1]

Between two polar antagonists, national socialism and communism, various groups kept expanding. Some would take up the Hitlerite program afresh, "trying to take it back to its initial 'purity.'" "They truly dream of a greater-German socialism, idealist in inspiration, hierarchical in structure, with a clearly racial and national orientation." Others ended up accepting "the Marxist postulate of class struggle." But even the most promising of these movements "patch up threadbare old doctrines" rather than attempting renewal, or displaying constructive courage.

Over against the "recycled" Nazis and Communists, Marc held up the *Gegner*. "Young and likeable" Harro Schulze-Boysen and his comrades who published *Gegner* held meetings, lectures, work camps and multiplied contacts with other non-conformist circles, forming groups in various German cities and in other German-speaking countries. "It would be premature to consider that movement as likely to directly influence the political situation," but Marc provided a Schulze-Boysen parable which captured the *Gegner* spirit:

One day, Schulze-Boysen said, two funeral processions were crossing a small country village at the same time: two mutually hostile groups of political adversaries were burying young militants fallen in a fight. The coffins were followed by uniformed figures, faces marked by hatred. But those who ... had killed one another were unconsciously pursuing the same ideal. He decided on discovering in all the different camps, parties, groups, in all the classes of the population, men "of the same sort" prepared for struggle and deserving of victory ... yesterday's adversaries became today's allies.[2]

Marc pictured the *Gegner* as "convinced of the inanity of efforts directed towards ... ameliorating the present situation," much like the Ordre Nouveau (ON) group, "radically opposed to all political, social, or spiritual reformism."[3] ON and *Gegner* had a common notion of the true "revolution":

Harro Schulze-Boysen, Fred Schmid, Adrien Turel ... show that the coup d'état ... the raw seizure of power which so much preoccupies so-called "revolutionaries", does not ... constitute a revolution: that title only fits a total spiritual change which reveals the very foundation of a new life ... true Revolution – only bloody to the degree that it is badly prepared, as Robert Aron and Arnaud Dandieu in France have pointed out – is a renewal of all values ... a flashing transformation of society and, above all, the creation of a new man.[4]

Thus, a few weeks after the Reichstag fire, as Hitler was dismantling republican institutions, Marc was still hoping for that "true revolution" eluding Hitler's "ambiguous" movement – but which the most innovative of the young National Socialists wanted. Marc focused on the spiritual factor as essential to the creation of the "new man," as effecting genuine and lasting conversion in people.

Marc regretted *Gegner*'s tardiness in grasping "the reality of the person" central for ON. But Schulze-Boysen "recognized the ultimate meaning of Revolution" in the creation of the new man, as far from egoism as from altruism.[5] Marc also claimed that *Gegner* shared the decentralist and regionalist ideal of the Black Front and the federalism of ON. According to him, Harro Schulze-Boysen's group envisaged Franco-German cross-fertilization, once a common working vocabulary was found: "contemporary political problems – the *Anschluss*, the Polish corridor, the debts, disarmament – are perhaps badly posed". Schulze-Boysen argued that "only a new 'socialism,' a revolutionary 'socialism' could ... defuse the threat of imperialistic war." The upcoming generation's socialism would be "something completely different from that represented by the old parties."[6]

Although Marc saw Schulze-Boysen and his comrades as challenging the Hitlerite reaction, it was more as national socialist rivals than as representatives of an antithetical political culture: he worried about his allies' blatant "contempt for reason," "opposition to any effort at doctrinal clarification," and tendency to think that what they did was more important than what they said or wrote.[7] The Adversaries disregarded all parties with programs or parliamentary ambitions as sterile, even those claiming to be in the line of National Socialism or communism; their own search was for the elite who would make up tomorrow's *active minority*. Marc saw the *Gegner* as having a direction very similar in spirit to *Esprit*'s Third Force declaration, which said: "We do not have the time to create a party, and do not want to contribute yet another division to those which already exist. The only practical thing to do now is to work for unity among the forces who truly represent the people. We are not asking anyone to leave a political grouping to join us. But we want our friends to derive a fighting spirit from us to pass on to their comrades."[8]

Marc admitted that Adversaries' ideas could be "fragmentary, vague, at times even dubious" and granted that the ON movement's doctrinal rigour – "the secret of its strength" – was "a bit lacking" among the Adversaries, who had not yet grasped the depths of the person and so discovered the human fundamentals of the revolution.[9] ON also had to concede that the Strasserites, National-Bolsheviks, and certain *Gegner* movement people, however likeable, tended to sacrifice to the cult of the collective "we" at the expense of the "I."[10] But Marc admired the Adversaries' will to start over again, the youthful and focused enthusiasm demonstrated so well by Harro Schulze-Boysen, which resulted in the French having something to offer, since France "is generating an ideal of a *new order at the service of man* in which the Adversaries will, perhaps, recognize their own aspirations."[11] Hitler only confirmed Marc's belief that *ohne Theorie, keine*

*Revolution*: a true revolution needed to be founded on a proper theory and an accurate sense of the human person. The Nazis, unless they turned to Marc's friends, would lead the revolution in a disastrous direction.

Marc's warnings about Hitler's overtures toward the Right seemed prescient in February 1933, as the new chancellor used the burning of the Reichstag as a pretext to ban the Communist party and its affiliates. On the evening of the fire, there was a gathering of the range of radical youth leaders in a restaurant near Berlin's Stettiner railway station. Approximately two hundred representatives of the radicals of the Hitler Youth, the Socialist Youth, the Young Communists, the Red Boy Scouts, the National Revolutionaries, and Otto Strasser's Black Front – "antagonists only yesterday" – met and agreed to cooperate. Hitler's alliance with the conservatives had shocked many Hitler Youth, and other young people resented the dividing of the nation into Right and Left. Youth leaders such as Harro Schulze-Boysen got agreement on common social revolutionary aims. But the Reichstag fire that evening and the subsequent repression of the Communists and Social Democrats killed this ecumenical spirit.[12]

It was clear, in succeeding months, that Baldur von Schirach's Hitler Youth was not the only youth movement within the NSDAP, much less in Germany. Robert Ley, head of the Kraft durch Freude organization and of the Arbeitsfront, was still a serious rival to Schirach, and welcomed members of Strasser's Black Front into his organization, which, with Ley's cover, even edited their own newspaper. During the early years of Hitler's regime it was still possible to join one of the national socialist movements with the hope that national socialism would lose its worse features or that it was having temporary trouble with an unstable buffoon. But as Adolf Hitler consolidated his position, the issue became how much the bad elements in National Socialism could be fought from within the movement, or how much involvement could be maintained without sacrificing fundamental principle or becoming accomplice to criminal activities.[13]

The German non-conformists whom Marc imagined as the true German revolution were under great pressure in this period. After the Reichstag fire, Ernst Niekisch, like Ernst Jünger, had his house searched; his *Widerstand* was finally banned in December 1934.[14] Ernst von Salomon, author of *Die Geächteten*, the classic account of the Freikorps, a regular at *Gegner* meetings, was arrested.[15] In the spring, Otto Strasser fled to Prague, still posing as a viable National Socialist alternative to Hitler.[16] In April, *Gegner* was closed down. In the fall, Schulze-Boysen, after a severe beating from the SS, confided to von Salomon that he had "put his plans for revenge on ice."[17]

The rapid series of setbacks for Strasserism in December 1932, Hitler's rise to the chancellorship in January, the burning of the Reichstag in February, the brutal repression of the German Communists, and Hitlerite intimidation of Marc's friends or associates led Marc to shift his attention to countries like Britain and Belgium for substitutes.

French fascist writer Pierre Drieu la Rochelle mused over Ernst von Salomon and the lessons of the *Gegner* experience and, in his journal, promised himself "never to adhere to a regime, whatever my political convictions. The only man I recognised as a brother was Ernst von Salomon in Berlin. He fought in the Freikorps, served a six-year prison sentence for Rathenau's murder, and yet was no Nazi and refused to participate in Hitler's triumph. Hitler's ideas were close to his own. But there is an abyss between the ideas of an intellectual ["un homme d'esprit"] and those of a man of action."[18]

Schulze-Boysen's dream of restoring Germany's *Volksgemeinschaft* through a socialist resolution of class struggle, his idealistic notion of *Arbeitsdienst*, were transformed into a harsh totalitarian regimentation by the Nazi regime. Hitler and his henchmen translated uplifting ideas into brutal and unscrupulous political reality. But Marc was still certain that liberal democracy had no future and that therefore the *Gegner* and ON represented the only viable path: that of the great spiritual revolution, the revolutionary brotherhood of tomorrow.

After Hitler seemed to set back ON's hopes for Germany, Marc and several of his friends became more preoccupied with the religious dimension of the spiritual revolutionary experience, in order to help the French movement avoid some of the Germans' mistakes and to clarify their special tenets for creating the "new man." The review *Ordre Nouveau*, which appeared in May 1933, focused on the pure elaboration of theory (without *Esprit*'s attention to day-to-day political events, literature, or the cultural scene). Robert Aron and Arnaud Dandieu's *La révolution nécessaire*, in November, soon went through six printings, while René Dupuis and Marc's book *Jeune Europe* (essays celebrating several national manifestations of the generational groping for a new order) was also widely remarked, and honoured by the Académie française.[19]

Religion was more important for Marc than for his comrades across the Rhine (despite the Strasserites' relative sympathy for Catholicism, and the *Tat*-Kreis vein of reformist Protestantism). ON had always attracted young men with a special sympathy for efforts to devise a Nietzschean religiousness. Marc took the lead in melding the non-conformists' interest in the "human person", the "new man" aspirations of ON, with his religious preoccupations. The thuggish perversity which surfaced in the German youth movement led him to mine France's Catholic tradition and the idealistic vein of her revolutionary heritage for energy for that post-liberal and post-democratic "Necessary Revolution" which would better Germany's poisoned effort. Marc's turn to Catholicism in 1929, as for other converts of his generation and ethnic background, also was a conversion to France – or to a certain idea of France.

## POSITIONING FRANCE'S NEW ORDER

Hitler dealt swiftly with the Strasserites, the National-Bolsheviks, and the *Gegner* and *Die Tat* circles – putting down the so-called German non-conformists or left-wing Nazis with a decisiveness and finality that dated Marc's patronizing dismissal of flabby Hitlerite national socialism. Marc, shaken but undaunted, now adopted the attitude that the Hitlerite triumph was a perversion of the best part of the German youth movement. In reaction, Marc and his friends reaffirmed the basic aspirations of the spiritual party in France, their own role as the indispensable theorists of that "Necessary Revolution," that "New Order" which the pseudo-revolutionary societies – Russia, Italy, Germany – had driven off course.

The new journal *Ordre Nouveau*, directed by Arnaud Dandieu and Robert Aron, was rigorous and austere, intended for an elite readership (publishing less than a thousand copies, in contrast to the large dissemination of books popularizing ON ideas written by Daniel-Rops and the others). The first issue (May 1933) announced that it would set out "the true revolutionary creed" for French young people disappointed by all the failed insurrectionist experiences, the "révolutions manquées" which marked the contemporary world. French youth would find "the same élan, the same intensity" as the Hitlerites, Stalinists, or Fascists, but without the disillusionment which followed in the wake of experiences which had been "heroic but blind"; their route, drawing on the authentic anti-statist and personalist spiritual tradition of their country, would be to defend "a true revolutionary doctrine" and the human personality against deforming dictatorships and demagoguery.[20]

ON took what we now call a "good European" perspective. Daniel-Rops pleaded, from a Christian perspective, for ethnicity and decentralization over against the modern state,[21] de Rougemont for rethinking economic structures in the interests of *la personne*,[22] Arnaud Dandieu and Robert Aron for a recognition of the "bankruptcy" of the American liberal capitalist system,[23] Jean Jardin for appreciating the Italian Fascist alternative to liberal individualism (despite its excessive "statism").[24] René Dupuis denounced the Soviet Union as "inhuman" for failing to subordinate economic to "spiritual" interests, to the interests of "the person."[25] It was left to Alexandre Marc to put the German situation front and centre, in both the first and the second issue of *Ordre Nouveau.*

"German youth, after having awakened immeasurable hopes in the world," Marc lamented, "was beginning to betray them." The German "national revolution" was turning sour: "After spending so much energy, to end up with that caricature of a Third Reich! The German revolution certainly seems botched ... at least for the moment!" But Marc would not then, or ever, dismiss the National Socialist revolution as unfounded, a fluke, accident, or irrational collective delirium. For Germany, before the advent of the Nazis, *"Parliamentary democracy brilliantly demonstrated its incompetence,* faint-heartedness, depravity" as liberal democracy, the Social Democrats, the Communists, and Marxists in general had displayed their impotence. The German Left had demonstrated that all politics in "the spiritual atmosphere of materialism" would be sterile. For some time, National Socialism, "whose triumph my friends and I have predicted since 1931," had been the real master of Germanic destinies.[26]

Marc continued with his customary and unique fraternal, or "insider," critique of the National Socialist movement as excessive, even dangerous, but always based on something solid. He distinguished what was dissident and rebellious in National Socialism, granting that this dissidence was sometimes well founded, from its constructive aspirations, which were sadly "dangerous and insufficient." There were those "National Socialist excesses and brutalities": they had to be understood in perspective, since "all insufficiently prepared revolutions are accompanied by brutality and excess." Nevertheless the Nazis' attack on liberal, parliamentary democracy, their struggle against the "egotism, corruption, and impotence of parliamentary parties," had been justified, as was the National Socialist revolt against the myths of decadent liberalism, against the injustices and hypocrisy of the Treaty of Versailles, against "the slavery of lending on interest," against both capitalism and Marxism and the deformed human being engendered by those systems. In contrast, the National Socialists advocated natural equilibrium, the reestablishment of human environments – family, trade, region, the small landholding, and direct relationship to work and to the land. ("We must not forget that article 17 of the National Socialist program requires the pure and simple expropriation of large landed property holders.")[27] "National Socialism, on the *cultural and spiritual plane,* demonstrates a determination to break with materialism ... refusing to accept the dominance of the material. It fights free thought ... immorality, licence, moral degradation."[28]

Marc dismissed liberal and Marxist critiques of the Nazis: "their criticisms of National Socialism constitute praise in our eyes". The true insufficiencies of National Socialism were beyond their grasp because *"The deficiency of Hitlerism begins at the point where the liberal critique ends."*

Young Germany had so far failed to free the national idea from its economic, administrative, or police baggage, and "to restore to it its pure dimension of spiritual intensity." They had been right to be aware of the dangers of state-centred nationalism ("Mussolinian fascism") or economic nationalism ("Stalinist fascism"), and this had led them to supplant economic and statist abstractions by founding the nation on the more concrete, earthier idea of race. But this was done in a way which tended to subordinate the spiritual dimension to biological considerations, resulting in a slide toward a racist nationalism using economic statism to institutionalize an unparalleled form of slavery. Behind a *mystique of the masses,* and National Socialist glorification of heroes, there might be lurking "a leader who manipulates crowds, a master who dominates slaves ... cruel paradox, National Socialism ... constitutes ... a veritable plebeian democracy, but which, rather than ... parliamentary, is a new type of *caesarism.*"[29]

Marc predicted that National Socialist youth, "intoxicated with slogans, marching, and illusions," would, "like the 'shock troops' of pan-Russian National Socialism" (Bolshevism), experience "weariness and disappointment," once the orations and grandiose ceremonies were over. Hitler was a multifold disaster: their just and promising critical focus, vibrant anti-materialism, and uplifting revolutionary spirit were deformed by a personality cult, by racist teachings, by a "biological mysticism" uncharacteristic of the better side of the national-revolutionary current.

National Socialism, a worthy idea, by no means "intrinsically perverse," had promised an "anti-materialist" revolution of an unprecedented rapidity and scale. Lack of intellectual clarity in the ideology, and the unforeseen advent of Hitler, had dashed great hopes. High tragedy would be the lot of the younger generation in Germany.

CONVERSION

Thierry Maulnier, a Jeune Droite writer hailed for his precocious book on Nietzsche, contributor to the first issue of *Ordre Nouveau,* described the basic problem of the age as a crisis "within man" ("La crise est dans l'homme," as an essay of his put it). Gabriel Marcel, Daniel-Rops, Denis de Rougemont–like Marc – passed from crises into religious commitments. Arnaud Dandieu, however, following Nietzsche, sought a new philosophy of desire, a "morale du devenir" based on the spiritual value of pleasure. The spurious German theologian Otto Neumann allowed Marc to publicize his private hope that non-conformists such as those of ON might keep that faith in youth, its values, in the properly spiritual dimensions of the human personality.

Dandieu was older than his ON peers, and much vaunted for his lively, multifaceted intelligence, but did not seem a likely Führer of an ON regime, for while the movement had an elitist conception of authority (rooted, like the German groups with their *Führerprinzip*, in a culture of homoerotic male bonding), it was more collegial. Authority in the French movement was built upon the founding group of so-called consuls, and on a revolutionary council issuing from them, which was to be staffed by cooptation, as the movement produced its own cohort of leaders. True, the admiration for Dandieu seemed excessive to Mounier (who would come to play an analogous role in the *Esprit* group).

By the end of July 1933, and *Ordre Nouveau*'s third issue, Dandieu and Aron had finished *La révolution nécessaire*, and Dandieu had set out to further delineate the movement's precepts with Alexandre Marc and others. But just before going on summer vacation, he contracted a lethal infection, and after days of feverishly expounding his ideas on his deathbed, died on 6 August 1933.

This tragedy for his close ON friends was noted by prominent thinkers such as François Mauriac and Gabriel Marcel as an important loss for an entire intellectual generation. Marc met a sobbing Jean Jardin, sitting on the Neuilly hospital doorstep, who told him "our movement is dead."[30] Daniel-Rops commented "Dandieu was a genius ... he would have been the Bergson of our generation."[31] Marc remained haunted by this death for the rest of his life: "After Dandieu, we continued, but things never went as well as they had done ... He was the common bond. The group never blended in the same way."[32] Robert Aron remembered the loss of Dandieu, the memory of him, as defining and shaping Alexandre Marc:

[Marc was a] man of absolute material disinterestedness, of complete loyalty to his ideas, to his friends, and to himself, he lived in permanent state of venerating Dandieu's memory: naming his son, Arnaud, his daughter, Mireille, after the sister of our friend [and secretary of ON]. A man of great spiritual exigencies ... one regrets that he has too literally repeated, all his life, the same initial program and that, convinced of being right, he did not sufficiently adapt his certitudes to the evolution of ideas and the new pressures from events. Solid and immovable like a rock, planted in the middle of the ... counter-currents of a volatile period, he played a defining role in the persistence of the movement to which he dedicated his life.[33]

Marc would regularly remember Dandieu, wonder how ON's genius would have reacted to a particular situation. Thanks largely to Marc, Dandieu became a mythic figure, a *lieu de mémoire*, in ON circles ... and even among post–World War II federalists. Dandieu and Aron's *La révolution nécessaire* established the basic ideology of the ON movement. Dandieu's personalism continued to inspire serious philosophical reflection – not the least in Emmanuel Mounier's *Esprit* movement, which, in contast to Marc, preferred to forget its origins.

The memory of Dandieu's death stayed with Marc not only because of the loss of the perceived great mind of the age, but also because Marc learned that, during his feverish deathbed ramblings, this Nietzschean culture-Catholic addressed the absent Marc as if Marc were a Catholic and Dandieu had undergone a deathbed conversion, leaving a believing Catholic's testament.[34] Marc was shaken by his great friend's *in extremis* perception of him as Catholic. And then about a month later, Denis de Rougemont challenged Marc's perspicacity in religious matters because he had never had the experience of belonging to a Church. Piqued by the remark, Marc resolved that fall to convert to Catholicism.

Jean Plaquevent, a young priest active in student circles in the Latin quarter, and a contributor, advisor, and, secretly, ecclesiastical censor to *Esprit*, became Marc's spiritual director in spring of 1931 and baptized him on 29 September 1933.[35] Already, for some time, a particularly creative and enterprising Dominican and Jesuit intelligentsia had been interested in Marc's melding of his new-found religiosity with the novel anti-liberal and anti-communist philosophies of ON. Marc had long disparaged Protestantism as engendering the individualism behind Western decadence; his castigation of Protestantism for engendering capitalism – at a joint meeting of his religious circle and the Club du Moulin Vert – had sparked the founding of the original ON movement. The fusing of spiritual and worldly energies in Roman Catholic religious communities, their joining of the personal and the social, encouraged Marc's involvement in a succession of communitarian experiences with dedicated, tightly knit groups of bright young men, united by common ideals. He thought, for a time, that commitment to revolutionary ideals precluded marriage, and considered joining the Jesuits – the "Soldiers of Christ." His diaries reveal that his new religiousness led to a J.-K. Huysmans–like torment over the tension between his libertine Latin Quarter ways as a compulsive womanizer and the austere moral standards which his pending conversion implied.

This sort of sexuality versus spirituality strain was common and intense in Marc's milieu and helped explain the common interest in Nietzsche. Denis de Rougemont, a highly sensual but repressed pastor's son like Nietzsche, was writing his classic and provocative *Love in the Western World*: profoundly anti-modern, puritanical, anti-feminist, it defended an uplifting Christian spiritual ideal of marriage against a deeply ingrained ideology of erotic passion in Western culture.[36]

ON, like *Esprit* – and particularly like the German[37] non-conformist youth movements – counted very few women in their ranks, aside from a few doing secretarial or administrative work. One of Marc's girl-friends from Sciences Po, the Flemish Yvonne Serruys, was an exception, as was – after 1934 – a certain Eugénia Hélisse (apparently the mistress of a famous French film-maker),[38] but their presence seems to have generated tensions in the ON band. Given their aggressively masculine language and style, it is difficult to imagine a Simone de Beauvoir in Marc's immediate circle.[39] There was only the odd female contributor to *Ordre Nouveau* and while there were more at *Esprit*, which published a special issue on the status of women, the sole ON article touching on women's issues (in a number on the home and city planning) implied that an orderly, traditional model of the family would prevail in the New Order.[40] ON remained a gang of angry young men, part of that Young Europe in turmoil which Alexandre Marc described in his first book.

Marc was increasingly involved with the Dominicans[41] of the lively Juvisy convent near Paris: they were on the cutting edge of the progressive wing of their Order and, by the late 1930s, committed to Catholic spiritual renewal – a general Catholic Renaissance.[42] He was a member of a dynamic team of journalists transforming Catholic publishing with the Dominicans' progressive weekly *Sept*, and organizing their projects and publications, creating a national support network in the guise of circles of "friends" like the Amis de *Plans*. Catholics taken by the personalist vision of French spiritual regeneration met and formed contacts and friendships from one end of the country to the other. (One of the first friends of *Sept* was a young Jesuit-educated army officer named Charles de Gaulle, a *protégé* of Daniel-Rops.)

The Dominicans helped Marc avoid the police and deportation. When Marc met Suzanne Jean, the Dominicans encouraged the match, and on 18 November 1933, just a few months after meeting, and only weeks after Marc's baptism, the couple were married in the privacy of Marc's circle at Juvisy – the only marriage ever celebrated in that institution.[43] The marriage came as a surprise to Marc's first great spiritual love, Margarita Abella Caprile.[44] Marc and his New Britain spouse became involved in the Société de Saint-Louis – a new "order" of lay people, married and single, living in a kind of Christian commune, applying Catholic and personalist principles to both the community and their workplace. The community's new publishing project, Les Editions du Seuil, began by publishing religious children's literature by Marc's spiritual director the abbé Jean Plaquevent, and eventually became one of most important publishing houses of post-war France. Similar projects and experiences with Emmanuel Mounier and some Belgian *compagnons* were also soon in the works.

Alexandre Marc, as Robert Aron put it years later, was the convert's convert, and "brought to the practice of his new religion the passions of a neophyte who felt obliged to justify his choice." Still, "less gifted for a practical life than for managing ideas, he had great difficulty holding himself to the step-by-step and consistent life-plan necessary for forging a career."[45] When he married amid the progressive Dominicans, one of the most dynamic and influential Catholic communities of the time, Alexandre Marc brought European youth revolution, and helped them evolve the new religious discourse that would have great and unexpected influence, and even ecclesial consecration at the Second Vatican Council. But since Marc was tainted by his German connections and inspirations, his role was subsequently minimized, and he has never been given credit for his role in originating what became a world-historical force.

## NEITHER OF THE RIGHT, NOR OF THE LEFT: THE NECESSARY REVOLUTION

We are neither of the Right, nor of the Left, but ... at the half-way point between the extreme Right and the extreme Left, behind the president, with our backs turned to the assembly.[46]
Robert Aron and Arnaud Dandieu

Works ... being peddled about nowadays as the philosophy of National Socialism ... have nothing to do with the inner truth and greatness of this movement (namely the encounter between global technology and modern man).[47]
Martin Heidegger

We believe that at the spiritual origin ... of the national socialist movement are seeds of a new and necessary revolutionary position.[48]

Alexandre Marc and Henri Daniel-Rops

ON deigned to address the general reading public in the fall of 1933. Daniel-Rops explained the group's main ideas in successive articles in the conservative *La Revue hebdomadaire*, and then the book *Eléments de notre destin*. Alexandre Marc, with René Dupuis, portrayed European youth swept up in post-liberal revolutions, as in their book *Jeune Europe*.[49] Robert Aron and Arnaud Dandieu's *La révolution nécessaire* manifesto was widely reviewed, and soon went through seven printings; Emmanuel Mounier hailed it as "the first work with allows us to confront *Das Kapital* on the level of basic principles."[50] Appearing just weeks after Germany left the League of Nations, it was the arrogant, anti-republican tract of young men "neither of the Right, nor of the Left, behind the president, with [their] backs turned to the assembly."[51] And in it, the ON claimed a decisive, world-historical role for France ... and their own cutting-edge revolutionary thinking:

The revolution which is in the offing, and which the Russian, Italian, and German revolutions only incompletely and imperfectly symptomize, will be accomplished by France. All kinds of arguments join to prove this: first, spiritual reasons, because France is ... the country which can find in its history the personalist and anti-statist tradition so necessary today, and for which the concept of liberty ... keeps all its vigour and necessity.

But the new French revolution also involved a strong authority component because "for us the idea of revolution is inseparable from the idea of order. The true revolution could have no other goal than the creation of a new order." Or as the book put it: "When order can no longer be found in order, it must be found in revolution: and the only revolution we envisage is the revolution of order."[52]

This litany to order meant that ON endorsed the trend toward dictatorial, authoritarian regimes, but also that order could not be an end in itself, as it was in those incomplete and imperfect regimes in neighbouring countries. France, drawing on her special personalist tradition, could encourage the completion of all the other revolutions. Dandieu and his comrades thought that the unique French notion of the personality made ON unlike the authoritarian alternatives. Their denunciation of capitalism and Marxism as two complementary forms of contemporary materialism "cannot link us to Hitlerism which, however, from its beginnings, attacked both capitalism and communism as the twin faces of materialism and of abstract thinking," since the "statism" of Hitler ("like that of Roosevelt"!) was damnable. And so "even if racism were not, itself, a kind of materialism," the "Hitlerite inspiration" fitted with "the Marxist system" in the modern world's "gallery of horrors."[53]

*La révolution nécessaire* was supposed to clarify those revolutionary longings which Denis de Rougemont had tried to elucidate in the *Nouvelle Revue Française* the previous year. The authors provided weighty philosophical and historical allusions to Marx, to Bakunin, or to the "men of '89." They had statistics on comparative unemployment in Europe, and on exchange and credit, and long digressions on what they called "the dichotomic function of the revolutionary spirit." The book suggested that a new, anti-parliamentary, anti-Jacobin French revolution, inspired by a genuine spirituality, was both necessary and inevitable. This militantly anti-materialist uprising, effected by youth, would avoid the blunders concerning State or Race that the previous authoritarian revolutions had made. The "Necessary Revolution" in France would see the flourishing of the human personality in local communities suited for it.

This agenda did not easily translate into parliamentary political activities. During the summer of 1933 Marc went on a joint speaking tour with the "young Turk" neo-socialist Gaston Bergery and, returning disillusioned with the opportunism of this dashing young politician, began to take some distance from him.[54] The October 1933 *Ordre Nouveau* reviewed the established French political groups for their revolutionary potential (demonstrating, of course, how they all fell short of ON standards). Former Action Française supporter Jean Jardin described that organization as representing "the only genuine revolutionary movement in France since the Commune," but complained of its playing the parliamentary game.[55] Engineer Robert Loustau depicted the Radicals as devoid of idealism and vision.[56] Robert Aron described authentic Communist militants as being "in search of a true revolution."[57] René Dupuis saw the bankrupt French parliamentary system playing its last card in the person of this charismatic Third Force idol, Gaston Bergery, and his neo-socialists:

The neo-socialists ... and M. Bergery, above all, pretend to embody the nation's élan, passion, destiny; they appeal to a mystique of the masses and to a conception of authority which very much resembles that of Fascism or of National Socialism and which is, in fact, the French variant of them.

Their victory (improbable, if not impossible) ["The Front commun of M. Bergery seems a foredoomed failure, an abortion"] would inevitably lead to a dictatorship which, in spite of being exercised within parliamentary forms, would be no less absolute. Dictatorship seems, then, the uncovering of the last parliamentary card, the supreme flowering of parliamentarianism.[58]

Alexandre Marc and Dandieu's friend Claude Chevalley (who had two years of graduate study in mathematics in Germany) insisted (despite Gaston Bergery and the Third Force) that "There would be no 'Ordre Nouveau Party.'"[59] "*We have but one tactic: allegiance to our beliefs.*" ON had grown organically; one did not join by accepting its program and a membership card. "*One joins by a radical break with the established disorder, and by the slow maturation of new ways of thinking and living.*" This gave lives "meaning and their revolutionary edge."[60] The organization was crowned by "*spiritual communities*" and "among the most exemplary ... the Ordre Nouveau cells which achieve the revolutionary community or community of persons, and so assure the victory of the ... revolution."[61] In sum, the ON movement – like religious orders such as the Jesuits – emphasized changing young people through intense, unique communitarian experiences, for as the title of Thierry Maulnier's new book had it, "the crisis is in man" (*La crise est dans l'homme*.)[62] The new spirit of communitarianism, the vigorous experience of group living, having changed people, the "complete" and "sufficient" revolution could finally be realized by "new men" who would lead it.

Having established authentic spiritual communities, Marc and Chevalley claimed that "THE TACTICS OF 'ORDRE NOUVEAU' RESTORES THE FAMOUS 'TRANSITION PERIOD' TO ITS TRUE PLACE: BEFORE THE REVOLUTION, AND NOT AFTERWARDS." These communities knew that their New Order was already fending for itself: "Rather than sacrificing vital revolutionary energy to the interests of that purely artificial agent called a party, we are already fabricating the ON society. So the tactics we envisage will thus counter any ... treason ... and render impossible any 'annexation' of the revolutionary élan by a Bonaparte or a Fouché, a Stalin or a Hitler."[63]

So Marc and his comrades – contemptuous of fatuous intelligentsia – envisaged their tiny group enkindling a total conversion of France by, first of all, "changing men." Marc had convinced ON that a youth movement could transform an entire country in a matter of months: a whole German generation had risen from crude capitalist or Marxist materialism to a collective celebration of youth, the countryside, the outdoor life, virile fraternity, and the surmounting of class differences. The young in the countries neighbouring France were already savouring revolutionary experiences: Marc received inquiries about ON positions from José Antonio Primo de Rivera in Spain (also on the lookout for a more "humane" revolution than that of the Hitlerites), from his wife's New Britain movement, from intrigued Italian officials, and from young Belgians noted for their religious preoccupations. "Young Europe" seemed the vanguard of world-historical change.

Aron and Dandieu's proclamation of ON's positions chided "the Hitlerite inspiration" but not German national socialism as a whole. Marc and his friends were given to distinguishing between "the Hitlerites" and a wider movement, including the broader NSDAP with positive qualities and interesting personalities. The Aron-Dandieu tract announced the coming "Necessary Revolution" in France alongside a special issue of ON that positioned it over against the "incomplete" and "imperfect" attempt in the Reich. Hitler forced a rethinking upon Marc and his friends, and it is interesting to compare it to the thinking of Martin Heidegger, a famous German theorist of spiritual Revolution.

## MARTIN HEIDEGGER

During the first months after Hitler came to power, in early 1934, his regime was supported by some serious intellectuals, despite the muggings of people like Marc's *Gegner* friends. One was Martin Heidegger, Husserl's successor as predominant phenomenological philosopher.[64] Heidegger had been named rector of the University of Freiburg in April 1933 and then joined the National Socialist party. Heidegger later explained that he had accepted the rectorship with "the hope that I could win over the university professors and persuade them to turn National-Socialism into *national socialism* ... develop the spiritual, the intellectual, powers of the movement."[65]

A former aspirant Jesuit, from Black Forest peasant stock, Heidegger felt much attached to the German countryside but repelled by Germany's industrial cities: "At most the townsman is 'stimulated' by his stay in the country," he wrote, "but my whole work depends on the world of these mountains and peasants."[66] A "return to the land" was important in Nazi rhetoric, and Hitler extended the Arbeitsdienst (Labour Service), created by the Weimar Republic to alleviate unemployment: students were to spend a few months in manual labour each year, in daily contact with workers and peasants, getting into shape. This was Heidegger's favourite Hitler project, and he encouraged his students to seek a "conversion experience" in one of these labour camps – to become a "new man," an intellectual labourer.[67]

The Arbeitsdienst also interested Marc and his friends in France, since ON, condemning the separation of "thought from action, theory from practice," had its own *service civil* from 1931, described in Dandieu's *La révolution nécessaire* as a unique and creative response to the new technological culture created by changed in industrial production. ON's "civic service" was to highlight the fact that one social class did most of the repetitive, numbing, uncreative tasks marking modern industrial production. ON wanted to show how creative leisure could come out of modern industry – not just more profits and unemployment. So ON people did unskilled industrial work without pay, freeing workers for paid vacations for the first time in their lives. (In the summer of 1935, as we shall see, fifty ON activists worked in four different factories in the Paris area.)[68]

Several of Hitler's other ideas were less attractive to French nonconformists. On 14 October 1933, Germany withdrew from the League of Nations, which she had joined under Chancellor Gustav Stresemann – Aristide Briand's counterpart in the heyday of Franco-German *rapprochement*. Nevertheless, Martin Heidegger exhorted his students to support the Führer's foreign policy: "It is not ambition which made the Führer leave the League of Nations," he assured them, "nor a craving for glory, nor blind obstinacy, nor a need for violence: it is nothing other than the clear desire to be unconditionally responsible for assuming the mastery of the destiny of our people."[69] Soon, however, Hitler's rivals and opponents, and Jews, were being oppressed, and Heidegger seemed to take his distance from the Party, lamenting, in 1935, "the works which are being peddled about nowadays as the philosophy of National Socialism but have nothing to do with the inner truth and greatness of this movement (namely the encounter between global technology and modern man)."[70] Heidegger always remained an admirer of a pristine German national socialism much the same as that which interested Marc and the *Plans* and ON circles: an attempt to create a "new man," "converts," in the face of industrial society's unprecedented challenges to the spiritual rootedness of culture.

A LETTER TO HITLER
ON GERMANY'S "RÉVOLUTION MANQUÉE"

Like Martin Heidegger, the ON group chided the Führer and his cronies while paying respect to certain basic national socialist ideas. In November 1933, one month after Hitler's clamorous abandonment of the League, *Ordre Nouveau* published – alongside the new books of Aron and Dandieu, of Daniel-Rops, and of Marc and Dupuis – a special "Letter to Hitler" which addressed Hitler in a presumptuous, even insolent, manner (yet appeared shockingly familiar, even congenial, to some). Composed in the name of ON by Marc and Daniel-Rops,[71] it congratulated Hitler – "*Gravedigger of the League of Nations, bravo!*" – for "giving a loud slap on the hypocritical face" of the League,[72] but warned him that if he only addressed the old

French elites and traditional French interest groups, so notoriously blind to German problems, he would be guilty of "a singular intellectual laziness and revolutionary deficiency"; there were French young people around movements like ON who grasped the larger importance of Hitler and of the national socialist movement: "We believe that at the spiritual origin, if not in the tactical evolution, of the national socialist movement, is to be found the seeds of a new and necessary revolutionary position."[73]

The ON group had been able to achieve what "neither you nor Mussolini have had the time to do: formulating the doctrine before moving into action." The new young French revolutionaries were "neither communist nor fascist but ... had successfully set out the principles of that New Order essential to resolving the crisis and saving the human person." ON could evaluate national socialism "not as foreigners or émigrés, like your adversaries, but from a deeper, revolutionary point of view," in their impatience with hypocritical French liberals, with their own scandals, who "suddenly adopted a moralistic stance regarding your 'tyranny' and 'atrocities.'" [74] could not approve "your troops' excesses" or forgive "the murders, the imprisonments, the beatings" and concluded that because it was "*spiritually insufficient, your revolution was condemned to drift into brutality.*"[74]

So Hitler's brutality was not sufficient justification for parodying National Socialist doctrine any more than was Hitler's contempt toward the League of Nations, as Hitler's attitude was "one of the rare proofs of having a sense of fair play ("loyauté") which a European people has given in the last fifteen years."[75] The new ON, anti-liberal generation in France assumed a nuanced attitude toward Hitler and the German National Socialists: "we by no means overlook the fundamental differences which separate Germany from France, differences of instinct and temperament, of geography and history. The answers which you propose, even supposing them achieved in Germany, would not be uniformly valuable for other countries ... Each country, each nation, ought to find in itself ... the strength for its own deliverance. We will leave to a few of your pale imitators the ridiculous chore of pretending to establish a national socialism carbon-copied from yours."[76]

ON assessed National Socialist strengths and achievements over against weaknesses, errors, and misconceptions ... from the point of view of their own superior, more universal, revolutionary vision. On the substantially positive side[77] were the Nazis' putting an end to the "lie" of liberal democracy (a phrase we encountered in *Gegner*'s ON-sounding manifesto of May 1932), their struggle against the "dictatorship" of the economic factor in society (points 13, 14, 16, and 18 of the 1920 program elicited great hopes), nationalization of trusts, sharing in the profits of large industry, communalization of department stores, expropriation of land for the general interest without indemnity, abolition of unearned income from and speculation in land.[78] Nazi principles reflected some sense of the communitarian aspect of personalism, though they fell short of embodying it: "You have understood ... that against the Americano-Bolshevik or democratico-capitalist ... one must juxtapose the experience of the organic collectivity, rich in fraternity and love. Your departed young heroes witness to that great truth. But have you been able to institutionalize it? That is another matter."[79]

ON granted that the National Socialists had also had the courage to "face the ridicule entailed in defending morality." "Agreed: your comrade Röhm exclaimed that one does not make a revolution just to close a few homosexual lairs. The revolution is not *just that*, but it is *also* that."

In the final analysis, what was most inspiring, worthy, and empowering about the national socialist movement was its zeal: "The genuine greatness of your movement is that it is ... heroism, sacrifice, and abnegation ... a challenge to contemporary materialism. We will shortly turn to what we see to be incomplete and deviant about your heroism from our point of view; but it exists. To a world which only lives for the frenetic satisfaction of instincts, which offers ... mass-produced furniture as the great goal of mankind (capitalism and communism being the same in this respect), you have answered (like Mussolini, by the way) that one could demand other things of people ... a voluntary acceptance of rigour."[80]

ON commended the positive side of national socialism – its *mystique* set against the old liberal political culture – but rejected its rough, opportunistic, totalitarian *politique.*

We have repudiated all complicity with this soulless world, diagnosed the American cancer ... We agree with the struggle against materialism. And yet we are not in your camp. An abyss separates us.

Who among your theorists have accomplished that effort which we have been making, for several years now, to grasp the very root of the evil, to assess not only the consequences of this materialism but its causes? And if your February 1920 program hit upon a few of the truly essential points, why, Chancellor of the Reich, have you not acted upon them? Do you forget promises more easily than insults?

YOUR MOVEMENT POSSESSES, IN ITS ROOT ORIGINS, SOMETHING TRULY GREAT. WHAT HAVE YOU MADE OF THAT GREATNESS? ABOVE ALL, WHAT ARE YOU GOING TO MAKE OF IT TOMORROW?[81]

The 1920 Nazi program, important for the German Strasserites, led ON to reproach Hitler for keeping the old framework of a party (for parties "degenerate sooner or later into bureaucracy or police") even after the burning of the Reichstag,[82] hesitating to implement the original NSDAP economic program,[83] for a distorted notion of race ("an axiom as theoretical as it was dubious"), and, above all, for ignoring the danger of the totalitarian state: "At the beginning of your movement, while hallowing the local *patrie* and its virtues, did you not fathom the crucial danger of rigid centralization? Had you not said that the *patrie* and the nation are the only realities and, Nietzschean that you are, seen 'the state as coldest of ... Leviathans?' "[84]

In the final section of the "Letter to Hitler," ON highlighted Hitlerite insufficiencies "with more rigour and more justice than you yourself when judging the Marxists and liberals," by juxtaposing National Socialist vagaries to the clear exigencies of ON.[85] The National Socialists had not had "the courage to rediscover the realm of the human in all its breadth and richness," having "lacked the boldness, faith, and creative spirit" to go beyond mere band-aid solutions and reforms. But the only way the Nazis could have done this would have been by developing a sense of that cornerstone of the New Order: "l'homme intégral," the *person*.[86] Here again there was the conviction that ON had something invaluable to offer the Nazis.

The Nazis may have had a muddled ideology, but the ON people, rather than regretting the disappearance of the values of German liberal democracy, kept insisting on the inevitability of, necessity for, a "Revolution of Order" in France. Would France "remain eternally fixed to the rotting frame of a democracy which had lost all spiritual meaning," while wondering "if you, Germans, who have begun a revolution, who have discerned *the* revolution, will be able to bring it to fruition"?

Is it not too late? Are you not already bound hands and feet, prisoners of ideological deficiencies and practical mistakes? In that case, there is little hope. Rather than gloating over French inadequacy, lucid Germans should want "a young and spiritually vigorous" France, and such a neighbour was a distinct possibility, because:

IN THE SOULS OF A COURAGEOUS YOUTH IN FRANCE, AN IMMENSE WAVE OF ENTHUSIASM AND REVOLT, OF FURY AND DISGUST, IS RISING.

We are all fed up with the parliamentarian charade, productivist madness, moral flaccidity, and partisan treachery. "We will build our home," young people sing in one of their ballads. We too will build our own. Soon we will tear down all the disintegrating walls.

ON admitted that a pre-revolutionary situation was hardly evident in the France of November 1933, either in the press or in the streets. Nevertheless, the movement, claiming to speak for an entire generation as it had in the *Nouvelle Revue Française* (*NRF*), already forming a sort of government in exile, warned that the powerful "anxiety" of this generation would soon emerge:

We have neither *faisceaux* of fighters, nor millions of adherents grouped under banners. But while less raucous, the activity of young France is no less efficacious. A project is under way which may still be unnoticed but tomorrow the results will be there for all to see. Mr Chancellor, we know that few can understand what we are saying. We think that you, who have been carried to power by the enthusiasm of youth, can. MUSSOLINI HAS UNDERSTOOD. He openly considers it unproductive to deal only with the present French government, which he recognizes as provisional, inefficient, and useless. He is awaiting a true government to assume, with political power, the mission of France. On that day, a dialogue can be undertaken. On that day, Mr Chancellor, you will have to opt for the true revolution by finally discarding those mere appearances in which you currently luxuriate. *If you are still able ...*

... faced with a revolutionary France conscious of its mission, liberated from all attachments to autarchy and imperialism, you will have to either renounce *your* own dream of autarchy, or allow the outbreak of that bloody conflict whose repercussions will, in turn, sweep you aside.

On that day, tell us, once and for all, whether Franco-German differences, none of them insurmountable, have to be settled by machine-gun fire, or if, finally united in the one essential task, we will cooperate in founding a New Order on earth.[87]

The ON letter confronted Hitler with an important choice regarding the ultimate meaning and purpose of national socialism and the New Order: was it strictly a means for establishing German strength and hegemony or was it meant to foster a new, regenerated Europe? Hitler would have to choose, come post-republican France, between supporting the young French fighting for a revolutionary European New Order and dealing with the tired old elites from the old liberal democratic regime. Harro Schulze-Boysen's "Open Letter of a Young German to France"[88] in the February 1933 *Esprit* had warned the French that they would have to make a similar choice in dealing with a Nazi-controlled Germany.

The attitude toward the newly victorious Nazis in ON's "Letter" proves that while it may have been hard for German National Socialists to have their program taken seriously by many of their country's intellectuals, their movement was taken very seriously by bright French elites who self-confidently claimed to speak for their whole "new French generation" in France's leading literary review in 1932. Many of them would always look back to the early 1930s as a turning point, and play significant roles in French life – not least after 1940, when Hitler would have to choose between supporting revolutionary change toward a New Order and treating with the old power structure of a German-occupied France.

ON's focus on early National Socialism's communitarian, idealistic, anti-materialist impulse and ability to radically change young people along positive and constructive lines led to the conviction that nascent German national socialism, like Russian communism and Italian fascism, partook of a general twentieth-century struggle to create order beyond the "disorders" of capitalist materialism. So ON denounced Hitler's conservative influence on national socialism and supported Otto Strasser and the Black Front, and the young intellectuals of the *Tat*-Kreis and especially of *Gegner*. But even after Hitler's brutality put down or coopted ON's German friends, Marc's group still respected the basic inspiration of national socialism: an authentic rebellion against the spiritual decay of modern society.

ON's personalism embodied a whole approach to life which, the group believed, neither of the leading fascist powers (much less the Soviet Union) had been able to conceptualize: personalism captured what was distinctive and valuable in the French revolutionary tradition, giving the French an edge in the search for new men who would ignite a spiritual revolution unsullied by racism or party or state worship. France's New Order would be more humane – and more open to religiosity – than its crude predecessors, since it transcended nationalism, racism, and statism, and was programmed to counter totalitarian impulses. The French personalist revolutionary example could inspire a "personalization" of off-kilter European experiences by improving on their errors and imperfections, and thus helping achieve the "necessary revolution" in Europe as a whole.

Was ON's abstruse review, publishing a few thousand copies, voicing the unspoken longings of an entire French generation? Some French young people, for whom they pretended to be the spokespersons, were in an anti-parliamentary and anti-establishment mood, and the violent riots against the French republican government through the night of 6 February 1934, just some weeks after Marc's letter to Hitler, fitted ON's prophecies.

*L'Ordre Nouveau*'s "Letter to Hitler" drew a great deal of criticism, as this young circle of *polytechniciens*, Sciences Po alumni, journalists, writers, librarians, architects, critics, and historians had neither a popular base nor a very clear plan for the group who would effect their French New Order. While the Soviet and fascist experiences had been blatantly self-interested, pushing the primacy of the party and the state, the Nazis embodied the spirituality of the youth movement which converted people to a new sense of region and country, to fraternity in joyful communion, beyond class struggle and the alienation of the cities.

ON was interested in transforming the best and the brightest of the young into a spiritual aristocracy of anti-materialistic personalists, revolutionary leaders shaped by their sense of the historical inevitability of their course, ignoring the possibility that their anti-liberal and anti-capitalist New Order might require violence to be effected. France's shining example would serve as an uplifting antidote to the deformed and incomplete revolutionary experiences of her neighbours.

Marc's assumption that one might seriously appeal to Adolf Hitler in the name of national socialist principles did not last very long. A little over a year after the original Marc/Daniel-Rops letter, *Ordre Nouveau* published a "Post-Script to the Letter to Hitler" which wondered how the Nazi party's radical program could still be put forward by a reactionary regime constantly compromising it. ON claimed to feel "great compassion for the German people," whose revolutionary aspirations had been disappointed by an old-style political apparatus with foreign and economic policies antithetical to that of Nazi rhetoric. The "back-to-the-land" initiatives had freed some people from "the abstract life of cities" but seemed largely intended as "an economic weapon to promote autarchy." Nothing had been done to "deproletarize" the masses of industrial workers, since the vaunted corporations of the trades were simply "a way to mobilize all the forces of the Nation for the benefit of the State." The Third Reich responded to unemployment as would an imperialistic police state, and so abandoned the revolutionary principles that once inspired the National Socialist movement: "War production, police, that is all you offer to the young men, arms itching to be put to good use, who finish the labour camps where they are supposed to get in touch – at least momentarily – with the real and deep dimensions of human life in its struggle with nature and the land."[89]

ON saw the Nazi regime's dubious "achievements" as confirming the gloomy original 1933 "Letter to Hitler": "Now you are doomed to go down the slippery slope that leads from nationalism to statism, from statism to autarchy [national economic self-sufficiency] and from autarchy to war."[90]

The ON circle and Heidegger shared a sense of how the National Socialist revolution failed to transcend the alienating features of modernity. Heidegger had relied on the broad historical force manifested as National Socialism, Marc's circle believed in the youth movement being shaped and reshaped by different ideas, leaders, and institutional projects. With his always stronger belief in the positive, providential role of man in history, Marc could never admit that he was dealing with unstable, peculiar people with whom one could hardly reason, even by appealing to the values they repeatedly affirmed.

Heidegger, realizing that the spiritual revolution he had hoped for in the national socialist movement was not easily achieved, appeared to dismiss History altogether. Jacques Derrida later observed that Heidegger, despite many references to "spirit" in his public pronouncements from 1933 to 1935, avoided using the word for nearly twenty years after his public estrangement from National Socialism.[91] The "spiritual revolution" that Heidegger yearned for had proven to be a disturbing oxymoron, and he was led to stand back from both spirit and historical movement in the light of this ill-fated junction.

But in his *Einführung in die Metaphysik* (1935), Martin Heidegger could still assign a historical task to the German people – the most spiritual of peoples, the "metaphysical people" in the face of the "spiritual decadence" of a Europe caught between Russia and America. Their mission was to take "the great decision" that would bring about the continent's destiny, the deployment of "new *spiritual* forces from this middle place."[92] ON had also claimed such a role for France – as the most spiritual, personalist nation, the "terre décisive" (in Dandieu's last words of *La révolution nécessaire* in 1933) of European civilization's spiritual forces against the barbarism of the East (Russia) and the West (the Americans).

The words "spirit" and "spiritual" (partly for political reasons, partly because of differences embodied in language) did not mean the same thing on the different sides of the Rhine: whereas in Germany these words meant the impersonal unfolding of Being in historical becoming,[93] for the French around Marc they designated the human person, and "new man" shaping the course of history.[94] In the "Letter to Hitler" he had seconded the Nazis castigation of "that world of abstraction and unreality ... of 'modern' man" which gradually isolated the person from realities, and remade him into a standard type: the numbered being. "We know that a civilization which encourages the eradication of the *patrie*, the family, property, the *métier*, or offers nothing more than a deformed or odious image of them, is not a civilization."[95] By taking the rhetoric of the Nazi regime very seriously in a formal, civilized "Letter to Hitler," *Ordre Nouveau* appeared to be in collusion with a spurious, manipulated "spiritual revolution."

In fact, this "Letter to Hitler" was aimed at the revolutionary German youth whom Marc had been in contact with, and several bundles of the special issue had been sent to German addresses, in the hope that some at least would get past border control; the polite and deferential tone of the "Letter to Hitler" may have been deliberately non-confrontational so that its substance would escape Nazi censors. But not a single copy of the "Letter to Hitler" made it into Germany at that time (although it would be requested in the next few years by Third Reich academics for use in classes studying interesting French political movements).[96]

Most reaction to the "Letter to Hitler" occurred in France where Gabriel Marcel, one of ON's founders, had already threatened to quit the movement. Arnaud Dandieu warned that his old teacher would bridle, and the "Letter to Hitler" proved the last straw. Alexandre Marc met with Marcel and tried to mollify him, as well as Robert Garric (leader of the Equipes Sociales, whose *Revue des Jeunes* portrayed ON's non-conformist revolutionism as troubling). When the three met in front of the Gare Montparnasse, Gabriel Marcel made a scene in public, shouting: "You don't exchange letters with Hitler; you march on Berlin!" A bellicose Garric approved him, bellowing excitedly: "*Oui, à Berlin!*", startling passers-by.[97] Marcel had pointed out something important: the letter had been an "exchange," an internal rather than an external critique of Hitlerite national socialism. Marc may have claimed to be of neither Right nor Left, but it was unthinkable, in the circumstances, that he would address Stalin in the familiar, bantering tone he used with Hitler. It was a letter written by someone who had been brought, as a European youth leader, to the Brown Hall in Munich by an aspirant leader of German national socialist youth. Daniel-Rops responded to an irate Marcel letter by defending Marc, responding to what he thought was Marcel's only substantial argument, that the ON writers were weakening the French government: he claimed that the government did not really represent the country, which it was leading down the path of war, just as "Hitlerites a year back also denied their democratic government the right to represent Germany." Daniel-Rops stood behind the "Letter to Hitler,"[98] and cited the "many demonstrations of sympathy we are receiving."[99] In fact strongly negative reactions to the controversial text had, within a few months, provided the catalyst for a definitive turn for French young people and French communitarian personalism: it was salvaged, transformed, and widely disseminated by the Catholic intellectuals of *Esprit*, who were also, but in their distinctive way, out to create "new men."

# 5  The Sohlbergkreis Heritage, the Paris Riots, and the French Popular Front (6 February 1934–June 1936)

> The Germans are further along than us.
> Emmanuel Mounier

The spectacular changes in Germany in early 1933 encouraged Marc and his friends to imagine that they would soon be mapping out France's place in the European New Order. By the end of that year, bands of their bold young street fighters were challenging the French republic; the rioting they joined in on during the evening of 6 February 1934 nearly brought down the government. The grave threat to liberal democratic institutions sparked a defensive Popular Front coalition of the Left, which was elected and began taking defensive measures in May and June 1936.

French and Belgian "Europeanists," self-confident in their prophetic stance, refused to be unsettled by the horror stories which began coming out of New Order Germany as they took it for granted that "their" national socialism would prevail. After Hitler seized power, Otto Strasser came to say the German revolution was not yet completed, urging his French comrades to keep faith in the European youth revolution. In November Marc and Ordre Nouveau (ON) published their notorious "Letter to Hitler," suggesting that the true spirit of the German youth revolution survived in the Strasser wing of the National Socialists. Marc's ardent tract *Jeune Europe*[1] portrayed an entire European generation on the march for a New Order from one end of the continent to the other, thus implying that Adolf Hitler was a minor, ephemeral player on the scene.

The very day after Hitler came to power, *Esprit* published Harro Schulze-Boysen's "Open Letter of a Young German to France," with its plea that French youth reject any notion of a Western capitalist "crusade" against the Soviet workers' state.[2] When the Nazis took over, Marc's comrade was arrested and beaten, but Schulze-Boysen's mother was a friend of Hitler's close comrade, the flying ace Hermann Goering, who got him released. Although his *Gegner* was soon closed down,[3] Schulze-Boysen was appointed to a responsible position in Goering's new Air Ministry, and began playing an active role in the ideological struggle in the Nazi party. Assuring Marc of his commitment to their common vision of a European New Order, Schulze-Boysen, in January 1934,[4] organized conferences on ON's ideas in Berlin and Göttingen,[5] and urged ON to publish in Nazi youth journals and to establish an ON support group in Berlin as part of his attempt to gain support for a leadership role among national socialist youth. He even got briefly transferred from the Air Ministry to Ribbentrop and Abetz's Foreign Affairs Ministry so that he might serve as an advocate for the importance of the French New Order forces on the European scale.

Meanwhile back in France (June 1934), Germanophile writer Pierre Drieu la Rochelle presented Third Force *chef* Gaston Bergery to the führer of the German students' association, who reported back to Berlin that Bergery could be categorized a socialist politically, but was a receptive listener.[6] On 25 June, Bergery presided over a meeting of five thousand supporters in a Salle Wagram adorned with quasi-Nazi trappings.[7] Concurrently, Eugen Meves, a friend of Schulze-Boysen who had presented the early Nazi party program in *Esprit*, brought Otto Strasser to meet Mounier.[8] Mounier went to see the French Fascist party founder Georges Valois to discuss joint projects.[9]

Gregor Strasser was murdered by the Hitlerites on 30 June, the "Night of the Long Knives" in Germany. That drama found Marc less focused on Germany than busy networking French non-conformists in economic policy discussion cells (these were mostly set up around Robert Gibrat and Robert Loustau, and, from time to time, with their fellow "X-Crise" group technocrat comrades like Jean Coutrot), as well as the distinct Ligue d'Action think-tank on financial policy (led by E. Pillias and E. Primard).[10] At this time[11] Mounier was worried about the French Communist party's new openness toward religion and its effect on the Third Force's "spiritual revolution" rhetoric; he concluded that it was incumbent upon his comrades to formulate "a constructive critique of communism" from a "firm spiritual foundation." A few weeks later Izard reassured Mounier that the Third Force would transcend the lacklustre "conformity of the Left," and the "new" *Esprit* and a renewed Third Force could quickly reunite. In what became a habitual pattern of duplicity, Mounier eagerly kept working with his radical friends while maintaining an image of independence in order to mollify some of his eminent mentors like Berdyaev and Jacques Maritain.[12]

In October a Hitler Youth delegation was hosted by Christian pacifist leader Marc Sangnier, innocent pioneer of that European youth hostel movement which the Nazis would find useful for their purposes. French young people visited Abetz's Karlsruhe, made the ritual climb up the Sohlberg, and admired local German popular piety, but discovered the Hitler Youth "a little too pagan" in their body language when devouring the Führer's radio speeches.[13] Sangnier invited the Hitler Youth for a return visit, and the Sohlbergkreis started its own Sangnier-linked *auberge* in Germany. The Nazis saw only advantages in having their people "dialogue" with others: the Nazis never wavered in their convictions, while the others were sometimes captivated by national socialist communitarian zeal.

Soon after the 6 February 1934 insurrection in Paris, Abetz started *Sohlbergkreis* to husband and expand the spirit of the original meetings by publishing "our French comrades,"[14] and it went on to admit the differences but laud the similarities for the next three years.[15] "Good European" Abetz regretted the anti-Germanism of the Action Française but held up Drieu's new nationalism as exemplary[16] – his *Socialisme fasciste* as furthering Franco-German understanding.[17]

Another *Sohlbergkreis* article discussed the French personalists' notion of communitarian revolution: "You young French people prefer to follow the guidance of your individual reason. [We Germans] having suffered ... from strictly materialistic undertakings recognize that the problem ... [is] moral before anything else ... capitalism must first be resisted in ourselves. ... the horrible physical misery around us can only be alleviated ... by economic leaders who are [both] technically accomplished and profoundly socialist ... [this is the reason for] our confidence in the *chef*."[18] Robert Aron organized meetings involving various French, German, Belgian and English representatives.[19]

The effervescent fellow-feeling among the French and Belgians was husbanded by solicitous Germans: Hitler Youth held ski camps for young people from Grenoble and Lyon during the Christmas 1934 holidays;[20] *Sohlbergkreis*, suggesting that the French were not all inferior, mongrelized racial stock, published articles on France's Alpine peoples, illustrated by photos of handsome women in Savoyard dress. The publication also warmly signalled *Esprit*'s critique of liberal democracy and praised its communitarian politics.[21]

Unknown young Frenchmen, self-important with their vague and lofty ideas, were flattered by some of the top young Nazis: leaders of obscure organizations numbering a few hundred were treated as peers by young Germans responsible for millions. *Sohlbergkreis* noted that one of the hosts of the French visitors, the German-American Baldur von Schirach, at twenty-seven was both head of the Hitler Youth – six million young people from fourteen to twenty-two – and *Chef du service d'Etat de la conduite de la jeunesse* for all of Germany.[22] Could the French non-conformist librarians, theatre-managers, architects, editors, or popular journalists administer massive organizations including millions of their peers? The Germans, like their friend Schulze-Boysen, matter-of-factly assumed that (with a little help from their friends) it was a real possibility. The Germans' own ascent from relative obscurity to total power had been dazzling, and so, in a few years, would be that of some of their French and Belgian comrades.

In January 1935, Paul Marion, forceful French neo-socialist youth leader and editor of the journal *L'Homme Nouveau*, explored in Abetz's review the prospects for effecting a general societal "Plan," like that of the leading trade union (the CGT), in France.[23] Abetz showed that he liked this kind of progressive French thinking more than he liked Action Française's Henri Massis underscoring France's *Latinité* against Germany. Abetz envisaged new, self-confident nationalisms reinvigorating Europe, and one of his comrades predicted that the new, rejuvenated Nordic and Latin peoples would confront the barbaric materialists threatening from the East.[24] In *Jeune Europe*, Bertrand de Jouvenel, for the Comité d'entente de la jeunesse française pour le rapprochement franco-allemand, called for an understanding with Germany. *Sohlbergkreis* described young francophones enchanted by the "anti-individualism" they had experienced in the Hitler Youth work camps.[25]

Harro Schulze-Boysen was giving seminars on international politics for the Hitler Youth when, in March, he proposed the creation of an ON Berlin Action group.[26] ON people were already meeting with Nazis in Paris, particularly when Abetz or his colleagues visited, and this paralleled ON activities in Brussels.[27] Since Schulze-Boysen wanted to publish ON essays in Nazi youth publications,[28] Marc, believing his German friend was trying to orient the ideology of the Nazi regime in the right direction, counselled his French comrades to collaborate, but guardedly and on specific projects.[29]

*Sohlbergkreis* praised the non-conformist fascist tract *Demain la France* by New Right thinkers Thierry Maulnier, Robert Francis, and Jean-Pierre Maxence – despite their penchant for a Latin peoples' hegemony rather than the German-Latin mixing Abetz favoured.[30] And non-conformists, especially those employing personalist language, were much more interested in national socialists than in Fascists. In April 1935, *Sohlbergkreis* published a "Jeune Europe" program which downplayed Latinité but emphasized the search for peace and a European federalism.[31] As if to show where their primary loyalties were, a few weeks before a fascist congress in Rome to which French non-conformists had been invited, members of the French contingent got together for study sessions in Paris with Nazi youth leaders.[32] Bertrand de Jouvenel's "Comité d'entente de la jeunesse française pour le rapprochement franco-allemand" was involved in an intense discussion (which lasted from 23 to 26 April) on the possibilities for a true socialism for France, where a French representative identified only as "F"[33] voiced misgivings about the Hitler revolution: "We stood out in France for defending the Hitlerite system [as] socialist and revolutionary. But June thirtieth [the night of the long knives; the obliteration of the Strassers] profoundly discouraged us ... the 'guarantors of socialism' were liquidated." "F" complained that a band of "reactionaries" had taken over national socialist Germany. A number of the French took up the invitation to return to Germany to see for themselves, and after the meeting they attended the Hitler Youth's Reichsberufwettkampf (Championnat National des Métiers de la Jeunesse Hitlérienne) in Sarrebruck, where they met with Baldur von Schirach and Dr Ley. The French president of the Fédération universitaire internationale[34] was particularly impressed by the Hitler Youth and their role in the future of the German nation.

Abetz's publication praised the French technocrat-futurists known as *planistes*, Bertrand de Jouvenel's conception of the "directed economy," and the efforts of the Esprit and ON circles: Esprit for seeking a new religious underpinning for work, ON for facing the problem of the monotonous nature of the labour required by several sorts of machinery, and for their labour service project for young people. These organizations could produce the builders of a French national socialism – as could the national students' union, the Jeunesses patriotes, the Scouts, the Croix de Feu, and the youth branch of the French Catholic Action movement. But the most promising nucleus for French national socialism, as of May 1935, were the ON and Esprit groups and the youth division of French Catholic Action (ACJF).[35]

Non-conformists had a limited interest in certain elements in the Italian Fascist movement. Robert Aron led the same groups from the April meeting with the Hitler Youth to a three-day Fascist congress in Rome in May, organized by Professor Ugo Spiritu (cited as an original fascist theoretician in *Esprit*). ON was represented by Aron, Claude Chevalley and René Dupuis, Esprit by Mounier and André Ulmann, Bergery's new "Front Social" by Louis-Emile Galey, neo-socialist youth by *L'Homme Nouveau*'s Paul Marion, and the Young Right by Jean de Fabrègues. The delegation, treated as if they were the cream of

European New Right, were invited to meet with the Duce in his palace in Venice.[36]

Marc favoured elements in the German model, and now Emmanuel Mounier reacted similarly toward the Italian, recognizing "at the heart of the regime, a fascist Left, comparable to the Hitlerite SA, for whom the revolution is unfinished business. [They are] *syndicalist* ... with a power base in Milan and in workers' organizations. These people organized this congress because they wanted foreign backing in their struggle for power ... Mussolini would tolerate them if they won.[37] Rossoni's rousing anti-capitalist concluding speech was moving": "it must be said – some are already afraid to admit it – we were all swept up in the feeling." The whole congress ended in "a sort of spirit of friendly enthusiasm."[38]

It was striking how, despite similar fraternal public rhetoric, private enthusiasm was noticeably absent from Mounier's encounters with Communists or Socialists. High-profile "man of dialogue," Mounier was privately much more interested in the German experience than in political moderates or the Left. ON, too, concluded that they had been relatively disappointed with Ugo Spiritu and their Italian experience,[39] and that dialogue with the Germans was closer to the real thing: professors in Nazi Germany's universities remained interested in non-conformist ideas.[40] While Jean de Fabrègues was representing the Right wing non-conformists in Rome, Fabrègues's comrade Thierry Maulnier spoke in Berlin.[41] *Sohlbergkreis*, warmly encouraging dialogue, raised ON's protégé Charles de Gaulle's *L'Armée de métier*, and cited at length *Esprit* articles sympathetic to Germany.[42] But were there real similarities between the French non-conformists and Hitler's war-veteran street brawlers? Abetz said that each self-respecting, confident *Volk* should effect their own revolution, and not undertake "pale imitations" of the special German experience. Marc's French New Order appealed to Abetz's sort of national socialism, and he reassured Marc when news came of his becoming an official, high-level Third Reich advisor and strategist, specializing in policy toward Western European countries.[43] Marc, unmoved by reports from the Rome congress, encouraged focusing on projects with the Germans, and the new de Becker movement in Belgium.[44]

The non-conformist–German contacts in summer 1935 culminated with a mid-August to mid-September Sohlbergkreis youth camp at Evian-les-Bains, which had been scheduled by Abetz's group the previous May. In July, Bertrand de Jouvenel, flamboyant stepson and lover of Colette, and leading apostle of concessions to Germany, had envisaged a New Right French national socialist coalition involving the Volontaires Nationaux, the Bergery group, and Jacques Doriot's circle:[45] then, in August, he signalled "striking verbal resemblances" in the generation's rhetoric, a common political discourse emerging. It is ironic to note that three of the most important advocates of transcending old French royalism by means of French generational solidarity in harmony with Nazi Germany – de Jouvenel, Bergery, and Marc – were of Jewish or partly Jewish background. Marc and his circle were certain that it was just their personalism which could become this generational discourse and, as we shall see, they were right.

ON people, in a classic New Right pattern, ignored grass-roots politics to take hands-on jobs as top-level administrative assistants, where they could work for their ideas from behind the scenes. Jean Jardin, short, immaculately dressed, discreet and efficacious, romantic and royalist culture-Catholic, began writing under a pseudonym in *Ordre Nouveau* once he became private secretary to the formidable French transportation czar Raoul Dautry – who, as head of the French national railways system, shared Jardin's interest in fostering practical contacts with Germany. Before long, *Cahiers Franco-Allemands* singled out Dautry for praise, for employing his train network to promote exchanges among European youth. Germanophile Jardin maintained a cordial private relationship with Abetz and Abetz's Paris agents such as Ernst Achenbach (functionary in Abetz's German embassy in Paris during the Occupation – when railroads were vitally important and Jardin was private secretary to Pierre Laval).[46]

While working for his mother's friend Hermann Goering's Air Ministry, Harro Schulze-Boysen remained in touch with ON group and was, in turn, asked for reports on them by Nazi officials.[47] He assured an ON contact[48] that interest in them was "still important" both in Ribbentrop's Foreign Office and in the Deutsche Studentenschaft, and that they should write for *Wille zum Reich*, a Nazified version of the *bündisch* organ *Die Kommenden*. Although he understood French wariness at this suggestion, he still thought articles on the ON's 1931–32 efforts to create an Arbeitsdienst in France would be timely. In candid letters,[49] Schulze-Boysen proudly claimed to have, with *Gegner*, introduced radical notions such as the Arbeitsdienst into the German revolution; he also reiterated his conviction that "the power of the capitalist society ought to be *definitely* broken: that is the pre-condition for any spiritual life and to any fresh 'personalism,' for which there are more and more disciples in Germany ... I am closer to that conception today than I was two years ago." Since becoming interested in communitarian commitment, he had also begun to develop more respect for the communists, who had "undeniably gained in quality," and he planned on having a good talk with Denis de Rougemont toward the end of August.[50]

In December, after meeting with Otto Abetz, de Rougemont went to the University of Frankfurt as his guest for the spring term to experience Hitler's Germany for himself and host a visit by Mounier and his wife.[51] As the anti-fascist "Popular Front" political coalition was coming together in France, non-conformist intelligentsia persisted in making contacts with the Nazis: for example, Abetz's key Belgian contacts, the Belgian "Jeune Europe" group ("Europeanists" frequenting the colourful salon of the rich, elegant young socialites Edouard and Lucienne Didier) sponsored a ski camp in the Bavarian mountains during the 1935 Christmas vacation. It was held in the Sohlberg spirit, and included not only young Belgians and Germans but also delegates from France and England, and led to a series of four camps being organized for the following summer.[52] The first volume of the *Deutsch-Französische Monatshefte/Cahiers Franco-Allemands* (successor to the review *Sohlbergkreis* and listing Otto Abetz and Friedrich Bran as founders) appeared in January 1936, calling attention to Dautry's promotion of youth exchanges through the railroad system. Despite the Nazi regime's growing brutality and exclusionary politics, the high-minded Europeanist youth movement seemed flourishing, supported in the highest business and social circles.

Hitler's rise to power did not put the New German philosophy beyond serious intellectual interest for the French, as Stalin had Marxism-Leninism. Alexandre Marc discovered that German thinking remained of much interest among advanced intellectuals such as Father Yves Congar, an astute, pioneering young Dominican communitarian theologian who had been sympathetic to the Action Française until it fell foul of the Vatican.[53] In mid-February 1936, Congar urged Marc to explicate that current of the new German *Existenzphilosophie* which had Karl Jaspers melding Nietzsche and Christianity, but to be careful to explain the origins of this thinking *"in making allusion only to Gabriel Marcel and Martin Heidegger."*[54] Was Congar worried that references to Max Scheler, or to Henri Bergson, would cause problems for the Dominican review *Sept?* Or about the orthodoxy of Jaspers's position on the compatibility between Christianity and Nazism? In a follow-up letter a few weeks later, Congar said he wanted a disquisition from Marc on the Heidegger-Jaspers parallel or, even better, a thorough explanation of the existential point of view, and an explanation of the contrast between *Geisteswissenschaften* and *Naturwissenschaften*, in contemporary German thinking.[55] Thus, in 1936, despite the Aryanization of German academic life by the Nazis, serious French intellectuals were still taking German professors and their philosophizing seriously – and as early as 1936 one could provide an erudite "explanation of the 'existential' point of view" employing the new conceptual language of Martin Heidegger and Gabriel Marcel.

This stirring philosophy, capable of electrifying culture-Catholics, ex-Catholics, and Catholic converts alike, had set the Dominicans to employ the serviceable, energetic, and well-connected Alexandre Marc, who could neatly catholicize this new German philosophy, as he had catholicized personalism with "Otto Neumann." In 1940, Vichy France's Uriage National Leadership School study group, with its remarkable chaplains René de Naurois and Jean Maydieu, carried on this interest in the new German thinking. Yet a decade later existentialism was described as yet another invention of the Resistance and its heroes J.-P. Sartre, Gabriel Marcel, and Albert Camus.

The new German societal model interested non-conformists, and on the eve of the election of the Popular Front government, *Esprit* economist François Perroux hardly deigned to mention the petty concerns of French political parties as he called attention to the world-historical innovations of the Third Reich. While critical of the National Socialist model for being constructed on pseudo-values (*Volk, Rasse,* etc.) which undermined respect for human persons, Perroux insisted that certain structures of Hitler's regime, analysed in greater detail in his book *Les mythes hitlériens,* were "personalist."[56] If contemporary German philosophizing could not be dismissed because of anti-intellectualism, their societal model should not be rejected out of hand because of ethnocentricity and racism. While other French editors were preoccupied with the implications of the Popular Front government's Matignon agreements, Mounier left for two weeks in Germany with Denis de Rougemont,[57] returning on 24 June intent on carrying discrete, if not secret, dialogue with the Hitler Youth[58] in the orbit of the Jeune Europe group which, as both *Sohlbergkreis* and *Esprit* indicated,[59] advocated appeasing Germany.[60]

After a week-long seaside dialogue with the Hitler Youth in Belgium in July, which we will describe later, Mounier settled in an isolated Belgian farmhouse and constructed, in five weeks, an aggregate of the positions worked out over the previous months.[61] This "common *Esprit* statement" was to confirm personalism as a "third way" between capitalism and communism, a striking, radical alternative to the Popular Front.[62] In this *Personalist Manifesto,* Mounier firmly rejected Marxism and Italian fascism, but provided nuanced analysis of national socialism: borrowing from leading corporatist theorist François Perroux, he outlined the "structure of a personalist regime" which would constitute an entire political culture very different from that engendered by Léon Blum's shaky left-wing coalition.

ON people were no more interested than Mounier in working with the Popular Front; they wanted something totally different. In June, just when the Popular Front seemed most promising, Marc urged *Esprit* co-founder Izard to quit the Socialist party for Bergery's "non-conforming" Frontist party (which Marc was promoting to the Catholic readership of *Sept*): "[Bergery's paper] *La Flèche* is well done," Marc assured Izard, "[with] interesting and lively articles ... What a shame that you ally yourself with old factions and outdated politicians."[63] ON's Robert Loustau, who, like Izard, was also interested in serving a highly visible political grouping from behind the scenes, approached rene-gade Communist Jacques Doriot, who, in June 1936, founded the mil-itantly anti-Communist Parti populaire français. Loustau was given responsibility for devising its social program, and even published a book outlining the movement's goals. ON was "neither Right nor Left," and so its members, like Loustau, could move easily into groups of zeal-ous communitarians or insurrectionists who were anti-Communist but difficult to situate on the traditional political spectrum. For all of its confusing rhetoric and posturing, ON's basic values were really those of the twentieth-century New Right: total rejection of the capitalist eco-nomic system, hostility to liberal democracy, commitment to create a new political culture, elitism, belief in spiritual revolution. The gifted technocrat Loustau, as we shall see, worked efficaciously for his deals in projects with the neo-socialist branch of the Socialist party, as a high-level advisor to Doriot, to Colonel de la Rocque of the Croix de Feu, and then to the National Revolution of Marshal Pétain.

When the Popular Front did not offer the non-conformists the new sort of France they craved, it rekindled their determination to find a Third Way, a New Order, more in line with the hopes of those insur-rectionists of February 1934. Europeanists, rather than abandoning German contacts, fabricated, by the summer of 1936, a new personal-ist revolutionary language and comportment. It had been uncovered by intellectual elites steeped in Nietzsche and the new *Existenzphiloso-phie*, circulated to support groups and their German comrades, and was becoming understood and experienced by the masses. For the next four years there would be a sustained effort to network various groups – in France and Belgium, but also in Germany, Switzerland, and Britain – committed to this new non-conformist New Order. They would create an elite cohort of dedicated and competent young men with faith in, and blueprints for, a New Order – political, social, eco-nomic, religious, and cultural – which would engender converts and create "new men." They made little effort to create a popular political base, since they never imagined that they would come to power by nor-mal liberal democratic political processes. But they did believe that their time would come, and here, again, they were right.

## THE FEBRUARY RIOTS, A POPULAR FRONT, A PERSONALIST MANIFESTO (FEBRUARY 1934–JULY 1936).

From the 6 February 1934 riots in Paris, through the era of the French Popular Front in 1936, and the debates over the Italian invasion of Ethiopia, the Spanish Civil War, and the Munich agreements, there was steady progress in bringing together a French non-conformist coalition. Over against individualism, materialism, and capitalism, personalist discourse promised its French and Belgian adepts a rejuvenating spiritual and moral communitarian experience. Once the common ground was established, networkers like Alexandre Marc could bring the disparate non-conforming groups into interactive relationships with one another, as technocrats responding to this rallying cry made the plans for taking France into the New Order. This broadened from Nietzschean Germanophiles and Europeanists to involve visionary technocrats, army officers interested in Catholic social doctrine, Dominicans, and Catholic laymen looking for new forms of communitarian experience – all united by the dream of "another France," or "another Europe," after the demise of liberal democracy and the Third Republic. In this chapter we shall trace the non-conformist coalition in France from the important riots of 6 February 1934 to the creation of a Popular Front government in June 1936 and, after an electrifying meeting with young Germans, the promulgation of an anti–Popular Front Manifesto in response.

### NEW MEN FOR THE NEW ORDER: TECHNOCRATS, ROYALISTS, "X-CRISE"

Philosophers, historians, mystical royalists, engineers, ecologists, and even world-class mathematicians were drawn to the new thinking of ON. In 1933, for example, Robert Aron recruited two brilliant and proven young engineers, Robert Loustau and Robert Gibrat, from the Centre polytechnicien d'études économiques, better known as X-Crise – a sophisticated and fraternal discussion group of technocrats trained at the Ecole Polytechnique.[64] The pair were soon sparking ON's "technical cells," formulating concrete applications for ON's doctrine, preparing L'Ordre Nouveau thematic issues, promoting ON ideas to X-Crise leader Jean Coutrot and his circle.[65] Technocrat and ON interaction would continue and intensify until the defeat of France in 1940, and then serve subsequent attempts to institutionalize a French New Order.[66]

Robert Loustau, the older of the two at thirty-four, became – like his comrade Jean Jardin – an important éminence grise of the 1930s.

Army veteran, alumnus of both the Ecole Polytechnique and the Ecole des mines, Loustau had a brilliant career in iron metallurgy[67], while taking a serious Catholic's interest in, and approach to, economic and social problems. Robert Gibrat, five years younger, a mathematician who had also studied law, became one of the period's rare econometricians, taught at the Ecole des mines at Saint-Etienne, and was *ingénieur-conseil* to the Societé générale d'entreprise. Gibrat worked with Loustau in X-Crise between 1931 and 1933 and followed him into the ON.[68] Loustau and Gibrat were already involved with ON when they experienced their frustration with the unfocused anti-republican riots on 6 February 1934. Loustau became an ideologue for Colonel de la Rocque's large right-wing veterans' organization, the Croix de Feu, in 1934 (the year in which it created a youth auxiliary, the Volontaires nationaux, open to the post-war generation), and than again in 1937 when, as the Parti social français, it experienced a period of dramatic growth, exceeding by 1937 the membership in the Croix de Feu (as many as 450,000 in 1936). In a graphic demonstration of the facility with which intellectuals could pass from one extremist organization to another, Loustau simultaneously became, as we shall see below, a member of the politburo and drew up a program for Jacques Doriot's crypto-Nazi Parti populaire français. Loustau worked with Gibrat at a scheme to employ the latest electronic communication techniques to network the French non-conforming groups and to coordinate the revolt against French liberal democracy of the 1930s. The two engineers would have their chance to help establish their own notion of an authoritarian, planned, post-republican New Order after June 1940.[69]

While some ON people were working at drawing in engineers, Marc and his comrade Xavier de Lignac were approaching monarchists. Using pen-names, the two wrote, in 1933–34, for the *Courrier Royal*, semi-official publication of Henri, Comte de Paris, the pretender to the throne of France, who was trying to distance himself from the Action Française. De Lignac, a student of politics at the Ecole libre des Sciences politiques and literature at the Sorbonne, and an Action Française–type Catholic, had encountered the ON in late 1933 thanks to Daniel-Rops and Jean Jardin.[70] It was Jardin, railway administrator but romantic Catholic royalist (hating automobiles, loving to cross the old French provinces by rail) who connected ON with the Bourbons. De Lignac, after becoming administrative secretary of the review in 1936, would downplay his royalism.[71] But at the Liberation of France, it was de Lignac, then working for de Gaulle as an expert on media, who would set up a meeting between Henri Bourbon and the General when the latter considered restoring the monarchy.[72] Also joining

ON at this time were Albert Ollivier and his brother Louis, who would, like de Lignac, be active both at Vichy and then in the media in de Gaulle's post-war RPF (before becoming ... French manager of the Disney corporation!) R.-P. Millet, an ethnographer interested in racial theories, also became active at ON in this period as ON appealed to young dreamers and activists, militant anti-Communists all, who combined, often in the same person, radically modernizing and strikingly anti-modern visions for top-down changes to republican France.

### PARIS RIOTS FOR A NEW ORDER: 6 FEBRUARY 1934

Prominent *Esprit* non-conformist André Déléage led a group of forty Third Force militants among the crowd who charged the French police defending the barricades protecting the Chamber of Deputies in Paris on 6 February 1934.[73] ON saw the February attack on democratic institutions as a significant, if disappointing, prelude to the veritable French Revolution. But there was no unanimity about the reasons for the non-conformist frustration. *Esprit* set down its differences from ON, while the Jeune Droite's *Revue du Siècle* in turn set down its differences from both *Esprit* and *L'Ordre Nouveau* (which had published a special manifesto), but no post-February common front immediately materialized. ON's own line showed signs of hardening into a sectarian dogma.[74] Robert Aron mused that the riots must have been caused by Dandieu's ideas: they had erupted six months, to the hour, from his death.

Alexandre Marc, always the busy networker against the communist menace, was joined by several of his comrades in sending feelers to other movements, and finally joining several (*planiste* Christian Pineau's syndicalist Nouvelles Equipes, the Front national syndicaliste,[75] and *Préludes* – heir to the defunct *Plans*), in a Club de Février to broadcast and circulate the new non-conformist thinking so as to avoid any more confusing fiascos like the February riots.[76] Some ON people followed Marc in working within, or even consciously infiltrating, large Catholic organizations or media channels amenable to their new ideas, such as the Croix de Feu or the communitarian Catholics in its orbit. This largest and most important group in the February street demonstrations had seemed particularly unmilitary and indecisive that night: Colonel de la Rocque sent his troops home early, perhaps saving the republic. The brand-new *Sept* seemed to suggest that Saint Dominic might have seen barricade-storming as a healthy reaction against parliamentarianism but stopped short of recommending it as a regular policy; still, this *Sept*/Dominican popularization of non-conformist views among Catholics at this time was significant.[77] ON Catholic Loustau would join the Croix de Feu, and Catholic convert Marc would join *Sept*, after 6 February, with the agenda of clarifying the political perceptions, and focusing the communitarian energies, of their large, and largely Catholic, constituencies.

### CATHOLIC COLONELS IN THE WINGS: DE LA ROCQUE AND DE GAULLE

In the wake of the February riots, when ON's Loustau and Gibrat joined the Volontaires Nationaux of the Croix de Feu to help clarify the movement's social philosophy, Colonel de la Rocque met formally with the ON people to discuss the possibility of their organization serving as official ideologues of his movement.[78] Loustau was soon at work providing it with an agenda of social policy. The ON's new fondness for mobilizing large groups to block the Communists and fight for the New Order had already led Mounier, in mid-February, to warn Berdyaev that a new sort of strong-armed anti-worker fascism might be surfacing in their movement.[79] There certainly was a new interest in military men: a few months later, *Sept* interviewed a friendly Colonel de la Rocque who appeared much the devout Catholic. At the same time[80] ON's *Sept*-group Catholics were becoming enthusiastic about the ideas of Marshall Pétain's erstwhile protégé Charles de Gaulle.

De Gaulle was already a member of Marc's "Amis de *Sept*" because of his interest in new Catholic social and religious thinking.[81] But it was Robert Aron who took this unusual officer-intellectual to a couple of ON meetings in late 1934 and early 1935.[82] This was a period when de Gaulle's ideas interested German planners more than the French, but at the first meeting, in the apartment of Daniel Halévy (friend of Péguy, contributor to *L'Ordre Nouveau*,[83] admirer of Arnaud Dandieu), Marc remembered the young officer dazzling the company with his vivid evocation of the nature of the next world war and his novel conception of reforming the French army: de Gaulle's elitist and authoritarian approach to rejuvenating France would not have offended them.

Roused by de Gaulle's ideas, the ON sent a brash open letter to all of the French deputies and senators warning of the dangers in the international situation and of the French army's deficiencies. There were only five replies; four merely polite, and a very supportive fifth from up-and-coming government leader Paul Reynaud, who already admired de Gaulle. Some of Marc's non-conformist colleagues like P.O. Lapie (whom the general would name to an important post in liberated France) and the fascist-leaning neo-socialist Marcel Déat particularly liked de Gaulle's elitist *Vers l'armée de métier.*[84] The ON's high-profile popularizer Henri Daniel-Rops published de Gaulle's *La France et son armée* in his new "Présences" collection; Alexandre Marc gave de Gaulle–inspired talks at the Saint-Cyr officer's school and at the Air Academy. Despite de Gaulle's efforts to present his new ideas to the French military as being backed by Marshall Philippe Pétain himself,[85] the officer who introduced Marc's Gaullist talk chided Marc for lending credibility to Jules Verne–like fantasies and, when privately confronted, snorted that the haughty de Gaulle was "le grand hurluberlu de l'armée française!"[86] But de Gaulle's thinking did find solid support among people open to the Catholic social thought represented by the *Sept* Dominicans, or to the blueprint for the New Order of Marc and his friends.

By May 1935 the Gibrat-Loustau efforts[87] to promote ON ideas among the Croix de Feu's war veterans seemed more successful than the Marc–Daniel-Rops initiative to disseminate de Gaulle's thinking in the military. The overtures toward the Croix de Feu were critically evaluated in ON technical cell meetings and serious progress reported back to the plenary ON meeting.[88] In June Loustau's high profile in de la Rocque's organization,[89] his manifesto for it, his fiery lecture to a crowd of three thousand, even made Robert Aron and others worry that Croix de Feu would become a personalist fascist movement, employing ON discourse but caricaturing ON's ideas, and that ON should hurry to organize its own people throughout France. For some ON leaders like Aron, Loustau seemed to have distorted what ON was really about, but Robert Gibrat, while understanding their misgivings, wanted to stick with Loustau to get beyond pretentious talk and theory and accomplish something.[90]

Loustau and his comrades in the Croix de Feu were soon chafing under the leadership of the cautious de la Rocque and being approached by others with more urgent agenda and more radical programs. In late June, Bergery's *La Flèche* announced that a new political coalition would meet in renegade communist Jacques Doriot's territory of Saint-Denis: this new "neither Right nor Left" "Front social" would be particularly attractive to the disgruntled young people[91] from the Croix de Feu's youth wing, the Volontaires Nationaux, In July, Loustau and Gibrat left it, taking other young intellectuals with them.[92] That summer's discussions toward forming a broad movement involved a spectrum of ex-Volontaires Nationaux, and Jacques Doriot, Paul Marion, Louis-Emile Galey and Bergery, among others. Out of this ecumenical encounter came Gibrat-Loustau's Mouvement Travailliste Français[93] – which modestly announced itself as a world-historical anticapitalist force superseding the Second and Third Internationals.[94]

In fact while Loustau was working for the Croix de Feu he was also helping Doriot – publishing *Justice sociale, économie humaine* (Saint-Denis: Parti populaire français, 1936) to summarize the initial program of Doriot's new Parti populaire français. Although this party was made up largely of ex-Communists, Loustau was made a politburo member[95] – along with Germanophile political theorist Bertrand de Jouvenel and fascist novelists Raymond Fernandez and Pierre Drieu la Rochelle. Loustau would keep a low profile in, and resign in frustration from, Doriot's movement in 1938, after having demonstrated that an astute non-conformist technocrat and ideologue could easily move from one kind of alternative to liberal democracy to another.[96]

### THE RADICAL DOMINICANS OF *SEPT*

Like the Croix de Feu and the groupings of non-conformists, the Dominican order was a dynamic, militantly anti-communist, often anti-republican, force in inter-war France. Like the aesthetic, home-grown fascists at their friend "Corbu's" *Plans*,[97] and the Europeanists at *Esprit* and ON, they created a journal backed by a network of support communities. The cream of the Dominican elite assembled *agrégés*, Third Way political theorists, converts to Catholicism, metaphysicians, novelists, avant-garde theologians, and politicized military officers to launch highbrow, large-circulation publications. Alexandre Marc was converted, baptized, married – and employed – by the famous Juvisy Dominicans, who were running a plethora of activities. In February 1934 they announced what would become their best-known project: a large-circulation "neither Right nor Left" review called *Sept*.[98]

The Juvisy community were, despite their traditional tonsure and flowing white robes, experimental communitarians, operating from a modern convent structure in the middle of a "Red Belt" (Communist-leaning) Parisian working-class neighbourhood, a bit like Daniel in the lion's den. These Spartan elite priests, who "prayed seven times a day" and were all the more "loved for that,"[99] were visited by social workers and professors, pastors, chaplains of Catholic Action groups, film producers, and trade unionists. Lively, charismatic, innovative, erudite, they represented the best and the brightest of the French Catholic church – a spiritualist, communitarian alternative to Marxism in tough "pagan," Stalinist territory.

A key Juvisy personality was Father Marie-Vincent Bernadot, founder of some of the leading Catholic intellectual reviews in the world – including *La Vie Spirituelle* (1919) and *La Vie Intellectuelle* (1928) – a man of peasant background who had been a staunch supporter of the Action Française. Unlike many of his fellow Dominicans,

Bernadot had quickly taken the papal side during the 1928–29 Action Française controversy – even advising the papal nuncio in France and thus earning some gratitude in Rome. This resolute anti-communist was, despite his rural and monarchist background, an important fashioner of the "progressive" and "neither Right nor Left" orientation of *Sept* and the publishing house, Editions du Cerf, which he also founded.[100]

Alexandre Marc, with his publishing and networking experience and innovative personalist, federalist anti-Stalinism, was just the sort of man to help in Bernadot's projects. Marc soon became the Dominicans' resident convert, seen as a Europeanist and described as an ex-Bolshevik who had seen the light. If a smart Russian Jewish revolutionary could be converted, "turned inside out like a glove"[101] by the neo-Dominicans, why not a whole French workers' suburb? The Dominicans began to flaunt "converts from Communism," even if of good bourgeois family.[102] Marc was valuable both as window-dressing and as a dedicated, skilled professional organizer behind the scenes.

Father Pierre Boisselot signed the front-page editorials for *Sept*, along with Joseph Folliet, a well-known professional Catholic activist and its editorial secretary.[103] *Sept*'s administration may have been top-heavy with Dominicans but they numbered only six (including Marie-Dominique Chenu, Yves Congar, Jean Maydieu, and A.-D. Sertillanges) among the forty contributors to the review, most of whom were under forty years of age (including Marc and Daniel-Rops), with several not yet thirty (Etienne Borne, Maurice Schumann, P.-H. Simon, and Congar). There were seven *agrégés* (Borne, Henri Guillemin, Etienne Gilson, Rops, Maritain, P.-H. Simon), several former *normaliens*,[104] Catholic leftists, right-wing authoritarian corporatists, and apostles of the special communitarian spirituality of *Esprit* and of the "revolutionism" of ON.

As *Sept* was on the cutting edge of French religious thought and experience, it proved vulnerable to attack by unreconstructed right-wing Dominicans loyal to the Action Française. The celebrated Notre Dame preacher Father Marie-Albert Janvier hated Father Boisselot and successfully schemed against Boisselot's *Sept* in the Vatican. But despite the rapid physical disappearance of the review, its intellectual and spiritual influence proved remarkable: young *Sept* Dominicans Marie-Dominique Chenu and Yves Congar (whose advice Marc often sought for *Sept*'s orientation)[105] would go on to be among the most famous and influential Catholic theologians in the world.[106]

Dominicans invited Marc to address their seminarians on "the dreams of contemporary youth, particularly in France,"[107] as if Daniel-Rops, Scheler, and Marc were representative of European revolutionary youth moving toward Catholicism. The Dominicans arranged for Marc's clandestine marriage to fend off the threat of deportation, high-level political support for his visa application, and a job with *Sept*, and once things became difficult in Paris, a priest friend arranged for housing in the provinces. For his part, Marc worked for a Dominican editorial committee with whom he met twice a week, and made his living as a freelance journalist.[108]

Father Jean-Marie Maydieu (1900–1955) was distinguished among the new generation of Dominicans as a strong personality particularly influential at *Sept* (as later at Vichy's national leadership school at Uriage, where he served as chaplain and spiritual guide). Maydieu had been a student at the elite Ecole Centrale, and a former *camelot du Roi* and member of Charles Maurras's personal bodyguard: "when Maurras went about town he was accompanied by two or three young men with cudgels to protect him. Maydieu was one of them."[109] Maydieu had taken his vows as a Dominican on 23 September 1926, the year of the Action Française crisis. A few years after that he had played a role in Marc's conversion and so now, when Marc argued that the review's image was too Dominican, Maydieu helped him establish a national network of *amis* like those behind *Plans* and *Esprit* which would involve a fraternal, committed, community experience.[110] Laymen such as Charles de Gaulle (one of the first members) joined the "amis de *Sept*"; before the end of that year Marc would be helping the young lieutenant-colonel disseminate his ideas.

The first *Sept*, appearing as a new Catholic Third Way publication just a few weeks after the February attack on parliamentary institutions,[111] soon had a much larger circulation than the more detached and philosophical "idea" reviews *Esprit* and *Ordre Nouveau*. *Ordre Nouveau*'s Marc and Daniel-Rops were prominent contributors. By early 1937 *Sept* had special issues pushing a "Catholic alternative" for France – imposed by a military man if necessary – which sold over one hundred thousand copies. The interviews with Colonel de la Rocque and the presence of Charles de Gaulle in the support group suggested an openness to an authoritarian Catholic order imposed from above.

*Sept* announced itself as "Neither of the Right nor of the Left" but wanting "to realize the Catholic order in France"[112] (the February 6th uprising having failed), and it was soon instrumental in setting out an agenda for Catholic Action in France.[113] *Théologiens en veston* (lay theologians in street clothes) published chapters of their upcoming books (Jacques Maritain's *Humanisme intégral*, Etienne Gilson's *Pour un ordre catholique*)[114] in its pages. Msgr Emile Guerry, Catholic Action leader trying to wean young people from the Action Française, drew on *Sept*'s ideas for what became the important first full study of the goals and inspirations of the *L'Action Catholique*.[115] *Sept* demonstrated "an admiration which was quickly tempered" for certain anti-parliamentary organizations and for Italian fascism.[116] When the neophyte *Esprit* literary critic P.-H. Simon argued in *Sept* that the state should exercise "authority" through a host of new or rethought intermediary bodies, his fellow teachers in the National Teachers' Union were alarmed and accused him of becoming a sophisticated apologist for fascism.[117] Alexandre Marc positioned *Sept* on the new Germany in his regular two-page column "Les idées et la vie," which came just after its editorial; he introduced the latest German thinking and the novelty of the German youth movements,[118] in the guise of presenting an overview of the foreign press.[119] Each issue concluded with a page of "Amis de *Sept*" news, and Daniel-Rops' "Chronique ouverte," which might have a letter, or the gist of a debate. Father Maydieu urged Marc to keep increasing the lively review's circulation,[120] but the Dominicans were soon investigated by the police about Marc's activities and Marc (who still lacked proper legal status in France) had to be discreetly moved to a haven within the walls of a convent in southwestern France, near Pau, where Father Plaquevent was chaplain.[121]

*Sept* announced "A New Order in the offing, we must not let it be made against us." The review proposed private property, tied to resettling families on the land, and business on more human dimensions, as means of providing some relief from the afflictions of the age – a little garden on returning from one's day at the factory, small farms, middle-sized enterprises. Paul Chanson, well known in Catholic circles as the innovative president of the Fédération du port de Calais, recommended corporatist structures as a salvific alternative to liberal economic and social relationships.[122] This was part of a larger discourse which set society's highest priority as returning the "mère au foyer." It was proposed that married women be forbidden to work, and there be "prudent" reserve about the notion of female suffrage, because a woman's place was in the home: the idea that she might find self-fulfilment in work was not worth considering.[123]

While the brash *Esprit* non-conformists were belittling Colonel de la Rocque as old-fashioned and moralistic,[124] the December 1934 *Sept* published a friendly interview with him, in line with the Marc circle's openness to right-wing authoritarian figures interested in their own program for national renovation. The 15 February 1935 issue had Daniel-Rops arguing that the French had not completely succumbed to "materialist productivism" because their peasants were the repository of "ancestral" values. A romantic Péguyist notion that peasants were not materialistic but instinctive communitarians was common among Catholics in this period ... much as communists imagined proletarian communities transcending selfishness. A man like Daniel-Rops thought it very important that peasants were Catholics, while the industrial workers were not. And Daniel-Rops's whole ON-Esprit-*Sept* circle considered the bourgeoisie materialistic like the proletarians, but hoped that, like the Germans, they could radically spiritualize the new generation of the middle class. This oblique interest in the German experience did not go unnoticed: that same February 1935 when Daniel-Rops was advocating peasant socialism in *Sept*, the Juvisy Dominicans told Mounier that police were watching them and had even come to question them about Raymond de Becker.[125] *Sept* published a special issue on "L'Allemagne d'Hitler" a few months later[126] as its circulation – along with arcane, elitist *Ordre Nouveau*'s – continued to grow.[127]

In the January 1936 *Sept*, Pierre-Henri Simon, undaunted by his colleagues' invective, endorsed Jacques Maritain's idea of a French Third Party melding left-wing economic and social policies with religious and family values.[128] Implying the time was ripe for a new political option, Simon suggested that Catholics "synthesize ideas and reconcile hearts" to prepare a Third Force, neither capitalist nor communist, like that envisaged by Georges Izard, L.-E. Galey, Georges Duveau, and Gaston Bergery.[129]

In fact, while calling for a Third Force, *Sept* was still a relatively parochial operation which "had a hard time getting beyond a moralistic discourse which tended to obfuscate the facts [and] to make moral reform the key to all amelioration."[130] The *Sept* group considered it obvious that economic liberalism was de-Christianized, liberalism in general corrupting; a neat remedy could be found in social Catholic teaching. To people largely innocent of modern economic analysis, Catholic economist François Perroux's learned corporatism seemed the most persuasive alternative to the capitalist system. While Marc came from a very different political culture from these ingrown Catholic circles, he shared their assumption that liberalism was perverse, and he lumped together the capitalist and Soviet systems as destructive of workers.[131] But *Sept* – unlike Marc – also saw all forms of socialism (even Henri de Man's "spiritualized" kind) as destructive [132] – as was to be expected of a Dominican review censored[133] to be in line with the Catholic doctrine.[134] Thanks largely to Marc, however, the ON Catholics were able to help *Sept* move beyond sclerotic Catholic thinking and attack both Stalinism and capitalism with a Third Way communitarian option that seemed promising in the circumstances.[135]

By spring 1936, ON's quest for a Third Way New Order involved working with the Catholic communitarians in the Société de Saint-Louis order, and with its leaders Paul Flamand and Eugène Primard[136]

– particularly on Third Way publishing projects.[137] Marc got Flamand's communitarian Catholics to interact with the Catholic ON theorists.[138] This sort of networking effort was not made toward the Communists or Socialists who were (despite some warm public overtures) in another camp. Marc's Amis de *Sept* networked a certain bourgeoisie and clergy which felt itself threatened by the Popular Front.[139] The review by early 1937 had become one of the most important Catholic or Third Way publications in France:[140] it was disseminated as a progressive Catholic publication by the young Catholic factory and agricultural workers in the Jeunesse ouvrière chrétienne (JOC) and Jeunesse agricole chrétienne (JAC).[141] Alexandre Marc saw this as a worthy effort of propaganda or popularization, part of his larger project of creating a communitarian, idealistic, Christian press, which could employ the ideas of the ON elites.[142] But *Sept* suddenly encountered (spurious) "financial difficulties" in 1937 owing to the machinations in Rome of jealous Dominicans close to the old Right of Maurras and the Action Française. While *Sept* was officially scuttled, the review reappeared, with the new name *Temps présent* and under official lay editorship, to continue Dominican networking for the New Order.

As the French Popular Front began to materialize Marc was working simultaneously for ON, for the Catholic communitarianism around Flamand and the Société de Saint-Louis, and for the Dominicans at *Sept*: what had seemed very different initiatives were coming together. In Germany different groupings of the so-called Conservative Revolution had been brought together (by force) into the National Socialist Revolution. In France, where a Popular Front government to defend liberal democracy had been formed, Marc was working at creating a solidly anti-Communist alternative coalition to that shaky progressive pro-republican political alliance. Elitist and authoritarian nonconformists, activist Catholics, and radical communitarians were merging into a linked confederation which was beginning to operate as a French political culture distinctly different from that of the parliamentary Left and Right. Young Germans and young Belgians were showing the way by their failures and successes at melding spiritual revolution with political action in ways which only a few individuals like Marc had envisaged a few years before.

Non-conformists promoted modernizing theology, which inevitably annoyed Catholic conservatives. One way to avoid the ecclesiastical antagonism which had undermined *Sept* would be to convince the Vatican of the real possibility of their suddenly moving from the margins into leadership positions in which they would favour Catholic interests.[143] Cardinal Pacelli, soon to be Pius XII, saw the possibility of a European New Order and was trying to strengthen French Catholics by working to remove the condemnation from the Action Française. In fact, in 1940, a mixture of theological dinosaurs from the Action Française and non-conformists charged up by avant-garde theology would come to positions of some influence in France, work together in the effort to "re-Christianize" young people, and bring an intense new communitarian religiousness to the centre of public life.

## GASTON BERGERY'S COMMON FRONT

Given the self-conscious exclusiveness of Catholic political culture in the inter-war period, it was easier to network Catholics with one another than with religiously indifferent communitarians and Third Force people. But already in the fall of 1934 Georges Izard had proposed placing the Third Force – the activist offshoot of *Esprit* which had joined in the rioting against the government on 6 February – under the command of the maverick radical Gaston Bergery. Although the *Esprit* orbit was overwhelmingly Catholic, 90 per cent of the Third Force people voted to follow Izard and leave the *Esprit* groups for Bergery's Common Front. The resultant new grouping was to be the "Front Social" – a militant Third Way political option for France.[144] In November when Mounier visited his Strasbourg *Esprit* group headed by ON's Pierre Prévost, two to three hundred people came to his lecture and subgroups of doctors, and of jurists, were created as a result.[145] But despite the positive signs in Strasbourg, Mounier privately noted a problem of *Esprit* group recruitment in the face of the tempting alternative of joining Bergery's party.[146]

While *Esprit* people were joining areligious political activists, religious communitarians were approaching the officially areligious ON group. Also in November, Paul Flamand, militant in the Catholic Action movement and the Société de Saint-Louis, future non-conformist leader, taxed ON that their "purely intellectual doctrine" was insufficiently religious: "les problèmes de la personne humaine, de la Primauté du Spirituel, s'accrochent aux questions spirituelles, à une religion, à une Foi." Flamand warned that without a religion, without a living faith, no society could be saved; there could be no creativity.[147] Several innovative pre-war projects involving dedicated Catholic laymen – notably the Société de Saint-Louis, the Editions du Seuil, the Rotoir commune – and then the Jeune France cultural movement under Vichy – would be inspired by the communitarianism of the dynamic and charismatic Flamand. Like other Catholic Action activists, Flamand shared ON's belief in the role of a new generation of elites, except that their whole project had to be ruralized and spiritualized by interaction with the new breed of Catholic. The same month

Mounier visited the Communist-Catholic discussion group at the Ecole Normale Supérieure at Sèvres to discover the Communists there so interested in the new breed of Catholics that they wanted to form their own *Esprit* group. This was simultaneous with Georges Izard's working toward an *Esprit*-Bergery juncture.[148]

By the end of 1934 several non-conformists had begun to employ personalist communitarian discourse for the first time. In December, *Esprit* published Mounier's first essay concerned with the "person," and an article by Paul-Ludwig Landsberg, a German disciple of Max Scheler, on the "Christian person." Like personalist communitarianism, the thinking about the future known as planism was flourishing in the personalist milieu and also offering promise of a non-communist alternative to the Popular Front of the Left which was just beginning to take shape.[149] *Ordre Nouveau* lured bright young activists such as Xavier de Lignac (*nom de plume* of Jean Chauveau), Albert and Louis Ollivier (both, like Lignac, serious Christians fed up with party politics), and R.-P. Millet.[150] Other newcomers included the Greek Jew I.-S. Révah, introduced by Mireille Dandieu, and the syndicalists Pierre Prévost, Albert Hayon, and Roger Boulot. Boulot, who dropped from sight, seems to have been the one working-class member of a movement which was claiming that it would totally change the lives of the working classes.[151] *L'Ordre Nouveau* tended to attract, and be read by, impecunious young intellectuals from well-to-do backgrounds.[152] The influential young Dominican Maydieu, former stick-wielder for Maurras, now wrote Marc that even he was becoming a personalist.[153] And as the anti-fascist coalition of the French Left took shape during 1935, the French non-conformists and personalists strengthened their relationships with one another and with their young interlocutors in Belgium, Germany, and Italy, as we have seen, but also in Quebec[154] and England.[155] This swelling of personalist rhetoric was not universally welcomed. Jacques Maritain made it clear in December 1934 that he had serious reservations, particularly about Marc and Denis de Rougemont,[156] and since Maritain still remained the prestigious patron of *Esprit*, Mounier tried to edit de Rougemont's personalism to placate him.[157] Although Alexandre Marc published in their *Dossiers de l'Action Populaire* that month, the French Jesuits remained much more guarded about personalism than were the Dominicans – perhaps because of those German or Germanophile contacts which had caused the Dominicans to come under police surveillance.[158]

Besides enkindling Dominicans, non-conformist circles also continued to inspire communitarian initiatives among lay people such as that ambitious Societé de Saint-Louis of Catholic lay people in which Paul Flamand had become active. A fundraiser for that society assured Marc that while others had built cathedrals, people like them had the task of "rebuilding a world: a project worth living and dying for."[159] That this world would be the "New Middle Ages" Berdyaev had foreseen is shown by distinguished medievalist Etienne Gilson, who coupled his sympathy for the Société de Saint-Louis with his good feelings toward *Sept*. An agricultural commune called Le Rotoir grew up out of the Société de Saint-Louis order and it was thought that communities like it would mushroom, offering a French variant to the Belgian Communauté movement, or a laymen's version of the Juvisy Dominican community.[160]

When Mounier went to network non-conformists in the provinces in March, he discovered, among other things, the avant-garde, ecologically oriented Bordeaux ON/Esprit group, run by Bernard Charbonneau and Jacques Ellul, working out a pioneering critique of technological society. For Mounier they were "a little Protestant circle [who] only think revolution," "a bit Jansenist, but [with a] solid, peasant, worker bent (they exchange mimeographed copies of a handwritten journal). ... practically committed to celibacy as a precondition for effecting the spiritual revolution ... a bit tense, a bit immature, but ardent."[161] In retrospect we can discern, in this ardour, the first serious and important manifestation of the "Green" movement in France. But Mounier/ON/Bergery personalist communitarianism, progressively more disciplined and centralized, was less open than it might have been to the novel ecological critique and wilderness camping experiences of the Bordeaux people ("Camping, camping, outside of camping no salvation!" Mounier sneered.) Mounier and his ON friends like Marc called themselves non-conformists, but they were becoming more and more obdurate, insisting that even the Bordeaux campers conform to the discipline required for a kind of government in exile being federated over against French liberal democracy.

In Toulouse, Mounier encountered another dreamer in the person of "a turbulent seminarian, sympathetic to us" who would have a colourful career. René de Naurois quickly took his comrade Mounier to see his sympathetic mentor, Msgr Jules Géraud Saliège, "the socialist bishop" of the city, who confided to his young visitors his sympathy for the personalists, along with his belief that Marxism was "the most beautiful spiritual revolution of the nineteenth century,"[162] Mounier kept up his ties with de Naurois. This would prove important after the defeat of France in 1940 when the robust cleric would be named chaplain and *de facto* spiritual director to Pétain's new National Leadership school – l'Ecole Nationale des Cadres d'Uriage. De Naurois would then be instrumental in having Mounier invited to try to orient the school in the direction of communitarian personalism.[163]

In June 1935 *Le Temps*, France's leading daily, pointed out that the French delegation to the Fascist Congress on Corporations in Rome represented a sort of Common Front among French youth which involved not only *Esprit, Ordre Nouveau,* and Jean de Fabrègues's "Young Right" but also the group from *L'Homme Réel* – men who also transcended right-wing paradigms in their involvement with veteran trade-unionist/fascist theorist Hubert Lagardelle and another colleague[164] from the old *Plans*, in their work on the plan of the trade union Confédération Générale du Travail (CGT), and in their new interest in the spiritualist socialism of Henri de Man.[165] In fact ON, *Esprit*, and *L'Information Sociale* were already working in concert to bring together like-minded local personalities across France and Belgium; ON's leaders had taken to making friendly overtures toward *Esprit* people[166] and meeting with them to work out common position papers.[167]

During that summer of 1935, fifty young ON enthusiasts, many "of good family," attracted some attention as vacation replacements for workers in four factories in the Paris and Beauvais regions.[168] (This was an idea whose time had come: the next summer, paid vacations for workers would be one of the most popular innovations of the Popular Front.) During that same period, ON held a series of meetings to clarify its anti-capitalism[169] over against liberal democratic structures. De Rougemont argued that their movement represented the only hope for "real" democracy (i.e. local government). Claude Chevalley maintained that the people engendered a collective person: he favoured indigenous elites, natural aristocracies rooted in local traditions.[170] Marc forewarned his comrades that "Our only chance is to become a rallying point" for everyone fed up with normal politics – a genuine Third Way beyond Right and Left; he agreed with Chevalley's circumventing of democratic prattle by focusing on the formation of local meritocracies via a three-way system of "élections-cooptation-nomination": new elites in which a certain continuity with the founding elite would be respected but not institutionalized. The "spiritual" element in education (left unspecified) was to be crucial.[171] "Real democracy" involved decentralization, but rather than levelling and egalitarianism, it favored the emergence of local elites, often rising naturally from privileged backgrounds and "instinctively" exercising authority over the less equal. This was another ON notion which would find its way into the blueprints of Vichy's top-down Révolution Nationale.

While the ON and Esprit movements pretended, for several compelling practical reasons, to be quite distinct, they were quietly working together more and more. At a September meeting, the groups that had been excommunicated at Maritain's insistence – Third Force, ON

– were formally reunited with an Esprit movement which was claiming to be "born again" in its effort to gather a Third Force drawn from all parties.[172] Mounier, behind Maritain's back, worked with Robert Aron and Denis de Rougemont at renewing a regular relationship between ON and Esprit,[173] calling a first working meeting for 10 October,[174] just a few days before de Rougemont[175] would utter yet another call for a Third Force, a new sort of youth-based revolutionary movement, inspired by a personalist approach, transcending the outdated and sterile Left and Right, in an *Ordre Nouveau.*[176] Once the two Third Way movements had quietly decided to minimize their philosophical differences and work hand in hand for a French New Order,[177] Gibrat and Loustau went to see Mounier, proposing a sort of *centrale téléphonique* for the youth movements.[178] In November *Esprit* began regularly featuring a column entitled "News of the Third Force" recording the progressive coming together of the coalition being created over against the French Popular Front – a discreet movement, ripening among "a small group of men," avoiding taking "electoral or partisan positions."[179]

At this time Georges Izard seemed tempted to take some distance from Bergery to join the ex–Volontaires nationaux in shaping a new, larger coalition,[180] while the other *Esprit* co-founder and Bergeryist L.-E. Galey came out for what he called an "anti-fascist fascism" in France.[181] Politicized apoliticism, paradoxical discourse about fascism, began to characterize the non-conformists: Bergery's Common Front against Fascism was evolving into what began to look like an innovative form of fascism – or a new French national socialism. Informed foreign observers noted in January that what seemed to be a broadly based "spiritual revolution" was taking shape in France.[182]

This impression of a nascent French spiritual revolution was reinforced in February when a widely circulated[183] special edition of Bergery's *La Flèche* officially endorsed personalism much as *Sept* was already recommending it to the Catholics. Bergery called for a "National Revolution" in the Front Social publication.[184] In contrast to the coalition of the Left which was beginning to take shape in France, *this* National Revolution would be technologically sophisticated, avantgarde, and characterized by top-down initiatives in areas such as air travel,[185] and its concern for the spiritual dimension of revolution implied a more favourable attitude toward religion than the French Socialists or Communists had demonstrated.[186]

The Europeanist dimension to this national revolution resurfaced with Hitler's remilitarization of the Rhineland in March: the French Right joined the Briandists in opposing armed resistance; *Esprit*/nonconformist appeasement of Germany was less isolated than it had been just a few months earlier.

## THE FRENCH POPULAR FRONT:
## THE MATIGNON AGREEMENTS

On 7–8 June 1936, the new government of Léon Blum worked out the so-called Matignon agreements, which helped provide some of the most important benefits gained by French workers up until that time. But French non-conformists seemed relatively uninterested because of their zeal for the kind of Third Way politics led by rebels like Gaston Bergery, and shunned "old factions and outdated politicians."[187] ON declared that the best response to Hitler was the promotion of a New Order in France – and the movement was roundly criticized for this.[188] But Marc noted that *La Flèche* had become a weekly, and Georges Valois's *Nouvel Age* a daily, with ideas "*beaucoup plus incertaines et mélangées*" than those of his own Catholic/ON circle, and he worried that his own people were being left behind.[189] Among Marc's ON comrades, however, was Robert Loustau: when Jacques Doriot founded his Parti populaire français that June, Loustau produced its social program, and a book outlining its ideas.[190]

While the Popular Front coalition encouraged edifying, fraternal public dialogues between high-profile figures of the Left like Paul Nizan and André Malraux and non-conformists like Mounier,[191] non-conformists were planning and networking with one another behind the scenes to replace it with a different kind of political order. Marc was particularly insistent that the ON establish good working relationships with people open to radical alternatives to liberal democracy like Nobel laureate Dr Alexis Carrel, Jacques Doriot, Gaston Bergery, historian Lucien Romier, and Pierre Dominique. He urged the Société de Saint-Louis Catholics to keep in touch with people like Jean de Fabrègues, Jean Jardin, and the young non-conformist essayist Guy Frégault and his comrades in Canada,[192] as Catholic non-conformists, often inspired by *Sept*,[193] seemed to be proliferating.[194] While Marc thought Thierry Maulnier and Jean de Fabrègues's *Combat* group and the Comte de Paris's *Courrier Royal* people interesting, he was concerned that their right-wing images might undermine the efforts of anti-communists and non-conformists, to reach out to trade-unionists.[195]

The heterogeneous collection of anti-republicans on Marc's mind had little to do with one another at the time, but he envisaged them as becoming key figures in a non-conformist network shaping an alternative politics for France.[196] They also shared a particular attitude toward German bellicosity, as was shown by the July *Esprit*'s claim that the only "positive response" to Hitler's latest demands had come from individuals like Bergery (who is "close to our position") and ON's "Réponse à Hitler" pamphlet, which, rather than calling for no-quarter resistance to Nazis, focused instead on the possibility for a French internal revolution.[197] Marc had a good eye for potential Third Way revolutionaries: four years later most of these people would be fashioning the alternative political culture initiated by the Vichy regime's national revolution.

What did the non-conformists have in common? Leaders of the movement were soon using Mounier's *Personalist Manifesto*, composed in Belgium in August after the decisive interaction with the Germans,[198] to explain it. This tract provided the non-conformists with a handy discourse – a communitarian personalism structured, if need be, by the economics of Perroux – to represent their Third Way alternative to the Popular Front.[199] Convergence was concretely demonstrated on 26–7 September, at an important meeting at the Auberge de Jeunesse at Plessis-Robinson, when the Amis d'*Esprit* were required to contribute to the support of their organization and accept the principles of the *Personalist Manifesto*, while Robert Aron and Denis de Rougemont suggested that the various local Esprit and ON groups combine. There was talk of the new initiative of allying with Izard to create a serious political alternative to the Popular Front. While the effort to merge people was generally accepted by the representatives of the thirty-two groups there, several of them – some of whom would become famous intellectuals (Jacques Ellul from Bordeaux, philosopher Maurice Merleau-Ponty from Chartres) bridled at this effort to instil commitment to a central authority, conformity among the non-conformists.[200] But despite the dissidents and complainers, the Esprit movement, particularly, seemed to be growing by leaps and bounds.[201]

# 6 Otto Neumann in Belgium, Networking for the New Order (January 1933–September 1938)

The Nazi revolution in early 1933 quickly generated neutralist, anti-war sentiment in Belgium which spread from the avant-garde circle of Germanophile intellectuals – described in Alexandre Marc's book *Jeune Europe* that year – to a serious political force. This dowdy, complacent, inward-looking francophone enclave – like French Switzerland or Quebec – became a vibrant centre of new religious experience and political discourse, melding spiritualist socialism and revolutionary Christian communitarianism, extolling the world-renowned social psychology and political theory of Henri de Man. As in Germany and France, youthful Europeanist idealism was soon being exploited by Nazi agents with their own agenda.

In January 1933, on the eve of Hitler's seizing power, *Jeune Europe, le front européen pour les Etats-Unis d'Europe* appeared as the Belgian voice of a Swiss-based European movement supporting the "European federation" ideal of the *Union Jeune Europe* (UJE). It championed a federated, integrated Europe, with a common army, no customs barriers, peace and prosperity for all member countries.[1] At ten thousand copies its circulation was much larger than that of the so-called "international reviews" *Esprit* or *Ordre Nouveau* in France. Abbé Jacques Leclercq, the leading contributor, was an alluring professor at the Institut Saint-Louis of Brussels who had even impressed eminent intellectuals like Jacques Maritain with his philosophy of non-violence;[2] his founding of *La Cité chrétienne* helped make him one of the most influential authors of the Europeanist movement. Leclercq's comrade

Henri Nicaise, editor of *La Cité chrétienne*, was an ultra-pacifist and neutralist who wanted Belgium to steer an independent course in the face of the German threat and, to further "the Christian City," promoted fraternization with the Hitler Youth. *Jeune Europe* published in its pacifist vein until June 1936,[3] with Nicaise's review appearing alongside, the two working in concert to foster Belgian Europeanist anti-war sentiment.

Raymond de Becker, magnetic Belgian Catholic Action youth leader close to Leclercq, attracted attention with his book-length manifesto for a new order, *Vers un ordre nouveau*,[4] contending that the dawning New European Order would be totalitarian, but in the same beneficent way as medieval Christian Europe. Stirred by Berdyaev's *New Middle Ages*, de Becker championed the idea that "a special type of monastic life in the world would arise, a kind of new order" – a community of charismatic, godly laymen who could convert the world.

Strikingly short and moody, a curious mixture of activist and contemplative mystic, de Becker had abandoned his studies before university for full-time involvement in the Belgian Catholic Action movement in which he found Christus Rex, Catholic Action leader Léon Degrelle's activist offshoot organization, particularly significant. But while the bullying, pugnacious Degrelle turned more and more toward street brawling, de Becker, accompanied by two comrade-disciples, left for a cabin on a barren Alpine plateau above the lake of Annecy, in the spiritual orbit of the Trappist monastery of Tamié.

After two years of zealous asceticism, but deserted by his comrades, who bridled at taking an oath of perpetual fidelity and at innovative liturgies involving the Mass in French, de Becker set off alone on foot, like a medieval mendicant, begging his food and shelter along the way, for Sainte-Beaune in Provence. After another period in a mountain cabin without water or electricity, de Becker appeared in Paris in October 1933 (where he was known for having started his own review, *L'Esprit Nouveau*, with Catholic activist Henri Bauchau), and began fascinating Berdyaev, Mounier, and Jacques Maritain with stories of his two years of spiritual experiences.[5] By this time de Becker's *L'Esprit Nouveau* had become a sort of Belgian Catholic *Esprit* – directed toward bringing together Right and Left, and engendering a new Middle Ages superseding the old liberal civilization.[6] De Becker quickly became central in the Europeanist movement, and in pre-war Germanophile and neutralist circles in Belgium.

Mounier had been wanting to get involved with de Becker for over a year;[7] in March 1933 he had praised de Becker's notion of "personalist revolution" (although better suited to a "spiritual elite" than to the masses)[8] and de Becker and Bauchau's *L'Esprit Nouveau* as remarkably similar to Mounier's own *Esprit*.[9] For himself, Mounier preferred spiritual types to street brawlers (who tended to consider him an effete intellectual). Alexandre Marc, too, tended to find Mounier indecisive and ineffectual but claims to have introduced him to de Becker, probably when Marc and Mounier had adjoining offices in the De Brouwer publishing house on the Rue des Saint-Pères.[10]

In November 1933, after Ordre Nouveau (ON)'s notorious "Letter to Hitler," Mounier was pressured by Maritain to turn from Marc's group and so decided to work closely with the Belgian mystic.[11] But in turning toward de Becker, Mounier was less taking his distance from ON than again following Marc: Marc's celebrated[12] December 1933 book *Jeune Europe*[13] described Raymond de Becker's *L'Esprit Nouveau* as one of the most interesting of European youth movements. *Jeune Europe* (titled as per the Abbé Leclercq's review) described those Belgians as having the same values as ON with their appropriate motto – "spirituel d'abord, politique ensuite, économique à leur service" – but as distinctive because "the crowning and end of future social organization, and to which they subordinated all economic and political elements, was the Christian Spirit, Catholicism." Marc cited de Becker as holding that "The basis of a Christian order will always be the realm of God ... The New Order will only find its origins and justification in love ... the love of men for men and the love of men for God."[14] De Becker's was a new form of Catholic communitarianism, a "Christian Revolution" which could institute the New Order best suited for the Belgians. For Marc, "L'Esprit Nouveau's inspiration sometimes echoes that of Otto Neumann" whose ideas he had outlined in *Esprit* the previous March – a serious effort to meld Catholicism with the national communitarian socialism to produce a personalist revolutionary option. Marc could only be optimistic about Belgian youth: "on the spiritual plane, which takes precedence over all the rest, they seem ready to confront all the basic problems, to rethink, even recreate them ... to pioneer new spiritual perspectives and even a new philosophical system, a totalitarian *Weltanschauung* ... the Belgian example confirms that in all the world's countries, an ardent younger generation ... [is] preparing, by its very erring ways and excesses, a New Order at the service of *l'homme intégral*."[15]

Marc had transformed the original ON inspiration into a Catholic personalist revolutionary discourse suitable for Germany in the guise of Otto Neumann. For France, in turn, Mounier and *Esprit* (with Neumann's help) transformed Dandieu's recondite philosophical reflections into the inspiration of a broadly based personalist communitarian revolutionary movement. Now Raymond de Becker and Henri

Bauchau were creating a variant suited to the particular Belgian national genius.

De Becker called for an "army of saints" to be "the dynamite of the Christian revolution" in the January *Esprit*,[16] as his band of personalist revolutionaries were taking over *L'Avant-Garde*, the Louvain University Catholic student newspaper in which Léon Degrelle had famously promoted a new political discourse for Belgian youth (publishing as many as ten thousand copies, bringing the brewery heir sudden political prominence).[17] In early March the French Dominicans' *Sept* appeared, with Marc as resident expert on European youth movements, to popularize new Third Way Catholic thinking. It conveyed de Becker's call for a "Christian Revolution" to a large Catholic audience.[18]

The French Catholic intelligentsia were interested in de Becker, the Belgians in French political methods. In January 1934 *L'Avant-Poste* in Brussels published a special issue of essays by ON – a movement depicted as led by Catholic generational spokesperson Daniel-Rops[19] and set into context by Marc's timely book on *Jeune Europe*: "la plus saisissante et la plus aigue 'prise de conscience' qu'ait inspiré notre chaos continental."[20] In that issue Marc, seconded by Chevalley, showed that ON transcended "cosmopolitanism": although they were anti-imperialists, anti-Statists, even anti-nationalists, they were nevertheless resolutely "national." Every revolution which did not take national diversities into account was abstract, lifeless, cold, incapable of attainment. "The Revolution of Order will incorporate 'elements very important in historical development ... the particular characteristics of races and peoples.'" "The Revolution of Order [would incorporate] all the concrete riches of man."[21]

Just after the riots of 6 February by the fascist youth leagues in Paris, the *Ordre Nouveau* had de Becker's *L'Esprit Nouveau* in its round table on "French values viewed from the outside." The admired values were not those of France's fragile liberal democracy. Alphonse Zimmer de Cunchy, Catholic youth leader editor of *L'Esprit Nouveau*, ally of l'abbé Leclercq and Jeune Europe, described France diminished by the "bourgeois self-satisfaction" which deflected French young people from merging into "true personalism ... revolt against the social order which is disfiguring her."[22] *Ordre Nouveau* held up *L'Esprit Nouveau* as a sister undertaking.[23]

Léon Degrelle later claimed that he would recreate the historic realm of Burgundy. Marc thought that such discourse about tradition and heritage showed that while the nineteenth-century revolutionaries worked from abstractions about "man," the Nietzschean revolutionaries of the twentieth century were right to address blood, soil, ethnic communitarian feelings – particularly those infused with religiousness.

Belgians saw what *L'Avant-Poste* called ON's "new message" as fascist, or quasi-fascist, albeit with a more sophisticated and intellectualist, or perhaps "national socialist," line than Degrelle's Rex movement.[24] The interest in ON was illustrated when King Albert I died (in a mountaineering accident) and a copy of the movement's *La Révolution Necessaire* was found open on his desk, along with an issue of *Ordre Nouveau*[25] – left untouched for weeks as mourners filed past, adding to the prestige of *L'Ordre Nouveau* in Belgium.[26]

Nazi leaders also took an interest in Belgian youth. The Belgian government reacted to the Nazi victory by putting aside 150,000,000 francs for fortifications along the Meuse, and then constantly increasing defence appropriations. Otto Abetz, and his boss von Ribbentrop, both culture-Catholics, believed that Belgians could be pacifistic or benevolently neutral about, if not openly sympathetic toward, German national socialism: by early 1934 there were, besides Degrelle's legions, six thousand supporters of *Jeune Europe* (up from five thousand the previous June).[27] In late 1933 Abetz met,[28] and became fast friends with, the wealthy socialites Edouard and Lucienne Didier, who began to promote the European movement – and "understanding" for Germany – in Belgium.

On 6 March 1934, Prime Minister Broqueville declared Belgium neutral and was vigorously supported by de Becker and the student editors of *L'Avant Garde* (which much increased its circulation). When Hitler occupied the Rhineland two years later, *L'Avant-Garde* would oppose French and English resistance.[29] *La Cité chrétienne* (Henri Nicaise and Marcel Grégoire) also applauded Broqueville, arguing that the new Europe had to accommodate Germany, with the Versailles treaty revised.[30] From April, when Alexandre Marc moved from Paris to southwestern France, de Becker began to strongly influence Mounier, who, more and more, established himself in Brussels. In the May *Esprit* de Becker foretold a "national Catholic revolution" in which saintliness would be the cutting edge of social change. To be sure, fascism and communism were totalitarianisms, but Christianity "is itself totalitarian" and could appreciate "national values and racial values" subordinate to its own. De Becker's national Catholic revolution would be effected by an "Order" obtaining the primacy of Christianity and also determined to "develop national values, vital values of blood, of the race, of the fatherland against the dissolution of Marxist, Jewish, free-mason internationalism."[31]

By May 1934 Mounier believed something "very big" could grow out of his involvement with de Becker – despite the man's occasional unsteadiness (especially in that muddled mystical state in which he pretended to think and write in Russian). But Jacques Maritain (whose wife was Russian-Jewish) was disturbed by de Becker's invective against Jewish internationalism and escorted Mounier to seek assurances from abbé Leclercq – who granted that his protégé was given to impetuous behaviour and flamboyant gestures (such as that "premature and unfortunate" brochure on a national Catholic Order), but argued that these were attributable to his youth rather than to his basic character.

There were those in Leclercq's circle who wanted a political party, while others, like Mounier and de Becker, wanted to create a large Order which would be a catalyst for radical change, surmounting party divisions. De Becker may have seemed a bit unhinged at times, but he captivated people. The old Esprit-Brussels contingent became so large that it had to be subdivided into four sections, and the energetic new Brussels Esprit/Esprit Nouveau group (referred to as "the de Becker group" by Mounier) began discussing the possibility of combining with Esprit-Paris, producing a weekly publication, and promoting more interaction among the "Amis d'Esprit" groups scattered across France and Belgium. These latter were to continue meeting independently from the get-togethers of the Order, even when their members became members of it, because the "Amis" groups were afforded the possibility of good contacts with non-Christians. Mounier began planning a communal residence-headquarters-school for the international "Amis d'Esprit."[32]

While Esprit offered daring contacts with non-Christians, L'Esprit Nouveau offered electrifying contacts with well-connected Germans: the afternoon after the discussion with the Leclercq group found the director of the Reich's German Student Exchanges Office, well dressed and polite, calling on Mounier and inviting him to lecture to his students. Esprit's editor mused that "after eighteen months we may still be only a few meters from the dock but sea winds are already beginning to caress the sails."[33]

The 25th of May 1934, Mounier marked his third Pentecost in Brussels. The day before a Wednesday evening lecture, organized by L'Avant-Garde in Louvain, Mounier was surprised by a telephone warning that de Becker's group was subsidized by the Germans;[34] he ignored it for a heartening encounter with a "young, vigorous group, out to conquer that old reactionary fortress of the Louvain," some of whom claimed to have been inspired by Esprit from the beginning. Twenty people joined the new "de Becker" Esprit group after this talk, and the L'Avant-Garde circle promised to publicize Esprit in various ways. Mounier had a cordial meal with several of them afterwards, including the bright social theorist Emile Hambresin, whose critique of extant corporatisms over several issues of L'Avant-Garde would soon be studied in the Esprit groups. Hambresin was one of those Belgians with a special interest in Germany and would soon represent his circle in ski expeditions ornamented by the presence of top leaders of the Hitler Youth.

Perhaps because of Mounier's dubious new frequentations, the wealthy De Brouwer and Desclée Belgian sugar-manufacturing and publishing families decided that they would no longer provide Parisian office space and secretarial help for the review (although they did continue their F10,000 yearly subsidy). After teaching on the French side of the border in nearby St Omer, and getting romantically involved with Paulette Leclercq, an enthusiast of Esprit-Brussels, Mounier approached rich Catholics in his home town of Grenoble, as well as in Lyon, for financial support. But Eugène Primard, leader of the Catholic businessmen organized in the Société de Saint-Louis (which – like the de Brouwers – discreetly funded "friendly" publications), displayed what Mounier called "a certain number of the reflexes of the old Right that he seemed unable to get over" when Mounier approached him in February 1932.[35] After an afternoon discussing their project, Mounier provided de Becker with a list of potential financial backers, hoping he might do better.[36] At the end of May 1934, de Becker approached various youth groups which were interested, but Mounier thought that, like Primard, they too "would take a long time to be free of their old right-wing reflexes." Mounier and de Becker also spent an evening with young National Socialist students who, in contrast, in Mounier's words, "tried with remarkable politeness and a sustained and attentive enthusiasm to defend the spiritual values of obedience, total commitment to the leader ('let a man risk everything, his whole life' one of them said to me)." At a meeting of the left-wing Association des Ecrivains et Artistes Révolutionnaires, on the other hand, Mounier and de Becker were disgusted to see the "petits camarades" like Aragon dump their "hatred and lies" on Drieu la Rochelle. Esprit supporter Humeau was not allowed to speak his mind, while another old Esprit person, Ramon Fernandez, was goaded by Communist antics to resign from the association. In the back, de Becker and Mounier clutched their new manifesto: "A bomb in that Communist lair? The future will say," Mounier mused.[37]

But Mounier returned to find a letter from Esprit mentor Jacques Maritain enclosing a copy of his remonstrances to de Becker, expressing regret that de Becker had not shown up for a private confrontation with him, and warning Mounier that while he (Maritain) much liked de Becker and appreciated his great "generosity, dynamism and charisma," the man's "intellectual and spiritual formation" was still deficient. There was "a lack of proportion and equilibrium" in what de Becker was undertaking which could prove "very dangerous," and while

Mounier had had to be warned against hotheads before, there was now the risk of "an experience even more dangerous," for a political involvement with de Becker could jeopardize Mounier's basic values.[38]

Mounier, typically, tried to mollify Maritain while simultaneously encouraging de Becker's new role as leader of "the movement" among the new French Catholic elite – despite the Maritain-like reservations of at least some of them.[39] Several months earlier Maritain had insisted that Mounier and *Esprit* take their distance from the "goose-stepping" style of Marc and ON and Mounier pretended to comply. By this time, Marc had left Paris for the safety of a convent in southwestern France. Mounier had found a new comrade-inspiration and did not want his unworldly mentor to interfere anew.[40] For the rest of that year Mounier accelerated contacts between the French and Belgians: de Becker visited the Esprit people, the ON group,[41] and had dealings with Izard's street-fighting Third Force. Mounier wanted the Belgian to move to Paris to "spiritualize" the city.[42]

De Becker was an unusual spiritualizer in that he was making furtive approving references to Adolf Hitler. In the July *Esprit*, for example, he described the timetable of a spiritual revolution as "slow when only average men are working at it. But then heroes, geniuses or saints come along: a Saint Paul, a Joan of Arc, a Catherine of Sienna, a Saint Bernard or a Lenin, a Hitler and a Mussolini, or a Gandhi and suddenly everything picks up speed ... human irrationality, the human will, or, for the Christian, the Holy Spirit, suddenly provides elements which men lacking imagination could never have foreseen."[43] De Becker's sense of a Nazi-Catholic compatibility missed by the unimaginative helped lead him to support the Leclercq/Jeune Europe/*La Cité chrétienne* concessions toward Germany.[44] He became a leader in several movements that transformed Brussels into a centre of exciting Europeanist enterprises melding Christian renewal with the neo-socialism of Henri de Man.[45] Mounier began to forsake the Left Bank to spend more and more time in Brussels; de Becker broadcast his call for "Christian Revolution" to France in *Sept.*[46]

Henri de Man's "spiritualist" socialist communitarianism seemed tailor-made for Belgium, and his Plan du Travail had been adopted by the Belgian socialists in 1933 to fight the economic depression. In February 1934 *Esprit* published admiring commentaries on it by Jean Lacroix and André Philip. In *L'Avant-Garde* Raymond de Becker urged Catholic students to meet and talk with socialists as de Man, the new president of the Parti Ouvrier Belge, met with the admiring de Becker and forty Catholic students at Louvain. De Man and de Becker exchanged a series of letters in the socialist newspaper *Le Peuple*, agreeing on the urgency of rethinking Belgian politics. De Becker dismissed

Degrelle's Rexists as a sterile offshoot of the old Catholic party, and backed de Man's vision of a new third way joining Catholics, nationalists, and socialists. Otto Neumann had been a figment of Alexandre Marc's imagination; Raymond de Becker had moved the syncretic dream to concrete political initiative.

In the wake of the de Becker–de Man dialogue, Jeune Europe began to attract socialists to supplement its Catholic core – and to have still more contact with Germans, which encouraged its appeasement line until the Hitlerite invasion.[47] One person who stood out among the high-culture appeasers was the beautiful and brilliant Lucienne Didier, in her early thirties, distaff side of what was known as one of the most glamorous couples of pre-war Brussels. From January 1935 she held a bi-weekly salon with her distinguished and wealthy printer husband, Edouard, in their elegant turn-of-the-century villa at Ixelles. An informal talk was followed by amiable fraternization among the guests. The Didiers were known for their lively conversation, luxurious automobiles, and hospitality to writers, politicians, and intellectuals – most very young – and to the German emissaries to francophone youth, Otto Abetz and Max Liebe. Young anti-war activists progressed from Jeune Europe meetings to the heady charms of the Didier salon – a daring neutral ground where Catholics primed in the world-historical prophecies of Berdyaev and Maritain could encounter visionary non-Catholics. The least anti-clerical of the young socialist leaders – Léo Moulin, Henri de Man, and Paul-Henri Spaak – met with the new Catholic intelligentsia of de Becker and Bauchau's *L'Avant-Garde*[48] and Nicaise and Leclercq's *La Cité chrétienne*.[49] The Left had castigated war as the device of armament manufacturers; *L'Avant-Garde* pacifists had rebuked the arms industry since their March editorials favouring Belgian neutrality.

As the Jeune Europe movement[50] was expanding, Hitler's rise to power was calling into question its Europeanist idealism. But in the face of warnings about the naïveté of the anti-war movement, *La Cité chrétienne*'s editor, Henri Nicaise, defended the goals of *Jeune Europe*:[51] there was no essential contradiction between German nationalism and the aims of the European movement; there were genuine commitments to avoid war, agreement was still possible, it was important to go beyond prejudices.[52] Then, after having sent a petition to Belgian youth leaders and obtained their support, Nicaise reiterated his position in *La Cité chrétienne* in September, and increased his work with Mounier, serving as spokesperson for the "sub-group on international questions" of the Brussels *Esprit* group.[53] "We should work with Nazi Germany in a pacifist spirit ... collaborate with her for the common good to the extent possible," the *La Cité chrétienne* editors declared, on

20 February 1935, just after Germany's annexation of the Sarre.[54] This position of the new editors at the review (activists who were involved in the Jeune Europe movement) bolstered Nicaise's appeasement line.[55]

In the February *Esprit*, de Becker published documentation on the Communauté movement for its upcoming April founding congress in Paris. The members of this new type of monastic community, an order of laymen dedicated to the re-Christianization of art and culture, and of political, social, and economic life, were to undergo "profound ascetic and contemplative training," live an intense communitarian and liturgical life, and accomplish "the Christian revolution in all areas of life," the building of "a new Christianity," "the divinization of the human, of the created." The thirty-three communitarian theses of Communauté were authoritarian, hierarchical, elitist, and undemocratic; Catholicism was the only legitimate totalitarianism and so Communauté members were, like Jesuits, to find a "true freedom" in obedience and submission to the rule. Paragraph 33 subordinated the individual *patrie*/nation-state to the international "revolutionary community": if a conflict arises between the two, "the defence of ... the latter, whose ideal is universally human, is more essential than that of *patries*."

Once again, Jacques Maritain warned Mounier of the implications of de Becker's thinking – comparing traditional religious communitarianism with the new de Becker *Gemeinschaft* experience: "When religious assemble in a monastery, it is not for the pleasure of it, but to attain perfection – and to be together for that reason. The feeling of togetherness ... is indispensable, certainly, but secondary ... the Germans, starved for emotional unity ... are asking *much more* of temporal community than it can possibly provide: mystical communion."[56] Maritain demanded that de Becker be excluded from the *Esprit* special military issue planned for June.[57] And Maritain was not the only one worried about the Belgian: on 17 February the police paid a visit to the Dominicans of Juvisy to question them about de Becker's relationship with the Germans.[58]

In fact Nazi operatives were using avant-garde Europeanist idealism and Christian-socialist dialogue to infiltrate both the Belgians and their Catholic sympathizers in France. On 21 February, when Abetz came to give one of the bi-weekly talks on German youth in the Didiers' salon in Ixelles, he encountered a significant contingent of Belgian youth leaders: directors of *La Cité chrétienne* and of *L'Avant-Garde*, as well as the sprinkling of socialists who were now frequenting this milieu.[59] The next day Mounier and his group held a meeting at the University of Liège which also involved socialists, liberals, and

Catholics, and "a rather precise and very cordial agreement between the diverse elements came out of it."[60] The Europeanist milieu offered Mounier a subsidy.[61] The next month Henri de Man was made Belgium's minister of public works with the firm support of the Parti Ouvrier Belge, just as de Man's "spiritual socialism" seemed to be melding more and more with the communitarian personalism and Europeanist anti-war movements.

While *Esprit* people were meeting with Nazis *chez* Didier in Ixelles, ON's Robert Aron was organizing a delegation of French young people to attend an official Fascist congress on corporations in Rome in May. But ON's priority interest remained Germany: they met with Nazis in Paris and their old comrade Harro Schulze-Boysen, now working for the Reich, proposed to establish a special Berlin Action group for ON.[62] For their part, the Sohlbergkreis Nazis, while granting worthwhile qualities in the thinking of French "new Rightists" Thierry Maulnier, Robert Francis, and Jean-Pierre Maxence, scolded them for visualizing the future of Europe in the Latin peoples rather than a Germanic-Latin alliance.[63] The communitarian personalists of Belgium and France – unlike the French right-wing generational spokesmen Henri Massis and his fellow Maurrasians – saw more interest in exchanging views with National Socialists than with Mussolinian Fascists.[64] The April *Sohlbergkreis* published the Belgian "Jeune Europe" call for peace and European federalism.[65] From the "Europeanist" point of view, Fascist congresses in Rome were vacuous pomp, while in little Belgium genuine world-historical change was being engendered – the meeting and melding of spiritualist socialism and religion, the revolution of the twentieth century, Europe's future.

Mounier (who would soon be marrying, residing, and teaching in Brussels) was trying to propagate the Belgian spirit in France, notably by presiding over the first congress of de Becker's Communauté movement which was held in Paris, on 14 and 15 April at the Hotel des Sociétés savantes. Communauté was supposed to replace the old Third Force (which had abandoned the "Amis d'*Esprit*" in July 1933 to join Bergery's Frontists). The forty young people who attended the Communauté congress discovered elders Jacques Maritain and Nicholas Berdyaev "sitting and listening like schoolboys" in their midst.[66] It was decided that different "Amis d'*Esprit*" and Communauté people, when in the same city, were to form common study groups and projects.[67] ON advertised de Becker's *L'Esprit Nouveau*, and had its own supporters and meetings in Brussels in this period.[68]

Mounier married Paulette Leclercq on 20 July and moved into an apartment in the house of another *Esprit* backer[69] on the outskirts of Brussels; he became a teacher in the city's Lycée francais. While other intellectuals might have found Brussels stodgy and provincial, Mounier was at the centre of Third Force politics, of a youth revolution generating its own philosophy, art, and literature, and of a momentous fusion of Catholicism and socialism. The Belgian working class, less alienated from its Catholic roots than the French, favoured a melding of Christianity and socialism which could engage trade-union and workers' party leaders.

Henri Nicaise, as editor of *La Cité chrétienne*, became a leading champion of "Jeune Europe" pacifism, declaring in the 5 September issue of his review that, despite all the foreboding over Nazi Germany, Jeune Europe would never abandon striving for peace with her.[70] His manifesto to "all the *chefs* of the leading youth groups of the most disparate sort" in support of this position had got their unanimous support. "Members of Jeune Europe [would] boycott press inspired by war psychosis."[71] But it was well known by this time that *La Cité chrétienne* was much involved with Abetz's *Sohlbergkreis*, and this was causing undisclosed but serious dissension among Nicaise's editorial board.[72] At the end of September, Mounier organized the first meeting of the Esprit/Communauté groups at Villeneuve-sur-Auvers, in a large open barn belonging to a youth hostel. Besides the major delegations from the Belgian cities of Brussels and Ghent, nineteen other cities were represented. From 26 December 1935 to 5 January 1936, the Belgian branch of "Jeune Europe" (in effect, the Didiers) organized a Christmas vacation at a Bavarian mountain ski camp in the spirit of the old Sohlbergkreis for Belgians and Germans, with some English and French in attendance. A series of four follow-up camps were being organized for the next summer.

At the beginning of 1936 a New Order seemed considerably closer in Belgium than in France (whose political scene was dominated by the left-wing anti-fascist coalition called the Popular Front). So French non-conformists were particularly active in Brussels, where the ON movement held a joint meeting with de Becker's Communauté movement and several other Belgian groups on 18–19 January, and then a follow-up in April.[73] The leading Brussels daily *Le Soir* noted that a January Mounier lecture on "the spiritual revolution" indicated the formation of a Popular Front of French and Belgian spiritual revolutionaries, trade-unionists, and neo-socialists (who had attended the Italian Fascist congress together a few months earlier): Marc's *Ordre Nouveau*, the syndicalists' *L'homme réel*,[74] and Paul Marion's "young" or "neo" socialist *L'homme nouveau*.[75]

The February 1936 *Esprit* special issue, "Pour un ordre nouveau en Belgique,"[76] portrayed Belgium showing even France the way with the Esprit-inspired groupings Communauté and L'Avant-Garde while the

Rexists were portrayed as outmoded and Right-wing. (In fact Léon Degrelle's men did have an old-fashioned Catholic side – making a show of chanting the Magnificat in the streets of Rome. And, at least at this point, they tended to find Italian Fascism more attractive than Nazism.) De Becker dismissed Rex as a right-wing clerical party and called for a true Third Force in Belgium – one closer to the de Manian spiritualist socialist positions of *Esprit*. A final appendix in *Esprit* discreetly noted that Jeune Europe–Brussels was working for a "Fédération Européenne" by organizing frequent international study trips and vacation camps, "a permanent cultural contact between the new generations of different countries,"[77] and that there was considerable interaction among French, German, and Belgian "spiritual revolutionaries" in Brussels. In March, when Hitler occupied the Rhineland, *L'Avant-Garde*, as we have noted, urged accommodation and opposed French and English resistance.[78] This was almost two years to the day after Broqueville had proclaimed Belgian neutrality and been supported by de Becker and the other pacifists of *L'Avant-Garde*, as well as by *La Cité chrétienne*.[79] In April, Otto Abetz's new bilingual, lavishly illustrated *Deutsch-Französische Monatsheft/Cahiers Franco-Allemands*, successor to *Sohlbergkreis*, brought out a special issue on Belgium. Abetz published this review from his native Karlsruhe "to encourage Franco-German understanding"; it also tended to ignore the Rexists while having Max Liebe praise the "Arbeitsplan" of Henri de Man. H.N. [Henri Nicaise?] vaunted the importance of "the Walloon groups" (the monthly *Terre Wallonne*, the Communauté movement, the Belgian Esprit circle) for uniting socialists, former communists, and Catholics "against [the treaty of] Versailles and for a policy of understanding with Germany."[80] ON held another meeting with Communauté that month in which the prospects for publishing a newspaper, and a common Franco-Belgian declaration, were discussed.[81]

Nicaise, with "a few collaborators and friends" of *La Cité chrétienne*, visited Germany from 14 to 22 April, returning with "a durable sympathy for those ardent young people" which caused him to lose the few negative prejudices he retained toward the Nazi regime.[82] He was active in the Brussels Esprit group and on 6 May announced the conclusions of its "sub-group on international questions":[83] French foreign policy was "dangerous for European reconciliation," and "while some clarification of Hitler's intentions in Eastern Europe is needed," his peace proposals were "very healthy."[84]

The previous December, the Swiss personalist philosopher Denis de Rougemont had taken up the post in the University in Frankfurt am Main secured for him by Otto Abetz. There Henri de Man, after writing *Der Kampf um die Arbeitsfreude* (1927), had been named to a new chair of social psychology and taught from 1929 to 1933, writing *Le socialisme constructif* (1933) while also being named director of the "social studies office" of the Belgian workers' party and producing his "Plan du Travail." De Man was fluent, even wrote his books, in German; de Rougemont, too, was one of the rare Parisian-based intellectuals to be fluent in that language (several others among them belonged to the ON movement), and after arriving at Frankfurt described his conception of personalism *auf Deutsch* in Abetz's *Cahiers Franco-Allemands*. Rougemont's unusual analysis of Nazism as a crypto-religious phenomenon was, by April, being reported in the French Catholic press.[85]

Appeasement of Hitler did not sit well with everyone in the personalist milieu. The de Brouwer family withdrew their last subsidy to *Esprit* by the end of April.[86] Mounier complained about this to Maritain, inviting his mentor to visit him and his wife in their new Brussels residence, but to no avail:[87] Maritain disapproved of the continuing involvement with de Becker and began distancing himself both from de Becker, and, eventually, from Mounier.

The May 1936 electoral successes of Léon Degrelle's Rexist party represented a serious threat to Belgian liberal democracy, and the summer brought a major struggle between Rex and the traditional Belgian parties united behind Prime Minister Van Zeeland. Degrelle planned to march on Brussels with 250,000 militant Rexists in October and press the king to grant him total political power.

In June 1936 Léon Blum's French Popular Front government worked out the so-called Matignon agreements, affording some of the most important benefits gained by French workers to that time. While most French reviews were preoccupied with the implications of this new progressive government, Esprit's Mounier left Brussels two days after the Matignon settlement to spend two weeks with Denis de Rougemont in Germany.[88] De Rougemont took the Mouniers to a night-time Nazi rally and remembered explaining it to them as a quasi-religious experience – a drama "inspired by the Protestant liturgy: Decalogue, confessions of sins, promise of grace, credo."[89]

Emmanuel Mounier returned from Germany determined to learn more about the young Nazis first-hand but wanting to be discreet about his contacts with them.[90] By the summer of 1936 Otto Abetz had become a regular at the Didier salon near Brussels, occasionally speaking under the auspices of *Jeune Europe* – still promoting rapprochement with Germany.[91] The *Jeune Europe* blueprint for a federal Europe was reported in Abetz's *Sohlbergkreis* as well as in *Esprit*.[92] Mounier called for a revision of the Treaty of Versailles and for a European Federalism in *Jeune Europe*. He was invited to the Jeune Europe international camp that summer, intended to promote dialogue with the Hitler Youth. The Didiers organized the get-together for 11–19 July at a Belgian seaside property lent by Count Lippens near the resort town of Zoute.[93] Although there were discreet notices about Jeune Europe in *Esprit*,[94] Mounier did not report on his acceptance of the invitation or the meeting itself to the Esprit movement.[95]

The week-long encounter between the Hitler Youth and the young Belgians, led by Mounier and Louis Carette of the Belgian Esprit group,[96] interspersed political explication and dialogue with beach sports. The experience was "amicable, but not conclusive," Carette and Leo Moulin remembered years later. The young Germans seemed extremely *sympathiques*, sang in harmony beautifully in the evenings. In frank discussion with the German delegation led by M. Schultze, Führer of the Hitlerjugend, Mounier "remarked how he understood the historical reason for the German national movement but also how most of us thought that the national aspect of Hitlerism had suffocated its socialist tendency." Mounier and his comrades objected to the Nazi identification of the state with the *Volk* and even to "the underlying attitude of Nazism regarding life": "we think that the popular community [should allow] each person to accomplish himself, while the Hitlerites think community an end in itself. Schulze [*sic*] honestly recognized that there one touched ... the essential divergence between the Personalist and the National Socialist conception of life." But "On international affairs, in contrast, everyone remarked an almost complete agreement and real possibilities of collaboration."[97] Abetz, who figured in the background of the deliberations, must have been satisfied.[98] Mounier's philosophical differences with the Hitler Youth were identical to those regularly put forward by Marc and the ON people. Esprit made a show of forging its own distinctive "personnalisme communautaire," but basic similarities between Esprit and ON remained as Mounier went off to an isolated Belgian farmhouse to collect his thoughts and write up a manifesto for his movement.

For his part, Raymond de Becker travelled to Hamburg in July 1936, for an International Congress on Workers' Vacations, and then on to Bavaria and to Berlin, where he was invited by Nazi foreign minister Joachim von Ribbentrop. De Becker was much flattered[99] by his evening as von Ribbentrop's guest and heartened by the "democratic origins" of the young men in his circle. On his return he described his and Mounier's Communauté movement in *Monatshefte* as, with the Rexists, a significant organization representing Belgian nationalists and Catholics; he went ahead and organized the first visit of the National Socialist press to Belgium. This was the last straw for Jacques Maritain, who definitively broke with him.[100]

Over against the spectacular (if – in retrospect – ephemeral) rise of Degrelle and the Rexists, there were the more refined, de Manian spiritual-socialist, germanophile, and Europeanist young intelligentsia with their selected reviews, support groups, Didier salon, ski camps, and seaside discussions. Raymond de Becker then seemed to embody what Alexandre Marc had only imagined for Germany in the guise of Otto Neumann: a mystical Catholic personalist who could distil the thick foreign current of the German youth revolution into something appropriate for Catholic Belgium. The Belgian search for a "new man," while originally much inspired by the French, seemed by the summer of 1936 in many respects more developed, articulate, mature. From Otto Abetz's German point of view, it even became an item of export to France.

As in the case of France and Germany, the situation seemed ripe for some bright young person to "non-conform" to the previous approaches to religion and politics and come up with a new set of ideas conforming instead to the dawning European New Order. This new style of individual and communitarian living, embodied by converts, would then have a top-down effect and perhaps, even, in a very short time, dramatically change Belgium. Once again, a new mixing of religious and philosophical and political language was effected and taken very seriously by young convert elites, certain they had a lucid vision of the future. As in the other countries, not much effort was put into trying to find converts to the "new thinking or being" among the masses, much less among the simple working people, whose lives would presumably be dramatically changed by the dawning New Order. Working stiffs were presumed to be irrecuperably manipulated, if not brainwashed, by political ideologies, denatured religiousness and the new technological world forced upon them by rampant capitalism and communism. True converts were a chosen few, but their world-historical responsibilities were enormous.

## FROM CATHOLIC COMMUNITARIANISM TO NATIONAL SOCIALISM: ABETZ AND THE BELGIAN PARADIGM

While the French Popular Front government of Léon Blum caught the attention of the world in the early summer of 1936 as a daring experiment in social-democratic coalition politics, Belgium continued to march to a different drummer and pioneer Third Way way initiatives, particularly those of special appeal to Catholics. With its uneasy cohabitation of Flemings and Walloons, its multiracial and multilingual heritage, that country could hardly embrace the racialism of Adolf Hitler.

But Mounier and his fellow Bruxellois Catholic youth leaders were stirred by the selfless, energizing communitarianism of the young Nazi elite. And the Hitler Youth leaders, who had gone from marginality to a directing role in transforming the new generation in their country, took the non-conformist intelligentsia of Belgium and France – despite their lack of a popular constituency – seriously. And so, Hitler or no Hitler, German-Belgian interaction continued.

In November of 1936, Raymond de Becker gave a lecture at the University of Berlin in which he confidently predicted that Belgium would adopt "a new position in international politics." At the same time Mounier informed the Germans of the nature of the communitarian personalism behind this new Belgian politics with his synopsis "Was ist der Personalismus?" in the same issue of Abetz's review, which reported de Becker's talk.[101] De Becker, however, not only called attention to the personalism of *Ordre Nouveau* and *Esprit* but also focused the Germans' friendly interest in the French young socialists open to Paul Marion's neo-socialist review *L'homme nouveau*, as well as in the syndicalists involved with *L'homme réel*.[102] All of these groups were sensitive to the role of spiritual experience in creating "new men."

The day after Christmas 1936, several well-known Belgian youth leaders – including the personalists Emile Hambresin and Marcel Vercruysse – joined Max Liebe, Abetz's man in Brussels, and some leaders of the Hitlerjugend for a ten-day ski camp at Winkelmoos, held in a good Europeanist spirit of promoting dialogue among the peoples.[103] Both Hambresin and Vercruysse had come out of de Becker's *L'Avant-Garde*; Hambresin had contributed review essays on corporatism to *Esprit*.[104] Participant Henri Nicaise, as an early Belgian Esprit supporter, expressed fascination with the Hitlerjugend's "communitarian idea": it was "really fundamental," "transcended all the barriers of class and religion"[105] – it had overcome regional, caste, and sectarian barriers to help the Germans form a national community of "new men."

In January, de Becker, reviewing Mounier's *Personalist Manifesto* in the well-known tennis-player and socialist Paul-Henri Spaak's publication *L'Indépendance Belge*, visualized "enormous possibilities" in personalism's inspiring a communitarian revolution in Belgium.[106] Otto Abetz's *Deutsch-Französische Monatshefte/Cahiers Franco-Allemands* had already discussed the long range aspirations, the "Planisms," of Henri de Man, Marcel Déat, and Paul Marion, and what it called Drieu la Rochelle's "fascist socialism." Now after that Winkelmoos camp the review offered an extended, serious critique of the personalism of Denis de Rougement and also that of Emmanuel Mounier.[107]

For a few of the non-conformists, *Grenoblois* Mounier was interesting for his racial qualities as well as for his communitarian ideas. Raymond

Millet, in a pamphlet vaunting "alternatives to communism," described "idealist" Mounier as seeming "of Nordic origin, tall and blond like the Scandinavians, at once gentle and rough like them; his eyes – pale but changing like the water of the cold seas – show friendship, will, and irony in turn."[108] In the *Monatshefte* François Berge, director of Esprit's "ethnology study group," portrayed the populations of Savoy and Dauphiné as a sort of blue-eyed, pink-skinned, "Nordic" race in France.[109] Millet's profile of Mounier as Nordic *Grenoblois* was echoed by a German author[110] describing new French movements which might be of interest from the Third Reich's point of view (he situated Esprit's position as somewhere between that of ON and that of Marcel Déat).[111] The February 1937 *Deutsch-Französische Monatshefte* suggested that there had been a Germanic people in the high Alpine valleys southeast of Grenoble: the legendary "Alleman" family, holding all possessions in common in their mountain fortress, had periodically descended, "bearing the banners of Uriage or Valbonais," to reassert their hegemony over the people of the Grenoble plain.[112] Could Otto Abetz have imagined that, four years after he published these romantic musings, he would be the German ambassador in Paris, and Mounier would be teaching "Knight-Monks" to administer New Order France in the medieval Chateau d'Uriage, perched high in those same mountains?

In February, Millet and *Ordre Nouveau* launched *A nous la liberté* to foster a "revolutionary awareness" among French trade-unionists. *A nous la liberté* was supportive of several Nazi domestic programs: the second issue exhorted young Frenchmen to meet young Germans in the Auberges de la jeunesse, and it praised Wilhelm Frick, the German interior minister, for decentralizing German administration along federalist lines, "according to ethnic, linguistic, and cultural realities."[113] But there were still some important issues separating the Belgian and French non-conformists from the Nazis.

In March, Denis de Rougemont, fresh from his Abetz-arranged teaching stint in Frankfurt, contrasted the Nazi and the personalists' sense of the person for Abetz's review (abutting Catholic Nazi Alphonse de Chateaubriant's celebration of the new Germany).[114] De Rougemont contrasted the German feeling of national *Gemeinschaft* with the French concern for the person – while granting that the common aspirations of European youth movements were at least as important as their differences.[115] In May, Mounier, in dialogue with Abetz, seconded Rougemont's position, asking "is the person the *primacy* of man over nature, or indeed only a fusing of the individual to the collective spirit? Our disagreement with fascism and national socialism lies ... in that sense of the person ... we think, counter to the *Cahiers'* editors, that German socialism can only be a stage on the way to integral personalism, the natural and spiritual goal of Western civilization."[116]

Once again, Mounier suggested that the French personalist communitarians, the fascists, and the Nazis were groping their ways toward the same "new man" – but that the personalists were arriving there sooner than the others. That same month (May 1937), de Rougemont reiterated his view that Nietzsche, admired by the Hitlerites, was really an anti-statist;[117] and de Rougemont's ON comrades kept writing in favour of "pure," "anti-statist" national socialism – the antipode of fascism.[118]

Thus de Rougemont and Mounier continued a nuanced analysis, dialogue, a sort of internal critique, which admitted the possibility of a maturation of Europe into a New Order of "personalized" national socialism. Stalinism and liberal capitalism, on the other hand, were doomed by the "revolution of the twentieth century." The Hitlerite Nazis were too racist, but the earlier Strasser wing of the German national socialists and the current, nascent Belgian national socialists around the socialist deputy, Paul-Henri Spaak, achieved a healthier balance. The non-conforming solution was to wait and see what German national socialism might become, as well as the result of the Belgian and French "national experiences."

So ON refused to choose sides in the European civil war:[119] the review took no position on the Italian invasion of Ethiopia and, in the Spanish Civil War, was "against both Fascism and Stalinism, and for a federalist Spain."[120] ON implied that while both Communism and Nazism were pernicious, national socialism might still be redirected. This was a stance not unlike the Vatican's.[121]

In April 1937, two days before elections, Cardinal Van Roey formally condemned Léon Degrelle's Rex movement, thus sundering Belgian Catholics. Degrelle's ensuing defeat marked the beginning of Rex's decline: his lack of urban support corroborated the de Becker–*Esprit* line that Rex was hopelessly conservative and the personalist communitarians were needed to help spark a new political coalition.[122] Already in February Paul-Henri Spaak had announced that the time for a Belgian national socialism had come, and in May, Max Liebe, still Abetz's man in Belgium, cited this Spaak declaration as a watershed in Belgian politics. Liebe called for a de Man–Spaak–Rexist alliance.[123]

During the summer and fall of 1937 there was much discussion and networking by members of the Communauté and the Brussels Esprit groups in an effort to work out a "new socialism,"[124] as well as another discreet seaside encounter at Zoute. At the end of July, Mounier, working more and more in Belgium with "the young de Manian socialists ... the living elements of the party,"[125] summoned a large international *Esprit* congress in France which included 154 representatives from twenty different cities. After that, from 7 to 24 August, Jeune Europe sponsored a youth camp on l'île Marguerite – also with less publicity than that given previous Europeanist encounters.[126] Jeune Europe and the Didiers organized a visit of German industrialists and journalists to Belgium in August. Despite Hitler's growing brutality, Nazi intellectuals still pretended to take French and Belgian non-conformist thinking seriously,[127] subjecting it to critical analysis duly reported back to France.[128] The non-conformists continued to evaluate German communitarian thinking – often reproving its racism and anti-Semitism.[129]

Although the non-conformists rejected participation in traditional political parties, they sent agents to infiltrate them. The best example was Georges Izard, who, in December 1937, left Bergery's Parti Frontiste – becoming notorious for its crypto-Nazi style and appeasing line on Germany – to accompany old Esprit comrades (L.-E. Galey, André Déléage, and others) into the French Socialist party (SFIO) and encourage its "personalist element" (i.e. Bergeryist appeasement of Hitler)[130] as well as the spiritualist, "neo-," "national socialist," or even "anti-fascist fascist"[131] currents such as those by which the young de Manians were transforming the Belgian political scene. These new "socialists'" efforts to influence the SFIO and the CGT trade union were co-ordinated, secret, opposed to the pessimistic temper of anti-fascism, and geared toward promoting total national renovation.[132] They were particularly committed to countering French communist efforts to draw syndicalists into any "anti-fascist crusade."[133]

In contrast to the French, the Belgian non-conformists' and personalists' efforts were relatively public, and connected with socialist leaders, in their contact with the Germans. By December 1937, the Belgian Esprit group was working with Henri de Man and following his advice in working for a new political coalition.[134] Abetz and Lucienne Didier were among those present at the 1937 Jeune Europe Christmas vacation ski camp in Bavaria, which was remembered for *L'Esprit Nouveau* co-founder Henri Bauchau's informed analysis of the Belgian situation. Abetz and Catholic activist Bauchau seemed to see eye to eye,[135] which was important, since, in February, Abetz's employer Joachim von Ribbentrop was made German minister of foreign affairs.[136]

In January 1938 Esprit-Brussels[137] had regretted the Belgian government's inability to institute a credible anti-capitalist program and pictured the country divided, waiting for the crystallization of a new political force.[138] That same month Raymond de Becker told that group of his new journal, *Les Cahiers Politiques*, which would be backed by Spaak and devise a political discourse inspired by "a politics of the person" and transcending all of the old orthodoxies.[139] Albert Lohest (of Communauté, the Didier salon, and Esprit's special Liège-based study group on "social renovation") and Esprit economist François Perroux would be important contributors.[140] In the May *Esprit*, Perroux even called for a "national anti-Marxist socialism." So while Robert Loustau was drafting a program for Doriot's French national socialism, de Becker, Perroux, and Spaak were framing a Belgian one. (And, after the war, Xavier de Lignac would define something not completely dissimilar for de Gaulle.) Alexandre Marc was not alone in his sympathetic interest in German communitarian thinking and experience.

When de Becker and Paul-Henri Spaak opted for a Belgian national socialism in early 1938, the worst fears of Paul Nizan and Jacques Maritain were realized, as communitarian personalist platitudes were beginning to become, at least for de Becker and Spaak, the working language for a crypto-Nazi New Order Belgian political culture. The Belgian Esprit group admitted concern in their ranks about "certain patronages," "possibilities of deviation," and "ideological exaggerations."[141] Some of the best-known people in the Belgian Esprit group, alarmed when de Becker's lecture to them was denounced in the press and Esprit-Belgium decided to close its meetings to outsiders,[142] began insisting that Belgium reaffirm her alliance with France.[143] In February Henri de Man, claiming frustration at the parliamentary game, resigned his ministerial post. When the German *Anschluss* with Austria took place in March 1938, the fears of anti-Nazi Belgians were confirmed as Henri de Man joined Spaak in urging Belgian neutrality.[144] Mounier, in contrast, criticized the denial of spiritual liberty, of a civilization founded on it, represented by the *Anschluss*.

The following September there was the Chamberlain-Hitler conference at Berchtesgarden, and by the beginning of October the Munich agreements were being fiercely debated in Belgium and France. At first, the Munich agreements seemed to shatter the unity among the Belgian non-conformists, but soon what they had in common would prevail over what divided them.

## CATHOLIC COMMUNITARIANISM IN FRANCE: THE *SEPT* EXPERIENCE

Catholic non-conformist communitarians in France largely directed their efforts to their co-religionists rather than to the country at large, as they might have done in Belgium. A smaller percentage of the French than of the Belgians were active Catholics, and so Catholic communitarianism did not become as mainstream as quickly there. Perhaps the best-known French non-conformist, Henri Daniel-Rops, became less active in an ON movement whose influence he considered disappointing,[145] and instead created, in early 1937, a collection called "Présences" for his publisher, Plon. His own essay *Ce qui meurt et ce qui naît* was followed by a collective work, *Le communisme et les chrétiens*, where his thoughts on the relationship between communism and Christianity were set alongside those of the Christian intellectual elite (François Mauriac, the Dominican Father Ducattillon, Nicholas Berdyaev, and Denis de Rougemont) and an essay on the Soviet Union by the convert Alexandre Marc.[146] The review *Sept* had followed up its highly successful issue on Communism in December 1936 (110,000 copies) with one on "Le Christ et l'ouvrier" in February 1937 (150,000 copies). In it, Daniel-Rops had romantically depicted the similarities between the life of Christ and that of humble working people.[147] Marc advocated squarely confronting the de-Christianized context of working people as described by Cardijn and the Jeunesse ouvrière chrétienne (JOC) by treating them with the dignity due them as Christians. He was optimistic about the possibilities for a re-Christianization of the working classes thanks to young people building a Catholic New Order out of the JOC, the Scouts, and the general Catholic Action Youth (ACJF) movement.[148]

On 19 February 1937, *Sept* published an interview with Léon Blum, president of the Council of Ministers – a daring thing for a Catholic review to do at that time, since Blum was a socialist, a Jew, a "materialist," and making friendly overtures.[149] One week later, more consistently, it published another cordial interview with Colonel de la Rocque[150] in which the Croix de Feu *chef* reaffirmed his devout Catholicism and claimed that French national reconciliation could follow·upon a consolidation of all of the "spiritual forces" in the country.[151] *Sept* considered fascism a possible "spiritual" force, as it underlined the following month when it published a list of the accomplishments of Mussolini;[152] if the review tended to be unambiguously anti-Nazi, it had a more nuanced attitude toward Italian fascism. Some ON people faulted *Sept* for an approach that was too Christian, not sufficiently "revolutionary."[153] And such was Catholic sympathy for fascism that the review was severely reproached, in July, for its reservations about the Italians' invading Ethiopia[154] – an imperialistic project endorsed by both the Italian episcopate and the papacy.[155] The interview with Blum and the misgivings over Ethiopia were held against the review by its Maurrasian enemies. Despite healthy financial and circulation figures, and a vigorous network of partisans and supporters, *Sept* announced, in late August (as we have seen) that it was closing for alleged "financial reasons"[156] – in fact the culmination of behind-the-scenes Vatican manoeuvres by friends of Maurras and the Action Française.[157]

The demise of *Sept* made the personal situation of Marc – a Jew lacking citizenship papers and dependent on his salary from the review – "desperate,"[158] and, from Pau, he set about looking for a new place to live, in Montpellier or Aix.[159] He urged his clerical friends to start up "a new *Sept* ... run by laymen ... watched over by the Amis de *Sept* and a group of theologians (including some Latour-Maubourg 'bolsheviks')."[160] Father Boisselot wrote that, while the guidelines for the new *Sept* were being worked out, a like-minded pedagogue, Gilbert Gadoffre, had created a well-appointed Collège d'altitude which was to open at Mégève in the Alps in October and was in need of professors.[161] Meanwhile Marc kept working at creating a national, and international, network of people sympathetic to an initiative like training young men in a radically new way – and Gadoffre (later a key figure in Vichy's National Leadership School) would be one of them.[162]

In November 1937 the new *Temps Présent* appeared, seemingly a laymen-directed successor to *Sept*. Marc had been kept regularly informed of its beginnings in the Sociéte de Saint-Louis/Editions du Seuil milieu and of Stanislas Fumet's getting commitments for regular contributions from Maritain, Simon, Mauriac, Daniel-Rops, and even Paul Claudel (overcoming his pro-Franco annoyance with the others). Despite Vatican disapproval of *Sept*, the new review had the behind-the-scenes support of French bishops.[163] Father Boisselot invited Marc to take up his old *Sept* position there, noting that despite the public withdrawal of the Dominicans, the new review would not in fact be the sole charge of laymen.[164] Because of the threat of being expelled from France, however, Marc could not oblige. By early 1938, living on a farm near Aix-en-Provence, keeping a low profile, exercising self-censorship in many of his writings, Marc felt frustrated at being far from many projects he had initiated.[165] He was a sort of pet convert of the Dominicans (in a period when the Catholic church, if often indifferent to the plight of European Jews, was attentive to converts), making a living from articles published in middlebrow Catholic publications, diffusing ON ideas in the Catholic intelligentsia, urging Catholic–Third way interaction.[166] The Catholic avant-garde milieu employed Marc as a professional networker and authority on the new German and Belgian communitarian ideas, and worked toward gaining him legal status in France, after having arranged his discreet marriage with a French citizen.[167] But by 1938, obliged to lie low on his farm in Provence, Marc was becoming – despite vigorous efforts[168] – "out of the loop" of Paris-based Catholic publishing. When he was involved with devout Catholics experiencing the European youth revolution they usually were, like Mounier and de Becker, dramatically affected. Marc had reservations about his Europeanist *confrère* Abetz, but was unshakeable in his vision of the true importance of nonconformism and of the Sohlbergkreis experience, and so he worked tirelessly and selflessly, in whatever circles he could, to bring it to fruition.

### NETWORKING THE COMMON FRONT

In early 1937, Mounier's *Personalist Manifesto* confidently set out "the fundamental doctrines of a movement, taking shape among the young, which may well be destined to have as much influence as socialism or fascism."[169] Among the several initiatives to circulate nonconformist ideas were the "Clubs de presse," a network coordinated by Raymond Millet to promote the non-conformist alternative press in the different regions of France.[170] Exhortations by Denis de Rougemont, Mounier, and Jean Maze of *La Flèche* (which was publishing as many as sixty thousand copies at the time) launched the project, which involved *Esprit*, the ON movement, and Bergery's organization.[171] By June it was claimed that there were already a hundred of these groups in operation.[172] There was also the new weekly newspaper *A nous la liberté!*[173] which was put out by ON and published the ideas of Millet, X-Crise, etc.[174]

A remarkable contingent of what we would call militant "Greens," a nascent French ecological movement, became one of the most significant spin-offs of non-conformist activity. Even *Esprit*, now regularly publishing sympathetic notes about ON,[175] began celebrating the vitality of the joint Esprit/ON communitarian personalist organization in southwestern France, which Mounier had visited, as we have seen. Drawing upon a whole network of Esprit and ON groups in the Bordeaux region, it had become one of the most original personalist communitarian attempts to "change men," under the aegis of Bernard Charbonneau and of legal scholar, Protestant theologian, and social critic Jacques Ellul. Ellul was working out what would become his world-famous critique of the technological society[176] in the midst of a sustained communitarian effort built around wilderness camping experience, parallel to the earlier practices of the *Wandervögel*, and becoming a charismatic teacher and mentor who would attract lifelong disciples.

Christian Roy has argued from his study of previously unexplored primary sources and interviews that it was as a local variant of personalism, based on a sort of conversion experience engendered by "feeling nature as a revolutionary force,"[177] that ecology was first articulated as a radical political position beyond Right and Left. Thus the ecological movement can be seen as having been invented by non-conformists in southwestern France, not by visionaries in Germany or in America (as is often assumed, given the belatedness of general environmental awareness in France).[178]

In general, ecological awareness continued to be a marginal, regional thing among the non-conformists, as was shown by the variety of topics discussed at the important Esprit congress at Jouy-en-Josas in late July 1937, which attracted 154 representatives from twenty different French cities as well as from Tunis, Casablanca, The Hague, London, Cracow, Naples, Zurich. The two-day program included presentations by Maurice Merleau-Ponty, director of Esprit's psychology study group, and François Perroux talking on "authority," "the function of the leader," "a new philosophy of democracy," and his plans for a "personalist economy" that would take a "radically new direction." The brilliant mystic Simone Weil, who was, like her English parallel George Orwell, living the life of working people, was encouraged to continue to lead the group's study of the industrial proletariat.[179] Mounier saw the gathering as marking "a great growth in the size of our movement."[180] The ideas put forward here, once they were in final form, were to be spread by the now combined ON/Esprit groups among economists, technicians, industrialists, and trade-unionists.[181]

François Perroux's new high profile among the non-conformists marked an unprecedented authoritarian and anti-democratic bent in personalist communitarianism, as did Mounier's continuing interaction with the de Manian socialists in Brussels and Zurich. Rather than debating all of this, Mounier was critical of the secessionists who refused to meld into the new force. He had become, in the words of Jacques Ellul, "extremely authoritarian," no longer tolerating any critical opposition within the personalist movement.[182] Merleau-Ponty, Esprit's representative in Chartres, signatory of several progressive Catholic petitions, left the Esprit movement after the Jouy congress despite Mounier's appeals. "Merleau" kept his differences with the non-conformists to himself and went on to become a prominent phenomenologist and Marxist political theorist.

Mounier's troubles with the Bordeaux group were significant, as it represented one of the most active personalist regions in France, even publishing its own bulletin, *Le Journal Intérieur des groupes personnalistes du Sud-Ouest*.[183] By the time of their All Saints Day weekend camp meeting high in the Pyrénées near Lesponne, the personalist communitarians in Bordeaux, Bayonne, Pau, and Toulouse had already published four or five issues of their *Journal* and had had much inter-action and common meetings. (For example, Marc's old sponsor, Father Plaquevent, was the leading personalist educator in Pau.) The ten people at the Lesponne camp discussed Esprit, and Charbonneau made several controversial remarks about the movement.[184] Jacques Ellul (who would live an anti-modern counter-culture life while a bour-geois academic in Bordeaux, mentoring his own devoted circle) bri-dled at Mounier's new authoritarianism and let him know as much. Mounier ridiculed the ecological bent of the Bordeaux group in the private interior bulletin of the personalists: "camping, above all camping: outside of camping no salvation."[185] Annoyed, Ellul and Charbonneau and the whole network of the personalist groups of the southwest took their distance, and the following March it was announced that they had resigned from the Esprit movement.[186]

ON was represented (by Aron and Rougemont) at the Esprit con-gress as well as at a Jeunesse et socialisme meeting; their people tend-ed to see their first loyalty to Marc and the ON inner core (which did not include, for example, Charbonneau and Ellul). Mounier's *Journal intérieur* became a private publication as his group, in tandem with *Ordre Nouveau*, was trying to establish ties with Georges Valois's *Nouvel Age*, the Jeunes Groupes Duboin, and the "revolutionary elements" in the Catholic trade union movement (CFTC).[187] From even farther afield, *Espagne nouvelle* showed itself very sympathetic to ON ideas at this time.[188]

In August, Alexandre Marc, who had earlier moved to Freiburg to be around Husserl and Heidegger, settled in the Aix-en-Provence of Maurice Blondel, who was regularly cited by Marc in *Ordre Nouveau* at the time.[189] Marc now tried from southern France to gather all French non-conformist movements and circles into a coalition of so-called *fédérés*, networking a broad counter-culture of young people inspired by personalist ideas. This continued to be done in a semi-secret way which has hitherto escaped the attention of historians.[190] The broader network would furnish the new elites who would run various French institutions from the advent of the Vichy regime onward. (A portion of this elite remained in influential positions through a succession of political regimes until recently.)

By the end of 1937, as we have seen, Georges Izard, Galey, Déléage, and others had made a show of leaving Bergery's Parti Frontiste (noto-rious for its pacifist line on Germany) for the divided SFIO,[191] where they worked for Bergeryist pacifism and for reorienting French social-ism along the spiritualist and Europeanist lines that the de Manians were advocating in Belgium. These newly minted socialists kept up their secret efforts[192] to realign the SFIO and the CGT in conjunction with the personalist/non-conformist network and its program of total national renovation.[193] A lack of any genuine hope in the French Socialist party was suggested when, after a few months of Izard's efforts, Mounier asked him to write an essay on "the uselessness of political parties."[194]

In January 1938, Mounier directed his followers to enlarge their perspective on possible alliances by working with the review *Jeunes*, Jean Coutrot's X-Crise think-tank, Bergery and *La Flèche*, *L'homme réel* (a syndicalist review influenced by Sorel and Proudhon, to which the grand old man of French left-wing Fascism Hubert Lagardelle, and the Le Corbusier-linked businessman François de Pierrefeu contributed articles),[195] and particularly with *Nouveaux Cahiers* – founded by Auguste Detœuf (*polytechnicien* become managing director of the Alsthom electrical machinery company) – which had been publishing since the previous March. Several *Esprit* and ON people were active at *Nouveaux Cahiers*, such as Denis de Rougemont and Jean Jardin,[196] as well as Jardin's boss Raoul Dautry, head of the French state railway system and benefactor of European youth exchanges; the stunningly original Simone Weil, the Esprit/ON group's authority on the proletarian condition after being backed by Detœuf in her factory work experiences, published some of her most important essays there.[197] Although Weil is now remembered as an Orwellian anarchist, her study of the proletarian condition was worked out in the *Nouveaux Cahiers* milieu of cerebral, imaginative, but militantly anti-Communist French industrialists sponsoring non-conformist authoritarian-communitarian reflection. Here an elite of brilliant young businessmen, architects, and engineers worked alongside mystical communitarians in advocating efficient, humane, but top-down and post-liberal, communitarian structures.[198]

Other non-conformist ideologues spreading ON ideas in other organizations at the time included Robert Loustau, writing up a program for, and serving on the executive committee of, Jacques Doriot's Parti Populaire Français (PPF), and Robert Aron, who, with Claude Mauriac,[199] wrote up a party program for, and became a leader in, Bergery's Parti frontiste – which had also evolved from left-wing anti-fascism toward militant crypto-fascist anti-communism.[200] Doriot adopted more and more Hitlerite language, and Bergery and Aron tried to keep up a dialogue with the Nazis, as non-conformists turned more authoritarian, and militant anti-fascists moved further from liberal democracy in the direction of what looked more and more like French national socialism.

In February 1938, Esprit formed a central committee to coordinate its study projects. It was made up of old Esprit hands Jacques Madaule and François Perroux, joined by the German expatriate Paul-Ludwig Landsberg, and Pierre-Aimé Touchard, former leader of the Third Force street fighters become director of Bergery's new Front Social, precursor of his Parti Frontiste; they met bi-weekly in the apartment of Marcel Moré, former *polytechnicien* become wealthy *agent de change*, expert on Marxism, and publisher of the surrealist review *La Bête Noire*.[201] The new tone of French and Belgian personalist meetings[202] was now frankly anti-liberal.[203] ON was planning an "International Summer University," what Marc envisaged to be an "Ecole de vie et de sagesse révolutionnaire," inspired by Dandieu's ideas. It would run from July to October and have a substantial library.[204]

During the night of 12–13 March, Arthur von Seyss-Inquart, the new Austrian minister of the interior and a Nazi, requested German troops to intervene in his country. The next day the *Anschluss* was proclaimed; Vienna prepared for the triumphant entry of Hitler. The general French non-conformist response to the growing external threat was to focus on the need to spark an internal revolution, a New Order, in France, which would allow her to set her own course. An ON meeting the following week decided to publish at least six new numbers of a more issues-oriented, "less abstract and utopian" *Ordre Nouveau*. The non-conformists were privately coordinating their responses to the European drama with Bergery, which meant, in practice, Xavier de Lignac's publishing a series of articles in *La Flèche* to counter any revival of the World War I anti-German "Union Sacrée" in France.[205] Marc wanted the reincarnated *Ordre Nouveau* to take a "violent and critical line." He thought ON involvement with *La Flèche*[206] worthwhile on the condition that de Lignac and several others get over their "intellectualism"[207] and speak out against parliamentarianism, the party system, "reformism," and "statism" – against liberal democracy in general. For himself, Marc had to be careful about keeping a low profile, since his naturalization application would be "paralysed within a matter of weeks" if he rejoined public debate.[208] Official concern over his activities was understandable: he was, after all, an alien working hard to undermine the very liberal democratic structures which had granted him political asylum.

The difficulties of the French Popular Front coalition were sufficient by March to inspire Mounier to write an obituary for it in which he showed no sympathy for that coalition's defence of liberal and democratic values. It had failed because it had lacked "a strong spirituality which could have inspired, formed character,"[209] and he called for a new politics inspired by Nietzsche and Dostoevsky, André Malraux and Henri de Man.[210] *Esprit* demanded "a disciplined revolutionary politics," "leaders with the required authority" who might "create new values for France."[211]

In April, Marc began to make personal overtures to Gaston Bergery, saying he found the issues supported by *La Flèche* interesting and had called attention to the review in his page of *Temps Présent*, even when Bergery did not reciprocate in his own paper. Marc and some friends wanted to meet with Bergery in Aix and have a serious conversation; Bergery agreed.[212] Marc outlined the ON reservations about Bergery and his *frontisme* to his comrades; rather than the Parti Frontiste's new appeasing line on Hitler or the growing quasi-fascist style of its meetings, the problems with the movement were:

1 Its questionable attachment to party structure
2 Its being devoid of any intransigent federal ideas
3 A certain wishy-washy reformism
4 Its failing to transcend a parliamentary mentality
5 Its holding to a vague concept of nationalization.[213]

Or as Marc put it in a subsequent letter: "we have several complaints against the attitude of Bergery, we are anti-parliamentarians ... opposed to all grouping in parties, resolutely anti-statist ... we do not want to nationalize trusts, but to decentralize them and transform them into independent and federated workshops, cooperatives, etc." "Nevertheless, we think that collaboration between *frontisme* and us is not impossible, we will try to clarify that possibility."

In sum, Marc's priority was creating a network of *trusted* comrades, resolutely anti-democratic and anti-establishment,[214] and so he began to employ a tactic to subvert and eventually gain control of the ineffectual, "too democratic" movement of Bergery by taking over its support group. Marc was willing to contribute a column called "Les Faits parlent, la Presse commente" to *La Flèche*, but he found Bergery's idea of what this contribution was to be too narrow. Marc wanted the majority of the "Comité directeur" Amis de *La Flèche* to come from ON, and confided that he was "very disappointed with Bergery who, at no time, gave the impression of being a revolutionary ... we can and ought to use him. But on one condition: that he be oriented ... Robert Aron ... [is] sometimes too weak in dealing with Bergery. [That is] a danger."[215] Marc thought that Bergery, like Mounier, could be used for ON purposes by ON people loyal to ON, who had a special vocation to manipulate weak public figures. Marc played the role of intransigent anti-democratic conscience of the ON group, while Robert Aron became more and more involved with a *frontisme* "party" given to more and more crypto-Nazi choreography and discourse in its public meetings. Marc planned to subvert *La Flèche* both by his articles and by having ON people get *de facto* control of the Amis de *La Flèche* in Paris, Lyon, Marseille, Grenoble, Bordeaux, and Toulouse (these were the largest groups, and ON was well represented in those places).[216] Annoyed at the reticence of his colleagues,[217] Marc circulated the statutes of the extant Club des Amis de *La Flèche* and a list of its Comité d'honneur (which included well-known figures such as André Gide, and composers Arthur Honegger and Darius Milhaud).[218] The ON people were, first, to become involved in promoting *La Flèche*; second, to form a study circle to criticize the content of the articles in *La Flèche*, and to orient the activities of the Parti frontiste; and, third, the Amis de *La Flèche* (with ON and *Esprit*) would get involved in the Clubs de Presse as a "means of centring their activity toward a precise goal and toward penetrating indirectly in the milieux more or less susceptible to being influenced." "Copains surs" were to form Clubs des Amis de *La Flèche*, where they did not already exist, and when there were ten or fifteen of them they would have a general meeting and then discuss and adopt the new statutes which the ON leaders would propose.[219]

In this period, Marc, who believed in the important role of the *chef* and regularly took a harder line than the other ON leaders,[220] was also ordering his comrades "in the name of revolutionary discipline" not only to take over the Amis de La Flèche but also to infiltrate meetings of groups like *Nouvel-Age*, the review *Recherches philosophiques*, and *L'Ordre Réel*.[221] His goal was to draw these different groups into a disciplined Ligue fédérale des non-conformistes.[222] In fact, really "free" dialogue was declining in non-conformist circles: Mounier announced in April that only recommended individuals would be allowed to attend the next Esprit congress.[223] And in June he was more specific: while personalist groups should try to draw different philosophers (including people like Gabriel Marcel and Maritain) into discussions on personalist communitarianism, future congresses of the movement should be limited to those who had regularly participated in the work of a group.[224]

In spring 1938 ON's Chevalley, Marc, Rougemont, Lignac, André Boutier, and Prévost discussed setting up a full-fledged school for revolutionary formation, what they called their "Free University," by the summer of 1939. They envisaged Rougemont's lecturing on the book he was writing and, at the top of the list of people from the outside, Georges Bataille, former comrade of Dandieu and animator of that "Collège de Sociologie" study group which was doing such important and original thinking about the nature of community élan and experience.[225] They envisaged renting a country property to help put "federalism into practice."[226] (And in fact a community named "La Galéjade" would result.)

In mid-June 1938, *Ordre Nouveau* reappeared in the form of a thirty-two-page issue put together "after a year-long interruption due solely to financial difficulties" during which "the various members of the group multiplied their contributions to the major press, [and] their contacts with political or professional groupings" spreading ON's ideas and preparing to seize power.[227] Seizing power proved not, however, as simple as it had appeared. Marc's plan to take over the Amis de *La Flèche* became difficult because of Bergery's personal authority in the statutes and because Robert Aron's intentions had become suspect to certain members of the Conseil National of the movement. Georges Valois and some of his people were also suspicious of ON overtures. Still, the idea of networking through a "Fédération des groupements non-conformistes" seemed workable, especially around the nucleus of innocent-seeming Clubs de Presse in the provinces. In Paris, where there were the "Etats Majors" of the different movements sending out directives to their troops, some contacts were possible, but not the top-down "federation," which was practical only in a smaller setting. The effort was directed toward multiplying provincial contacts "between the activists of ON, *Esprit*, *La Flèche*, *Temps présent*, on one side, and *Nouvel Age*, perhaps anarcho-syndicalists, on the other"; the publication of regional bulletins was envisaged. ON would establish the firm linkage between the ON leadership (Marc's *Agir*) and the federated non-conformists in the provinces. And it was one of Marc's most trusted comrades who promised to "make the 'clandestine' link between the two without the Parisians being aware of it as that is, for the time being, indispensable." Thus the coalition of marginal groups began to take shape and offer an alternative political culture to that of established liberal democracy. Zeal for the New Order transcended the old ideological differences, as Marc and his ON cohorts planned to infiltrate a range of organizations, and network the non-conformists in their different regions[228] – particularly with the Clubs de Presse.[229]

National socialism was never mentioned as an adversary of Marc's proposed network of non-conformists, and his ON people were important ideologues in the two French mass movements taking on Nazi characteristics: the PPF of Doriot (with Loustau) and Bergery's Parti Frontiste (with Robert Aron and Prévost influential at *La Flèche*). Marc's non-conformists were so opposed to liberal democracy, and so desirous of a New Order, that they could "conform" to a sort of French national socialism disguised as "revolutionary federalism." In this way, innocuous-seeming discourse about non-conformity, and persons federating into living communities to create "new men," really promoted an authoritarian political culture which embodied values quite different from its slogans. As Bergery moved from a "Common Front against Fascism" to a left-wing French national socialism, so Marc grouped non-conformists into a federation to institute a communitarian personalism enforcing rigid conformity and centralized authority to introduce the New Order. Unfortunately, as Franklin Roosevelt observed, when the heralded New Order finally arrived, it was not "new" and it was not "order."[230]

Marc advocated frankly duplicitous tactics: "the two organisms remain distinct, their coordination will remain discrete." The revived *Ordre Nouveau* seemed happily "inspired by that federalist formula" and evidence that "an agreement between all the non-conformists of right and left is becoming a possibility."[231] The July 1938 issue, devoted mainly to "twenty years of public finance," was announced as intended to "show the application of our ideas to the most concrete cases."[232] The first issue included contributions from non-conformists ranging from Thierry Maulnier of *Combat* (a review which the young François Mitterrand was promoting in the Latin Quarter) and Jean Maze of *La Flèche* to René Belin of the CGT trade union. *Ordre Nouveau* declared itself a meeting place for people putting aside outworn labels, working together to "contribute to the revolutionary rebuilding of France."[233]

This coming together of French non-conformists recalled what had happened in Germany six years earlier. In the 15 July 1938 *Ordre Nouveau*, Claude Chevalley showed the continuity between French non-conformists and the German youth movement: he employed the texts of Heidegger (and, to a lesser extent, Heidegger's French expositor Jean-Paul Sartre) to clarify the special sort of activist temperament which ON fostered. *Esprit* then endorsed this view. For Alexandre Marc, *Ordre Nouveau* was beginning to resemble the broadened review *Gegner* on the eve of Hitler's coming to power.[234]

The coming together of the German non-conformists had been aborted by the brutal power grab of the Hitlerite Nazis. By July 1938 those same Nazis began to interfere seriously with the French non-conformists' efforts to create a "youth front": more and more of them were being called into military service. The non-conformists' focus, however, remained steadfastly fixed on internal revolution in France rather than on threats posed by her external enemies. A comrade of Marc's, seconding his appeal to the French non-conformists (if not, in effect, to the whole French "New Right") to achieve "l'Union ou la Mort," asserted: "It is a question of federating the efforts of all who, protesting against the impotence of parliamentary democracy, want

the Revolution of Order in France which – consciously or unconsciously – all of Europe is awaiting," and which would put all of society
at the service of the person.[235]

A succession of meetings cemented the ties among the young communitarian enemies of liberal democracy. The organizers of the second Jouy Congress of the Esprit groups, held 26–31 July 1938, found
two-thirds of the editors already in uniform and only seventeen groups
represented. François Goguel described *frontisme* as having certain
"anarchistic" traits, particularly excessive anti-communism, but
promised that the personalists in the movement were working to cor-
rect its faults.[236] For its part, Bergery's group lent Pierre-Aimé
Touchard, who had founded and directed Bergery's Front Social
before it merged with *La Flèche*, to run a small bulletin called *Le
Voltigeur* to network the "Voltigeur" cells of like-minded non-
conformists/personalists. These people were already, as we have seen,
meeting in the so-called Clubs de Presse, the loose network of "ecumenical" groups to share information which had been launched in
speeches by Mounier, de Rougemont, and *La Flèche*'s Jean Maze early
in the previous year.[237] Touchard soon endorsed the term "anti-fascist
fascism," as employed by Bergery, to describe *Le Voltigeur*'s aspirations,
and this, too, was seconded by Mounier.[238] It was Touchard, rather
than an old *Esprit* hand, who would take over the management of *Esprit*
when Mounier was drafted into military service.[239]

Emmanuel Mounier, pushing for discipline and ideological conformity in the Esprit network, did not particularly like Marc's term "non-
conformism" to describe the common aspirations of the new anti-
liberal, anti-parliamentary, personalist-communitarian generation. But
he was, like Marc, a strong advocate of generational unity in the circumstances,[240] and in early August he sent Marc a draft of his questionnaire on the usefulness of political parties (*Enquête sur les Partis*)
which the coalition was planning to circulate among the representatives in the Chamber of Deputies. The brash covering statement –
"Pour une Refonte des Doctrines Démocratiques" – announced that
sixty-five people had been asked to "rethink" democracy. These included François Perroux, Jean Lacroix, Robert Aron, Yves Simon, Raymond Aron, Gabriel Marcel, Nikolai Berdyaev, Jacques Maritain,
Simone Weil, Jean Grenier, Henri Guillemin, Paul-Louis Landsberg,
Jean Maze, Gaston Bergery, and Alexandre Marc. Mounier asked Marc
to contribute to the special issue of Esprit that would come out of it:
"a dozen pages, as precise, sober, technical and concrete as possible"
on certain passages of the questionnaire which were obviously "very
ON" in orientation.[241] Marc (typically patronizing a man he considered
"un faible") responded that he would be glad to write, but wanted to

avoid being eliminated at the last minute by Mounier's Comité de lecture" because his articles were "too revolutionary." Marc urged Mounier to attend the meeting in Gap on 27–8 August because their people were very dispersed and needed to be brought closer together if they were going to accomplish anything. He also (disingenuously) reassured Mounier that "It goes without saying that I am not thinking of amalgamating but rather of pluralistic cooperation."[242] Mounier, in turn, reassured Marc that there was no unfavorable prejudice against him at *Esprit*, and that an article "against all parties" had an excellent chance of being published.

Erudite and arcane, the review *Ordre Nouveau*, having built bridges to non-conformists of all stripes, was made superfluous by the urgency of responding to the day-to-day issues to which ON people – now subverting various publications and organizations – were responding at *La Flèche, Le Voltigeur, Sept, Temps présent*, and other publications.[243] They were reaching a larger public and dealing with the succeeding crises by steeling the resolve of, and promoting ties between, the various groups out to displace liberal democracy with a revolutionary new order. The need for a pure theoretical review had passed: the theory and the discourse had been worked out and were now generally accepted. The time for *praxis* had come.

# 7 The Munich Agreements, the *Fédérés*, Defeat and Occupation (29 September 1938 to the Liberation)

> I knew that a doctrine which required conversion of its disciples
> could only appeal to the few.
>> member of *Esprit* group explaining low turnout at a
>> non-conformist meeting in Toulon, January 1939

The Chamberlain/Daladier settlement with Hitler at Munich in early October 1938 reinforced the non-conformists' resolve to jettison liberal democracy and create a different sort of France. Marc remained among the most resolved as he urged Gaston Bergery's right-hand man, Jean Maze, Catholic activist at *Sept* and editor-in-chief of *La Flèche*, "to profit from this respite – because it is only a respite – to redouble our efforts: coordinate, federate, revolutionary energies." He wanted connected people like Maze to organize the November non-conformist congress in Paris to follow up on the one held at Gap. Robert Aron would provide information on it, and Marc expected good progress to be made "if we kick out the sectarians and chatter-boxes."[1]

The invention of a kind of French national socialism was one non-conformist project, and in the October *Esprit* Mounier praised the Spaak-de Becker initiative in Belgium, because – like the Swiss socialists' version – it represented a vigorous and attractive new kind of socialist political culture: de Manian, spiritual, personalist and communitarian.[2] While marshalling support for a comparable French undertaking, Mounier sent Marc a copy of *Le Voltigeur français* ("our new rag"), urging him to write for it, and promising a preliminary *Esprit/Ordre Nouveau/Nouveaux Cahiers* meeting before the Paris non-conformists' congress to be held in Boulogne-Billancourt from 10 to 13 November. This projected interaction suggested that the non-conformists' leaders were now sending some discreet public signals of their fraternization (though not so much

as to shock the faithful), while seriously organizing across old political and religious divisions behind the scenes.[3] When Mounier
agreed to run the November meeting, Marc publicly praised
Mounier's new political drift in *Temps Présent* and privately congratulated *Esprit*'s editor "for taking a clearer, more vehement attitude
... The time has come to put an end to equivocations, don't you
think?" Marc hoped that the new *Voltigeur* would "clearly break with
democratic claptrap, eschewing the role (for which we have
reproached *Esprit*) of His Majesty's loyal opposition."

Marc, patronizing and bullying Mounier as usual, pressed him to
create "un comité fédérateur" of Robert Aron, Pierre Prévost, Joseph
Folliet, Paul Chanson, Paul Flamand, and a few others to help with
that November meeting.[4] Despite the risk of being arrested and
deported, Marc decided that he would spend two weeks at the centre
of the action in Paris to counsel Mounier and the others.

After the Munich agreements, the Belgian non-conformists
became the object of intense public controversy. When Raymond de
Becker explained Spaak's national socialism to an *Esprit* group plenary meeting there on 30 October, Communist spies infiltrated the
meeting and related the Spaak–de Becker appeasement line.[5] De
Becker's German contacts already worried Jacques Maritain (who
had refused to see de Becker since the previous year because of
them),[6] and Alexandre Marc remembers breaking with de Becker
over his suspicious involvement with Spaak.[7] But French non-
conformists were not agreed on the Belgian situation: while the
November *Esprit* portrayed Spaak as working with pro-Nazi groups
and urged France to do something before all of Belgium became
irretrievably pro-Nazi, the December issue contained both a defence
of Spaak and Mounier's conclusion that the verdict on the Spaak–de
Becker initiative was "still open."[8] De Becker, however, began to work
more and more openly with Nazi agents and to display contempt for
his old religious comrades, and he announced by the end of the year
that he felt "liberated" at leaving the Catholic church.[9] A visit by
Abetz to Brussels a few months later would precipitate a major scandal, as we shall see.

By early 1939, Emmanuel Mounier, seemingly less interested in
planning joint projects with de Becker in Brussels, was envisaging his
future in Paris: he and his wife were searching for a large property on
the outskirts of the French capital to serve as a community lodging,
headquarters, and experimental boarding school for the international Esprit community. Until the German invasion in June 1940,
Mounier remained curiously discreet about his relationship with de
Becker, and *Esprit* did not so much as mention the dramatic political

situation in Belgium. While some well-known Belgian Esprit figures had come out for firm resistance against the Nazis, Mounier's review had also encouraged "neutralism" and the hope that a "revolution-ized" Belgium might find a place in a New Order Europe. In general, Esprit, alongside Jeune Europe, can be seen in retrospect as having "softened up" Belgium and nurtured several of the key actors in the collaborationist regime in that country.[10]

As Bergery and his party were adopting a sort of non-racist fascism ("anti-fascist fascism," in their words), the review *Esprit* publicly criti-cized them for moving toward the Right[11] – while privately multiply-ing links, contacts, and meetings with them. Paul Flamand, repre-senting the militant Catholic communitarians of *Editions du Seuil,* and Pierre Prévost, one of Marc's chief henchmen in Ordre Nouveau (ON), fixed the meeting of the fédérateurs for 11–13 November as per Marc's suggestion while continuing to assemble people in the var-ious Clubs de Presse.[12] Mounier announced that the time had come for a "rebuilding of democracy," prompting Jean Maze and *La Flèche* to express how close *Esprit* had come to their positions; Mounier simultaneously intensified his involvement with both ON and the Christian Democrats of the Aube group.[13] The November Paris *fédéra-teurs'* meeting was the culmination of Marc's two-week effort to launch the *fédérés* movement in the Paris region and focus it on pre-cise revolutionary goals. A central directing committee for the Clubs de Presse was to be organized by Prévost, Maze, and Robert Aron. Paul Flamand was to direct the Paris secretariat of the movement, but the central secretariat of the *fédérés* was to be in Lyons under Joseph Voyant of the local ON cell, one of the most politically pragmatic and astute[14] of Alexandre Marc's closest collaborators. (Voyant was also one of Marc's first *compagnons* – Marc's equivalent term, for the personalist-communitarian revolution, to the French Revolutionary *citoyens* or the Bolsheviks' *camarades*.) Voyant and Marc would soon be joined by budding Europeanists Emile Noël[15] and Bernard Voyenne,[16] and by Jean Coutrot of X-Crise – legendary and mysteri-ous guru of the new generation of technocrats, relative of Marc's wife, now a supporter of Marc's new initiative.[17] A new top-down adminis-trative structure was to be functioning before the next congress, after the year-end Franco-Swiss personalist camping encounter, in Febru-ary, on Marc and Voyant's turf in Lyons.

An illustrative example of someone committed to the ON enterprise was Claude Chevalley, who had become by then, despite his typical ON misgivings about the United States, a mathematician in the Institute for Advanced Study at Princeton.[18] Chevalley was praised in the November *Esprit* for his intelligent use of Heidegger (and of the young

French expositor of *Existenzphilosophie*, Jean-Paul Sartre) to cast light on the nature of "the activist temperament," thereby clarifying ON's special approach, style, and personality. Marc found Chevalley's insight into ON political culture useful but thought that his friend – despite unflattering remarks about his American hosts – was getting soft on the United States.

Marc urged the general assembly of federators to interact with every true or potential non-conformist and keep in contact with distant *compagnons*. Delighted that "This time Mounier seems decided to march along with us to the end," Marc wanted close working relationships with the *frontistes*, the *Nouvel-Age* people, *Combat* (Jean de Fabrègues), *L'Ordre Réel* (Paul Chanson), and, above all, "real people": artisans, *coopérateurs*, trade-unionists, technicians, and so on. (Rank-and-file factory workers, the sorts of people who made up the bases of support for the French Communist party, were not mentioned.) Marc thought that the federators had "to completely reeducate our people before we can make them work in an ON spirit," before they could constitute the "new revolutionary force" which was the federators' goal.[19] A special two-day follow-up meeting was held two weeks after the general non-conformist congress for the leaders of the various Esprit groups in Paris and the provinces: it set as priorities an interior revolution in France and the avoidance of unreflective hostility toward Germany.[20]

*Fédérateur* networking continued in the cities and towns in the provinces. In Toulon, for example, the amalgamated ON and Esprit groups held their meetings in the Esprit locale on Sundays with "personalist readings" at hand – *Nouvel-Age*, a few *Nouveaux Cahiers*, a few issues of *Ordre Nouveau*. The group's secretary was a Catholic trade-union (CFTC) activist and they interacted with the Catholic idealists of the new Nouvelles équipes françaises (with whom they shared an office).[21] Their group discussions among "people of good will" on current issues such as anti-Semitism had broader appeal than the abstruse affairs of the earlier Esprit group. They associated with other groups to invite non-conformists on the lecture circuit to visit their region.[22] The Toulon group held a meeting two weeks after the Boulogne-Billancourt congress which drew twenty-seven people to meet the people in charge of the central office – Mounier, Perret, Touchard, and Landstey, who were introduced as "married, almost all fathers of families, and young (thirty to thirty-five years old)." Esprit veteran L. Maggiani then spoke on the newly clarified relationship between communitarian personalism and concrete political action: "Personalism, which has been faulted for not fostering concrete activity, has, on the contrary, a coherent doctrine on that subject. Action should be pure

... in its goals, in its means. What is [personalist commitment's] strong point? First it shatters the 'established disorder' by disengaging us from it. Then it invents, creates, immediately institutes in us, around us, the new order."[23]

Personalism was, then, a life-changing conversion experience of communitarian purity which fostered action in the surrounding world. A Toulon get-together was no mere discussion among marginals nostalgic for youthful communitarian religious experiences, but rather a microcosm of the completely different political culture of converts which the New Order would bring to France. Marc had seen 'unconventional young romantics and dreamers propelled to power in Germany overnight by "the revolution of the twentieth century" and foresaw something comparable – but different and distinct – in France.

The Toulon example shows the ON/Esprit melding on the local level which Marc had urged, and how the merged non-conformists imagined themselves part of an international network of young people thwarting Stalinism, supportive of spiritualist and communitarian alternatives to liberal democracy, and committed to a New Order in France. When one entered a group of *amis* or *compagnons*, one converted into a spiritual family which expected discipline, obedience, revolutionary vigour.[24] (Not surprisingly, a decline in attendance at meetings resulted. A Toulon comrade mused the next January: "I knew that a doctrine which required conversion of its disciples could only appeal to the few.")[25]

While Mounier continued with a high public profile in Brussels and Paris, Marc, obliged to lie low in the provinces, conspired to form elites shaped by the ON approach and bonded by factory and outdoor experiences. He was determined to convert the disorder of French individualism and liberal democracy into a communitarian new order.

While the non-conformists considered Belgium ripe for a new order, French non-conformist infiltrators had only met limited success in the Socialist party (SFIO). In November Marc admonished the best known of these non-conformist agents, Socialist deputy Georges Izard, for wasting his time in "an old impotent party (like all the others) ... it is a pernicious illusion to believe that one can accomplish more by working within such parties."[26] *Esprit*'s co-founder Izard seemed to have reached the same conclusion, and in December, with the victory of the strong anti-Nazi socialists over the anti-war Marcel Déat group, Izard, André Déléage, Georges Duveau, and L.-E. Galey announced their resignations from the SFIO with a polemical book calling for the disassembling of parliamentary institutions and the "radical interior rebuilding" of the country.[27] Marc congratulated Izard for the "brave" speech announcing his defection from the Socialists ("You know that I have no sympathy for parliamentarianism, or for parliamentary eloquence, but it is good that a breath of fresh air passes through that enclosure from time to time") and saw signs in Izard's book that he was "returning to Third Force positions which, as far as I am concerned, I always regretted your abandoning." He expected fellow convert Izard to work with the *fédérés*, "particularly come the day when, fed up with parliamentarianism, and pathetic social democracy too, you rediscover the revolutionary spirit of our youth."[28]

Some of the Marc group's 1939 networking projects were more successful than others – as their *compagnons* were called to the military, leaving the exempted to carry on their efforts. Despite "inextricable material difficulties," Marc and his comrades threw themselves full time into the *fédérés* movement and what Marc saw as "urgent revolutionary projects": the publication of the projected *Cahiers fédérateurs* and a small review called *Agir* (which Marc thought "could be the seed of something important").[29] The Clubs de Presse, though hard to get going in the confused circumstances, at least institutionalized contacts with the *Nouveaux Cahiers* groups.[30] Bernard Voyenne helped Marc publish *Agir*, whose subtitle and motto was *Fédérer les Forces Françaises*.[31] It had much the same purpose as the resurrected *Ordre Nouveau*, but seemed to elicit more of a response, especially in the Lyons area. One reason for this was Mounier's move from Brussels to play a larger role in the French project for national renovation.

Marc, gratified by Mounier's support for the *fédérateurs*,[32] urged him to help put together "a group of men disengaged not only from any party, [but] even from any political 'identification.' " Marc saw Esprit's image as left-wing, so if it gave public support to the *fédérateurs* project it might draw many people who might not otherwise consider it. As it was, Paul Flamand complained that Esprit people were not sufficiently supportive of the *fédérés parisiens* despite Mounier's efforts. Marc began preparing a major meeting in Lyons to iron out the theoretical and practical problems and asked Mounier to articulate "all the non-conformist impulses, from *Combat* to *Esprit*, from *Nouvel-Age* to *L'Ordre Réel*, et al." so as to launch "our very own 'Communist Manifesto' " at Lyons.[33]

The monthly meeting of the Esprit/ON groups in the provinces provided the faithful with an abundance of readings from friendly publications from the "neither left nor right" non-conformist political spectrum. In Toulon, for example, it took three large tables to lay out the plethora of theory reviews – *Collection Esprit, Ordre Nouveau, Ordre Réel, Travail et Liberté, Nouveaux Cahiers,* and *L'Abondance* – as well as the more directly political non-conformist organs such as *Le Voltigeur Français, Feuilles Libres,* and *La Flèche,* along with other personalist readings.[34] The Lyons Esprit group led the way in firming up contacts with economics guru François Perroux, André Philip, *Les Amis des Feuilles Libres, Ordre Nouveau,* the Nouvelles Equipes Françaises (NEF), the Centre des Fédérateurs, and other non-conformist personalities and groups. A philosophical task force set about recasting democratic doctrines in the light of the political group's ideas. They planned camp meetings in the high mountains, again at Gap in the southern Alps, and in the Pyrenees, ending the year with a Franco-Swiss winter camp at Argentière during Christmas vacation. ON's influence on *Esprit* was evident in the February 1939 issue in essays urging revolutionary action (Bernard Charbonneau) and calling for a "totalitarian orthodoxy" in the personalist community (Pierre Prévost).[35]

Marc's comrades fretted over his *Agir's* simply repeating the line of *Ordre Nouveau* and other non-conformist publications,[36] but in places like Toulon ten or fifteen non-conformists from different groups got together "in a communitarian spirit" for bi-weekly discussions according to *Agir's* instructions.[37] Intending to help federate non-conformists in a way which neither *Ordre Nouveau* nor *Esprit,* by itself, could, *Agir* urged such regular meetings of ten to fifteen people all across France and particularly including the readership of *Combat,* the new review co-directed by Jean de Fabrègues and Thierry Maulnier and involving the elite of the New Right intelligentsia (individuals such as Maurice Blanchot, and supporters like young François Mitterrand). Marc even envisaged *Esprit/Ordre Nouveau/Combat* coalescing into a triumvirate interacting on "efficacious, precise common activities" geared toward replacing liberal democracy with a New Order.[38]

Marc pressed ("Cher Ami et Compagnon") Mounier to further the common effort in *Esprit* and *Le Voltigeur* as Marc sent *Agir* directly to all *Esprit's* local representatives. But Marc warned that this bulletin, larded with a few passages from Mounier "conceived, of course, in the purest *fédérateur* spirit," was addressed not to the "grand public," but rather to the "initiated." Marc's secret networking of an inner circle of the non-conformist movement had to contend with a Mounier who was vague and irresolute in contrast to *compagnons* who were more *purs et durs,* and deferential to Marc, such as Prévost and Chevalley.[39]

Marc's efforts to integrate Georges Valois and Jean Coutrot into the *Agir/fédérateurs* project resulted in Valois giving him the addresses of his own people,[40] and Marc's calling the attention of the *fédérés* initiative to Valois's *Nouvel Age* readers, providing the addresses of his closest colleagues, and promising to publish in *Agir* the addresses of non-conformist publications mentioned in *Nouvel Age*: *Juin 1936, Le monde à l'envers, La Révolution prolétarienne.*[41] Simone Weil was a prominent contributor to this latter, and both she and Valois, like Marc, were planning for a New Order incorporating Catholic spiritual values. Jean Coutrot offered contributions from his CEPH technocrat study group for *Agir* and invited a *fédérés* leader to one of its meetings.[42] Paris gatherings began to coordinate heretofore independent initiatives like the Estèbe group, France vivante, and the Comité du Plan, as Coutrot was turning his experience in networking in industry, business, and the liberal professions to networking non-conformism via his Bureau d'Etudes Economiques, Sociales et Humaines. Like his comrade Marc, Coutrot was trying to meld an elite of technocrats, planners, engineers, social thinkers, and idealistic communitarians into a sophisticated new political culture, countering the Bolshevik model, transcending liberal democracy.[43] Marc urged the Coutrot group to become involved with Catholic activists, such as those at the upcoming congress of the Amis de *Temps Présent* which Marc was planning, as well as with several smaller meetings and encounters, and a possible general meeting of the *fédérés*. For this latter Marc wanted Coutrot personally present along with "the most open and dynamic" representatives of groups such as France vivante, Maximisme, and the Comité du Plan. Paul Flamand was to organize the next *fédérés* meeting.[44]

Marc was unique for promoting links between Catholic activists (e.g., of the *Sept/Temps Présent* circle) with non-conforming *fédérés*, technocrats, and Third Way revolutionaries such as the Frontists involved in national planning schemes but not normally working with religious groups.[45] Marc also encouraged ties with the Jeune République group, and the backers of *L'Abondance, La Nef,* and even the monarchist *Courrier Royal,* as well as with trade-unionists.[46] Jean de Fabrègues, for the Young Right, welcomed *Agir* and asked how *Combat* could help it; he wanted Marc to write on the movements attempting to renovate France for the review *Civilisation* as, overcoming earlier reservations, Fabrègues became interested in the *fédérés* project.[47]

Marc's constituency ranged from the extreme Left to the Right and included anti-communists, people critical of liberal democracy, capitalism, and the United States, supporters of some sort of European New Order, and mavericks in the political and economic establishment. Marc's coalition-building had Coutrot's group now overlapping with ON, the *fédérés*, Gaston Bergery's neo-socialists, and the Catholics of *Temps Présent*[48] as Marc cast the net ever wider toward those he considered of a non-conformist bent.[49] This "ecumenism" ignored the old parties in its effort to gather non-conformist revolutionary forces for an assault against the old order,[50] as the communitarian commitment was to provide a conversion and bonding experience superior to that of the old religions and politics.[51] Marc, and a few comrades like Jean Maze (the *La Flèche/ Esprit/ Sept* activist), circulated freely between religious, political, and religio-political groupings.[52] Through all of these networking efforts, as if husbanding the original non-conformist flame, Sohlberg alumni kept in touch with Marc.[53]

The Amis de *Temps Présent* were part of a non-conformist lecture circuit of communities of "Social Catholic" lay people.[54] The subjects of these talks give an idea of the variety of non-conformist Catholic interests: in spring 1939, the exiled German non-conformist Ernst Erich Noth spoke on Franco-German relations,[55] Stanislas Fumet on Léon Bloy, Joseph Folliet on averting war, Georges Hourdin on the worthlessness of political parties, Alexandre Marc on "Le Salut de la France par l'esprit de Péguy." François Perroux would also speak, along with Pierre-Henri Simon,[56] who defended the "pure" German national socialism of Otto Strasser over against the Hitlerite aberration.[57]

### THE ABETZ AFFAIR IN BELGIUM

We have seen how, in early 1939, Nazi intellectuals pretended sympathetic interest in the ideas of communitarian personalist Denis de Rougemont[58] while criticizing Emmanuel Mounier's.[59] Undaunted, Mounier asked the German embassy in Paris in February to keep lines of communication open by inscribing him on their "service des revues allemandes,"[60] but in an April review of Robert Aron's *La fin de l'après-guerre* Mounier described his non-conformist comrade as "underestimating the negative realities of the situation" in encouraging continuing dialogue with Hitler. Rougemont, after some post-Munich indecision, also adopted an anti-Nazi position at this time.[61]

By the spring of 1939, some well-known political leaders were involved with the personalist communitarian network in both Belgium and France. In May, Henri de Man, with Spaak's backing, was elected president of the Parti Ouvrier Belge – representing a Belgian national socialism enlisting proletarians and bourgeoisie to overthrow capitalism and establish Belgian neutrality. The May *Esprit* published several ON contributions[62] and the proposal of Hubert Beuve-Méry[63] – well-known *Le Temps* Eastern Europe correspondent, and active layman in Dominican circles – that France be saved by a select elite: new *équipes* of men thirty to forty-five years old, aloof from both Hitlerite propaganda and the republican establishment. These shock troops could effect France's *own* revolution to the New European Order without its having to be foisted on her from the outside, as had been the case for the Czechs.[64]

In June, *Combat*'s Thierry Maulnier proposed a "provisory" fascism for France. *Esprit* agreed: the country needed "an original form of national socialism."[65] Abetz, now Ribbentrop's foremost advisor and an unapologetic francophile, had always claimed to want each people to achieve their "own" national socialism and so that summer, forbidden entry into France, he visited "neutralists" in Belgium. There he joined Max Liebe, attaché to the German embassy, in encouraging "young intellectuals of the Spaak–de Man–Van Zeeland school" to oppose Belgium's entering the war on the Allied side. The alarmed French government set up a special counter-espionage unit to monitor the influence of the "Ribbentrop stable" in Brussels.[66] On 16 July the first of a series of articles appeared in the Belgian daily *Le Soir* in Brussels denouncing Abetz's camps and colloquia, and the whole history of Europeanist propaganda in Belgium.[67] It was implied that naïve Belgian Catholics and spiritualist socialists had been manipulated by Nazi agents into a pacifist-neutralist position and were now helping to soften up France.

In fact, when war was declared two months later, Belgium remained resolutely neutral, and Europeanist guru Henri de Man was taken into the government as a special minister.[68] In October, Raymond de Becker, discreetly supported by Spaak and aided by the writers Robert Poulet and Pierre Daye, founded the weekly newspaper *Ouest* to reinforce this neutralist sentiment. In the spring of 1940, on the eve of the German invasion, it would receive a generous subsidy from Abetz's man in Brussels, Max Liebe.[69]

## THE "DROLE DE GUERRE"

The 1930s non-conformists responded to the danger facing France by abandoning parliamentary institutions for the "Fascism of the Left" put forward by Gaston Bergery and his Frontists, or the appeasement position of maverick young Socialist leader Marcel Déat. On the eve of Germany's September 1st invasion of Poland, Déat invited Marc to lunch in Paris because he had read his newpaper article condemning war as disastrous for Europe.[70] There Déat realized that, though against war (declared on 3 September) Marc did not advocate submission to Germany. Although de Gaulle had convinced him that France was sorely unprepared for war, Marc was still, like de Gaulle, ready to fight for France: although still not a citizen, he volunteered for, and was accepted into, the French army.[71]

In December 1939, a remainder of the Groupements Non-Conformistes met in Paris at their provisional headquarters at 204 Blvd Saint Germain under the aegis of Jean Coutrot[72] and Paul Flamand, including Pierre Prévost, Georges Pelorson, Braibant, Coutubaud, Estèbe, Guillaume, Groener, Heruteaux, Isambert, Mirlès, Polin, Reybaud, and Pierre-Henri Simon. Flamand got the group's support to start a new review with a circulation of two to five thousand to coordinate their projects. Pelorson suggested that the different groups, movements, and individuals clarify their respective positions beforehand, since their supporters wanted congruity rather than disparate opinions from this new central office: the common "opinion fédérale." But, given the urgent circumstances, each group was to define "its" position, indicate how many copies it could use, and explain just what its specific contribution to the "revue fédérale" would be.[73]

On 20 March Edouard Daladier resigned and the following day Paul Reynaud formed a new French cabinet making a place for Charles de Gaulle. On 10 May the German army invaded Belgium, the Netherlands, and Luxembourg. Neville Chamberlain resigned as British prime minister and a Resistance-oriented coalition cabinet, including Conservatives and Labourites, took office under Winston Churchill. On 28 May King Leopold III of Belgium, advised by Henri de Man, ordered his army to cease fighting and, in response, Belgian government officials on French territory declared Leopold deposed.

While Belgian non-conformists faced invasion and surrender, French non-conformists brought out a June 1940 *Esprit* to provide "a free voice for French youth": heterogeneous contributors drawn from the networking efforts of federators like Marc (imprisoned by the French army for a week during the height of the invasion of France for possessing "defeatist propaganda").[74] Jean Maze of *La Flèche*, Jean-Pierre Maxence of *Gringoire* and the Jeune Droite, Georges Lefranc from the corporatist branch of the trade-union movement, and Pierre Prévost of ON summoned their readers not to lose heart in the face of the Nazi onslaught but to "turn their attention toward that ray of light … to catch a glimpse of the after-war years" and the "new elites" which were emerging in France: Mounier's "post-war militia," Prévost's "technocrats with a sense of grandeur," and Georges Lefranc's new trade-union elites. The new generation would form "men of character" (Prévost), spark a "French interior renaissance" (Maze). Mounier recalled "The whiplash that Hitlerism gave Germany in six years, the strength, the vitality, the aggressiveness, the imagination that he, in the face of massive despiritualization, blew into the flabby Weimar Republic," and foresaw "entirely new conditions and realities" which might be harrowing "but at least will bring us out of the blind alleys of the past."[75]

In those fateful months which preceded the invasion and defeat of France, Mounier, Flamand, Maze, Coutrot, Aron, Marc, and their non-conformist band did not try to steel opinion in *Temps Présent*, *Agir*, *Esprit*, or other publications, but rather to firm up friendships, alliances, and habits of mind for replacing the liberal democratic order with something else. An elite of converts would advance its agenda through a network of communities, cells, relationships, and institutions. The central role of Paris in French life, and of the clergy in the life of the Catholic church, allowed small-circulation reviews such as *Sept*, *Ordre Nouveau*, *Temps Présent*, *Le Voltigeur*, and *La Flèche*, or publishers such as the early Editions du Seuil, to create a network of committed *compagnons*, people with similar ideas and ways who would get together from time to time, and who, once in influential positions, retained their original loyalites and did what they could to help one another and so advance the common cause.

By the late 1930s the *fédérés* and other communitarian movements committed to the primacy of the spiritual were engaged in vital regular interaction, even a kind of confederation. This helps explain how – with the collapse of Third Republic institutions – non-conformists and communitarian personalists were ready, able, and available to run publishing, planning, recreational, military, educational, and youth organizations and extra-parliamentary political movements, to reorganize government services, and to do innovative speech writing, film, radio, liturgy, philosophy, theology, literature, physical education, and spiritual renewal projects – in short, to create a different kind of France.[76]

Non-conformist influence went far beyond the direct readership of their publications as they worked at creating institutions which could engender elites of converts committed to fostering a post-liberal, post-republican political culture when the occasion inevitably presented itself. This network, however, included some volatile characters, and some incompatible personalities, who sometimes acted in unexpected ways. The new prominence and influence of the "new order" men did not necessarily produce the behaviour or have the political results one

might have anticipated from the patterns of behaviour we have discerned over the previous decade. The war severely tested these people
and produced some unexpected heroes and villains. But the movement as a whole gave some encouragement to the leadership of
France's mortal political enemies and hardly reinforced liberal democratic attitudes, or liberal democratic institutions.

### DEFEAT AND OCCUPATION IN FRANCE (1940)

On 10 June 1940 – ten years after the first Sohlberg meeting – Otto
Abetz invited a group of his key Belgian contacts,[77] newly liberated
from French prisons at his behest, for a celebratory lunch in his
German ambassador's quarters in Paris. Abetz's rise from humble
francophile drawing teacher, to advisor to the German foreign minister, to ambassador to Paris was to be paralleled by his Belgian friends'
rise from political marginality to central roles in building a place for
Belgium in a New European Order. Abetz's Belgians were soon employing confiscated media to shape a new politics, and directing new organizations meant to revitalize Belgian youth. Max Liebe, German
cultural attaché, continued on as Abetz's agent in occupied Brussels,
but did not find the Belgian Pétains or Quislings he might have expected (Spaak was out of the country and would only return to Belgium at
war's end to become one of the great unifiers of post-war Europe,
Henri de Man soon exiled himself to France, while Léon Degrelle
became a much-decorated Third Reich hero on the eastern front).
Liebe was, however, able to make New Order enthusiast Raymond de
Becker editor of Belgium's leading daily *Le Soir*, and Louis Carette, a
stalwart from de Becker's *L'Avant-Garde*, director of Radio Brussels.

On 10 July 1940, the day on which the French National Assembly
voted the Third Republic out of existence by confiding full powers in
Marshal Pétain, maverick radical Gaston Bergery presented a declaration to that body which condemned the war as having been unneces-
sary, unwise, and unconstitutional and demanded that the republic be
replaced by a new and radically different regime which would "collaborate" with Germany and institute a progressive, authoritarian, national and social "new order" at home. This proclamation recognized a
universal aspiration toward "a national form of socialism" and urged
that the new France have "a regime which corresponded with those of
continental Europe." The sixty-nine parliamentarians who signed
seemed eager to abandon all resistance to the Germans and were
"clearly in an indecent hurry to bury the Republic and replace it with
an authoritarian alternative."[78] Soon left-wing disciples of Bergery

were active in the Vichy administration, such as the well known non-conformist communitarians Louis-Emile Galey, Maurice Gait, Jean Maze, Georges Pelorson, Armand Petitjean, and François Gaucher, while Bergery himself was sent as the Marshal's ambassador to the Soviet Union.

At Vichy, Paul Baudouin, Action Française–style Catholic, named minister of foreign affairs, was charged with planning the new youth administration and took on Robert Loustau of ON as his chief of staff. Baudouin named administrators who were either Catholics, non-conformists, or, like Loustau, both. He particularly mustered Catholics from Robert Garric's *équipes sociales* and from the *scoutisme routier* (Rover Scouts) movement. Among the non-conformists called to Vichy were Paul Flamand and Pierre Schaeffer from the Poitevins editorial cooperative, which had founded Editions du Seuil. Flamand and Schaeffer created Radio Jeunesse – broadcasting daily propaganda aimed at the revitalization of young people – and the new regime's umbrella cultural organization, Jeune France.

The first secretary-general for youth, Georges Lamirand, had been involved with the Dominicans and Garric's *équipes sociales*, and, like many early enthusiasts for the National Revolution, he fused religious idealism with practical hands-on interests and abilities. Lamirand's ministry was able to orient the regime's tone and style, words and symbols, the whole of *maréchalist* discourse in the area of youth policy. From the French collaborationist and German point of view, Lamirand was too Catholic, but for non-conformists he represented just the right mixture of religious idealism and technical competence.

The Catholic/non-conformist milieu had several plans and projects for reconstructing French youth. Pétain mused about founding "maisons de jeunesse" in all the villages of the country, and Lamirand wanted obligatory "maisons des jeunes" in each canton. Catholics and non-conformists agreed that France needed new leaders, so these places were to cull France's new elites, who would be distinguished for ideological commitment, "spirituality," as well as for practical abilities. Masons, Jews, atheists, "effete intellectuals," communists, and other undesirables would be replaced by new men, with the spirit of converts and a new agenda.

Paul Flamand, an important pre-war bridge between Alexandre Marc's non-conformists and Catholic communitarians, headed the Jeune France organization in the occupied zone, with noted non-conformist writer and literary critic Maurice Blanchot as his literary director, and became influential in shaping an official state culture. This state culture would have a pedagogical elite create a whole new generation of young people in specialized regional schools, and these "new men," in turn, would spread their fresh communitarian zeal in all the workplaces, in every corner, of France and thus enkindle a new kind of national community, a community of communities.[79]

Another pre-war Catholic non-conformist was Radio Jeunesse co-founder Pierre Schaeffer, who came from *scoutisme*, and Editions du Seuil, and also displayed the *polytechnicien*'s technical expertise typifying X-Crise and *planistes* circles. Discharged from the army in 1940, Schaeffer learned that his comrades were at Vichy, where the national radio needed a youth program. Emmanuel Mounier urged Roger Leenhardt of *Esprit* to join him, and the latter discovered that Vichy's Secrétariat à la Jeunesse was run by a happy mixture of Christian activists and non-conformists charged with just that "neither right nor left" zeal to create a new generation which had electrified their network before the war.[80] Jeune France, founded to produce shows for Radio Jeunesse, soon became crucial to the non-conformists as Schaeffer and Flamand used its structures to build an ambitious cultural movement, directed by personalists and ON people, which would draw artists into a community experience and so produce new and better sorts of artists. The non-conformist network had ideas at the ready, for they had been working on the guidelines for creating a culture for the New Order for years.[81]

Jeune France did not intend brutal cultural expurgation but much of the Third Republic's artistic establishment, held to be tainted by its socialist, Jewish, Masonic, and foreign elements, was to be encouraged to early retirement. The new culture would neither be pluralistic nor fashioned by just anyone: Jeune France's members were to be neither foreigners nor Jews, recommended by two sponsors, and undergo a one-month trial period before being selected by the organization's administrative council. France's new official state culture was going to be virile, anti-liberal and anti-democratic without being Nazi or fascist; it would be more Catholic and spiritualist, populist but hierarchical, creative but traditionalist, innovative but rooted, Péguyist and communitarian.[82]

In December 1941 Schaeffer claimed that Jeune France had been able to assemble all the young artists and writers of France into a veritable community. Mounier, who had given much thought to the communitarian dimension of art before the war, thought that rather than living in ivory towers and being prostituted by the rich, artists would now experience *un retour paysan* to contact the hard realities of daily life and authentic human emotions and draw new riches and inspiration from the popular soul. Already in 1934 Mounier had envisaged neighbourhood *maisons des arts* allowing fresh kinds of artists to flourish in communities and transcend "snobbish [academic] aesthetics" and undertake "communitarian projects in which architects, painters, musicians, film-makers, theatre directors [would] aspire to a common goal [while accepting] free collective discipline." Mounier gave Schaeffer a list of comrades who could run Jeune France projects, including the poet Pierre Emmanuel, Albert Camus's mentor Jean Grenier, Garrone of the Ecole des Roches, the philosopher Gabriel Marcel, Henri-Irénée Marrou (folk musicologist as well as historian), François Berge (a Musée de l'Homme expert on folklore), and his old comrade Alexandre Marc (described as "very devoted to the youth movement"). A wary Vichy official described a wholesale infiltration of Esprit people at Jeune France.[83]

### THE KNIGHT-MONKS OF URIAGE

The establishment of a national leadership school, an Ecole Nationale des Cadres, at the end of the summer of 1940, with a coherent vision for providing new leaders for the transformation of France, was neither the isolated brainstorm nor the happy accident that alumni of Uriage later claimed. In fact the school was staffed by a number of individuals who had been preparing for such a pedagogical role for years – militant anti-communists, and anti-liberals, a disproportionate number of them serious Catholics. The new thinking about spiritual communities made up of "persons," not individuals, and producing "new men," formalized into the theories of communitarian personalism, was introduced at the Uriage school from the reviews *Esprit* or *Ordre Nouveau* and seemed the perfect rallying cry to many of their members,[84] a useful language for introducing the spiritual dimension into the movement for national renovation. Almost effortlessly, communitarian personalism became the watchword, even the unofficial ideology, of the national leadership school.

As we have seen, militant non-conforming Third Way revolutionaries, a number of them self-styled communitarian personalists, had joined in the insurrection of the revolutionary Right which nearly brought down the Third Republic during the riots of 6 February 1934: they were comfortable with the prospect of an anti-democratic, authoritarian, antipode to the republic.[85] There were conservative revolutionaries who described themselves as enemies of parliamentary democracy in the name of personalist democracy, as the representatives of a new youth politics, "neither Right nor Left" but dedicated to the advancement of the human person.[86]

Although many of their German friends[87] had been brutally put down by the Hitlerians by 1936, the French personalists had still felt themselves part of a growing transnational movement and were assured of the continuing fidelity of their friends back in Nazi Germany.[88] Bright young Third Way ideologues from the ON group had approached the large, mostly Catholic, veterans' organization, the Croix de Feu, to serve as theorists, advisors, and propagandists.[89] They worked with the "planists," trade-unionists interested in rationalizing the French economy and countering the rising power of the Communist unions.[90] ON activists had worked at linking certain Catholic youth groups with the secret *X-Crise* group of polytechnicians who were envisaging long-term, authoritarian political projects to achieve the modernization of France.[91] The Communists would be stopped in their tracks by a youth movement espousing authority and efficiency, with remedies for the abuses of capitalism. The new order in France would foster more humane, more personal, creative relationships in the workplace, and generate richer, more spiritual human communities than were possible in liberal democracies.

When France fell in June 1940, the network we have described of visionaries and enthusiasts for the Third Way in France already knew one another through the efforts of Alexandre Marc and his comrades at *Esprit, Ordre Nouveau,* and other reviews, and a variety of organizations, and had established a radical agenda touching on a range of issues. Once the parliament voted the republic out of existence, new leaders were ready to be named with the contacts and programs for what the Uriage elite school would call "the Revolution of the twentieth century"[92] – leaving liberal democracy behind for the first totally counter-revolutionary government France had known since 1789.

On October 1940, on his first official visit outside of Vichy, Marshal Philippe Pétain came to assist at the "Baptism" of the Pétain cohort of his government's new national leadership school, the Ecole Nationale Supérieure des Cadres, at the Château de la Faulconnière, near Vichy. The next month the school was moved to an even more impressive setting, the romantic Alpine Château Bayard, at St Martin d'Uriage above Grenoble. The Château d'Uriage then began producing new elites, new leaders for a whole network of new leadership schools, which were to form young people dedicated to national renewal and to the Marshal in what school publications soon described as a personalist spirit.[93] The Ecole Nationale Supérieure des Cadres d'Uriage was directed by a strikingly handsome and charismatic young officer from an old, noble, and very Catholic family of the southwest, Pierre Dunoyer de Segonzac. Although superior *chef* Segonzac had been close to the *Action Française,* his chaplaincy and Study Bureau were soon dominated by young Catholic progressives from the circle of the review *Esprit.*[94] Decisive to the ideological orientation of the school was the return from Portugal of another strong, wilful, and charismatic personality,

Hubert Beuve-Méry, who was made director of studies in early 1941. This professor of law, foreign correspondent, and former collaborator (with Emmanuel Mounier) in the propaganda office of Jean Giraudoux was a recognized authority on Nazi Germany and an admirer of Salazar's Portugal with a particular interest in the virtues of the *Mocidade portuguesa* (the Portuguese youth movement).[95] Young Beuve-Méry quickly demonstrated the qualities which would make him the most important person in post-war French journalism: devout and taciturn, but religiously innovative, Dominican-raised, this born leader was soon master of novices for a Uriage school become a laboratory, even a sort of think-tank, for the National Revolution.[96]

While Beuve-Méry had a certain interest in the personalist philosophizing of a Jean Lacroix or an Emmanuel Mounier, and a genuine interest in the heady theological speculation of the banned Jesuit evolutionist Teilhard de Chardin, "Beuve" was more a leader of men than a speculative thinker: he showed a particular interest in order communities of laymen in his effort to work out a "Règle de Communauté des Chefs" to provide efficacious guidelines for his teaching corps and their charges. Elites, authority and obedience, and the mystical élan of male community life were his watchwords, although he also displayed sympathy for a kind of *völkisch* federalism. Several of his ideas paralleled those of other lay orders established at the time, such as that Communauté group around the ex-Catholic become crypto-Nazi Raymond de Becker in Brussels, or in the ecumenical community founded by Protestant Brother Roger at Taizé near Cluny; the Société de Saint-Louis had already founded the Editions du Seuil and its leaders were now important in thinking out guidelines for a new culture in Vichy's cultural association Jeune France; the still largely unknown Ordre des compagnons de Péguy was also organizing amid the ruins.

At the height of its power and glory from the fall of 1940 to Christmas 1942, the key figures among three dozen or so permanent staff of the Uriage school – many of them of aristocratic background, as the "de" particle in their names suggested – worried about their lack of success in drawing peasants and workers into their orbit. Their relationships with the peasants of the Uriage area were not good either. One barrier to attracting working people was the emphasis on what Professor Jean-Jacques Chevallier, bicycling up into the mountains from his home in Grenoble each day, trumpeted as *l'ordre viril*; this entailed vigorous morning *décrassage* and a rather harsh program of physical training dictated by the instructor Vuillemin, a relatively anti-intellectual apostle of the "sweat and suffer" Hébertiste method of putting people into shape. Vuillemin's Uriage set people to climbing fences and rock faces, fording icy mountain streams, and embarking on gruelling Alpine ski expeditions. Visiting Pétain counsellors such as the Pétain hagiographer René Benjamin, and social thinker René Gillouin, found Uriage exalting, even a "Château de l'Ame" (Benjamin). Uriage lecturer and Jesuit Henri de Lubac synthesized this particular Uriage virility-emphasis with Christian values and traditions. Historian Joseph Hours provided historical perspective, while Paul Claudel read lyrical words on the heroism of Joan of Arc to the trainees.

The Uriage school's best-known publication offered uplifting advice and sophisticated matter for reflection to youth leaders around the country. Besides Beuve-Méry's exposition of the *Mocidade portuguesa, Jeunesse ... France!* published extensive analysis of Italian Fascist youth and then the Hitlerjugend by the distinguished young ethnologist Paul-Henri Chombart de Lauwe, all in the spirit of sifting and winnowing to find useful ideas. Although neither *Jeunesse ... France!* nor Uriage's mass-circulation, more popularizing *Marche, le Magazine Français* took positions on day-to-day political issues, both made it clear that Uriage found that the Free French who fought alongside the British in Syria, and at the battle of Suffren, in June and July 1941, had acted dishonourably.

It is not surprising that the Uriage school identified with the new Pétain government: while several Uriage, Esprit, or ON alumni or friends helped shape that government's social theory, youth initiatives, or propaganda organs,[97] the school had its own men throughout the Vichy apparatus, particularly in secondary administrative positions.[98]

Uriage's original and striking publications not only influenced the thinking of the few dozen young men who happened to be attending the school in a two- or three-week *stage* when they appeared, but they would be circulated through a cross-country network. The school also directed a whole variety of regional schools – at one point eleven in the free zone of metropolitan France alone – many of them lodged in *châteaux*, whose leaders were almost all Uriage alumni and intensely fraternal, loyal to the "Mother-School" and to Pierre Dunoyer de Segonzac, the *chef* of Uriage and his *moines-chevaliers*.[99] Segonzac and his men were much admired – were role models – in organizations like the Scouts and the Compagnons de France, and among the elite of young Alpine guides in Jeunesse et montagne. The Uriage alumni group, the Equipe Nationale d'Uriage, was well organized under Chombart de Lauwe, and the school regularly published and circulated not only practical Uriage training guidelines but doctrinal pronouncements, often personalist-oriented texts drawing from classic Esprit/ON formulations from the 1930s,[100] all of which reflected a determination to train new sorts of leaders, to place "new men," in all areas of national life.[101]

This was, in many respects, the fruition of the larger, Catholic, branch of the pre-war Third Way non-conformist movement: Uriage produced a new approach to ethnology, to psychology and to theology, as well as new thinking about physical education, new cultural symbols, art and theatre, and, in the end, in the guise of a "knight-monk," a "new man" – that dream of youth revolutionaries.[102] French young people were obliged to enrol in youth movements with strongly moralistic orientations, as Uriage rhetoric envisioned the transformation of France into a personalist community. While Uriage theorists and instructors condemned Nazi excesses, struggled against their critics and rivals within the Vichy government, and protected their Jewish friends, they continued to supply the guidelines, the conceptual apparatus, and the training (four thousand men passed through Uriage alone) for a very different kind of country – an authoritarian, technocrat-directed nation in which "individualistic" liberalism and "bourgeois" democracy would be abandoned, while moral and spiritual values would be officially fostered. While there were tensions with the occupying forces, and with powerful critics of Mounierist personalism such as government youth experts Henri Massis and Jean de Fabrègues, Uriage's new sort of France would certainly be more comfortable in a European New Order dominated by Nazi Germany than would a liberal democracy like the defunct Third Republic.[103]

Non-conformists had ranged from royalist authoritarians to neo-socialists before Marc and Mounier had brought them together on the eve of the war, setting the stage for their working together in places like the Uriage National Leadership School. But the sudden disappearance of communists and conformist parliamentarians, and the new possibilities for orienting Pétain's French state in a rapidly changing situation, encouraged the reappearance of the Right versus Left tendencies in alternative politics. Maurrassian Jean de Fabrègues, an inventor of the term "personalism" and pre-war non-conformist Right leader as editor of *Combat*, named director of Jeune France publications in the southern zone, always considered Mounier's personalism an unbridled, undisciplined sort of Bergsonian enthusiasm. Reappearing as a rival ideologue to Mounier, Fabrègues complained to non-conformist comrade Robert Loustau (ON ideologue become the foreign minister's chief of staff) that Mounier and fuzzy-minded adepts of his notions of "person" and "non-conformism" were grossly over-represented in the Vichy state apparatus. Despite his flattering of Mounier, Loustau had an authoritarian Catholic's impatience with

"Mounierism" and passed on Fabrègues's views to Pierre Pucheu, now one of the most influential of the pre-war non-conformists at Vichy.[104] Several of Mounier's colleagues recognized that Mounier generated a new breed of enthusiastic young people, but worried over what these would become in the long term.[105] They also suspected him of wanting to ignore other non-conformist groups and oversee the progressive transformation of the new generation of French youth in the hierarchical, top-down way of his Belgian comrades. As a Thomist philosophical realist, Fabrègues wanted less hope in progressive communitarian populism producing new sorts of human beings and more state authority with citizens mindful of their duties toward their national community. Thanks largely to Fabrègues's stratagem, *Esprit* was abruptly silenced for "its general tendencies" and Mounier eliminated from his influential positions in the search for the "new man" at Uriage and Jeune France. *Esprit*'s editor justly recognized the part of "the Pucheu-Marion group" (but not his comrade Fabrègues) in his setback.

After World War II, Mounier and the Uriage group built Resistance credentials from his silencing by Vichy – even if erstwhile non-conformist comrades, not Nazis or collaborationists, were behind it. In fact, Paul Marion and Pierre Pucheu, the new non-conformist heads of the propaganda and the interior ministries, were meeting daily with Henri Du Moulin de Labarthète, head of Pétain's civilian staff, and the three of them agreed that the National Revolution had to be rethought. So the two authoritarian non-conformists attacked the influence of the left-wing personalist non-conformist Mounier in the name of authoritarian, orthodox, neo-Thomist, Christian humanism, whose solid notion of human nature would be the best antidote to Germanic paganism. Soon National Revolution non-conformists (personalists and anti-personalists) got involved with Paul Marion's propaganda ministry, attempting to make the monthly *Idées*, run by René Vincent,[106] director of the regime's censorship services,[107] a serious and realistic voice of National Revolution thinking about the nature of the "new man," which would outclass the perceived undisciplined verbosity of the Uriage and *Esprit* groups. Marion also intended to eclipse the Ecole Nationale des Cadres d'Uriage above Grenoble with his own Ecole Nationale des Cadres Civiques at Mayet-de-Montagne, twenty-five kilometres from Vichy, training regional representatives and propagandists for the new French state. Besides Pucheu and Marion themselves, lecturers included non-conformists François Perroux and Maurice Gait, and the notorious anti-Semite Xavier Vallat. Pierre Laval visited the school in September 1942, and Pétain a month later.

Although soon blacklisting Mounier, Marion recruited willing old Mounier comrades to key positions in his propaganda machine. *Esprit* co-founder Louis-Emile Galey, director of propaganda for the Compagnons de France since August 1940, was named the regime's *directeur du cinéma*, over Robert Brasillach, a position Galey retained until August 1944. Galey became Marion's right-hand man, serving as his Paris-based representative for occupied France, where, aided by a former propaganda director of the PPF, he named Vichy's propagandists for the northern zone. Another Mounier intimate and Galey colleague, Jean Maze, an alumnus of *Esprit*, the Third Force, and Frontisme, directed the Compagnons movement until he quit in June 1941 annoyed at its overrepresentation of "Christian Democrats," and was put in charge of youth matters in Marion's ministry. So nonconformists and personalists were soon in key propaganda positions in France, as in Belgium, but after opposition to "Mounierism," the nonconformists around French propaganda minister Marion eventually came more from the pre-war royalist/Thomist/*Combat* milieu than the old *Esprit* network.

Jean de Fabrègues's band of authoritarian non-conformists particularly prized "prisoner" communitarianism. This form of revolutionary discourse had been devised by Jean Guitton, a former student comrade of Mounier, who wrote *Fondements de la communauté française* as a basic exposition of Vichy's communitarian aspirations. Fabrègues also helped initiate young right-wing non-conformist François Mitterrand to the Vichy political scene, remembering how the future president of the republic had zealously promoted the pre-war *Combat* in the Latin Quarter.[108] Fabrègues and Mitterrand, who spoke together to the major Chantiers de la Jeunesse meeting in Lyon in September 1942, were both ex-prisoners of war in Germany who believed that that defining communitarian experience was crucial to the National Revolution. Mitterrand recommended creating a new sort of elite in the chivalric spirit of the Service d'Ordre Légionnaire (SOL) and, like the later *Milice* (Vichy's official counter-insurgency force), Uriage, or *la Chaîne* groups,[109] "militias [*des milices*] which would allow us to transcend our fear of what might come out of the Germano-Russian conflict."[110]

Right-wing non-conformists like Mitterrand had ties to the tough, heavily armed anti-Communist conspirators of the Cagoule organization, several of whom who would go on to become new sorts of police in the *Milice*. While these people were rebellious non-conformists against liberal democracy, parliamentarianism, Fascism, and the Action française, their fanaticism began goading them into using brutal methods to force conformity to their own Pétainist alternative.[111] The review *Idées* marshalled authoritarian non-conformists by publishing well-known *Combat* writers but, rather than inventing something new, it orchestrated a "pamphletary discourse" inspired by that pre-war non-conformist dream of a "new man" which those legendary encounters, those conversions to non-conformism on the Sohlberg, had helped engender.

Some of the most powerful of Vichy's non-conformists, such as ON's Jean Jardin, Pierre Laval's wily chief of staff, kept up contacts with members of the French Resistance in London – before he left to manage important Vichy interests in Switzerland (and help provide a safe haven for Alexandre Marc). Others, such as Uriage *chef* Dunoyer de Segonzac, kept in touch with the anti-German but relatively pro–National Revolution *Combat* resistance network. Once again the leaders of movements considered mutually hostile were networking: there were secret *reseaux*, the La Chaine and Uriage rule-bound orders, and a discreet connecting of think tanks whose activities were oriented by an inner circle in touch with a centralized strategy and command posts.[112]

Both Paul Marion's propaganda ministry and the Commissariat aux Prisonniers supported *Idées*' fashioning National Revolution propaganda and promoting the "white fascism" of Fabrègues, which was alleged to be neither racist nor totalitarian but rather an alternative politics to build a new youth along the lines of the Belgian, Quebec nationalist, Salazar, Uriage, or José Antonio/Spanish models. So whether of Left or Right, whatever their differences, they put forward a host of ideas, a "pamphletary discourse," which helped orient the makeshift French National Revolution into an imposed, "top-down" operation which would neither summon forth a mass party nor violently seize power. Their revolution really consisted in a few months of establishing the bases of institutions which were going to build new men, which looked good on paper and had considerable impact on at least some of their first novices, but which soon ran into a host of problems. The French National Revolution was quickly torn by rivalries for prestige and authority among the diverse clans, personalities, and constituencies, and this led to talk, both among French non-conformists and in the highest government circles, of its collapse as early as August 1941.[113]

## THE LIBERATION: NEW MEN, WITH POWER AND INFLUENCE

A "Grande Fête," a national assembly of young people grouping as many as fifteen hundred youth leaders and young people from across France, was held with a pageantry worthy of Leni Riefenstahl from 31 July to 1 August 1942 on the plateau d'Uriage. It celebrated the baptism of the first (and last) intensive, six-month training session, and may be considered a high point in the life of the school. By that time Dunoyer de Segonzac had already had to defend himself in the face of critics at a meeting of the Conseil National. The return of Laval to power on 18 April 1942 had been correctly seen as a bad omen and, after the occupation of all of France by the Germans, and in the wake of a more and more open power struggle for the direction of French youth, the Uriage school was closed by the Laval government at the end of December 1942. The *Milice* were given the Château Bayard and its facilities and established their own, even more militantly Catholic, leadership school under the eccentric Acadian Thomist philosopher Dr de la Noue du Vair (whose mystical agenda included a struggle to the death against the communists and the restoration of the king). The militia's leadership school would function in the Château d'Uriage until it was attacked by the Resistance on 5 July 1944. Meanwhile the original Uriage network – its key members united in a secret order[114] – remained very much intact, and in a particularly close relationship with the Resistance movement *Combat* directed by Uriage friend Henry Frenay.[115]

At the Liberation, Hubert Beuve-Méry and the men and women of the Uriage Order had friends in all sorts of important positions and dreamed of making Grenoble capital of France.[116] Members of the Uriage network were present at the crucial discussions concerning the confiscated facilities of France's most distinguished pre-war daily newspaper, *Le Temps*, and, not surprisingly, proposed their being taken over by its former disgruntled employee, their old novice master. Under Hubert Beuve-Méry's firm, brilliant, and selfless directorship, the resurrected newspaper, now called *Le Monde*, became "another Uriage" – communal asceticism, personalist doctrine, and all. The post-war vitality of *Le Monde*, of Editions du Seuil, and of the revived *Esprit* were signs that former Uriage cadres, and friends of Uriage, were going to remain at the centre of post-war French intellectual and political life. Personalism and existentialism, the two great intellectual fads in post-war France, were no longer simply new and exciting ideas in the tiny circle of the Sohlbergkreis, or the Château Bayard, as they had been years earlier. The Uriage group and/or the personalist movement contributed some important ideas and some key men to the establishment of the Ecole Nationale d'Administration, to François Mitterrand's Socialist party,[117] to the federalist cause,[118] to the new post-war *tiers-mondisme*, and to the European movement in general.[119] In Poland the *Znak* group, from the immediate post-war period, claimed personalism in its role as parliamentary opposition. Key figures in the contemporary political transformation of Poland, including Prime Minister

Tadeusz Mazowiecki and Pope John Paul II, have had long ties with several members of the Catholic wing of the old Uriage group.[120]

Personalism was, then, something quite new and exciting in the early 1930s when it was discovered by those young Frenchmen and Germans of the Sohlbergkreis. Later in the Château Bayard, it had an important but somewhat paradoxical and controversial role during the war, only to emerge with great influence on certain European elites afterwards. The Franco-German youth movements of the early 1930s invented a language, an approach, which proved useful to these prophets of a very different kind of France, and a very different kind of Europe.

### PRELIMINARY CONCLUSION

A clandestine pre-war network among determined rebels, as revealed in newly available sources, did much to configure the Vichy National Revolution. The Sohlberg and Belgian seaside bonding experiences passed on electricity to Paris and Brussels, and inspired hopes for a new sort of person living in a new sort of European community. Those initiated found individualism and capitalism, materialism, Germanophobia, and ethnic rivalries outdated and destructive. German philosophical discoveries like existentialism (called *Existenzphilosophie* then) and phenomenology had helped point the way to the new European sense of self, rooted in defining community experiences.[121]

The early Vichy National Revolution partook of a more general communitarian "revolt against individualism and against liberal democracy."[122] Non-conformists encouraged moral and spiritual renewal as well as a general, progressive search for a "new man." Unfortunately, this soon led, in the circumstances, to a rigid authoritarianism and the establishment of an exclusionary society.

Their example illustrates the direct continuity between the German Conservative Revolution's utopian youth movement and Vichy France's right-revolutionary aspirations. It shows how this idealistic current passed first through Belgium, as German agents astutely saw that Catholic Belgium was the soft heart of republican Francophonie for buoyant, spiritualized national socialist ideology. The francophone communitarians were often good and idealistic, selfless, giving, future-oriented men who became (and remained) convinced, like Alexandre Marc, that original German national socialism represented a basically healthy reaction against that modern sense of weightlessness and breakdown of community which liberal individualism and brutal free-market capitalism had engendered. Despite the follies of Hitler, and his unfortunate racialism and violence, they held that national socialism was not intrinsically perverse: its fusing of ethnic and socialist communitarianism, "a national form of socialism," as the 1940 Bergery declaration put it, was a universal aspiration, as was the search for a "new man." After the horrors of World War II, those who had shared in this hopefulness found it inordinately difficult to explain to succeeding generations.

# 8 Alexandre Marc's Memories and the European New Right

Alexandre Marc's memory, though elephantine, was selective.[1] His memory-sharing disquieted his compatriots,[2] but he was as appreciative of historians situating him at the origins of personalism and of the French-German youth contacts of the early 1930s as he was hostile to those attributing him a central role in the formation of a French fascist ideology. For Marc, Harro Schulze-Boysen was the Germany which might have been: the dashing, selfless, German youth leader who shared the élan of the Sohlberg only to turn against lunatic Hitler and face martyrdom. Otto Abetz, who joined the Nazi party and served Hitler's imperialistic policies, was an unfaithful friend, better left undiscussed. Schulze-Boysen became progressively more important, Abetz less important, as Marc consciously or unconsciously fashioned his personal history for later generations so as to present himself as an architect of resistance to Hitlerite hegemony rather than a collaborator.

Marc's considerable archives – essential sources, unknown till now, for this reconstruction of his history – gave new life to what he had always remembered, while engendering in him involuntary memories which resurfaced at the rediscovery of documents, and were shaped by his notion of what the public at large should know. While she lived, his wife insisted on the unvarnished truth, but important materials may have disappeared after Marc's anti-materialist conversion experience, precipitated by unrequited love, made him into a "new man," determined to completely obliterate his Jewish identity, to be French, but still to be situated in his Russian past. In hosting lectures, conferences, and seminars, Marc invariably won the gratitude and good will of his guests, as he recalled the origins of modern European federalism in the noble, beautiful ideal at the beginning of national socialism,[3] a key to understanding the history of his generation.[4] He was less prone to discuss his responsibility, or that of his Ordre Nouveau (ON) movement, for the "neither right nor left" anti-materialist and anti-individualist fascist communitarianism which informed the Vichy government's early National Revolution.

Alexandre Marc's conversion to a committed anti-materialism defined a life of high-minded, selfless vocation, and this strong and authoritarian old man gathered sympathetic listeners to hear colourful anecdotes about it. Some of these tales had more of the ring of truth about them than others: Marc claimed to have had no Jewish cultural background, yet documents of the 1930s reveal it as one of his preoccupations; he offered increasingly detailed memories of comrades who were among Hitler's enemies, but, more and more, overlooked encounters with famous Nazis or collaborators.[5]

All of the non-conformists were Nietzscheans – several were authors of books on him – and the Nietzschean Marc's style was sharp, eloquent, and forceful (in contrast to his turgid, unrelievedly abstract essays on metaphysics). Marc's favourite essays from Dandieu (lauding the "intelligence sword") reflected a Stefan Georg Kreis Nietzscheanism[6] of the poetic man who "knew" the shape of the modern world better than the masses. ON mathematicians, architects, and engineers had met in an artist's studio on the Left Bank, bent on entering the circles of the powerful.[7] Several were nostalgic modernists: Jean Jardin loved both trains in the countryside and the *ancien regime*, and so helped run an efficient transportation system which came to be used to restore Old France by deporting alien human refuse to the north. Marc and Robert Aron, forgetting their own cultural origins, more French than the French, allergic to the "Jewishness" of the "American cancer," numbered among that Jewish or half-Jewish elite who admired German culture, and seemed deaf to rumours of the Holocaust.[8] Alain de Benoist, self-proclaimed heir of the non-conformists, also maintains lawyerly silences on this subject.

Fluent in German, admiring the new German philosophy, ON Nietzscheans reproached the barbarians while involuntarily admiring them, as when Marc blamed Hitler for being not sufficiently revolutionary, and thereby betraying his initial promise. Although it was recently alleged that "we still have no record of convinced men and women abandoning Hitler, because he had betrayed the high ideals of Nazism,"[9] Alexandre Marc demonstrates the contrary. Marc and his comrades tried to transmit the best and highest ideals of original German national socialism to France and Belgium, particularly after the sudden defeat of 1940. For Marc, Mounier, and several of their comrades, the spiritualist socialist and Christian Charles Péguy represented the noblest tendencies of a truly French national socialism.

The high ideals in Nazism betrayed by Hitler, perceived by Carl Schmitt and Martin Heidegger, as well as by the Stefan Georg Kreis,[10] touched a deep and secret region of the heart. Marc affirmed the "spirit of 1930s generation" for the rest of his career: Nietzscheanism, communitarian spirituality, and male bonding. It was youthful, anti-bourgeois, anti-egalitarian, anti-materialist, and so anti-American, anti-feminist, youth-oriented, thriving in gangs: young, male, and elitist. Not one woman is cited in the literature of the period as representing the spirit of the 1930s; only a few are decribed as non-conformists – and they are secretaries or relatives, marginal figures. The spirit of the 1930s was also truculent, devoted to *chefs*, against tradition and modernist but also anti-modern, and Eurocentric. Some of Marc's comrades described themselves as promoting an anti-fascist fascism and in the context of the times that made some sense. The non-conformists of the 1930s could also occasionally be anti-Semitic, while remaining responsive to avant-garde painting, architecture, and art, and trying to create meaning in a world after the Death of God. They were proud of their anti-materialistic non-conformity to bourgeois society, conventional Christianity and morality, and anti-feminist assumptions, and of their allergy to the basic values of liberal democratic political culture. The non-conformists encompassed the Right[11] and the Left,[12] and also self-styled national socialists[13] who wanted to leave the old Right and Left behind.

In all camps, Heidegger ("our Aristotle" for the young Germans) represented the cutting edge of philosophy, directly in the Nietzschean tradition. (Jean-Paul Sartre, convinced that the world had dramatically changed, lectured on the implications of Heidegger's thinking – which he had translated into French – to his fellow French prisoners of war in Germany in 1940.) Marc could envisage Heidegger's writing, translated into French, helping to sow the seeds of a home-grown, French, existentialist philosophy harmonious with a distinctive, home-grown, national socialist ideology in France.

After Hitler came to power, the generation of 1930 began to redefine the generational experience as a search for a new politics, unprecedented, domestically produced.[14] Alexandre Marc, definitively converted by his experiences with young Germans, remembered these German comrades as having been passionately interested in French ideas, while his memories of his own enthusiasm for German ideas and comportment became more selective.

While Marc remembered that it was encountering St Augustine in the reading room of the Bibliothèque Nationale that had made him a Christian, his diaries revealed his unrequited passion and desperate efforts to avoid expatriation, and his marrying a deeply rooted French Christian, making populist rooting central to his anti-materialist philosophy. Like other Jewish converts drawn toward Catholicism and/or national socialism, he was a selfless, sincere, dedicated revolutionary ... desperately avoiding deportation. It was only natural that he tended to remember what was altruistic rather than what was self-interested about his experiences.

Marc and his comrades tended to value fidelity, generosity, and courage as noble Christian qualities rather than kindness, compassion, and humility, and it is not surprising that Marc seems to have been dropped by most traditional Christian clergy after the war. Marc was of a generation of Nietzschean Catholics for whom friends[15] were more important than the institutional Church, who found people who wrote about Jesus[16] more interesting than Christians, and who saw nothing fundamentally incompatible between fascism or national socialism and the gospel teachings. Marc reconciled Nietzsche and Christianity by creating Otto Neumann, a pseudonym allowing a self-conscious Russian Jew to become an influential German Catholic communitarian theologian. Marc wrote much on reconciling Nietzsche and Christianity, but what remains is his zealous Christianity married to the German youth movement, the conviction that their melding could inspire, could change, the world.

Nietzsche encouraged the non-conformism of people with what he called "world-destroying thoughts" and so led ON architects, engineers, artists, mathematicians, composers, philosophers, writers, and theatre-producers to plan a new sort of Europe. When, after World War II, Nietzscheanism meant something different, they began to adapt their collective memory to fit the new circumstances.[17] These young male Germanophiles were deferential to born *chefs*, respectful of elite leadership, high culture, and art, contemptuous of materialists, communists, and other egalitarians, but tolerant of a "virilized" form of Christianity. Although many of them came from relatively well off families, and had upper-class educations, they had limited employment prospects in Depression France, but assumed that a Zarathustra could reveal the meaning of the modern world[18] and catapult them to directing roles, positions of serious responsibility.

Marc's generation experienced conversions: to Catholicism or to Marxism, to non-conformism or anti-materialism, if not to fascism. What Jacques Maritain and his circle found in Benedictine monasteries, Marc and the non-conformists found in the German Youth groups: a warm community of the chosen few, a tasteful setting and sexual purity, some avant-garde art and architecture, shared interest in certain basic inspirational texts, disdain for the degrading, vulgarly materialistic modern world.[19] There were generational spokesmen,[20] a celebrating of selected artists,[21] and nostalgia for the uniform faith of the Middle Ages. There was also a collective interest in new varieties of fascism and national socialism, and the search for a "new man." Marc converted from Russian to French, then from Jew to Catholic, then from bourgeois dandy to anti-materialist revolutionary non-conformist, in his search for a "new manhood."

Marc's conversion did not seem out of the ordinary for the times, but Jacques Maritain's contemporary efforts to convert people like Psichari, Gide, or Cocteau seem odd to our post-Freudian era in which exclusive, devoutly spiritual male circles, condemnations of homosexuality, and interest in the journals of individuals' conversion experiences have all become uncommon.[22]

Marc, the convert, had contempt for the "old man," and he and his fellow personalists soon tried to involve others in their communitarian, fraternal bonding. Marc's own conversion experience cemented unshakeable male friendships, and constituted a demarcating event more important than those colourful Russian anecdotes that he recounted as his background. He then lived as a faithful and committed member of the federalist/personalist/non-conformist network planning and plotting for a new kind of converted Europe for the rest of his life – a life which was a graphic illustration of the way ideas and values can arise and be propagated very differently from the way in which people prefer to remember.

A recent illustration of the problematic way in which Marc is remembered was provided by the UNESCO commemoration of Emmanuel Mounier from 5–6 October 2000 in Paris, which, more than a half-century after the death of Marc's comrade and *Esprit* co-founder, strictly limited the discussion of Mounier's or Marc's role in the origins of any sort of a French spiritualistic or "white" fascism; the gathering preferred to venerate and consecrate the exclusive memory of Mounier, who had, in fact, become a controversial historical personality. By 2000, Mounier represented for a generation their own purest, most generous and noble aspects. One had to be sensitive about that generation's memories of Mounier, particularly when archival materials such as Marc's contradicted the "Rémond school" thesis that France had been largely immune to fascism, or that Mounier had no involvement with the "white fascism" of the Vichy regime.

In 1944 Emmanuel Mounier led a number of former non-conformists, particularly Uriage school people, to refound *Esprit* as a progressive, Left-Catholic review interested in dialogue with the communists. *Esprit* worked closely with the Editions du Seuil publishing house directed by Jeune France's Paul Flamand, Beuve-Méry's *Le Monde* and *Le Monde Diplomatique*, and the other ex–National Revolution radical Left-Catholics who published *Témoignage Chrétien*. The old Vichy revolutionist anti-individualist ideology was repackaged as a new, Resistance-inspired, radical progressive Catholicism, and peddled in the rest of the world, particularly the USA and Canada, as the cutting edge of new Catholic thinking; it figured importantly in the background to the Second Vatican Council. Mounier, not Marc, became known as the founder of personalism and spokesperson for the generation of 1930.

François Mitterrand was another strikingly successful and influential figure on the Left, while discreetly faithful to his right-wing Barrèsian and royalist Catholic roots. Youthful supporter of the "Young Right's" pre-war *Combat*, leader of Pétain's prisoners' movement, Mitterrand – like Emmanuel Mounier – changed his image from that of zealous Pétainist into Resistance hero. He then called for a Third Way communitarian socialist France between the Stalinist East and the capitalist West, helping to create a powerful alternative to the French Communist party.

It was usually in a religious context, then, that an entire generation in the 1960s encountered, as "new theology" popular in progressive Catholic circles, the French non-conformism and communitarian personalism which are the subject of this book. Intellectuals from around the world were studying in the Murs Blancs community at Chatenay-Malabry, near Paris, a circle in which North Americans (even those involved with Dorothy Day's radical *Catholic Worker* movement) were suspect as tainted by the enemy: bourgeois capitalist culture.

Paulette Mounier, widow of Emmanuel (who died in 1950) and a venerated figure in progressive Catholic circles, set the tone during the 1960s at the Murs Blancs with Jean-Marie Domenach, Resistance hero and editor of what was now known as the avant-garde Left-Catholic review *Esprit*, become leader in the French Resistance against American economic and cultural hegemony. Commuting from the leafy Chatenay-Malabry community to *Esprit*'s offices near St Germaine des Pres on a black BMW motorcycle, Domenach welcomed a few anti-American Americans[23] and wary students from communist Poland. Dispassionate academic approaches to the Esprit movement, their archives, and Mounier's heritage were not encouraged in what was known to be one of France's several "chapels."[24] Besides the intellectual biography of Mounier by Domenach, a doctorate on his thinking was written and published under the direction of the prominent *Le Monde* literary critic Pierre-Henri Simon. A well-disposed Sciences Po historian was also in residence in the Murs Blancs community, writing an in-house history of the *Esprit* movement as of the mainstream Catholic Left, with the support of the movement and its related publishing houses and publications, such as Editions du Seuil and *Le Monde*. Mme Mounier ensured that the writings of well-disposed historians would have more documentation than rival interpretations; friendly historians skirted the subject of the links between the German youth movement and the non-conformists,[25] not to mention links with the European New Right (this was years before Domenach would become publicly involved with Alain de Benoist and the GRECE group.)

The taboo on the Germans included one on Alexandre Marc's role in inventing the French communitarianism of the 1930s. Marc, however, could document his and the German influence not only on Esprit and Mounier but also on a whole generation of non-conformists, and wanted his facts on record. His former colleague Jean de Fabrègues made special efforts to set the record straight about the Jeune Droite group. Because the history of the non-conformists involved the reputations of important political figures, and not just Charles de Gaulle and François Mitterrand, the highly centralized and discreetly politicized French academic establishment dealt gingerly with this subject.[26]

Modern Catholicism was altered by the invention of fascism, by the novel fascist experience. The origins of fascism can be traced from the counter-revolutionary thinking of early nineteenth-century reactionary Joseph de Maistre[27] to the radical anti-liberalism, authoritarianism, and anti-modernism of Louis Veuillot and Pope Pius IX, and then via the militant nationalism of Charles Maurras and the Action Française to the pontificate of Pius XII and the communitarian personalism which flourished in Vichy's National Revolution. Personalism was originally formulated by young disciples of an aging Charles Maurras who were looking for more dynamism, aggressivity, and political militancy. Their 1930s Personalist discourse was formulated to help precipitate anti-modern, anti-individualistic conversion experiences in a new generation impatient with the political Right and political Left of their day. It was proposed by contentious, self-styled non-conformists – most of them Catholics – as a the best ideology for a "neither right nor left" French New Order during the German occupation. It attracted young and old, activists and intellectuals – even traditionalist philosophers such as Reginald Garrigou-Lagrange, a Dominican authority on Aquinas and mentor of the young Karol Wojtyla. It was repackaged after World War II as a daring, progressive "new theology" suitable for dialogue with communists and helping to inspire the Second Vatican Council. As a quasi-official philosophy for the world's Catholics during the pontificate of John Paul II, it retained an ambiguous relationship to the political culture of European fascism.

Karol Wojtyla, personalist philosopher, populist anti-Stalinist, and benevolent authoritarian, was, as an anti-Marxist Third Way communitarian, an anti-liberal liberator of Poland. This anti-feminist devotee of the Virgin Mary, in his reverence for the European heritage and dislike of the modern world, advanced the process of canonization of harshly reactionary popes and pro-fascist Catholic clerical leaders such as Maximilien Kolbe and Monsignor Josemaria Escriva de Balaguer, founder of the *Opus Dei*. John Paul II is intelligent, intensely ascetic and spiritual, empathic and anti-materialistic, and like the original non-conformists, often best understood by an elite who grasp the implications of his positions or those with the psychological makeup to sympathize with his implacable hostility toward the women's movement and libertine sexual behaviour.

The personalism of John Paul II is hardly a dramatic popular success: in spite of it Catholic priests resign to marry, leaving more room for homosexuals in the Catholic priesthood. Despite the claims that obedience to dogma brings true liberty, there isn't much free debate of the troubled past or the contentious present. Despite the lessons learned from World War II, a marginal, repressive, and unhealthy politico-religious culture endures, even expands, in some parts of the world. It isn't really New, and it isn't really Order.

## ALAIN DE BENOIST AND THE EUROPEAN NEW RIGHT, NON-CONFORMISM AND THE FASCIST HERITAGE

Alain de Benoist, leader of the European New Right intelligentsia when Marc died in February 2000, admires Alexandre Marc and the non-conformists of the 1930s, and, like Marc, received an essay prize from the Académie française for a synopsis of his anti-materialist, Europeanist positions. De Benoist, too, liked the idea of a national Bolshevism, as, for him, liberalism and capitalism (particularly as represented by the United States) could be worse threats to Western man than Communism, and, as he liked to say, it was better to wear the helmet of the Red Army than spend your life eating hamburgers in Brooklyn.[28] Soon some prominent leftists[29] demonstrated sympathetic interest in him and the European New Right intelligentsia.[30] The political ambiguities of non-conformism, its positive and negative historical legacy, help explain this.

Non-conformism, nurtured by early national socialists, produced administrators of German-occupied Europe (and then, after World War II, astute managers of Europe's memory). While not always engendering collaborators with Hitler's New Order, it did foster an erudite and sophisticated consciousness of the superiority of white male European culture,[31] as well as of the well-foundedness of several national socialist or fascist ideas. Non-conformism's "crisis ideology" – assuming that conflict between peoples was a law of life – justified police-state measures against communists or North African immigrants, hereditary enemies who infiltrated the centre of the region's oldest cities. Socialists, liberal democrats, might build better schools to teach republican values, the modern Western sense of community, the feminine, and the self, but non-conformists assumed superior cultures must always defend their heritage against menacing "others" – an outlook with deep and ancient roots. Demographic and crime statistics, too, encouraged measures normally unthinkable in a liberal democracy, not in conformity with the principle that all people are created equal. Eurocentric non-conformity to enlightened values encouraged exclusionary and genocidal behaviour: enemies of the European heritage had to be repressed in the name of high culture; the condemning of Hitler and all genocides did not prevent reaffirmation of racial or cultural supremacy.

Non-conformism and nationalism could be united in their empathy for original, pure, national socialism. Original national socialism, ethnic pride manifested in a populist, socialist form, engendered both fascist, authoritarian regimes and liberation movements against fascism – but not historians lucid about a non-conformist experience which remained complex, tragic, paradoxical, framed in confusing terms, and difficult to explain.

When fascism and most of the intellectual Right was discredited after World War II, non-conformism continued in European federalism, de Gaulle's RPF, and progressive Catholicism. In 1968 Alain de Benoist and forty associates formed GRECE – Groupement de recherche et d'etude pour la civilisation européenne (Group for Research and Studies on European Civilization) – one of the most sophisticated think tanks for the non-conformist Right since the ON of the 1930s. Nietzschean de Benoist looked back to Alexandre Marc and ON for inspiration and parentage,[32] for a tradition of resistance to egalitarianism. He made cordial overtures toward Marc, and soon achieved a notoriety beyond that which Marc himself ever attained. The main tenets of GRECE were remarkably similar to those of ON; so were the paradoxes and tensions in the two movements.

Like ON, de Benoist's European New Right infiltrated elites, furnished second-level administrators, rather than trying to construct a popular base. De Benoist, said to maintain the best private library in Paris, published abstruse reflections, while calmly waiting for history to turn in his favour. People of colour and women would remain noticeable for their absence in GRECE, while the American free-enterprise circus and melting pot was a "cancer" worse than Stalinism. GRECE people were bright, articulate, anti-materialistic, and sure of their merit, even while their highbrow racial and cultural ideas were justifying lowbrow behaviour. As in ON, a shared, unspoken bond was often sympathy for original, pure, national socialism.

GRECE, the foremost movement of the European New Right, held its 1968 founding meeting in the Nice of the extreme-right *pieds noirs* and long-serving mayor Jacques Médecin. Both Alexandre Marc's CIFE (Centre international de formation européenne) and de Benoist's GRECE were supported by "Jacquo" – suspected of financial corruption, and a bitter enemy of the Left. Nice, like neighbouring Monaco, supported highbrow culture which did not directly challenge capitalism and justified strong-arm methods against undesirables, especially Moslems. Marc's federalism defended the regional heritage of Nice, and of the nearby french-speaking Aosta valley in Italy, thereby appealing to the locals – if not to those North African intruders doing their gruelling, dusty work under the hot Mediterranean sun. The nation-state, with its egalitarianism, liberty, and fraternity, undermined established regional structures with legislation coercing people to become more equal.

The GRECE movement had, by the late 1970s, penetrated various universities, mass media outlets, and publishing houses; de Benoist even published in *Le Figaro*. One had to go back to the non-conformists of the 1930s to find such a sophisticated, intelligent right-wing intelligentsia, and the GRECE group claimed to be the intellectual heirs of those very non-conformists, the German conservative revolutionaries, the inter-war anarcho-syndicalists, and those revolutionary right and fascist political theorists on whom de Benoist was a respected authority. European New Right (ENR) intellectuals, claiming to be among the few contesting liberal democracy and global capitalism, took it for granted that the Right produced the most analytically rigorous, intellectually coherent, and challenging ideas of the post–World War II era.[33]

The ENR drew on both the revolutionary Right and the New Left as they tried, like the old non-conformists, to incorporate features of both. But unlike the traditional French Right, de Benoist and the ENR rejected clerical and assimilationist Catholic nationalism for an anti-religious, life-affirming Nietzscheanism, which rejected both the religious and secular Christian heritage. The ENR surprised observers by being pagan, anti-Christian, and professedly anti-Western.[34] Historian René Rémond, categorizing the different political Rights in France, set historical thinking for a generation when he claimed that France had been particularly immune: there never had been a French fascism. De Benoist responded that he didn't "identify with any of René Rémond's 'Rights'": he represented a school of thought which rose above "obsolete divisions" – just as had the original non-conformists and national socialists.

The ENR thinkers, as a loose, heterogeneous school of cultural thought rather than a centrally coordinated movement, tried to open intellectual, political, and economic elites to alternative, counter-hegemonic conceptions of the world. Successful revolutions, for the ENR, have first overturned the spirit and culture of their ages, and GRECE's lofty metapolitical rhetoric has been serviceable, given the general public's negative attitude toward fascism and Nazism. The ENR's school of cultural thought, despite its origins in ultra-nationalism, the revolutionary Right, and fascism, does not unsettle with its long-term effort to win hearts and minds. For diehard Pétainists, and others sympathetic to the goals of Vichy's authoritarian and exclusionary National Revolution or "white fascism," a new post-liberal, anti-materialist order promised something other than hated individualistic and materialistic self-indulgence, the mixing of races, the fatuous liberal parliamentary game, and unbridled capitalism. ON had shown that even in liberal democratic France, anti-liberal and anti-democratic elite networks can suddenly appropriate power. After World War II, elements of the revolutionary Right surfaced in de Gaulle's RPF and among François Mitterrand's Socialists, although the French Revolutionary Right was supposed to endure only among isolated monarchist counter-revolutionaries, ex-Vichyites, Catholic integralists, extreme nationalists, Third Way political visionaries, neo-fascists, and neo-Nazis. And the French revolutionary Right looked like an irrelevant, loose collection of quarrelsome and eccentric personalities, with fragmented ethnic backgrounds. In this context, GRECE wanted to change people's ideas and world-views, basic values, ways of thinking.

De Benoist saw ideas shaping the world, for "like Herder, I believe firmly that the history of ideas is the key to the history of deeds. The great changes ... are ... those that have affected our intellectual life. Aristotle's revolution, Copernicus's revolution and Kant's revolution were without doubt more important than the French Revolution of 1789 or the Russian Revolution of 1917, which were ... the continuations of previous ideological transformations."[35] In 1994, he told the American New Left journal *Telos* that he would continue to "contribute to the development of ideas and wait for their impact." In this same period, the German New Right *Thule-Seminar*'s slogan was "Nothing can stop the arrival of a Europe of study groups," and a British ENR leader observed: "No Revolutionary could hope to change society permanently unless the educational system has been replaced with one with new priorities ... Education is political or it is nothing."[36] The ENR's notion of education, like the ON's, was political in so far as it was antithetical to the values of liberal democracies.

The ENR approached cultural and intellectual elites because the masses were not always receptive to their new ideas and arcane metapolitical exegesis. In contrast, decades earlier, ON had had tireless networker Marc to propagandize *Sept* and *Esprit*, and thus the convents and parishes of France, Belgium, and Quebec.[37] On their lofty metapolitical perch, ENR theorists observe the rise and fall of peoples and civilizations, the newest technology, modernity's effects on the quality of life, the evolution of communities – not mere daily political or military happenings such as the vulgar populist stratagems of the fascists, Nazis, and Le Penists. De Benoist and the ENR theorists warned of the universalist, egalitarian, and materialist poisons in liberalism and socialism, urging return to authentic pagan, Indo-European roots. De Benoist wrote in 1978: "The principal danger remains, more than ever, uniformity, robotization: universalism."

Alain de Benoist's denunciation of modern societies seemed humanistic, even Christian, as he admiringly cited the pastor Herder, the spiritualistic non-conformists (Marc, Thierry Maulnier, Bernard Charbonneau, Georges Bataille), and even North American Christian communitarians like Christopher Lasch, Alasdair McIntyre, and Charles Taylor.[38]

## FEDERALISM

In *Vu de droite*, de Benoist described federalism as preserving the piquant variety of peoples:

I have travelled widely on several continents. The *joy* experienced during a journey comes from seeing the differentiated ways of living which are still well rooted ... a different people live according to their own rhythm ... a different skin-colour, another culture, another mentality ... they are proud of their *difference* ... this sort of diversity is the wealth of the world, and ... egalitarianism is killing it ... it is important ... to affirm a personality which is unlike any other, to defend a heritage ... what one is. And this implies a head-on clash both with a pseudo-anti-racism which denies differences and with a dangerous racism which is ... the rejection of the Other ... of diversity.[39]

This seems sensitive, intelligent, and civilized, but if you don't like your "different" Third World neighbours, de Benoist also provides highbrow grounds for taking exclusionary measures against them, to cut off immigration to protect a Western political culture engendered by white, western European stock.[40] Contemporary ENR intellectuals, although endorsing most of the New Left (May 1968) ideals, reject "homogenizing" Westernized multicultural, multiracial societies, and de Benoist shocked even some in GRECE with his declaration about the Red Army and hamburgers in Brooklyn. The ENR stresses the cultural/metapolitical dimension as fundamental for politics, and the "right to difference" of communities and individuals, as did ON, but Marc's group – in a world threatened by Stalin – had a network of philosophers, architects, essayists, army officers, religious leaders, historians, technocrats, media and business executives, and public administrators behind them.

Like the 1930s non-conformists, de Benoist warned of "soft totalitarianism": "there are two forms of totalitarianism ... both dangerous. Eastern totalitarianism imprisons, persecutes and kills the body, but it maintains hope. Totalitarianism in the West creates happy robots. Such totalitarianism air-conditions hell and kills the soul."[41] When Raymond Aron called de Benoist's thinking national socialist or fascist, de Benoist answered (as Marc would have) that he was opposed to all genocides and that all societies, whatever their politics, required self-assured, well-trained, self-disciplined, and sophisticated leaders, with a communitarian and spiritual goal in life. If the Holocaust was of the very essence of Nazism, de Benoist, rejecting all genocides, claimed – like Marc or the Strassers – to be no Hitlerite Nazi even while respectful of the original, pure inspiration of national socialism, as were a number of his German ENR colleagues.

## WHAT THEY SAY AND WHAT THEY DO

The ENR's duplicities were also those of Marc and ON. There was tension between the ENR/ON focus on cultural metapolitics and their inevitable involvement with the "politics of politicians," as their vehement paganism clashed with the Judaeo-Christian values of the larger European population.[42] There was also a conflict between their intellectual elitism and aspiration for social change, their revolutionary Right heritage and New Left ideals,[43] and in their melding of conservative with revolutionary views of human nature, and communitarianism. ON and the ENR, avant-gardist and libertine in certain areas, could be repressive and conservative in the area of sexuality, equality for women, and family issues.

There was strain between scientific research, rigorous intellectual analysis, and their reverence for myths of origins, identity, and belonging. ON drew Le Corbusier's circle, the X-Crise elite from the Ecole Polytechnique, and world-class mathematicians, and yet promoted Heidegger's existentialism, frequented the myth-minded romantic Abetz and followers of the Count of Paris, pretender to the throne of France. The aggressively anti-modern modernists of GRECE could indulge in solstice rituals and organize Tolkien camps attracting upwardly mobile technocrats and philosophers of science. In both the ENR and ON there was simplistic anti-Americanism combined with an admiration for American federalism as a model for a "Europe of a hundred flags." ON juxtaposed healthy Young Europe to "the American cancer" during the European civil war of the 1930s, and also warned the Third World and working people of Americanization, consumerism, and robotization.[44]

The ENR's public pro–Third World anti-Westernism (e.g., celebrating Ché Guevara) disguised its Eurocentrism. ON, albeit against liberalism, capitalism, and individualism, was aggressively West-Europeanist against America and the "Asiatic hordes." ENR's communitarian ideal could undermine the rights of individuals and communities to intellectual freedom, and not to conform. ON claimed to be nonconformist, but wanted *chefs* to enforce anti-bourgeois and anti-communist conformity in its ranks. Le Corbusier's futuristic city was supposedly anti-individualist, anti-bourgeois, and communitarian, but, with its high-rise moderate rental (HLM) apartment buildings and elite-designed common playing fields and green spaces, it exterminated the variety and colour of the old working-class neighbourhoods, and seemed dehumanizing, even totalitarian.

Both the ENR and ON, while focusing on the metapolitical and ignoring the democratic political process, infiltrated political parties, public administration, universities, and the mass media, and drifted from being an aloof, long-term cultural force. After World War II, Alexandre Marc networked European elites as federalists, good Europeans, in European federalist institutions, rather than attending to economic, racial, or poverty issues: the great lost hope of the 1930s for him was represented by Harro Schulze-Boysen. The ENR, citing conservative revolutionary thinkers not usually associated with fascism and Nazism, are returning the highbrow Right to respectability. But prestigious names and lofty metaphysical speculation camouflaged a hidden agenda. Both ON and the ENR, in their ambiguous indefinable projects tied to the Nietzschean and conservative revolutionary heritage, had elusive visions of the future. The great lesson of the 1930s should be applied to them too: "Don't listen to what they say: watch what they do!"

Westerners were happy robots, McDonaldized or Disneyfied, drugged by the false doctrine of Progress, needing guidance from discerning *chefs*, according to the ON or ENR. But peoples' regional differences were worthy of the greatest respect – whether in the "Europe of a hundred flags," or in a Canada leavened by feisty Québécois separatists.[45] The levellers and universalists, American cultural and economic hegemony, destroyed differences, true individualism, and true freedom ("to be what you are").[46] The traditionalist peasant from the Piedmont was thought to be more an individual than the bank clerk and amateur guitarist from Omaha who rode with a Harley motorcycle club on the weekends. American civilization was diminishing and destructive of a West European/Christian (for Marc), or a Europeanist/Celtic (for de Benoist) or a Latin-Mediterranean (for the mayor of Nice) genius which affirmed life and created beauty in ways non-Europeans could not. European populist national socialism camouflaged anti–Third World, highbrow racism with lofty culture-chat. The European Idea *seemed* democratic, populist, pluralistic, and progressive – self-affirmation of their heritage and tradition against economic exploitation, capitalism, and the robotization of modernity – and so touched a profound chord. As memories of Hitler fade, and there is growing lawlessness in the streets of European cities, the ENR again challenges the old Left and Right, appealing to deep, hidden longings contrary to dominant modern, materialistic values.

Good, intelligent, people, with a populist and altruistic bent, believed in a "pure" national socialism or a "white" fascism. ON, the Uriage School, the federalist movement, and the ENR encouraged such people to think on a level of metapolitics which absolved them from responsibility for the base, day-to-day, ruthlessness of police and politicians, thus keeping this aspiration alive.

Foreign scholars have stepped in and written on sensitive subjects such as French fascism or the Vichy regime which had difficulty finding balanced treatment in France. The present study suggests that the movements known as non-conformism and communitarian personalism were parts of a important and influential revolt against liberal democracy central to French political culture in the twentieth century. This revolt manifested itself in both zealously religious and pagan form, and owed far more to German influences than has been thought. The new documentation presented here reveals in French political, cultural, and religious history some deep and largely unknown forces whose importance extends beyond the borders of France.

# Notes

1 This clandestine networking is largely ignored in the learned studies of the French non-conformists by Jean-Louis Loubet del Bayle, *Les non-conformistes les années 30* (Paris: Seuil, 1969) and by Loubet del Bayle's admirer Nicolas Kessler, *Histoire politique de la Jeune Droite (1929–1942)* (Preface de Jean-Louis Loubet del Bayle) (Paris: L'Harmattan, 2001).

2 This book was written in Quebec, which has long become accustomed to a provincial political culture which publicly proclaims fidelity to liberal democratic values while discreetly engaging in policies which support the local francophone heritage by limiting anglophone and immigrant influence and promoting, as much as possible, the political, economic, and cultural hegemony of old-family francophones. Old-family francophones avoid public embarrassment by simply assuming their consensus on taking measures to counter the influence of "others."

3 This tendency was pointed out by the self-exiled Yves R. Simon in his wartime analysis of how France drifted toward proto-fascism, *The Road to Vichy* (Lanham, Md.: University Press of America, 1988).

4 With France occupied by the Nazis, Raissa Maritain, a refugee to the United States, eloquently described her husband Jacques's pre-war conversion experience in her very influential book, *We Have Been Friends Together*, trans. Julie Kernan (Garden City, NY: Image Publishing, 1961). The importance of the "white fascism" of Charles Maurras and the Action Française was minimized in an intellectual itinerary described by

her as shaped by edifying religious and spiritual goals, and marked by democratic, liberal, philo-Semitic, even socialistic impulses.

5 In her *L'Eglise sans Vichy, 1900–1946* (Paris: Perrin, 1998), 150–4, Michelle Cointat provides, without citing her sources, rare critical reminiscences of the Uriage school experience which are notable for being unusual and without documentation. The memoirs of the thousands of young French people who shared experiences at the school are almost all positive and endorse the doctored public image of it as a Resistance institution. But alumni of the school were powerful and notably vindicative toward detractors, as B.-H. Lévy has suggested in his *L'Idéologie française* (Paris: Grasset, 1981).

6 See the classic study by Jean-Louis Loubet del Bayle, *Les non-conformistes des années 30*, and, more recently, that by Nicolas Kessler, note 1 above.

7 E.g., Mounier's fellow Uriage instructor, the Jesuit Henri de Lubac, was, like Yves Congar, a prominent theologian at Vatican II. He was subsequently, like early Esprit supporter Jean Daniélou, made a cardinal.

8 In Canada, where the influence of French non-conformism on francophone political elites was particularly strong, federalist leader Pierre Trudeau and his Quebec separatist rival René Levesque were both non-conformists. Canadian non-conformism, like that of Vichy France, assumed French Catholic cultural preeminence in a multicultural, pluralist society.

9 If the people wanted American culture (Hollywood, Ford's assembly line, Wall Street, McDonald's) the non-conformist elite would do everything it could to protect them from it (while also refusing them jazz, blues, country music, rock'n'roll, Orson Welles, Alfred Hitchcock, Jasper Johns, New York City, bluejeans, the Golden Gate, Death Valley, cowboys, the Simpsons, and Walt Disney).

10 Twice, while travelling abroad, Marc was severely injured by hit-and-run drivers (on one occasion in Washington, DC, where the driver swerved onto the sidewalk). He attributed these attacks to agents of the KGB.

CHAPTER ONE

1 Most of our information about Alexandre Marc, unless otherwise noted, is taken from various interviews with him (often in the lively critical presence of his wife, Suzanne) conducted for over two decades either by John Hellman or by Christian Roy. Confirmation of Marc's account was sought in unpublished material (mostly correspondence) in Marc's papers and these are the sources cited in this text, unless otherwise noted.

2 Founding group member Denis de Rougemont claimed that Joachim von Ribbentrop subscribed to *Ordre Nouveau*, and took the notion of

struggling for a New Order from it. See his *Politique de la personne,* 2nd edition (Paris: Je sers, 1946), 8.

3  When, after the king died, mourners were allowed to pass through his office where things had been left untouched since the time of his death, it was noted that Arnaud Dandieu and Robert Aron's book *La révolution nécessaire* (Paris: Grasset, 1933) lay open on his desk. Two months later, prominent Belgian Catholic youth leader Abbé Jacques Leclerc concluded his acclamatory biography *Albert Roi des Belges* (Brussels: Editions de la Cité chrétienne, 1934) with that telling fact: "Under the title [*La révolution nécessaire*], the King had written in his regular hand: 'morale et spirituelle' ... The last words he ever wrote. The story of his life." (230). (Christian Roy)

4  José Antonio wrote one or two letters to Marc endorsing *Ordre Nouveau*'s federalist ideas. After the war, Spanish dissidents close to Marc sought to retrieve them to demonstrate Franco's disloyalty to the original falangist inspiration, but they have not yet been found. The Falange's "Basic Points" celebrated "the spiritual dimension" and "the individual" as engendering "respect for human dignity, man's integrity and freedom." *Falange Española* 1 (7 December 1933), in José Antonio Primo de Rivera, *Selected Writings,* edited and introduced by Hugh Thomas (New York: Harper Torchbooks, 1975), 64–5. In the *Cortes* on 4 January and 28 February 1934, José Antonio analysed the modern state in the light of values which respected the geographic and cultural rootedness of Catalan and Basque patriots. Marc's Ordre Nouveau (ON) also distinguished the nation from the local *patrie* and its legitimate claims. José Antonio used the person/individual distinction to argue that the nation was obliged to embody universal values, over against the mere cultural survival of an ethnic group (ibid., 73–4, 84–7). Marc's movement sponsored noted Catalan critic Eugenio d'Ors in one of its first public lectures. (Christian Roy)

5  For a detailed account of *Esprit*'s founding, based upon Emmanuel Mounier's unpublished diaries, see John Hellman, "The Origins of *Esprit*: Ecumenism, Fascism, and the New Catholic Left," *Third Republic/Troisième république* 9 (Spring 1980), 63–122.

   After World War II there was a considerable effort to disassociate Marc and ON from origins of *Esprit* and the personalist movement – notably by editing and altering Mounier's diary for publication in his collected works.

6  John Hellman and Christian Roy presented a paper on contacts between German and French youth movements to the international colloquium on Franco-German cultural contacts in the 1930s organized by the German Deutscher Akademischer Austauschdient (DAAD) and the French Centre national de la recherche (CNRS) in Paris from 6–8 December

1990. Entitled "Le personnalisme et les contacts entre non-conformistes de France et d'Allemagne autour de l'Ordre Nouveau et de *Gegner* (1930–1942)," it was published in Hans Manfred Bock, Reinhart Meyer-Kalkus, and Michel Trebitsch, eds., *Entre Locarno et Vichy: Les relations culturelles franco-allemandes dans les années 1930* vol. 1 (Paris: CNRS Editions, coll. De l'Allemagne, 1993), 203–15. Several papers, such as Rita Thalmann, "Du Cercle du Sohlberg au Comité France-Allemagne: un exemple d'évolution ambiguë de la coopération franco-allemande" (67–86), Barbara Unteutsch, "Dr. Friedrich Bran – Mittler in Abetz' Schatten" (87–106), and Thomas Keller, "Katholische Europa-Konzeptionen in den deutsch-französischen Beziehungen" (219–39), demonstrated that German inter-war influence on the French has been much underestimated, as does Albrecht Betz's *Exil und Engagement: Deutsche Schriftsteller im Frankreich der Dreissiger Jahre* (Munich: Edition Text und Kritik, 1986); *Exil et engagement: Les intellectuels allemands et la France, 1930–1940* (Paris: Gallimard, 1991).

7  In 1982 the reviewer of John Hellman's *Emmanuel Mounier and the New Catholic Left, 1930–1950* (Toronto and London: University of Toronto Press, 1981) in the *Times Literary Supplement* called it "the best extant book on Personalism" – a philosophy influencing the French Socialist party and the pontificate of John Paul II – but went on to say that the book failed to explain "just what Personalism is." Patrick McCarthy, *Times Literary Supplement*, 12 February 1982, 159.

8  Denis de Rougemont was one of those who remained fully active in both the ON and Esprit groups through the 1930s. As a prominent Barthian Protestant essayist, he was also treated as a peer by Catholic, Protestant, and Orthodox theologians. See Bruno Ackermann, *Denis de Rougemont: Une biographie intellectuelle*, 2 vols. (Geneva: Labor et Fides, 1996).

9  Denis de Rougemont, "Alexandre Marc et l'invention du personnalisme," in *Le fédéralisme et Alexandre Marc* (Lausanne: Centre de recherches européennes, 1974), 51–69.

10  In 1939, de Rougemont published his broad historical classic *L'amour et l'occident*, translated as *Love in the Western World* (New York: Harcourt, Brace, Jovanovich, 1940), in which he shocked Catholics by contrasting his notion of the authentically Christian, spiritual (non-erotic) notion of conjugal love with the "heretical" (erotic) "Cathar" conception prevailing in the West. His puritanical attack on Western sexual mores, and his plea for the revival of repressed heterosexual relationships, contrasted with his increasingly libidinous personal behaviour, however.

Half a century later, de Rougemont told French Catholics that the birth of their personalism had involved several Protestant thinkers who became important figures in the ecumenical movement. See his *Journal d'une époque (1926–1946)* (Paris: Gallimard, 1968), 55–6, and Bruno Ackermann, *Denis de Rougemont.*

11  See Hellman and Roy, "Le personnalisme et les contacts entre non-conformistes." For a recent reiteration of the orthodox Catholic and Esprit group view, that Mounier worked out personalism largely by abstractly philosophizing on his own, see Gérard Lurol, *Mounier, I: Genèse de la personne* (Paris: Editions Universitaires, 1991), 143–229. The Amis d'Emmanuel Mounier awarded it a prize as part of their effort to manage Mounier's memory, and Lurol (and others) echoed this view in an international colloquium they sponsored, with the support of UNESCO in Paris on 5–6 October 2000. Sponsors included Jacques Delors, Paul Ricœur, Jean-Marie Lustiger (Archbishop of Paris), and Professor Stanley Hoffmann of Harvard.

12  Fifty years later, de Rougemont recalled his first encounter with personalism in the salon of Charles Du Bos. Marc handed him a "Manifesto" which was like "a burst of light" headed: "NOUS NE SOMMES NI INDIVIDU-ALISTES NI COLLECTIVISTES, NOUS SOMMES PERSONNALISTES." Cf. de Rougemont's comments in *Le personnalisme d'Emmanuel Mounier* (Paris: Seuil, 1985), 36–7.

13  One example is Jean Jardin of ON, who became Pierre Laval's administrative assistant at Vichy. See Pierre Assouline's *Une éminence grise: Jean Jardin (1904–1976)* (Paris: Balland, 1986). Jardin's home, on the outskirts of Vichy, became a safe haven for ON people (including Jews like Robert Aron), until Jardin was appointed French ambassador to Berne (overseeing Laval's interests in Switzerland?). Swiss archives would likely reveal more about Jardin's wartime activities.

Robert Loustau and Robert Gibrat, young engineers from the X-Crise group who had joined ON, tried to furnish a political platform for Colonel de la Rocque's Croix de Feu, and create a central telephone switchboard for French youth movements. After a brief effort to work with Jacques Doriot's PPF, both became high-level technocrats in the Vichy regime. See the three articles by Christian Roy, "Jardin, Jean," "Ordre Nouveau (review and group)," "Synarchy (*X-Crise*, Centre poly-technicien d'études économiques, Jean Coutrot, Plan pour un ordre nouveau en France, April 1941)," all in Bertram M. Gordon, ed., *Dictionary of World War II France: The Occupation, Vichy, and the Resistance (1938–1946),* (Westport, Conn.: Greenwood Press, 1998).

The collaborationist Brussels daily *Le Soir* was directed by Raymond de Becker, who had worked with Marc and ON in the early 1930s, before veering off toward Nazism. It published articles by neo-socialist theorist Henri de Man's nephew, the young literary critic Paul de Man, the recent discovery of which led to controversy over the origins of post-modernism.

On de Becker's evolution, which Mounier sadly regretted and Marc later attributed to psychological imbalance, see Hellman, *Emmanuel Mounier*, 87–95, 106–8, 121–6, and Xavier Dehan, "'Jeune Europe', le salon Didier et les Editions de la Toison d'Or (1933–1945)," *Bijdragen-Cahiers*, Navorsings – en Studiecentrum voor de geschiedenis van de tweede wereldoorlog/Centre de recherches et d'études historiques de la seconde guerre mondiale (Brussels) 17 (December 1995), 204–26.

14  For his part, Marc was involved with the *Témoignage Chrétien* circle. See Renée Bédarida's *Les armes de l'esprit: Témoignage chrétien (1941–1944)* (Paris: Editions ouvrières, 1977). Her *Pierre Chaillet: Témoin de la résistance spirituelle* (Paris: Fayard, 1988) further clarifies the role of Marc and certain of his friends in the Resistance against the German occupation. Some of these people remained loyal to Pétain all the while (cf. 141–2, 241–3).

15  Albert Ollivier of ON became political director of *Rassemblement*, the weekly publication of the Rassemblement du Peuple Français (RPF) movement created by General de Gaulle in 1949, and then director of Gaullist radio under the fifth Republic. ON's pre-war secretary, Xavier de Lignac, would, as "Jean Chauveau," head de Gaulle's press services. In the 1930s ON's Henri Daniel-Rops introduced the ideas of young Colonel Charles de Gaulle into Parisian salons, arranged to publish his writings, and gave lectures about them (Marc to military school cadets). During World War II, President Franklin Roosevelt was warned by, among others, philosopher Jacques Maritain (a sharp critic of the influence of the "goose-stepping" philosophy of ON), among others, that General de Gaulle, though he was leader of the French Resistance, had fascist ideas and tendencies (unpublished correspondence between Maritain and Yves R. Simon). The fact that de Gaulle was the great French hero of the resistance to fascism did not prevent the RPF from manifesting many characteristics of a fascist political party. The non-conformists of the 1930s had called for an "anti-fascist fascism."

16  Marc's post-war career is outlined in *Le fédéralisme et Alexandre Marc*. For a detailed account, see Isabelle Le Moulec-Deschamps's doctoral dissertation for the law faculty of Université de Nice (Institut du droit de la paix et du développement): "Alexandre Marc, un combat pour l'Europe" (1992).

17  In 1946, Marc became secretary-general of the European Union of Federalists for a year and, after helping found the European Institute of the University of Turin, a leader in the Mouvement Fédéraliste Européen (created in 1953). He taught, gave lectures, and authored several projects for a European or world constitution.

18  Marc's many post-war publications include *Proudhon* (Paris: LUF, 1945),

*Avènement de la France ouvrière* (Paris: Portes de France, 1945), *Principes du fédéralisme* (with Robert Aron; Paris: Flammarion, 1948), *A hauteur d'homme, la révolution fédéraliste* (Paris: Je Sers, 1948), *Civilisation en sursis* (Paris: La Colombe, 1955), *Europe, terre décisive* (Paris: La Colombe, 1959), *Dialectique du déchaînement, fondements philosophiques du fédéralisme* (Paris: La Colombe, 1961), *L'Europe dans le monde* (Paris: Payot, 1965), *De la méthodologie à la dialectique* (Paris: Presses d'Europe, 1970), *révolution américaine, révolution européenne* (Lausanne: Centre de recherches Européennes, 1977).

19 See below, p. 77.

20 Chevalley and Glady, "La Mort des Partis," *Ordre Nouveau* 4 (October 1933), 27.

21 Ordre Nouveau, "Lettre à Hitler," *Ordre Nouveau* 5 (November 1933), 31–2.

22 Harro Schulze-Boysen, "Lettre ouverte d'un jeune Allemand à la France" (translated from the German by A. Marc), *Esprit* 5 (February 1933), 732–4.

23 ON's Robert Aron saw it as significant that the insurrection occurred on the anniversary of ON guru Arnaud Dandieu's death.

24 "Chronique Permanente," *Esprit* 38 (November 1935), 280.

25 November 1935; Philippe Burrin, *La dérive fasciste: Foriot, Déat, et Bergery* (Paris: Seuil, 1986), 195.

26 When Mounier lectured in Brussels in January he was portrayed by *Le Soir* (30 January 1936) as representing "the spiritual revolution," a movement also represented by the reviews *Esprit, Ordre Nouveau, L'Homme Réel*, and *L'Homme Nouveau*.

27 Interviews with Alexandre Marc. For example, in a letter in the Marc archives (Dr Hans Espe to Marc, 19 October 1937), a professor at the Polytechnic School of Dantzig wrote Marc for a summary of ON ideas for his students.

28 For example, Hans Geschke in "Geist der Zeit" claimed to admire Denis de Rougemont's conception of man while faulting the personalist's understanding of the German *Blutverwandtschaften* and *Schicksalgemeinschaften*. This was reported in "Revue des revues," *Esprit* 76 (January 1939). Cf. Hellman, *Emmanuel Mounier*, 307n61.

29 Their activities were reported in the explicitly "private and confidential" *Journal Intérieur* of the Esprit groups (rather than the public "Chronique" of activities of the personalists regularly published in *Esprit*). The former remains an excellent source for understanding the dissimulated private, as opposed to public, non-conformist agenda.

30 E.g. Marc to Bergery, 2 April 1938. Marc assured Bergery that he found the issues supported by *La Flèche* interesting and was showing this by citing it in his page of *Temps Présent*.

31 For example, they facilitated his marriage. See further pp. 81–2.

32 It is amply documented by stacks of correspondence among Marc's papers of that period.

33 Marc to Coutrot, 12 March 1939.

34 Marc to Voyant (Lyon), 2 April 1939.

35 Cf. Voyant to Marc, 14 March 1939; Marc to Moosmann, 12 March 1939; Marc to Robert Aron, 12 March 1939; A. Boutier (Lyon) to Marc, 5 April 1939; Marc to L. Maggiani, 17 April 1939.

36 An illustrative example was André Moosmann, an employee at the Ministère du Travail, who had got to know Marc in the Sohlberg group (in which he had met a Polish woman whom he had married). In 1939 he was active in the discussions on communitarian personalism hosted by the Paris Esprit group, and wanted to start something similar among workers in the Belleville area. André Moosmann to Marc, 7 March 1939.

37 "Par la jeunesse, la culture se répandra dans tous les milieux et tous les métiers, par elle se reforgera une communauté nationale." Archives départmentales de la Gironde, Directives générales du Secrétariat général à la Jeunesse transmises aux préfets de la zone occupée. This directive is cited at greater length in Michel Bergès, *Vichy contre Mounier* (Paris: Economica, 1997), 46.

38 I am particularly grateful to the late Alexandre Marc for three decades of enlightening conversations, vigilant and friendly disagreements, over the nature of his non-conformism and federalism, and for generous access to his archives.

39 Mounier's classic essay to launch the Esprit project called on his generation to "Refaire la Renaissance" (the lead essay of the first *Esprit*, October 1932) and attacked modern individualism in the name of communitarian values. Berdyaev's most influential book in the period was his prophecy, *A New Middle Ages* (*Un nouveau Moyen-Age*, Paris: Plon, 1927), in which a merging of communist and Christian communitarianism would create a new era.

40 See Zeev Sternhell, ed., *The Intellectual Revolt against Liberal Democracy, 1870–1945*, Proceedings of the Conference in Memory of Jacob L. Talmon, 1990 (Jerusalem: Israel Academy of Sciences and Humanities, 1996), and Zeev Sternhell, "Morphologie et historiographie du fascism en France," preface to third edition of his *Ni droite, ni gauche: L'idéologie fasciste en France* (Brussels: Editions Complexe, 2000), 11–112.

41 For example, Marc was an intellectual model for the legal scholar Jacques-Yvan Morin, high-profile Parti Québécois leader and historian of federalism, whom Marc wanted to succeed him as head of his CIFE in Nice. Jacques Delors, an ascetic and progressive Catholic communitarian, discreetly supported Marc's projects when he was head of the European community.

42 The review *Więz* (the link, *le lien*), co-started with Tadeusz Mazowiecki in 1958 and directed for years by him, was central. It was directly inspired by, even a direct imitation of, the French *Esprit*, and like *Esprit* it could support communitarian initiatives of the government in the name of protecting against liberal and democratic excesses, of countering the ravages of the sort of unbridled individualism and moral permissiveness found in the West. Mazowiecki went from a position as *Znak* deputy to the parliament, to being a chief counsellor to Lech Walesa, editor-in-chief of the weekly *Solidarnösc* (1980–81) and, eventually, the first prime minister of post-communist Poland.

Karol Wojtyla, who did doctoral dissertations on the mysticism of St John of the Cross and on Max Scheler's notions of community, made his mark as a serious philosopher in the personalist tradition. Since becoming Pope, he has given a new life and orientation to several old personalist themes. See John Hellman, "John Paul II and the Personalist Movement," *Cross Currents* 30:4 (Winter 1980–81), 409–19.

43 Mme Suzanne Marc recalled that, years later, Mr Lipiansky offered her expensive jewels, ermine coats, or other extravagant gifts ... for delivery when his property was returned to him. She bridled at her husband's describing his father as a Marxist: "He liked money," she remarked. Marc's presentation of his background may be partially explained by the fact that, during the 1930s, converts from Marxism to Catholicism were celebrated and supported, converts from Judaism less so.

44 Marc later commented that his father "had a genius for business, but this genius did not work in a Western context": he did not enjoy the financial success in Berlin and Paris which he had expected.

45 Public comment by Marc on Catherine Baird's contribution to a colloquium in honour of his ninety years by the Réseau des historiens du personnalisme et du fédéralisme intégral at the Europäisches Zentrum für Föderalismus-Forschung of Ebehard-Karls University in Tübingen, 24 March 1994. On Berdyaev's impact on the formation of French personalism, see Baird's article "Religious Communism? Nicolai Berdyaev's Contribution to *Esprit's* Interpretation of Communism," *Canadian Journal of History/Annales canadiennes d'histoire* 30: 1 (April 1995), 29–48 (awarded a prize as that journal's best graduate essay in 1994). Berdyaev's book was originally published as *Novyie srednie veka* (Berlin, Obelisk-Verlag, 1924) and then translated by the Russian wife of French Catholic writer Stanislas Fumet as *Un nouveau Moyen-Age* (Paris: Plon, 1927) and *A New Middle Ages* (New York: Sheed and Ward, 1933).

46 Husserl's article in the review *Logos* with the tantalizing title "Die Philosophie als strenge Wissenschaft" particularly struck Marc, but he was disappointed with his teaching: "Germans, in general, made very dreary professors compared to the French. Husserl was terrible and 'he exuded

boredom' as the saying goes ... He gave me a very poor welcome when we first met, but when I left we were on good terms." Interview with Alexandre Marc by John Hellman (Cogne, Italy, August 1985).

47  "I went there for Husserl above all, and so, disappointed, I put aside philosophy , returning to France to study in the Faculty of Law and Sciences Po, as they called L'Ecole libre des Sciences Politiques. I said to myself: 'That's enough philosophy. I want to look a bit at Politics and Law' ... political studies most attracted me." Interview with Alexandre Marc by John Hellman (Cogne, July 1985). Thus Marc claimed he had not been taken with Heidegger any more than with Husserl.

48  Marc's comments on Roy, "Alexandre Marc and the Personalism of *L'Ordre Nouveau*" (MA thesis, McGill University, 1987), 14.

49  Interview with Alexandre Marc by Christian Roy (Tübingen, 24 March 1994).

50  Scheler had been a non-religious Jew but, at fourteen, converted to Catholicism. At Munich, Scheler had discovered Husserl, and contributed to the *Jahrbuch für Philosophie und Phänomenologische Forschung*. During World War I, he argued in quasi-Marxist language that Germany's struggle against bourgeois Britain represented the international proletariat, supported by the other have-not nations, displacing the bourgeoisie.

51  Remembering his encounter with personalist-communitarian Scheler half a century later, Marc recalled only his disappointment over the great "Catholic Nietzsche's" escapades: "I wasn't even twenty years old and he received me very amiably, much more amiably than was usual among the *Herren Professoren* of Germany who were usually terribly reserved. But he was very friendly, very lively, joking with me and talking about everything under the sun. He made a strong impression on me, with an element of mistrust. I found him a bit superficial – and he was. You know ... he tricked the Vatican. He was married, and had a mistress, and wanted to marry that mistress. So he took ... various initiatives with the Vatican to have his marriage annulled saying thirty-six thousand things that (I heard afterwards) were made up ... He said: 'But it's a scandal. I am the greatest Catholic philosopher but everyone knows I have a mistress." (... All he had to do was leave her.) Well, finally the Vatican listened and they annulled his marriage. Rather than marrying the mistress, he took another. So you see, he was not *un homme sérieux*. He ruined everything at the end of his life, turning toward a fanatical paganism, a bit to please the Nazis, to please *la nouvelle jeunesse*." Interview with Alexandre Marc by John Hellman (Cogne, August 1985)

In 1925, just two years after Lipiansky's visit, Scheler would turn from Catholicism, this time definitively. He died in 1928. Hans Kohn, *The Mind of Germany* (New York: Charles Scribner's Sons, 1960), 297–8;

Michel Mourre, ed., *Dictionnaire des idées contemporaines* (Paris: Editions universitaires, 1964), 612, 615.

52 Lipianksy was particularly impressed with his 1913 treatise on values, *Der Formalismus in der Ethik und die materiale Wertethik. Neuer Versuch der Grundlegung eines ethischen Personalismus* ("Formalism in Ethics and the Material Ethics of Values. A New Attempt at the Founding of an Ethical Personalism"), and his *Wesen und Formen der Sympathie.*

53 "[My professor] was not very appreciative, being an admirer of ancient philosophy. A great Latinist, conversant in Latin and Greek, he said: 'You know. It's a play on words. In German it's easy for Heidegger, also, to abuse that sort of thing, those word games.'" Interview with Alexandre Marc by John Hellman (Cogne, August 1985).

54 "For example, Scheler distinguished *Einfühlung*, to penetrate someone, in feelings; *Mitfühlung*, to feel with someone; *Einsfühlung*, to unite with someone, and so on. So when you translate it into French it is very difficult, or one must use jargon. And *se sentir, se sentir pénétrer dans quelqu'un, se sentir ceci*, etc. was much less forceful in French than it was in German. And that's why he told me not to do it. It was "a contortionist philosophy." [Similarly,] someone whom I admired very much from the philosophical point of view, Nicolai Hartmann ... a serious philosopher, said to me: 'Max Scheler! You admire Max Scheler! but he is not serious!' And it is true: he was a mixture of genius and yellow journalist [un génie, mais un génie peu sérieux]." Interview with Alexandre Marc by John Hellman (Cogne, August 1985).

55 Contemporary philosopher Paul Ricœur, intellectually nurtured in the Esprit milieu, remembered Landsberg as the determining figure in prewar French personalist philosophy. After World War II, Karol Wojtyla, the future Pope John Paul II, did a PhD dissertation on Scheler and translated his work into Polish.

56 "I was staying with a family of social democrats in Munich ... saw Hitler for the first time ... and he made a strong impression on me ... And my hosts asked 'Did you have a good time?' and I told them 'No'. 'What? Why not? he is strange this Hittel, no?' ( ... They didn't know his real name. He wasn't known.) So I said: 'Dieser Mensch ist gefährlich.' ... [My host replied]: 'He has no importance, let him talk.' And I answered 'No, because he is a fanatic.' [I vividly recall] ... that absurd little man with the overly tight raincoat. A worker who was sitting at my right, a big fat Bavarian drinking huge mugs of beer, shouted at one point 'Maul zu! (Shut up!) Germany will never follow you.' And the other responded, tit for tat, 'Germany? I am Germany!' And I thought to myself: 'Someone who is so outlandish as to be able to say that without imagining himself ridiculous is dangerous.' And that's what I said to my host the next day. And since I was impressed, I returned to Germany on study trips: two, or

three times ..." Interview with Alexandre Marc by John Hellman (Cogne, August 1985).

57  According to Marc, he changed his name on the advice of René Vaubourdolle, his boss at the Hachette publishing house. Marc told John Hellman that Pax-Press was an objective, independent press agency. Interview with Alexandre Marc by John Hellman (Cogne, August 1985). In the Marc archives and in a subsequent interview with Christian Roy (Vence, France, 7 October 1989), it emerged that Pax-Press was created by Marc with the inheritance of his Sciences Po comrade Charles-Edouard Glachant to promote Franco-German understanding, that the agency received at least F75,000 from the government's notorious secret funds, and that it had well-known Germanophiles like Jean Luchaire and Philippe Lamour among its directors. Glachant's inheritance disappeared in the project and, as late as 1937, he was still trying to get his money back from Marc, who reproached him for his pettiness.

58  "Manifeste" in *Réaction* 1 (April 1930); Jean-Louis Loubet del Bayle, *Les non-conformistes des années 30. Une tentative de renouvellement de la politique française* (Paris: Seuil, 1969), 440.

The novelist Georges Bernanos, another radical reactionary dissatisfied with the Action Française, was an enthusiastic supporter of the Fabrègues initiative. See John Hellman, "From the Radical Right to Resistance: De Gaulle, Maritain, and Bernanos," in *Chesterton Review*, "Georges Bernanos – Special Centenary Issue," 15: 4 (November 1989), and 16: 1 (February 1990), 513–27.

59  See H.-I. Marrou, "L'action politique d'Emmanuel Mounier," *Les Cahiers de la République* 2 (1956), 96.

60  Interview with Alexandre Marc by John Hellman (Cogne, August 1985); Edmond Lipiansky, *Ordre et démocratie. Deux sociétés de pensée: De l'Ordre Nouveau au Club Jean-Moulin* (Paris: PUF, 1967), 7.

61  André Moosmann to Christian Roy, 24 January 1986.

62  André Moosmann to Christian Roy, 24 January 1986; interviews with André Moosmann (Paris, 1 February 1988) and Alexandre Marc (Vence, 21 November 1989), by Christian Roy.

Some years ago, the *Bulletin des Amis d'Emmanuel Mounier* appealed to its readers for information about the nature of this "club," rumoured to play a decisive role in the origins of the review *Esprit*'s personalism. And yet, at the colloquium organized by these same Amis d'Emmanuel Mounier to celebrate the fiftieth anniversary of *Esprit* in 1982, André Moosmann seemed a ghost at the feast, his public recollections on the atmosphere surrounding the birth of personalism troubling to the custodians of the movement's history. We are grateful for his discreet, convincing eyewitness reports.

63  See Roy, "Alexandre Marc and the Personalism of *L'Ordre Nouveau*," 21.

64 Denis de Rougemont, "Alexandre Marc et l'invention du personnalisme," in ***. *Le fédéralisme et Alexandre Marc*, 55–6; interviews with
Alexandre Marc by Christian Roy, 1987–90. In a conversation with Marc,
Congar recalled suggesting to Marc the idea of such an ecumenical
group. Interview with Alexandre Marc by Christian Roy, 21 November
1990.
65 Ecumenical preoccupations would return to Marc in his later years, as he
tried to promote Catholic-Orthodox dialogue in the wake of the collapse
of Russian communism.

CHAPTER TWO

1 See Paul Ricœur, *Gabriel Marcel et Karl Jaspers* (Paris: Editions du Temps
présent, 1948)
2 This was a time for inventing new terms in intellectual life. Two years
after "existentialism" was used, Charles Renouvier, summing up his own
idealist system not long before his death, coined the term "personalism."
3 Christian Roy pointed out that rationalist critic Victor Basch dismissed
Kierkegaard's thought as "existential" in 1903. See P. Mesnard,
"Kierkegaard aux prises avec la conscience française," *Revue de littérature
comparée* 29 (1955), 456n, cited in Alessandro Cortese, "Kierkegaard," in
Vittorio Mathieu, ed., *Questioni di storiografia filosofica* (Brescia: La Scuola,
1974), 555. By 1930 Basch had become president of the liberal Ligue
des Droits de l'Homme; he and his wife would be murdered by the notorious Paul Touvier's *miliciens* in 1944.
4 For a general discussion of its reception in France, see Bernhard Walden-
fels, *Phänomenologie in Frankreich* (Frankfurt: Suhrkamp, 1983).
5 Jean-Louis Loubet del Bayle, *Les non-conformistes des années 30* (Paris:
Seuil, 1969), 422.
6 For example, in early 1932, Marcel would help find Marc an office
alongside *Esprit*'s Emmanuel Mounier in the Paris offices of Desclée De
Brouwer, the Belgian Catholic publishers.
7 [A] German ... book on Nazism ... accuses Jaspers ... Heidegger much
more, of being allies or pioneers of Nazism ... Jaspers I saw often and
knew very well at Heidelberg: he was as 'Nazi' as I was! – he detested
Nazism. Moreover his wife was Jewish, and he never wanted to disavow
her ... he hid her and then fled Germany rather than abandon her. He
went to teach in Switzerland ... but he was never pro-Nazi in any way ...
what Jaspers criticized was ... democracy as it was then functioning in
European countries ... the weaknesses of the Weimar republic – which I
criticized myself ... his book *Die geistige Situation der Zeit* ... much
impressed me. It was after reading that little book that I went to meet
him in Heidelberg." Interview with Alexandre Marc by John Hellman

(Cogne, Italy, August 1985). This meeting between the two men probably took place in early 1932.

8 Franco-German relations were important to French leader Aristide Briand, and it was well known that the review received government subsidies.

9 Daniel-Rops, *Le monde sans âme* (Paris: Plon, 1932), 12–13.

10 Ibid., 127.

11 Ibid., 225.

12 Ibid., 127, 225, 229.

13 Loubet del Bayle, *Les non-conformistes*, 86.

14 The manifesto was also signed by Gabriel Rey, an Hachette colleague of Marc's who later dropped from sight. Marc retained copies of the document in his archives.

15 Otto Abetz, to Alexandre Lipiansky, 6 April 1931. The meeting was to be held near the village of Rethel, in the Ardennes region.

16 The position of librarian in the French National Library was then known as a sinecure for erudite intellectuals. In those days access to the library's collections and reading room was severely restricted. Among Dandieu and Bataille's colleagues was Henry Corbin, an early French Heideggerian, soon to become known as an Islamicist.

17 Emmanuel Mounier, "Entretiens IV," 18 October 1932, in Mounier's *Oeuvres*, vol. 4 (Paris: Seuil, 1961).

18. Interview with Alexandre Marc by Christian Roy (Aoste, Italy, 12 August 1994). The historian of French spirituality abbé Henri Bremond (1865–1933), an important figure of the "Catholic Renaissance" of those years, had also had the same reaction as Marc on reading Dandieu's book on Proust: he went to meet its author at the Bibliothèque Nationale (according to Robert Aron's unpublished biography of his friend Arnaud Dandieu). When Marc first met him, Arnaud Dandieu was becoming known for his *Marcel Proust, sa révélation psychologique* (1930), which had been published ... in Oxford, thanks to the Anglicist and diplomat Abel Chevalley (whose son Claude, one of this century's greatest mathematicians, would soon join ON). Dandieu had joined the Association France–Grande-Bretagne at Abel Chevalley's instigation, and developed ties with T.S. Eliot's *Criterion* and A.R. Orage's *New English Weekly*. I am grateful to Christian Roy for this information.

19 This is evident from an unpublished text in the Dandieu papers and from Dandieu's article "Philosophie de l'angoisse et politique du désespoir," *Revue d'Allemagne*, 15 October 1932, 883–91.

20 Robert Aron and Arnaud Dandieu, *Décadence de la nation française* (Paris: Rieder, 1931), 133; Loubet del Bayle, *Les non-conformistes*, 44.

21 Denis de Rougemont was born in 1906 into a family which had moved to the canton of Neuchâtel from Franche-Comté in the fourteenth century,

and received a *reconnaissance d'ancienne noblesse* from the Prussian King Frederick II in 1784. The name sounded like French aristocracy, but the family owed their title to the Prussian court. A biography of Denis de Rougemont appears in a special issue of the Geneva review *Cadmos*, 33 (1986), 27. For more detail on the family see Jacqueline and Pierre-Arnold Borel, *Les Rougemont de Saint-Aubin* (La Chaux-de-Fonds: Editions P.-A. Borel, 1984).

22  Published in *Foi et Vie* 4, Paris (1928), 189–202.

23  Pierre de Senarclens, *Le mouvement "Esprit," 1932–1941* (Lausanne: L'Age d'Homme, 1974), 64; *Cadmos* 33 (1986), 127.

24  Denis de Rougemont, "Alexandre Marc et l'invention du personnalisme," in *Le fédéralisme et Alexandre Marc* (Lausanne: Centre de recherches européennes, 1974), 53.

25  Denis de Rougemont, *Le Paysan du Danube* (Lausanne: Payot, 1932).

26  Denis de Rougemont, "Alexandre Marc," 54.

27  Ibid., 52.

28  "Denis de Rougemont tel qu'en lui-même ... " (Interview, September 1985), *Cadmos* 33 (1986), 9.

29  Loubet del Bayle, *Les non-conformistes*, 94.

30  Robert Aron, *Fragments d'une vie* (Paris: Plon, 1981), 75.

31  Philippe Lamour, "Jeunesse du monde," *Plans* 4 (April 1931), 16.

32  Christian Roy pointed out that this is the year that René Clair directed *A nous la liberté!*, portraying modern man's alienation from modern industrial society, and potential liberation by employing technology to create leisure. This classic Clair film was particularly important for the ON group; they gave the name *A nous la liberté!* to a radical weekly which published ten issues in 1937. The Canadian ON used the same title the following year for a single issue it published on its own. See Christian Roy, "Le mouvement personnaliste *L'Ordre Nouveau* et le Québec (1930–1947): son rôle dans la formation de Guy Frégault," *Revue d'histoire de l'Amérique française* 46:3 (Winter 1993), 463–84.

33  Loubet del Bayle, *Les non-conformistes*, 96.

34  This tribute is Zeev Sternhell's in his *Ni droite, ni gauche: L'idéologie fasciste en France*, 3rd edition (Brussels: Editions Complexe, 2000), 128.

35  Ibid., 168.

36  Ibid., 170.

37  Ibid., 251.

38  For more on this see ibid., 169.

39  Cf. ibid., 169–72.

40  Ibid., 171–2.

41  Ibid., 240.

42  The account of the meeting is from a police report cited in ibid., 240. Lamour's affirmation of continuity with *Mouvement socialiste* is in Lamour, "Vers la deuxième étape," *Plans* 8 (October 1931), 10.

43 Sternhell, *Ni droite, ni gauche,* 112.

44 *Plans* 3 (March 1931), 31; Loubet del Bayle, *Les non-conformistes,* 95.

45 For more on Dami see Pierre de Senarclens, *Le mouvement "Esprit,"
1932–1941: Essai critique* (Lausanne: L'Age d'Homme, 1974). Dami was
a Swiss citizen who had served in the Italian army, lived in Hungary, and
spent two years studying at the University of Leipzig.

46 After meeting Emmanuel Mounier in Geneva in 1933, Dami would go
on to chronicle foreign policy for Mounier's *Esprit,* where he eventually
adopted an adamant pro-Munich agreement position. See John Hellman, *Emmanuel Mounier and the New Catholic Left, 1930–1950* (Toronto:
University of Toronto Press, 1981), 58, 98, 108, 109, 137, 139, 144.

47 Interview with Alexandre Marc by John Hellman (Cogne, August 1985).

48 Alexandre Marc diaries (unpublished).

49 The Manifesto of the Black Front was published in *Plans* (10 December
1931), and a long exposition of Strasser's positions was later published
by Emmanuel Mounier in three consecutive issues of *Esprit.*

50 This perception of French Europeanism was shared by Marc's future
comrade Harro Schulze-Boysen, who discovered *Plans* in Paris (where he
was employed as secretary to a Germanophile advocate of *rapprochement*
named André Germain). Schulze-Boysen described as "very astute, from
the French point of view," this "very fresh and lively" review's call for
European union. Harro Schulze-Boysen to his parents, 31 July 1931.
I am grateful to Christian Roy for providing this information.

51 G. M., "Deutsch-Französisches Jugendtreffen in Rethel 2-9 August 1931,"
4. Archiv der deutschen Jugendbewegung A 2-65. Christian Roy is grateful to Hans Coppi for communicating this document to him.

52 Marc to Lamour, 14 January 1986. Marc recalled in several conversations
with me that it was indicative of the spirit of these youth encounters that
Lamour's passionate oratory (in French; he didn't speak German) was
particularly effective in inspiring enthusiasm in young Germans who
didn't understand any French!

53 "Une exploration psychologique franco-allemande: Le Congrès de
Rethel 2-9 août 1931, Compte-rendu et exposés," *Notre Temps* 5, series 2,
nos. 103-4, 16-23 August 1931, 650-2.

54 Dieter Tiemann, *Deutsch-französische Jugendbeziehungen in der Zwischen-
kriegszeit* (Bonn: Bouvier, 1989), 83.

55 Marc recalled that he broke in disgust with a dismayed Abetz in mid-
1935. Marc claimed that during the war, he had his wife promise never
to resort to the intercession of Abetz, then German ambassador to
France, even if he were arrested for Resistance activities. In occupied
Paris, Abetz seems to have made friendly inquiries to find his old comrade. Interview with Alexandre Marc by Christian Roy (Vence, 22 November 1990), and Otto Abetz–Alexandre Marc correspondence.

56 *Plans* 8 (October 1931), 17, 235, and 9 (November 1931), 149.

57 Marc diaries (unpublished).

58 This document can be read, in retrospect, as the birth certificate of a particular and original school of thought, of post-war European federalism.

59 See excerpts in Edmond Lipiansky, *Ordre et démocratie: Deux sociétés de pensée: De l'Ordre Nouveau au Club Jean-Moulin* (Paris: Presses Universitaires de France, 1967), 15.

60 Marc's personalism was at least partially formulated as a reaction against the *völkisch* discourse of Nazis – including the Strasserites – who dismissed Marc's insistence on the dignity of the human person as religiousness or sentimentality.

61 Hans Coppi, *Harro Schulze-Boysen – Wege in den Widerstand: Eine biographische Studie* (Koblenz: Dietmar Foelbach, 1993), 61.

62 Until the end of his life, a romantic photo portrait of the young German remained in a prominent place in Marc's living room in Vence.

63 Interview with Alexandre Marc by John Hellman (Cogne, August, 1985).

64 William Shirer, *The Rise and Fall of the Third Reich* (New York: Simon and Shuster, 1960), 1354.

65 Marc diaries (unpublished).

66 Harro Schulze-Boysen had wide contacts through the special *Gegner* milieu. He had been named director of the publication by Franz Jung (1888–1963), a Dadaist writer and libertarian communist activist, who had edited it from 1919 to 1922, and then started it up again in June 1931.

67 Harro Schulze-Boysen to his parents, end of 1931. (I am grateful to Christian Roy for his archival discoveries on Schulze-Boysen.)

68 Cited in Christian Roy, "Alexandre Marc et la Jeune Europe 1904–1934: L'Ordre Nouveau aux origines du personnalisme" (Ph.D Thesis, McGill University, Montreal, 1993), 36.

69 Jardin would keep in contact with Marc's circle when he became right-hand man to Raoul Dautry, czar of the French national railway system, and then, during the occupation of France by the Germans, to Pierre Laval. Before the end of the war he would move to Switzerland to administer Laval's interests there. Pierre Assouline, *Une éminence grise. Jean Jardin (1904–1976)* (Paris: Balland, 1986).

70 Under the heading of "L'ALLEMAGNE EN REVOLUTION," *Plans* 10 (December 1931), 114–22. This article began as a review of a "revealing book" by Pierre Latercier.

71 Probably written by Philippe Lamour.

72 Cited in Loubet del Bayle, *Les non-conformistes*, 442–3.

73 Ibid. M. Loubet del Bayle was much aided in his research by Jean de Fabrègues and later contributed to the latter's *La France Catholique*. Michel

Trebitsch of the Institut d'Histoire du Temps Présent (IHTP), who directs a study group on French intellectuals on the period, has also tended to follow this view. Recent scholarship on German political culture in the period suggests that it is time for a broader perspective.

74 Christian Roy believes that the latter was a French term without a real equivalent across the Rhine, where *Lebensphilosophie* had made the Spirit into a pejorative "thwarter of the soul" – *Der Geist als Widersacher der Seele* – as in the title of Ludwig Klages's book, a principal influence on the *Gegner* milieu.

75 *Plans* 10 (December 1931), 14–23.

76 See Christian Roy. "Henriette Roland Holst-Van der Schalk et *Plans*, 1932: le personnalisme français, modèle pour le renouvellement du socialisme hollandais," *Canadian Journal of Netherlandic Studies/Revue canadienne d'études néerlandaises* 15: 1 (Spring 1994), 18–22.

77 "L'action – La rencontre de Francfort," *Plans* 12 (February 1932), 118–28. This latter group was known to the Esprit people through Hélène Iswolsky, daughter of the last czarist ambassador to France, who was one of them before immigrating to the United States, where she was long active in Dorothy Day's Catholic Worker movement.

78 André Moosmann to Christian Roy, 24 January 1986.

79 Denis de Rougemont, *Journal d'une époque (1926–1946)* (Paris: Gallimard, 1968), 92–3.

80 Christian Roy and interview with Alexandre Marc by John Hellman (Cogne, August 1985).

81 Alexandre Marc's closing address to the thirty-third session of the Collège Universitaire d'Etudes Fédéralistes in Aosta, 17 August 1993. Marc repeated the story every year to elicit commitment to federalism, in his closing address to the students of the graduate summer college of federalist studies he founded in Aosta in the Italian Alps in 1961.

The government of the autonomous, French-speaking Valle d'Aosta region of Italy was led for years by the Union Valdôtaine, a political party which explicitly claimed as its own the principles of "integral federalism" expounded by Marc and his followers. In 1993 the Northern League of Umberto Bossi distributed widely an Italian translation of a Marc federalist text as a brochure. Marc's personal base was in the stately summer hotel at Cogne (a traditional vacation site for Italian politicians), and he was treated with great respect in that establishment during the summer of 1985 when I spent several days interviewing him.

82 See his letter to his mother about the congress, February 1932.

83 Franz Mariaux, *Der Schutthaufen. Aufruhr einer Welt – Volk im Raum – Das Werden des Reichs* (Hamburg: Hanseatische Verlagsanstalt, 1931), 83.

84 H. Esbe (Harro Schulze-Boysen), *Gegner* 5–6 (1 October 1932), 12. The

larger context is provided in Roy, "Alexandre Marc et la Jeune Europe 1904–1934," 188–9.

85 Pechel served as editor of the *Deutsche Rundschau* from 1919 to his death in 1961 (except for the period from 1942 to 1949).

86 See Armin Mohler, *Die Konservative Revolution in Deutschland 1918–1932: Ein Handbuch*, 3rd edition (Darmstadt: Wissenschaftliche Buchgesell-schaft, 1989), section B 150.14 on Rudolf Pechel. Recent research has undermined his claim to have played a role in the Resistance against Hitler in his later career. It was Pechel who insisted on introducing Hitler to the June Club of Arthur Moeller-van den Bruck in 1922. Hitler's harangue made a negative impression on the young-conservative intellectuals in search of a Führer for Germany. Fritz Stern, *The Politics of Cultural Despair: A Study of the Rise of the Germanic Ideology* (Berkeley: University of California Press, 1961), 237.

87 Franz Mariaux to Rudolf Pechel, 17 February 1932, with the untitled report, dated 15 February 1932; Pechel to Mariaux, 19 February 1932, Pechel correspondence in Bundesarchiv, NL160. Christian Roy wishes to thank Hans Coppi for communicating copies of these documents, which he uncovered in the course of his research on Harro Schulze-Boysen. Quotations from Mariaux and Pechel in the following paragraphs are taken from this source. For an exhaustive French account (likely by Lamour) of the proceedings at the Frankfurt Congress, see "L'action – La rencontre de Francfort," *Plans* 12 (February 1932), 118–28. For the German organizers' assessment, see "*Plans* Treffen zu Frankfurt," *Gegner* 4/5 (5 March 1932), 13.

88 He would leave the meeting in protest, but reappear later that year in a leading role at *Gegner*.

89 Marc maintained this until his death in early 2000.

90 Untitled "Sonderdruck der Halbmonatsschrift *Gegner*, Mai 1932." This essay was never published. Hans Coppi kindly shared it with Christian Roy. Quotations from Schulze-Boysen in the following paragraphs are from this essay, unless otherwise noted.

91 "Räte oder Bünde," terms associated, respectively, with the Spartakists like Franz Jung, and with the Youth Movement.

92 See, for example, Marc, "L'état fermé ou autarchie," *Revue d'Allemagne* (5 January 1933), 1–19.

93 Untitled "Sonderdruck der Halbmonatsschrift *Gegner*, Mai 1932."

94 Alistair Hamilton, *The Appeal of Fascism: A Study of Intellectuals and Fascism, 1919–1945* (New York: Macmillan, 1971), 127.

95 He would demonstrate this during the war as leader of the Red Orchestra – though without going so far in his *Ostorientierung* as Ernst Niekisch, for whom the Soviet Union was less a workers' paradise, than an armed camp mounted against the West which Germany should join to form a

single Eurasian block ("ein Reich von Vlissingen bis Wladiwostok").
Cf. Otto-Ernst Schüddekopf, *National-Bolschewismus in Deutschland
1918–1933*. (Frankfurt: Ullstein, 1972), 365.

96  Hamilton, *Appeal*, 166.

97  Interviews with Alexandre Marc by John Hellman (Cogne, August
1985) and Christian Roy (Vence, 15 April 1988). In the middle of the
1920s, Robert Aron had written an article on "The Black Question in
France" for *Current History*: "I wrote a twenty-page study, very dense and
very precise, to explain that such a problem did not exist in our country." The editors were "satisfied by a point of view that was so unexpected for them." Aron, *Fragments d'une vie*, 75.

98  "The flame of a wonderful idealism is obscured by the fumes of disgust-
ing corruption," wrote Ernst Niekisch in his pamphlet *Hitler – ein
deutsches Verhängnis* ("Hitler – a German calamity," Berlin, 1932). Antici-
pating the title of a testament of the Youth Movement by a German
émigré close to the personalists, Ernst Erich Noth – *La tragédie de la
jeunesse allemande* (Paris: Grasset, 1935) – Niekisch saw "the tragedy of
German youth" in "the fact that national socialism could win the trust
of post-war youth," which "gave it its peculiar dynamism and political
weight ... Forces of revolt are surfacing among these young people that
challenge the bases of all that exists, of all established order." Ernst
Niekisch, *Hitler – une fatalité allemande et autres écrits nationaux-bolcheviks*,
edited by Alain de Benoist, translated from German to French by Imke
Mieulet (Puiseaux: Pardès, 1991), 221, 238. This was echoed by Marc's
memory of "a magnificent youth" ready to question every aspect of the
"established disorder," but that was led on and betrayed by "a madman:
Hitler." Interview with Alexandre Marc by John Hellman, Cogne,
August 1985.

99  Particularly in advertisements and articles. See "Jean Longueville" (Jean
Kuckenburg of *Europe*, a person close to *Plans*'s Franco-German network), "Allemagne. Nos amis allemands ont leur hebdomadaire," *Plans*
1 (20 April 1932), 30.

100  This was not such a bizarre idea, given the geopolitical focus of
Niekisch's thinking: ON – like the Pétain regime which a number of its
people would help administrate – claimed to be in opposition to both
Bolshevism and "the Yankee spirit" (albeit as political cultures more
than as rival power blocs).

101  Harro Schulze-Boysen, "Niekisch auf dem Holzweg," *Gegner* 9 (5 May
1932), 13.

102  Hans Coppi and Jürgen Danyel, eds., *Der "Gegner"-Kreis im Jahre
1932/33. Ein Kapitel aus der Vorgeschichte des Widerstandes. Tagung vom
4.–6. Mai 1990* (Berlin: Evangelische Akademie Berlin, 1990), 45–6;
Lutz Schulenburg, ed., *Der Torpedokäfer. Hommage à Franz Jung*

(Hamburg: Nautilus, 1988), 170. Christian Roy provided these references.

103  For an analysis of the fluid context in which the *Gegner* circle was trying to work out its position, see Alexander Bahar's dissertation, *Sozialrevolutionärer Nationalismus zwischen Konservativer Revolution und Sozialismus. Harro Schulze-Boysen und der "Gegner"-Kreis* (Koblenz: Dietmar Fölbach, 1992).

104  Robert Kiefé, a lawyer friend of Dandieu, led the criticism. Interviews with Alexandre Marc by Christian Roy (Vence, 6 April 1988, 3 June 1989).

CHAPTER THREE

1  Klemens von Klemperer, *Germany's New Conservatism* (Princeton: Princeton University Press, 1957), 133, 135–6; Peter D. Strachura, *Gregor Strasser and the Rise of Nazism* (London/Boston: Allen and Unwin, 1983), 117, 42.

2  By Alfred Werner, "Trotzky of the Nazi Party," *Journal of Central European Affairs* 11 (January April 1951), 38, cited in Klemperer, *Germany's New Conservatism*, 137.

3  Klemperer, *Germany's New Conservatism*, 137 8.

4  Ibid., 192.

5  Strachura, *Gregor Strasser*, 3.

6  Kurt Ludecke, cited in ibid., 30.

7  Ibid., 9, 104.

8  Ibid., 12.

9  Ibid., 43.

10  Ibid., 33.

11  Cited in ibid., 52.

12  Viktor Zmegac, ed., *Geschichte der deutschen Literatur, III (1918–1980)* (Königstein: Athenäum, 1984), 13.

13  Strachura, *Gregor Strasser*, 95–6.

14  William Shirer, *The Rise and Fall of the Third Reich* (New York: Simon and Shuster, 1960), 233, 246.

15  Joë Nordmann, "A l'étranger. Une interview d'Otto Strasser," *Mouvements* 2 (1 July 1932).

16  Daniel-Rops, "Les aspirations de la jeunesse française," *La Revue des Vivants* (July 1932), 104–5.

17  Marc, "Pour un communisme national: La revue *Die Tat*," *Revue d'Allemagne* (15 October 1932), 850–1.

18  Ibid., 852.

19  Kurt Sontheimer, "Der Tatkreis," *Vierteljahrshefte für Zeitgeschichte* 7 (1959), cited in Alistair Hamilton, *The Appeal of Fascism* (New York: Macmillan,

1971), 131n; Marc, "Pour un communisme national," 853. Fried's book appeared in translation in Paris in 1932 as *La fin du capitalisme*. He joined the ss in 1934 and worked for its Race and Colonization section. He went on to write (until his death in 1966) for the daily *Die Welt* after Hans Zehrer became its editor in 1953. See Armin Mohler, *Die Konservative Revolution in Deutschland 1918–1932. Ein Handbuch*. 3rd edition (Darmstadt: Wissenschaftliche Buchgesellschaft, 1989).

20  Marc, "Pour un communisme national," 857–9.

21  Ibid., 860–1.

22  Ibid., 860–2.

23  Denis de Rougemont, *Journal d'une époque (1926–1946)* (Paris: Gallimard, 1968), 93.

24  Marc, "Pour un communisme national," 865–6.

25  Ibid., 862, 864–7.

26  See Catherine Baird, "Religious Communism? Nicolai Berdyaev's Contribution to *Esprit*'s Interpretation of Communism," *Canadian Journal of History/Annales canadiennes d'histoire* 30:1 (April 1995), 29–48.

27  Christian Roy observed that the efforts of the Mounier group and many other non-conformists on behalf of the Vichy regime's spiritual "revolution of the twentieth century" at places like the Uriage National leadership school seem prefigured in Hans Zehrer's schemes for a "revolution from above," and according to Walter Struve after *Die Tat* "established a close liaison" with General von Schleicher early in 1932: "Throughout the next year, Zehrer pleaded for the destruction of the Republic by a coalition led by a 'neutral' chancellor with the support of the president, the army, and the ministerial bureaucracy. The hour of the intelligentsia and the Bünde would then have arrived. The 'real revolution' would depend upon them." Walter Struve, *Elites against Democracy: Leadership Ideals in Bourgeois Political Thought in Germany, 1890–1933*. (Princeton: Princeton University Press, 1973), 372; cf. chapter 11: "Hans Zehrer and the *Tat* Circle: The *Révolution Manquée* of the Intelligentsia," 353–76.

28  Alexandre Marc would hold to his grass-roots-based federalist version of it for the rest of his life.

29  Strachura, *Gregor Strasser*, 104, 106.

30  Shirer, *The Rise*, 246. However, Peter Strachura (*Gregor Strasser*, 112, 115) minimized the extent of the threat posed by the "Nazi Left" or "Strasser wing" of the Party.

31  According to Strachura (*Gregor Strasser*, 116), "this clearly was a rather clumsy piece of speculative optimism."

32  Shirer, *The Rise*, 247–8.

33  Ibid., 248.

34  Strachura, *Gregor Strasser*, 119.

35  For example, Otto-Ernst Schüddekopf.

36  Strachura argues that this depiction is "misleading," as Gregor Strasser proved to have little support (*Gregor Strasser*, 156).

37  Ibid., 120.

38  Ibid., 125.

39  Mohler, *Die Konservative Revolution*, A 2.8.

40  Marc, "*Die Tat*, son échec," *Mouvements* 4 (January 1933).

41  Marc. "L'état fermé ou l'autarchie," *Revue d'Allemagne* (15 October 1933), 19.

42  Pierre Bertaux, "Préoccupations de part et d'autre," in *Esprit* 5 (February 1933), 715, 717.

43  Marc, "Jeunesse allemande," *Esprit* 5 (February 1933), 727.

44  Ibid.

45  Marc also mentioned Hans Ebeling of *Der Vorkämpfer*, "who sees Strasser as 'fascist,'" Karl O. Paetel of the *National-Bolschewistische Blätter*, and Fritz Kloppe of *Der Wehrwolf*.

46  Marc never imagined that Mounier would appropriate and make over ON's personalism with far more popular success than Marc's own reviews. Interview with Alexandre Marc by John Hellman (Cogne, August 1985). Cf. Marc's remarks in Gilbert Ganne's inquiry on the generation of 1930: "Qu'as-tu fait de ta jeunesse?" III: "L'Ordre Nouveau," *Arts* 562 (4–10 April 1956).

47  This initiative eventually led to John XXIII and the Second Vatican Council, but the Holy Spirit took some extraordinary detours along the way.

48  Emmanuel Mounier to Georges Izard, 8 September 1932 (unpublished).

49  Nicolas Berdiaeff, "Vérité et mensonge du communisme," *Esprit* 1 (October 1932), 104–28.

50  Emmanuel Mounier, "Refaire la Renaissance," *Esprit* 1 (October 1932), 5–51, included in Mounier's *Oeuvres*, vol. 1 (Paris: Seuil, 1961), 137–74.

51  Mounier, *Entretiens*, *Oeuvres*, vol. 4 (Paris: Seuil, 1963), 508–9.

52  See John Hellman, *Emmanuel Mounier and the New Catholic Left, 1930–1950* (Toronto: University of Toronto Press, 1981), 44–5.

53  Marc, "Vers un ordre nouveau," *Esprit* 2 (November 1932), 330–1.

54  René Dupuis and Alexandre Marc, "Le fédéralisme révolutionnaire," *Esprit* 2 (November 1932), 316–24.

55  Mounier would conciously formulate his review's own communitarian personalism over against that of Marc and Arnaud Dandieu because ON's both fascinated and troubled him and nettled some of his review's older patrons, as we shall see.

56  Denis de Rougemont, "Cause commune," *Présence* (July 1932), 12–15.

57  De Rougemeont, "Cause commune," cited in de Rougemont, *Journal d'une époque (1926–1946)* (Paris: Gallimard, 1968), 94–5.

58  Cited in de Rougemont, *Journal*, 99, 100, 103.

59  De Rougemont, *Journal*, 105.

60 Jacques Maritain to Emmanuel Mounier, 2 November 1932, in Jacques Petit, ed., *Maritain/Mounier, 1929–1939* (Paris: Cerf, 1973), 59.

61 Mounier, *Entretiens* 6 (9 November 1932), cited in *Maritain/Mounier*, 63.

62 Maritain to Mounier, 10 November.1932, ibid., 67.

63 Mounier to Maritain, 11 November 1932, ibid., 64.

64 Mounier, *Oeuvres*, 4: 511–12.

65 Rougemont, a proud and prickly character, later aggressively rejected this charge – describing in minute detail the circumstances of Nizan's contribution, and claiming to be disgusted Nizan had lied to cover the Party's annoyance at having one of its official intellectuals in a "youth front" beyond its control. Denis de Rougemont, "Témoignage," in *Le personnalisme d'Emmanuel Mounier, hier et demain – pour un cinquantenaire* (Paris: Seuil, 1985), 130–3. Cf. Rougemont's *Journal*, 105–6.

66 He gave the example of Thierry Maulnier. Philippe Lamour, "Pour dissiper une équivoque," *Bulletin des groupes Plans* 1 (February 1933), 15.

67 "Sur un certain front unique," *Europe*, January 1933, reprinted in Paul Nizan, *Pour une nouvelle culture*, ed. Susan Suleiman (Paris: Grasset, 1971), 58–65.

68 Nizan, "Jeune Europe," *Commune* 3 (November 1933), 311, 313, 315. Nizan's quotation from Goebbels is in *Paris-Soir*, 20 September 1933.

69 Victor Farias, *Heidegger et le nazisme* (Paris: Verdier, 1987), 97–121; Alistair Hamilton, *The Appeal of Fascism: A Study of Intellectuals and Fascism, 1919–1945* (New York: Macmillan, 1971), 146.

70 Nizan, "Jeune Europe," *Commune* 3 (November 1933), 315.

71 Nizan, "Les enfants de la lumière," *Commune* 2 (October 1933), 105–112.

72 Many personalists would become cadres of the Vichy regime's National Revolution in its efforts of effect a renewal of French institutions – particularly in providing much of the brain-power behind this effort at the Ecole Nationale des Cadres d'Uriage, with a *maréchaliste* mystique which persisted even after the elite school was closed in 1942 and several of its students made their way into the Resistance. Alexandre Marc was invited to lecture there but claimed to have made it a pre-condition for accepting the invitation that the large portrait of Marshal Pétain hanging in the *château* of Uriage be turned to face the wall. Marc's distaste for Uriage contributed to his being frozen out by the Dominicans and other Catholic friends after the war, when they transformed the new Catholic discourse he had pioneered into a fellow-travelling left-wing communitarianism. Cf. John Hellman, *The Knight-Monks of Vichy France: Uriage, 1940–45* (Montreal/Kingston: McGill-Queen's University Press; Liverpool: Liverpool University Press, 1997).

73 This was one reason why both claimed Georges Sorel as an inspiration. On the Russian background to Marc's personalism, see James H. Billing-

ton, *The Icon and the Axe: An Interpretive History of Russian Culture* (New York: Knopf, 1966), 394; James M. Edie, James P. Scanlan, and Mary-Barbara Zeldin, eds., *Russian Philosophy*, vol. 2: *The Nihilists, the Populists, Critics of Religion and Culture* (Chicago: Quadrangle Books, 1965), 172–3.

74  Leopold Dingräve had the idea of a German Third Front of anti-capitalist struggle beside communism and fascism. This was in the final chapter of Dingräve's book *Wohin treibt Deutschland?* ("Whither Germany?") (Jena: Eugen Diederichs Verlag, 1932). (Christian Roy)

75  Interview with Alexandre Marc by John Hellman (Cogne, August 1985); Mounier, 26 November 1932, *Oeuvres*, 4:513.

76  Mounier, *Entretiens* (6 January 1933), *Oeuvres*, 4:518–9.

77  Izard, "Chronique du mouvement," *Esprit* 3 (December 1932), 493–5.

78  In interviews, Alexandre Marc suggested that the relationship never got beyond the Platonic because of his conviction at the time that he would become some form of pledged celibate. The turn of a convert from sexual promiscuity to celibacy, as part of an effort to recapture innocence and purity, was common among the convert intelligentsia in that period. Jacques and Raissa Maritain were also a model for many with their *mariage blanc* (unconsummated marriage).

79  Interview with Alexandre Marc by Christian Roy (Vence, 7 November 1987). Margarita Abella Caprile (1901–60) was an author whose "name figures among the first in her country in matters of poetry." Helena Percas, *La poesia femenina argentina (1810–1950)* (Madrid: Cultura Hispanica, 1958), 268. Although sometimes brooding and existential, her verse was "characterized by a measured romanticism and a marked inclination for the classical." Elida Ruiz, "Las escritoras," *Historia de la literatura argentina. 3 Las primeras décadas del siglo* (Centro Editor de América Latina, 1981), 302. Marc's diary reveals that when he was courting the Argentine poet (and trying to start ON) in the spring of 1931, he, too, envisaged himself primarily a poet. (Christian Roy)

80  Marc later claimed (to his wife's annoyance) that Mitrinovic was standing on his head at the time. For a scholarly portrait of the founder of New Britain and several other short-lived kindred movements (and a description of his relationships with painter Vassily Kandinsky, psycho-analyst Alfred Adler, and urban planner Patrick Geddes – whose disciple Lewis Mumford wrote Marc that he, too, admired ON), see Andrew Rigby, *Initiation and Initiative: An Exploration of the Life and Ideas of Dimitrije Mitrinovic* (Boulder: East European Monographs, 1984). See also the study edited by loyal New Britain militant Harry C. Rutherford, *Certainly, Future – Selected Writings by Dimitrije Mitrinovic* (Boulder: East European Monographs, 1987). In conversations with John Hellman on a visit to McGill University in the 1970s, Mumford revealed himself to be remarkably sympathetic to, and knowledgeable about, the French personalists.

81  Marc described the circumstances of their courtship at a meeting in
London in memory of Mitrinovic in 1954. *New Atlantis Foundation,
The New Europe Group and the New Britain Movement: Collected Publications
1932–1957*, cf. Christian Roy, *Alexandre Marc et la jeune Europe
(1904–1934)* (Nice: Presses d'Europe, 1999), 117–8.

82  Marc. "Jeunesse allemande," *Esprit* 5 (February 1933), 728. According to
Christian Roy, Marc had already used the phrase in his critique of "*Die
Tat: son échec*" in the January issue (no. 4) of the ON-inspired bulletin
*Mouvements.*

83  Marc was never given due credit for the terms and ideas he fostered.
French Catholic progressives were concerned to have orthodox origins
for their new religious ideas, which, of course, had absolutely nothing to
do with the linkage to German national socialism represented by Alexandre Marc. Marc's quality of being doggedly faithful to his inspirations
and to his friends – even when politically incorrect or disgraced – led
him to share his testimony and archives with me and my students when
his son had had enough of studying them.

84  Marc, "Le christianisme et la révolution spirituelle," *Esprit* 6 (March
1933), 934–72.

85  Marc only learned half a century later from me that Maritain's admoni-
tions were behind Mounier's reticence.

86  Marc, "Le christianisme et la révolution spirituelle," 959–60.

87  Mounier noted "L'individu n'est pas la personne" in December 1934, in
the first manifesto in which he defined his communitarian personalism
over against ON's. *Esprit* publicly disassociated itself from ON earlier that
year, but *Esprit* kept, adapting to its own ends, the Marc's group's notion
of personalism.

88  Mounier, *Entretiens, Oeuvres*, 4:510.

89  Ibid., 4:529.

90  Even Mounier did that for a while in this period.

91  Mounier, *Entretiens, Oeuvres*, 4:529.

92  Marc, "Le christianisme et la révolution spirituelle," 972.

93  Interview with Alexandre Marc by Christian Roy (Vence, 11 November
1987).

94  Interview with Alexandre Marc by John Hellman (Vence, August 1985);
unpublished letters of Mounier to Marc, from the end of 1933 to the
end of 1934.

95  Alexandre Marc later claimed he had discovered an obituary of Otto
Neumann with new biographical details and a more detailed account of
the tragic accident in a "serious" review of German affairs: his "German"
*Doppelgänger* oddly took on a life of his own! Interview with Alexandre
Marc by Christian Roy (Vence, 7 November 1987). An acquaintance
of Marc from the Sohlbergkreis, Otto Grautoff, head of the Deutsch-

Französische Gesellschaft, exiled in France under the Nazis, wrote in an unidentified German-language periodical an article entitled "Sozialismus, Kommunismus, Christianismus," where he reviewed the *Esprit* special issue "Rupture entre l'ordre chrétien et le désordre établi." In a few pages of an article found in the Marc archives (but unfortunately devoid of bibliographical reference), Otto Grautoff refers twice to Otto Neumann as an actual figure; once in reference to Marc, once in reference to André Philip. This makes Marc's recollection of an Otto Neumann obituary less improbable.

96 Mounier, *Oeuvres*, 4:515.

CHAPTER FOUR

1 Alexandre Marc, "Les Adversaires," *Revue d'Allemagne* (5 April 1933), 293, 295.
2 Ibid., 298–9.
3 Ibid., 289–99.
4 Ibid., 301–2.
5 Ibid., 303.
6 Ibid., 306–7.
7 Ibid., 308.
8 This manifesto's full French title can be rendered thus: "Manifesto of the Third Force, Movement for the rousing and grouping of forces fighting for the victory of a new social and international order."
9 Marc, "Les Adversaires," 308–9.
10 René Dupuis, "Le 'personnalisme' de William Stern," *Revue d'Allemagne* (5 April 1933), 314. Marc claimed to have written the bulk of Dupuis's articles at this time. Interview with John Hellman (Cogne, Italy, August 1985). William Stern's correspondence with *Esprit* concerning this article was with Marc, not Dupuis.
11 Marc, "Les Adversaires," 309–10.
12 H.W. Koch, *The Hitler Youth: Origins and Development* (London: McDonald and Jane's, 1975), 98–9.
13 Ibid., 214.
14 We have noted that, in 1935, he visited Mussolini, who stressed the left-wing origins of their common ideas, and told Niekisch that he considered Hitler's daydream of invading the Soviet Union foolish.
15 Alistair Hamilton, *The Appeal of Fascism: A Study of Intellectuals and Fascism, 1919–1945* (New York: Macmillan, 1971), 166.
16 Klemens von Klemperer, *Germany's New Conservatism* (Princeton: Princeton University Press, 1957), 240.
17 Ernst von Salomon, *Der Fragebogen* (Hamburg: Rowohlt, 1961), 397.
18 Cited in Hamilton, *The Appeal*, 220–1.

19 Marc later claimed that he had included Dupuis, the dull son of a prominent academic at Sciences Po, as co-author of this book in order to lend
respectability to its ideas, and that Dupuis's influence facilitated its being
awarded a prize by the Académie francaise.

20 Ordre Nouveau, "Mission ou démission de la France," *Ordre Nouveau* 1
(May 1933), 1, 3, 4.

21 "L'Etat contre l'homme," ibid., 5–9.

22 "Liberté ou chômage?" ibid., 1, 10–15.

23 "Faillite économique du libéralisme," ibid., 21–4.

24 "Misère de l'étatisme politique," ibid., 25–8.

25 "Misère de l'étatisme économique," ibid., 29–32.

26 "Faillite politique du libéralisme et du marxisme," ibid., 16–17, 20.

27 Marc, "Hitler ou la révolution manquée," *Ordre Nouveau* 2 (June 1933),
28–30.

28 Ibid., 30.

29 Ibid., 32.

30 Interview with Alexandre Marc by John Hellman (Cogne, August 1985).
By coincidence, Jean Jardin also died of septicemia after a benign operation in the same Neuilly hospital (in November 1976). (Christian Roy)

31 Interview with Daniel-Rops by Gilbert Ganne in "Qu'as-tu fait de ta
jeunesse?" III: "Ordre Nouveau," *Arts* 562 (4–10 April 1956), 7, cited in
Jean-Louis Loubet del Bayle, *Les non-conformistes des années 30* (Paris:
Seuil, 1969), 84.

32 Interview with Alexandre Marc by Gilbert Ganne in "Qu'as-tu fait de ta
jeunesse?" III: "Ordre Nouveau," *Arts* 562 (4–10 April 1956), 7, cited in
Loubet del Bayle, *Les non-conformistes*, 110.

33 Robert Aron, *Fragments d'une vie* (Paris: Plon, 1981), 103.

34 Marc knew that his comrade had dictated a text on his deathbed, but was
only able to read it much later: Dandieu's free-thinking family (except
for his sister Mireille, who suddenly became very religious after her
brother's death) concealed it for decades. Interview with Alexandre Marc
by John Hellman (Cogne, August 1985).

35 Plaquevent mentioned the conversion of "the Jew I told you about" in
one of his reports to the "Conseil de vigilance" of the Archdiocese of
Paris on the effects of reviews like *Esprit* in the Catholic milieu (archives
of the Archdiocese of Paris).

36 In fact it was only after the collapse of his first, spiritual marriage, during
his wartime exile in the United States, that de Rougemont became the
sort of seducer he had dissected, criticized, and rejected in his book.
Interview with Nanik de Rougemont (second wife of Denis) by Christian
Roy (Tübingen, March 1994).

37 Harro Schulze-Boysen and *Gegner* were somewhat different from their
French allies in being steeped in the *bündisch*, exclusive male-bonding

culture of the German youth movement. From the summer of 1932, the *Gegner* became a quasi-official organ for Fred Schmid's Gray Corps, an extreme example of one of those organically homoerotic political movements observed on both Left and Right, as is reflected in the closing chapter – "A Berlin Diary (Winter 1932–3)" – of Christopher Isherwood's 1945 autobiographical novel *Goodbye to Berlin*. A contemporary observer, Nicolaus Sombart (son of the sociologist Werner Sombart), whose account of the development of capitalism captivated ON), in a memoir of his youth in Berlin, described the spirit of the *Männerbund*, "the specific common trait of that German counter-culture," which saw nothing but decadence in the heritage of the Enlightenment: "For what is the opposite of that egalitarian, libertarian, democratic society they abhorred? The men's association, the élitist *Männerbund.*" Sombart can thus "see in the persistence of the masculine *Bund* syndrome the perhaps decisive factor in the stubborn resistance, in the passion with which German men react to the 'project of modernity', that is to the attempt to create a society that offers to each individual, whether man or woman, the opportunity of individual development, which means not only that corresponding political institutions and models of economic organization be put in place, but also that the opportunity be given to freely live out one's sexuality. Political emancipation and sexual emancipation cannot be separated." Nicolaus Sombart, *Jugend in Berlin 1933–1943. Ein Bericht* (München/Wien: Carl Hanser, 1984), 181, 188.

Harro Schulze-Boysen said much the same thing in an unpublished manifesto of May 1932 where he otherwise sounded closest to his French counterparts. As an outspoken libertine he was similar to Philippe Lamour, though he went further in dismissing the family as an outdated institution. He had what one now calls an "open marriage" and, in contrast to Niekisch, whose main reservation about the Soviet Union was the equality it supposedly granted to women, Schulze-Boysen's pro-Soviet Red Orchestra Resistance network had a striking number of women playing leading roles in its ranks. (Christian Roy)

38  Interview with Sabine Robert-Aron by Christian Roy (La Teste-de-Buech, July 1988).

39  The eccentric and brilliant political thinker and mystic Simone Weil, who affected masculine dress, could have been an exception. Marc had known her when she was a girl, and she did contribute to Rougemont's review *Nouveaux Cahiers* in the late 1930s, but, during World War II, Weil wrote a sharp and lucid critique of the elitist current in the personalist movement.

40  Henriette Cahen, "La femme dans la maison," *Ordre Nouveau* 13 (15 July 1934), 24–7. Marc the convert, like his comrades, seemed relatively uncomfortable with discussing, and intolerant of, the sort of heterosexual

promiscuity he had enjoyed as a young man. Homosexuality was almost a taboo subject, despite the high-profile homosexuals (e.g., Jean Cocteau, Maurice Sachs) in the convert milieu.

41 Our contemporary Jesuits and Dominicans – battalions in retreat in most of the world – have a mentality, and life-style, representing a religious culture very different from the disciplined, chaste, austere, young, and confident clerics of Marc's day. See André Ladouze, *Dominicains français et Action Française, 1899-1940. Maurras au couvent* (Paris: Les Editions ouvrières, 1989), an excellent study of the French Dominicans of the inter-war period. Father Ladouze was a Dominican of the striking avant-garde convent of L'Abresle near Lyon, designed by Le Corbusier (always happy to design innovative buildings for what he called "l'Autorité," forces which furthered modernist progress; his chapel at Ronchamp is considered one of the most architecturally significant French churches of the twentieth century). Father Ladouze seems to have had difficulty empathizing with his right-wing predecessors in the Order.

42 Father Ladouze, in his study *Dominicains français et Action Française*, reveals much about the struggle between Action Française sympathizers and progressives within the Dominican Order. But, in his sympathy for the embattled progressives (whose self-justificatory memoirs are an important source for him), he hardly mentions the fact that the progressives, like their Maurrasian rivals, were strikingly anti-liberal and authoritarian by our standards. Dominicans and other Catholics of the Left and the Right would come together for common goals, such those of Pétain's National Revolution, after 1940 (the date when Ladouze's narrative ends – like several other monographs by progressive Catholics stressing Right-Left splits in the 1930s).

43 Interview with Alexandre Marc by John Hellman (Vence, 1985); Marc to Christian Roy, 24 October 1985. Suzanne Jean remained a Protestant.

44 Interview with Alexandre Marc by Christian Roy (Vence, 21 November 1989).

45 Aron, *Fragments d'une vie*, 103.

46 Robert Aron and Arnaud Dandieu, *La révolution nécessaire* (Paris: Grasset, 1933; reprint Jean Michel Place, 1993), xii.

47 Martin Heidegger, "An Introduction to Metaphysics," translated from the German by Ralph Manheim (New Haven: Yale University Press, 1959), 199, cited in Alistair Hamilton, *The Appeal of Fascism. A Study of Intellectuals and Fascism, 1919-1945* (New York: Macmillan, 1960), 147.

48 Ordre Nouveau, "Lettre à Hitler," *Ordre Nouveau* 5 (November 1933), 4.

49 Dupuis's co-authorship of *Jeune Europe*, according to Marc, consisted merely of altering a word here and there (aside from the appendix on Central Europe, on which Dupuis was a specialist, having published a book entitled *Le problème hongrois* in 1931). The book was essentially

made up of the articles Marc had published on European youth movements for the Capriles' *La Nación* in Buenos Aires.

50 Emmanuel Mounier, *Oeuvres*, vol. 4 (Paris: Seuil, 1963), 537.

51 Aron and Dandieu, *La révolution nécessaire* (Paris: Grasset, 1933; reprint Jean Michel Place, 1993), xii.

52 Ibid., xiii–xiv.

53 Ibid., 271–2.

54 Interview with Alexandre Marc by John Hellman (Cogne, August 1985).

55 Jean Jardin, "Pourquoi ils sont Action Française," *Ordre Nouveau* 4 (October 1933), 1–2.

56 Robert Loustau, "Pourquoi ils sont Radicaux," ibid., 4–5.

57 Robert Aron, "Pourquoi ils sont Communistes," ibid., 6.

58 René Dupuis, "Le dernier carré," ibid., 13–4.

59 Claude Chevalley and Michel Glady (pseudonym of Marc), "La mort des partis," ibid., 19.

60 Ibid., 22.

61 Ibid., 24.

62 Thierry-Maulnier, *La crise est dans l'homme* (Paris: Rédier, 1932).

63 Chevalley and Glady, "La mort des partis," *Ordre Nouveau* 4 (October 1933), 27.

64 According to Christian Roy, Heidegger was the object of the critique of the political implications of Germany's contemporary philosophy in Arnaud Dandieu's article "Philosophie de l'angoisse et politique du désespoir," *Revue d'Allemagne*, 15 October 1932, and Alexandre Marc thought it regrettable that Heidegger's prestige came to eclipse that of the less brilliant, but less equivocal and more constructive Karl Jaspers. Cf. Marc, "Existence humaine et raison," *Revue néoscholastique de philosophie* 39 (November 1936), 518–24.

65 Heidegger to J.-M. Palmier, 10 January 1969.

66 Cited in Hamilton, *The Appeal*, 147. Marc particularly admired the rootedness of Heidegger.

67 Heidegger, *Freiburger Studentenzeitung* (30 June 1933); cited in Hamilton, *The Appeal*, 147.

68 See the favourable account of the experiment by André Maurois, *Paris-Soir* (23 October 1935), cited in Edmond Lipiansky, *Ordre et démocratie* (Paris: PUF, 1967), 78–80.

69 Heidegger, *Freiburger Studentenzeitung* (10 November 1933), cited in Hamilton, *The Appeal*, 146.

70 Heidegger, "An Introduction to Metaphysics," 199, cited in Hamilton, *The Appeal*, 148.

71 Interview with Alexandre Marc by Christian Roy (Vence, 14 November 1987). Probably because of the threat of extradition then being faced by the *heimatlos* Russian as an undesirable agitator, this issue did not name

232 Notes to pages 87–94

Marc among its contributors. Zeev Sternhell is sharply critical of "Aron and Dandieu's letter" – but Dandieu had died several months previously. Sternhell, *Ni droite, ni gauche: L'idéologie fasciste en France* (Brussels: Editions Complexe, 2000), 464–5. On Marc's authorship of the letter see Jean-Pierre Gouzy, "L'apport d'Alexandre Marc à la pensée et à l'action fédéralistes," *Le fédéralisme et Alexandre Marc* (Lausanne: Centre de recherches européennes, 1974), 5.

72 Ordre Nouveau, "Lettre à Hitler," 23.
73 Ibid., 4.
74 Ibid., 5.
75 Ibid., 7.
76 Ibid., 8.
77 Ibid., 8.
78 Ibid., 10–11.
79 Ibid., 11.
80 Ibid., 13.
81 Ibid., 14.
82 Ibid., 19.
83 Ibid., 19–20.
84 Ibid., 12.
85 Ibid., 15.
86 Ibid., 16.
87 Ibid., 31–2.
88 Harro Schulze-Boysen, "Lettre ouverte d'un jeune Allemand à la France" (translated from the German by Marc), *Esprit* 5 (February 1933), 732–34.
89 ON, "Post-scriptum à la lettre à Hitler," *Ordre Nouveau* 18 (February 1935), 30–2.
90 "Lettre à Hitler," 22.
91 References to the spirit reappeared, in very different forms, in his discussion of the poet Georg Trakl in 1953. (Christian Roy)
92 Jacques Derrida, *Of Spirit: Heidegger and the Question*, trans. George Bennington and Rachel Bowlby (Chicago: University of Chicago Press, 1989), 45. Jacques Derrida remarked of Heidegger's 1933 *Rektoratsrede*, in which he publicly announced his allegiance to the Hitler regime, that "one could say that he spiritualizes National Socialism": "By the same token, this sets apart Heidegger's commitment and breaks an affiliation. This address *seems* no longer to belong simply to the 'ideological' camp in which one appeals to obscure forces – forces which would not be spiritual, but natural, biological, racial, according to an anything but spiritual interpretation of 'earth and blood.'" It may be noted that the now infamous dyad of "earth and blood" had long been present in Arnaud Dandieu's writings in the "spiritual interpretation" of the Other as Other, i.e. in a heterology

he had been developing for over ten years before his friend Georges
Bataille's influential jottings on this basic theme of a philosophy of desire.
(Christian Roy)

93 As Derrida (*Of Spirit*, 37) notes, in Martin Heidegger's *Rektoratsrede*, "in a
sense which would, to be sure, *like* to think of itself not Hegelian, his-
toricity is immediately and essentially determined as spiritual. And what
is true of history is true of the world. On several occasions, Heidegger
associates, with a hyphen, the adjectives *geistig* and *geschichtlich*: *geistig-
geschichtlich* is *Dasein*, *geschichtlich-geistig* is the world. This association will
be constant, two years later, in the *Introduction to Metaphysics*." (Christian
Roy)

94 If Derrida's book highlights the mutual untranslatability of *Geist* and
*esprit*, the full scope of the correspondences and differences cutting
across and marking off the German and French spheres of "spiritual" discourse, as it directly pertains to our topic in a wider context, is explored
in the upcoming book of our colleague Thomas Keller (Université de
Strasbourg): *Deutsch-französische personalistische Diskurse in interkulturellem
Kontext.* (Christian Roy)

95 "Lettre à Hitler," 11.

96 Karl-Eugen Gass (Bonn University) to *Ordre Nouveau*, 18 May 1934; Hans
Espe (Dantzig Polytechnical School) to *Ordre Nouveau*, 19 October 1937.

97 Interview with Alexandre Marc by Christian Roy (Vence, 14 November
1987).

98 Although Marc later remarked that in writing it "Rops" seemed ready to
change any assertion into its opposite with disturbing casualness. Interview with Alexandre Marc by Christian Roy (Vence, 14 November 1987).

99 Letter from Daniel-Rops, 20 November 1933, among Gabriel Marcel's
correspondence at the Bibliothèque Nationale in Paris.

CHAPTER FIVE

1 It was published in Paris as a co-authored work with René Dupuis to lend
respectability to Marc's ideas. Dupuis was the intellectually lacklustre son
of a prominent academic, and his influence helped the book win a prize
from the Académie française (interview with Alexandre Marc). See
above, chapter 4, note 49.

2 Harro Schulze-Boysen, "Lettre ouverte d'un jeune Allemand à la
France," *Esprit* 5 (February 1933), 732–4. This reflects the impassioned
anti-liberalism and anti-individualism which would be behind his wartime
contacts with the Soviet Union. Western capitalism was always the principal enemy of the New Order for him, just as for his spiritual heir, contemporary New Right leader Alain de Benoist, who would have preferred
to "wear the helmet of the Red Army rather than living under the yoke

of American cultural imperialism, chowing down hamburgers in Brooklyn." Alain de Benoist, "L'ennemi principal," *Elements* 41 (March–April 1982), 48.

3 It was silenced in the month of April.

4 He was taking advantage of Claude Chevalley's visit to a mathematics conference in Germany.

5 Jacqueline Chevalley to Marc, 7 March 1934.

6 Philippe Burrin, *La dérive fasciste: Doriot, Déat, et Bergery* (Paris: Seuil, 1986), 123.

7 Ibid., 122.

8 "Entretiens VIII" (27 June 1934) (unpublished). They were to meet in the *Esprit* offices, but Mounier was, typically, unavailable, being at a meeting in volatile Brussels. Mounier did not make much of Strasser, or of this visit, in his diary.

9 Mounier went to see Valois on 28 June and privately concluded that Valois was a difficult man to work with. They discussed Valois's "cultural cooperatives" project as well as the possibility of creating a trade union for the press. Like Mounier, Valois had a mystical Catholic side. Ibid.

10 Marc circular letter to several colleagues (1 July 1934).

11 7 July 1934.

12 Mounier, *Carnets* VIII (26 July 1934) (unpublished). Recall that several important backers of Mounier's review – particularly Maritain – had serious reservations about the Third Force, which they considered a quasi-fascist, if not crypto-Nazi, initiative.

13 Gerhard Banaskiwitz, "Hitlerjungen auf Frankreichfahrt," *Sohlbergkreis* 1–2 (October–November 1934); Pierre Cherny, "Jeunesse française en Allemagne," ibid., 39–40. Cherny's muted acknowledgment of French reservations about the Hitler Youth are a rare note in what is a highbrow, but generally propagandist, Hitlerite publication.

14 Abetz wrote by way of introduction: "In Deutschland marschiert sie in den Reihen Adolf Hitlers, dessen Aufsteig sie schon damals den französischen Kameraden vorausgesagt und begründet hatte." "1930–1940 Rückblick und Ausschau," *Sohlbergkreis* 1–2 (October–November 1934), 1.

15 Ibid., 36. There were articles by Rudolf Hess and French war veteran become pacifist Georges Scapini. There was an admiring account of the interesting Decades colloquium held by Paul Desjardins (with writer Ramon Fernandez as secretary) at Pontigny, where one could meet people like Fabre-Luce, Denis de Rougemont, Roger Martin du Gard, Léon Brunschvicg, and Pierre Drieu la Rochelle. Fernandez had been an early supporter of *Esprit* and would, like Drieu and Fabre-Luce, subsequently move toward a collaborationist position.

16 Otto Abetz, "Französischer Nationalismus 1934," *Sohlbergkreis* 1 (October–November 1934), 23–6.

17 Hugo Rheiner, "Die dedachte Revolution," *Sohlbergkreis* 4–5 (January–February 1935), 119.

18 Carl Nabersberg, "Deux jeunesses en présence," *Sohlbergkreis* 1–2 (October–November 1932), 7.

19 Robert Aron to Dr Bremer, 26 November 1934 (planning a Franco-German meeting); Robert Aron to Raymond de Becker, 26 November 1934 (evaluating a Franco-English meeting and projecting a Franco-Belgian one).

20 "Französischer Frontkampfen führer spricht zu H.-J. Führer," *Sohlbergkreis* 4–5 (January–February 1935), 123.

21 "Im gleichen Heft wird aber auch ausführlich von der 'Krise der Demokratie und Staatsreform' gesprochen." "Zeitschriftschau/Revue des revues," *Sohlbergkreis* 3 (December 1934), 87. This sympathetic interest was displayed for *Esprit* despite Mounier's publishing an article (by Emmanuel Lévinas) which was faulted for its unfairly suggesting that Hitler was a power-hungry war-monger and so was seen as running against "the mutual comprehension of peoples."

22 "La jeunesse hitlérienne," *Sohlbergkreis* 3 (December 1934), 82.

23 Paul Marion, "Die lebendigen Kräfte einer französischen Wiedergeburt," *Sohlbergkreis* 4–5 (January–February 1935), 110–4.

24 Otto Abetz, "A la recherche de l'Occident," *Sohlbergkreis* 4–5 (January–February 1935) 117; Hugo Rheiner, "Das Germanentum und der Untergang des Abendlandes," *Sohlbergkreis* 6 (March 1935), 208–9.

25 Cf. March 1935. A francophone woman who returned from a visit to the Hitler Youth work camps remarked how they effectively eradicated nefarious "individualism." Claudine Chonez, "Réflexions au retour du camp de travail," *Sohlbergkreis* 6 (March 1935), 160–1.

26 This idea was put forward in a 7 March 1935 letter of Schulze-Boysen to Claude Chevalley and was another example of continued, if sporadic, ties between ON and Schulze-Boysen. The latter would pursue this matter in August, since he thought groups like this could help him acquire a position of influence in Hitler's regime.

27 Marc to ON group, 19 March 1935. Despite Marc's encouragement, however, the Paris ON people did not seem to pick up on the idea of working with Schulze-Boysen.

28 In March 1935, Schulze-Boysen was treating Chevalley as his new principal French contact now that Marc was difficult to reach in southern France. Although when Schulze-Boysen proposed creating an ON study circle and publishing ON articles in friendly Nazi youth publications he was already teaching international politics seminars for the Nazi party's youth wing, he later claimed to have been trying to subtly distance his young listeners from Hitlerism. Schulze-Boysen to Chevalley, 7 March 1935; interview with Helga Mulachiè (née Schulze) by Christian Roy (Vence, 11 September 1989).

29  Marc to Chevalley, 19 March 1935.

30  Hugo Rheiner, "Das Germanentum und der Untergang des Abendlandes," *Sohlbergkreis* 6 (March 1935), 208–9.

31  "Un programme des Revendications des Jeunes dans l'Ordre International," *Sohlbergkreis* 7 (April 1935), 213.

32  According to Otto Abetz's notes, 20 May 1935, *Inland I Partei/41/4*, cited
in Burrin, *Dérive*, 89.

33  It seemed to have become imprudent to publish the names of the
French involved with the Sohlbergkreis. Reports of contacts with the
Italian fascists, in contrast, were published.

34  President Jean Dupuy commented: "Lassen Sie mich ganz zu Anfang
sagen, wie stark ich durch den Gedanken beeindruckt gewesen bin, den
die Hitlerjugend in die Zukunft der deutschen Nation setzt." "Französischer Jugendführer über den Reichsberufwettkampf," *Sohlbergkreis* 8–9
(May–June 1935), 252.

35  "Der Kreis um Esprit bemüht sich um eine neue religiöse Unterbauung
der Arbeitsethik; die Gruppe Ordre Nouveau verfolgt die Frage, wie die
monotone Last der maschinellen Arbeit der ihr bisher lebenslang
erhafteten Berufsschicht abgenommen und durch eine Art technischen
Arbeitsdienst der Jugend in monatlichen Schichten getragen werden
kónnte." "Au sujet du socialisme./Eine Aussprache über den Sozialismus," *Sohlbergkreis* 8–9 (May–June 1935), 242.

36  The French ambassador intervened to prevent this encounter because
of growing tensions between Italy and France over Ethiopia. Mounier,
*Carnets* VIII, 29 May 1935 (unpublished).

37  Mounier also noted that, at the "camps of young fascists" which they visited, a black shirt said to Galey, "Why not work with the Communists?
That's the way of the future." Spirito was reputed to be "the philosopher
of the Left" but was prevented from speaking in the discussions.

38  Mounier, "Entretiens VIII," 29 May 1935, unpublished section.

39  Minutes of the ON committee meeting (Aron, Dupuis, Chevalley). Marc
archives. The Marc archives also contain a list of participants in this
meeting. Robert Aron's archives, in contrast, contain only a few interesting pre-war materials. The bulk of them deal with his post-war career as
prominent historian of the Vichy period and *academicien*.

40  For example, at the same time as the Fascist congress in Rome, Karl-
Eugen Gass, professor at the University of Bonn, wrote ON secretary
Mireille Dandieu (18 May 1935) to request issues of *Ordre Nouveau* –
beginning with the Letter to Hitler – for his seminar on present political
movements in France. This is one example from a few remaining letters
which show that professors in Nazi Germany universities interested in
new politics in France were particularly interested in ON. It suggests that
German intellectuals were less interested in French sycophants and

future collaborationists like Jean Luchaire and Alphonse de Chateaubriant perhaps because they believed – as Otto Abetz professed to believe –
that each *Volk* should find its way, effect its own revolution. Marc and
ON's self-confidence, independence, even arrogance, about the French
New Order might even have seemed refreshing to Nazi true believers.

41  *Sohlbergkreis* 8–9 (May–June 1935), 255.

42  Notably those of Maurice de Gandillac, a prominent proponent of
Franco-German rapprochement in the *Esprit* group. For more on de
Gandillac's overtures toward the new Germany, see John Hellman,
*Emmanuel Mounier and the New Catholic Left, 1930–1950* (Toronto:
University of Toronto Press, 1981).

43  Abetz to Marc (4 June 1935). The letter, on *Sohlbergkreis* stationery, also
urged the continuing exchange of publications.

44  Marc to Jacqueline Chevalley, 5 June 1935. Marc, unimpressed by
accounts of the Rome congress, asked for news of the "Moosman-Abetz
project." Marc was engaged in a continuing effort at ideological clarification with Aron, Daniel-Rops, and the others. He also encouraged an
exchange of publicity with de Becker's *L'Esprit Nouveau.*

45  Cf. Burrin, *Dérive*, 190.

46  After 1940, Jardin would be coopted from Dautry's service, via the inter-
vention of ON members Robert Gibrat and Robert Loustau (already
active Vichy government functionaries), to become right-hand man to
Laval. In the 1960s Jardin used his contacts with his old friend Achenbach – become an influential figure in the FDP – to help secure Ruhr
manufacturers their share in producing the new joint Franco-German
stock of armaments. Cf. Pierre Assouline, *Une éminence grise. Jean Jardin
(1904–1976)* (Paris: Balland, 1976), 320.

47  Cf. Schulze-Boysen to Chevalley, 5 August 1935. Schulze-Boysen planned
to meet Chevalley in Geneva. He also planned to meet with Denis de
Rougement at the end of August. In Schulze-Boysen's correspondence
with his family, Christian Roy found references to a report he was supposed to draft for Ribbentrop's office on the non-conformists.

48  ON mathematician Claude Chevalley visited Germany in this period.
Schulze-Boysen wrote a letter to his own father (13 June 1934) in which
he claimed to have prefigured much of the Hitlerite revolution in *Gegner.*
See Christian Roy, *Alexandre Marc et la Jeune Europe (1914–1934)* (Nice:
Presses d'Europe, 1998), 329n181.

49  We may assume that Schulze-Boysen did not have to be worried about his
correspondence with Claude Chevalley being intercepted because he was
in Geneva – with some friends from the SS – for a League of Nations
summer course. The other letter was to his father.

50  Schulze-Boysen to Chevalley, 8 August 1935.

51  Hellman, *Emmanuel Mounier*, 114.

52 Xavier Dehan, "'Jeune Europe', le salon Didier et les Editions de la Toison d'Or (1933–1945)," *Bijdragen-Cahiers,* Navorsings – en Studiecentrum voor de geschiedenis van de tweede wereldoorlog/Centre de recherches et d'études historiques de la seconde guerre mondiale (Brussels), 17 (December 1995), 204–36.

53 In this he was like many Dominicans, including his friend Maydieu, as we have seen.

54 Yves Congar to Marc, 15 February 1936.

55 Congar to Marc, 4 March 1936.

56 François Perroux, "La personne ouvrière et le droit du travail," *Esprit* 42 (March 1936), 881.

57 C.10 June 1936; cf. *Le fédéralisme et Alexandre Marc* (Lausanne: Centre de recherches européennes, 1974), 59; Hellman, *Emmanuel Mounier,* 114.

58 That Mounier returned on 24 June 1936 from Germany is recorded in Jacques Petit, ed., *Maritain/Mounier, 1929–1939,* (Paris: Cerf, 1973), 151. We have already noted that in early June a brief notice appeared that Monnier [*sic*] and a few others would go to a meeting with English and German youth at Zontéavec from 11–12 July. "Bruxelles," *Journal Intérieur des groupes d'amis d'Esprit* 8–9 (June–July 1936). The only young Germans allowed to travel abroad in this period were Nazis.

59 "Un programme des Revendications des Jeunes dans l'Ordre international," *Sohlbergkreis* 7 (April 1935); *Esprit,* 41 (February 1936), 791; "Tentation," *Jeune Europe* 3 (1936). This article is not included in the complete bibliography of Mounier's writings in his *Oeuvres,* vol. 4 (Paris: Seuil, 1963), but was found in the folder "Documents sur *Esprit*" (1936) in the Bibliothèque E. Mounier. The documents left out of Mounier's "complete bibliography" by his literary heirs often referred to contacts with the Young Nazis or ON. Mme Mounier told me that Mounier's diary on the period covering the Popular Front and this meeting with the Hitler Youth was lost by a researcher who was reading it on a park bench on the grounds of the Esprit community, Les Murs Blancs, in the 1960s.

60 For more on the Didier salon and "Jeune Europe" see J. Gérard-Libois and José Gotovich, *L'An 40: La Belgique occupée* (Brussels: Centre de recherche et d'information socio-politiques, 1971), 44–7; Xavier Dehan, "*Jeune Europe,* le salon Didier et les Editions de la Toison d'Or (1933–1945)," 204–36.

61 Mounier to Mme Guittet, 15 August 1936, *Oeuvres,* 4:597.

62 "Notre Manifeste," *Esprit* 49 (October 1936), 4.

63 Marc to Izard, 11 June 1936.

64 The school was nicknamed "l'X" by its students.

65 Coutrot was a trusted comrade of Alexandre Marc, since he was related to Marc's wife.

66  The Marc archives contain considerable correspondence between Marc and Coutrot. See also Jean-Louis Loubet del Bayle, *Les non-conformistes des années 30* (Paris: Seuil, 1969), 466–7; Robert Soucy, *French Fascism: The Second Wave, 1933–1939* (New Haven and London: Yale University Press, 1995), 232–3.

67  He worked as an engineer in the Loire basin until 1930.

68  Loubet del Bayle, *Les non-conformistes*, 463.

69  After 1940 both Loustau and Gibrat would be named to – and serve at least for a time in – relatively influential positions in the Vichy government, as we shall see. While his ON comrade Jean Jardin moved from being right-hand man to Dautry, the head of the French National Railway system, to being cabinet chief for Premier Pierre Laval, Loustau would move from working behind the scenes with Doriot to the position of cabinet director for Paul Baudoin, the Vichy government's minister of foreign affairs. Loustau would also contribute to the composition of the government's Charte du Travail and to the draft of that government's famous "Message de Saint-Etienne" on social problems. Gibrat would serve for a time as Vichy's secretary of state for communications, as ON's Albert Ollivier worked for Radio Vichy.

70  X. de Lignac to Christian Roy, 26 April 1986.

71  De Lignac (subsequently a prominent associate of General de Gaulle under the pseudonym Jean Chauveau) later claimed that he had been given a subject and its lines of development for the *Courrier* by Marc and was only required to make Marc's ideas as readable as possible.

72  Interview with Gabriel Jardin by Christian Roy (Vevey, Switzerland, August 1993).

73  Emmanuel Mounier, *Oeuvres*, vol. 4 (Paris: Seuil, 1963), 559.

74  This is the picture of the general situation presented in Loubet del Bayle, *Les non-conformistes*, 177.

75  See Pierre Andreu's memoirs, *Le rouge et le blanc 1928–1944* (Paris: La Table Ronde, 1977), 73–7, on this Front national syndicaliste of young spiritual revolutionaries looking to Péguy and Sorel as their masters, and on the "Young Europe" of anti-liberal revolutions described by Marc in his book as models to emulate; on the Nouvelles Equipes, see Andreu's *Révoltes de l'Esprit. Les revues des années trente* (Paris: Kimé, 1991), 69–73. (Christian Roy)

76  Loubet del Bayle, *Les non-conformistes*, 116–17.

77  Aline Coutrot, *Un courant de la pensée catholique: l'hebdomadaire "Sept" (mars 1934–août 1937)* (Paris: Cerf, 1961), 103.

78  Marc minimized the importance of this initiative. According to him, the colonel soon found himself being addressed in a brash "tone that makes me think you are forgetting who I am," and when he bragged of having

over a million men behind him, young Robert Aron, always the irreverent surrealist, responded that there were even more subscribers to the Gas Company! Interview with Alexandre Marc by John Hellman (Cogne, 1985), and Robert Aron, *Fragments d'une vie* (Paris: Plon, 1981), 108.

79  Mounier to Berdyaev, 15 February 1934. This letter is misdated 1936 in Mounier's *Oeuvres*, vol. 4, thus giving the (false) impression that there was a definitive split between the ON and Esprit groups after the 6 February riots. In fact the two movements were soon drawn to one another again, as we shall see.

80  *Sept* published this interview on 28 December 1934 (cf. Coutrot, *Sept*, 166–7).

81  De Gaulle was already a subscriber to *Sept* and an early member (card no. 7) of Alexandre Marc's Amis de *Sept*. Interviews with Alexandre Marc.

82  Aron knew Charles de Gaulle through a common friend, Colonel Emile Mayer.

83  In 1937.

84  Another acquaintance of Marc who was an early admirer of this book was the Christian Democrat Philippe Serre.

85  Jean Lacouture provides ample evidence for this in volume 1 of his biography of de Gaulle, *De Gaulle* (Paris: Seuil, 1984).

86  Interview with Alexandre Marc by John Hellman (Vence, 1984), and Pascal Sigoda, "Charles de Gaulle, la 'Révolution conservatrice' et le personnalisme du mouvement 'Ordre Nouveau,'" *Espoir* 46, March 1984, 46–7.

87  The two engineers worked so closely together, were so closely identified, that they are referred to in the ON minutes as Gibrat-Loustau. But Gibrat seems to have been more self-consciously faithful to ON ideas while Loustau would adopt a higher profile in the groups which he entered as an ideologue.

88  The minutes of a 29 May meeting of the technical cells on this subject was reported in the minutes of general meeting of ON held on 31 May. The assumption was that progress of ON ideas, whether in political parties or anti-parliamentary leagues, was of vital importance – but the group was more interested in extra-parliamentary movements than in organizations intent on working within the framework of liberal democratic institutions. Minutes of ON meetings remain in the papers of Alexandre Marc.

89  Burrin, *Dérive*, 190.

90  22 June 1935, Aron and Chevalley ON minutes to Marc. This demonstrates that years before Robert Loustau, as a hard-core Pétainist Vichy functionary, helped engineer Emmanuel Mounier's elimination as an ideologue for Vichy's youth movements, his fellow non-conformists saw Loustau as representing a danger that their movement would turn into a personalist fascism.

91 For example, Georges Izard's diary shows that in June 1935 he was interested in appealing to renegade Volontaires nationaux.

92 Cf. Christian Roy, "Alexandre Marc and the Personalism of *L'Ordre Nouveau* (1920–1940)" (MA thesis, McGill University, 1986), 152–3.

93 Mounier, "Entretiens VIII" (8 October 1935) (unpublished section).

94 Edmond Lipiansky, *Ordre et démocratie* (Paris: PUF, 1967), 76; Gérard Brun, *Technocrates et technocratie en France 1918–1945* (Paris: Albatros, 1985), 39; Hellman, *Emmanuel Mounier*, 314n43. Mounier saw their title as "Travail et Nation" in October.

95 Loustau was accompanied by Claude Popelin.

96 After resigning from the PPF in 1938, Loustau would, as noted above, resurface in the Pétain regime.

97 Le Corbusier (Charles Edouard Jeanneret), a French Swiss, had been a member of Le Faisceau of Georges Valois. His interest in religious architecture is demonstrated by his church at Ronchamps and the Dominican convent at l'Abresle near Lyon.

98 Even if it can now be seen, in retrospect, as a front for what became a sort of Catholic New Right.

99 A prominent Dominican medieval scholar and social activist/theorist involved with Juvisy, Père Marie-Dominique Chenu, described the community in these terms in 1935.

100 Les Editions du Cerf continues to be a major French Catholic publishing house.

101 This is how Jacques Maritain described his own conversion experience to Jean Cocteau. "Réponse à Jean Cocteau" (1926) in Jacques Maritain *Oeuvres (1912–1939)*, ed. Henry Bars (Paris: Desclée De Brouwer, 1975), 363.

102 Decades later, in her authoritative history of the review *Sept*, Aline Coutrot described its secretary Marc – the militantly anti-communist son of a wealthy Russian family ruined by the October Revolution – as "an Israëlite from central Europe who converted to Catholicism after having been a Communist" (Coutrot, *Sept*, 58). Another example was Marc's gently raised Esprit comrade Emmanuel Mounier, who was described by his first biographer, Candide Moix, as the son of rough peasant stock, a sort of reincarnated Péguy. In fact Mounier was the pride and joy of a Grenoble pharmacist who shared intellectual and religious interests with his friend, the Grenoble dean and Bergsonian philosopher who became his son's mentor before being named minister of education at Vichy: Jacques Chevalier.

103 Coutrot, *Sept*, 58. Folliet, the son of a Lyon silk manufacturer, was a well-known social Catholic. A journalist, public speaker, professor, theologian, poet, and balladeer, he would serve as general secretary and then vice-president of the Semaines Sociales program and director of

the *Chronique Sociale de France* from 1938 to 1944. He was ordained a priest in 1968 at age sixty-five.

104  Coutrot, *Sept*, 63.

105  Congar to Marc, 5 January 1934. Congar considered Marc the *de facto* representative of a projected review which Congar found generally good, well written, but a bit moralistic and eclectic. He told Marc that it was crucial to the Juvisy project to have a team of people who had the time to think and study. Unlike most of the Dominicans with whom Marc worked in the 1930s, Congar remained friends with Marc for life and, from his deathbed in Les Invalides military hospital in the 1990s, helped Marc reconstruct the story of the Moulin Vert group in the 1930s.

106  During the great changes which took place in the Catholic church in the period of the Second Vatican Council.

107  P. Bouessé to Marc, 11 January 1934.

108  Bernadot, Boisselot, Louvel ... Chéry and Maydieu when they were in Paris; only one other non-Dominican, Joseph Folliet, was in attendance at these meetings. See Coutrot, *Sept*, 57.

109  Father Yves Congar, interviewed by J. Feller (1980), cited in André Ladouze, *Dominicains français et Action Française. Maurras au couvent* (Paris: Les Editions Ouvrières, 1989), 144; *J. Puyo interroge le père Congar* (Paris: Centurion, 1975), 24. A quotation from Maurras's former bodyguard adorns the monument to the deportees and victims of the Holocaust just behind the Cathedral of Notre Dame, on the southern tip of the Ile de la Cité in Paris.

110  Marc to Boisselot, 7 June 1936. Marc advises his correspondents how to form a group of Amis de *Sept*: he suggests contacting a certain woman whose husband is a doctor and who has promised to see her friends, a priest, the directors of the JOC (Jeunesse ouvrière chrétienne), etc. (This letter suggests the bourgeois milieu in which *Sept* gathered its *amis* for support: the initiative involved organizing and instructing a certain clientele, many of whom felt threatened by the united Left of the Popular Front in general, and the Communists in particular, and sought a viable progressive alternative.)

111  On 3 March 1934.

112  17 March 1934. Cf. Coutrot, *Sept*, 39.

113  By c. March 1934. Ibid., 84.

114  Marc conceived of the idea for, and put together, Gilson's book.

115  Guerry had been based in Grenoble, where he had exerted considerable influence on the young Emmanuel Mounier. Mounier would go on to do much to shape a "neither Right nor Left" ideology attractive to young men who had been strongly influenced by, but wanted to leave behind, the Action Française.

116  C. March 1934. Coutrot, *Sept*, 107.

117  C. March 1934. Ibid., 105–6.

118  E.g., a young exiled German who had had an important function in a German youth organization published under the name of "Karl Turmer." (His real name was Solzbacher, and he eventually left for the USA.) Cf. ibid., 58.

119  Marc signed his essays with the pseudonym "Scrutator" or, sometimes, his own name. Interviews with Alexandre Marc. Ibid., 58.

120  Maydieu to Marc, 14 March 1934. Maydieu wrote that every time he came to Paris he was criticized for not giving sufficient circulation to *Sept*. He asked Marc to give a report on the review every two weeks, and to tell him every week what priests he had been able to see during that week.

121  The sisters in this convent worked with Plaquevent on rehabilitating prostitutes, who were given the choice of convent life (which included laundry and sewing work for locals) over prison. Marc, his wife, and his infant daughter lived in a separate residence within the convent walls. This was not so unusual in the period: after World War II, Paul Touvier and his family were only the best known among the fugitives hidden for many years in Catholic religious communities.

122  C. 1934. Cf. Coutrot, *Sept*, 126.

123  Ibid., 134–5.

124  Ibid., 166–7.

125  But rather than being upset, the Dominicans gave Mounier the impression of being proud about the police surveillance: an indication of the anti-bourgeois, rebellious spirit of the times.

126  *Sept*, May 1935.

127  Growth in subscriptions allowed *Ordre Nouveau* to expand from publishing editions of thirty-two to forty-eight pages in March 1935, and then to sixty-four in October 1936.

128  Pierre-Henri Simon in *Sept*, 3 January 1936, cited in Coutrot, *Sept*, 111. Simon was a well-known member of the *Esprit* group, so this is another example of non-conformists passing from one publication to another.

129  Simon in *Sept*, 10 January 1936, cited in Coutrot, *Sept*, 109.

130  Cf. ibid., 122, 124.

131  E.g., "Scrutator" [Marc] in *Sept* (13 March 1936) attacked the Soviet Union (as had Daniel-Rops earlier) for destroying workers just as "Yankee super-capitalism" had. Cf. ibid., 183.

132  Ibid., 125.

133  E.g., Boisselot to Marc, 30 June 1936. Boisselot understands Marc's annoyance (about being censored) but is under pressure to cut his article to make room to say something about the fascist leagues.

134  Marc's essays in *Sept* – such as a projected *sept jours* column on the

Front Populaire Espagnol – were, to his great annoyance, subject to *de facto* Dominican censorship. Cf. Father Boisselot to Marc, 28 March 1936. In another letter to Marc, dated 25 May 1936, Boisselot appealed to Marc to change his articles. "As a popular journal [we] have already lost too many subscribers."

135 Cf. *Sept*, 27 March 1936.

136 Primard to Marc, 16 April 1936. Primard told Marc that he and Flamand were working closely together.

137 A letter from Paul Flamand to Marc, 6 May 1936, describes publishing efforts involving La Société de Saint-Louis and ON, Gaston Bergery or Georges Izard.

138 Flamand to Marc, 6 June 1936. Flamand admired *La Flèche* and was making an effort to encounter ON Catholics like Xavier de Lignac.

139 A list of fifteen *Sept* supporters compiled around March 1936 included three engineers, a notary, a tailor, a doctor, a professor, a pharmacist, a *huissier*, etc. About one-third are priests (Marc archives). Marc advised the Dominicans on how to establish a support network for *Sept*. Cf. Marc to Boisselot, 7 June 1936.

140 Circulation increased from about 2,500 in June 1934 to about 25,000 in May 1937. The publication figures for special issues like that on Communism in December 1936 (110,000), or on "le Christ et l'ouvrier" in February 1937 (with an interview with Léon Blum) (150,000), contrasted favourably with that of mainstream Catholic publications such as *France Catholique* (8,000) or *Vie Catholique* (10,000) ... or the 1,000 or less of *Ordre Nouveau* or *Esprit*.

141 Marc to Boisselot, 21 June 1936.

142 In later June, in the wake of the Popular Front victory, Paul Flamand was envisaging moving to Paris the next October to create a centre for the Maison Saint-Louis, Alliance Louisienne, Editions du Seuil, etc. This project was to be kept secret. Flamand to Marc, 23 June 1936.

143 Mounier noted in his diary that the cardinal (probably Verdier) had told him that he had written papal secretary of state Pacelli that all censorship measures taken by the Vatican against French Catholics might prove catastrophic, given the prospective construction of an Ordre Nouveau in France (although Mounier found the cardinal's notion of what this New Order might be rather tender-minded and vague ... too naïvely influenced by Popular Front populist rhetoric). "Entretiens IX," 26 June 1936 (unpublished section).

144 See Hellman, *Emmanuel Mounier*, 90–1. About sixty members were present to vote at the meeting. At the time of the merger, the Third Force had around two to three hundred members, according to Galey. Burrin, *Dérive*, 118.

145 Mounier, "Entretiens VIII" (unpublished section).

146 Mounier, "Entretiens VIII" (22 November 1934) (unpublished section).

147 "Sans religion, sans une Foi vivante on ne sauve aucune société; on n'en crée pas ... Que ne pouvez-vous, Messieurs, vous abstraire un moment de Paris, de ses chapelles, de ses modes intellectuelles, pour aller vivre paisiblement quelques semaines dans un village ou une petite ville – et regarder la Vie ... La Vie, qui n'est ni très 'intellectuelle,' ni très 'logique' mais qui appelle aussi un Absolu: et ce n'est pas celui que vous proposez." Paul Flamand to ON, 29 November 1934.

148 Mounier, "Entretiens VIII" (30 November 1934) (unpublished section).

149 Cf. Burrin, *Dérive*, 154.

150 Albert Ollivier particularly admired Robert Aron. Louis Ollivier to Christian Roy, 16 January 1986.

151 Marc to Roy, 12 June 1986; Lipiansky, *Ordre et démocratie*, 77.

152 Cf. Loubet del Bayle, *Les non-conformistes*, 117.

153 Maydieu to Marc, 26 January 1935.

154 Claude Hurtubise to Claude Chevalley, 10 December 1934. This was the first of an exchange of five letters – running to August 1935 – between Hurtubise and Chevalley in which the French-Canadian journal *La Relève* promised to advertise ON in Quebec. It provides a list of bookstores selling *Ordre Nouveau* in Quebec. There was mention of young Quebec writer Robert Charbonneau being in touch with Daniel-Rops.

155 Robert Aron to P. Fontaine, 21 December 1934. In this letter Aron projects an ON evening in Brussels and envisages eventual contacts with the New Britain movement, and with the "young Belgian revolutionaries" publishing the paper *Le rouge et le noir*.

156 Maritain told Mounier that directly. Cf. *Maritain/Mounier*, 117.

157 Cf. ibid., 118.

158 The Jesuits' most prestigious journal, *Etudes*, refused to publish advertisements for the *Esprit* collection; the young Jesuit Jean Daniélou's favourable review of Mounier's *Personalist Manifesto* was not published. Mme Mounier told me that even Cardinal Henri de Lubac, SJ, was never as close to the personalists as were the Dominicans. (Cf. Mounier, Carnet VIII, 23 April 1935, unpublished.)

159 Eugène Primard to Marc, 2 January 1935. Primard's group of Catholic businessmen had also been an early backer of Mounier's *Esprit*, although he needed reassurances from Mounier that the publication would be sufficiently Catholic in orientation. See Hellman, *Emmanuel Mounier*, 43.

160 Father Plaquevent, who had already visited the Communauté group in Belgium, found the Rotoir group relatively ill defined, but strongly encouraged them when he, along with Jacques Madaule of *Esprit*, paid them a visit and found that everyone more or less shared the same spirit. Primard to Marc, 31 January 1935.

161  Mounier, "Entretiens VIII," 9 March 1935 (unpublished)
162  Ibid. During World War II, after some initial enthusiasm for Pétain's National Revolution, Saliège would be considered an outspoken leader of the small Resistance element among the French hierarchy – an exception which proved the rule for the French Church's apologists after the war.
163  When de Naurois left to become chaplain of the Free French Navy in London (where he shared the last days of non-conformist Simone Weil), he was replaced as Uriage chaplain by another powerful personality who had come from the extreme Right and developed strong ties among the communitarian personalists: Jean Maydieu.
164  François de Pierrefeu, an unorthodox businessman who had been interested in Le Corbusier's projects.
165  In an article by Raymond Millet, *Le Temps*, 30 June 1935. Millet was a militant anti-communist journalist who would contribute to a book on Marx by Robert Aron after the war.
166  Mounier recorded in his diary at this time that Robert Aron and ON were making friendly overtures toward Esprit. These passages were dropped from the published version of his diary in the effort to eradicate the memory of this pre-war convergence. Mounier, "Entretiens VIII" (29 June 1935) (unpublished section).
167  Aron, Dupuis, Daniel-Rops, Chevalley: ON meeting minutes, 28 June 1935 (Marc archives).
168  There was a favourable account of the experience by André Maurois, *Paris-Soir*, 23 October 1935, cited in Edmond Lipiansky. *Ordre et démocratie*, 78–80; Aron, J. Chevalley, Devivaise, R. Millet, X. de Lignac, A. and L. Ollivier sent a postcard to Marc on 11 August 1935 with the notation that it would be a souvenir of the "première expérience de service civil."
169  Denis de Rougemont and Robert Aron were planning propaganda brochures targeting "Bastilles à demolir" (e.g. gas, electricity companies, banks) as part of their involvement in the Comité de vigilance des intellectuels antifascistes – a committee which, despite its name, included a number of individuals like Gaston Bergery, who would soon be accused of complicitous attitudes toward German national socialism.
170  C. Chevalley to Marc, 29 July 1935.
171  Marc to Chevalley, 31 July 1935. Discussions on spirituality were common among the intelligentsia in the 1930s: in August 1935 Marc participated in a *Décade* discussion on asceticism with various personalities including Raymond de Becker and Martin Buber.
172  Hellman, *Emmanuel Mounier*, 100n32, n33.
173  "Entretiens VIII" (8 October 1935) (unpublished section).
174  Cf. Mounier, *Oeuvres*, 4: 576.

175 De Rougemont had been reading and writing as an independent scholar in the countryside. There he would write his famous classic *Love in
the Western World* about the destructive triumph of the erotic in modern
amorous relationships; in December 1935 he would take up Otto
Abetz's offer of a teaching position at the University of Frankfurt. Cf.
Hellman, *Emmanuel Mounier*, 114.

176 *Ordre Nouveau* 5 (15 October 1935), 1–7; cf. Burrin, *Dérive*, 194.

177 In February 1936 prominent Esprit personalist philosopher Jean
Lacroix, who was a specialist in clarifying the distinctiveness of *Esprit*'s
personalist line, would praise Arnaud Dandieu's *La révolution necessaire*
in *Esprit*: further evidence that the public break between the two movements was largely spurious. See Jean Lacroix, review of Robert Aron,
*Dictature de la liberté*, in *Esprit* 41 (February 1936), 837.

178 Gibrat and Loustau went to see Mounier on 17 October. Cf. "Entretiens
VIII" (24 October 1935) in Mounier, *Oeuvres*, 4: 576. Before they came
to see him, however, Mounier had already been considering this idea
on his own.

179 "Chronique Permanente," *Esprit* 38 (November 1935) 280.

180 November 1935; Burrin, *Dérive*, 195.

181 On 2 November 1935; cf. ibid., 200.

182 When Mounier lectured in Brussels in January he was portrayed by *Le
Soir* as representing "the spiritual revolution": a movement represented
by the reviews *Esprit, Ordre Nouveau, L'Homme Réel*, and *L'Homme Nouveau*
(*Le Soir*, 30 January 1936).

183 Four hundred thousand copies.

184 March 1936; Burrin, *Dérive*, 199.

185 The ON projected a "Fédération de l'aviation": the idea for this organization was to be "*spontaneous*," but it was to be subjected to ON influence by
its *chefs*. Bertrand d'Astorg of the Esprit and Uriage groups, and Xavier de
Lignac (through his work for de Gaulle), were involved with the planning
and organization of a national school for airline pilots and of the French
national airline industry, hence the founding of Air France in its modern
form. C. Chevalley to Marc, 16 May 1936; ON minutes, 7 June 1935.

186 But the ON Catholics like Marc had to be very careful to keep the ON
separate from the French Catholic organizations in which they were
involved. In a letter in which he tried to minimize the differences
between the ideas of Chevalley and those of Gibrat and Loustau, Marc
insisted that ON never make allusions to religious issues, as was de
Rougemont's bent, since that could endanger the whole review. Marc
to ON consuls, 29 May 1936.

187 For example, on 11 June 1936, Marc wrote Georges Izard of Marc's
continuing interest in *La Flèche* and chided Izard: "What a shame that
you ally yourself with old factions and outdated politicians."

188 On 17 June 1936, Marc wrote to the ON editorial offices that he had yet
    to receive copies of the movement's "Lettre [or "Réponse"] to Hitler"
    but noted that ON was being abused in the press for it.
189 Marc to Primard, 12 June 1936.
190 See Alistair Hamilton, *The Appeal of Fascism: A Study of Intellectuals and
    Fascism, 1919–1945*. (New York: Macmillan, 1971), 218; Robert Soucy,
    *French Fascism: The Second Wave, 1933–1939* (New Haven and London:
    Yale University Press, 1995) (passages on Robert Loustau) for a descrip-
    tion of the context in which Loustau wrote this book.
191 The three men shared the stage at a well-publicized public forum on 3
    July.
192 Marc to Primard, 3 July 1936. Frégault, who obtained a Ph.D. in Histo-
    ry from Loyola University in Chicago, would go on to become one of
    Quebec's best-known nationalist intellectuals. It would be interesting to
    learn more about his relationship with Marc, who sometimes envi-
    sioned ON pulling up stakes and creating a society devoted to a New
    Order among the "real French" (unsullied by the Revolution, founders
    of large families) in Quebec. Convert Marc wanted to be, as he imag-
    ined the French Canadians, more French than the decadent French.
    Cf. Christian Roy, "Le personnalisme de *L'Ordre Nouveau* et le Québec,
    1930–1947: son role dans la formation de Guy Frégault," *Revue d'histoire
    de l'Amérique française* 46:3 (Winter 1993), 463–84.
193 The Marc archives contain a c. September 1936 list of addresses of the
    Amis de *Sept* for Nimes, Montpellier. Half of *Sept* supporters seem to
    have been priests, therefore elites who were important transmitters of
    new ideas, of new religious and political discourse, to the French
    Catholic church.
194 Marc was informed that *Sept* was doing very well: publishing 40,000
    copies (much more than *Esprit* or *Ordre Nouveau*), expecting 300–350
    at a *Sept* banquet in Versailles (Boisselot to Marc, 22 July 1936); Flamand
    reported that an apartment on the rue de Seine in the Latin Quarter
    would be the new the Parisian headquarters of the SSL, the Alliance
    Louisiane, and Editions du Seuil. The Société de Saint-Louis is also pro-
    jecting publishing a review called *La Vie Temporelle*. Flamand to Marc, 13
    August 1936. (In fact, under pressure from Rome, *Sept* would suspend
    publication in a few months and be replaced by the Dominican-backed
    but layperson-directed journal *Temps Présent*.)
195 Prévost to Marc, 5 September 1936. Prévost wrote: "We should try to
    keep up contacts with *Esprit*. I will go to the annual meeting of the
    Amis d'*Esprit* – where Rougemont will be official ON representative. But
    we can't so easily work with *Combat*, the *Courrier Royal*, etc., because this
    would compromise our high-priority relationships with the *syndicats
    ouvriers*, etc. People like Thierry Maulnier must be avoided for this

reason." (This letter suggests how Marc and his ON comrades were consciously infiltrating various groups and organizations to advance their program.)

196 Marc to ON consuls, 2 July 1936. Marc suggested ON approach Carrel because a recent article of his seemed very much in the ON line. He urged his comrades to send their publications to Pierre Dominique, Doriot, Bergery, and Lucien Romier and suggested that ON create a weekly publication along the lines of *La Flèche*. This would be the short-lived *A Nous la Liberté* in 1937. During the war both Romier and Bergery would be advisors to Pétain, helping to the define the goals of Vichy's National Revolution.

197 M. de G. [Maurice de Gandillac], "L'Ordre Nouveau répond à Hitler," *Esprit* 46 (July 1936), 624–5.

198 Mounier to Mme Guittet, 15 August 1936, *Oeuvres*, 4:597.

199 "Notre Manifeste," *Esprit* 49 (October 1936), 4.

200 The *Journal Intérieur* of the Esprit movement – no. 10 (October 1936), 1–6 and no. 11 (December 1936), 2–5 – described the discussions leading toward the fusion between ON and Esprit groups. Merleau-Ponty kept the reasons for taking his distance from Esprit at this time to himself; Ellul described his own bridling at Mounier's growing authoritarianism in a letter to John Hellman (30 January 1976).

201 Mounier to Mlle Martineggi, 25 October 1936. Mounier noted that *Esprit* had four times more subscriptions than it had only five or six months earlier.

### CHAPTER SIX

1 Xavier Dehan, "'Jeune Europe', le salon Didier et les Editions de la Toison d'Or" (1933–1945)," *Bijdragen-Cahiers*, Navorsings – en Studie-centrum voor de geschiedenis van de tweede wereldoorlog/Centre de recherches et d'études historiques de la seconde guerre mondiale (Brussels), 17 (December 1995), 204.

2 Cf. Jacques Maritain to Emmanuel Mounier, 2 November 1932, in Jacques Petit, ed., *Maritain/Mounier, 1929–1939* (Paris: Cerf, 1973).

3 Dehan, "Jeune Europe," 208.

4 It was widely remarked and soon out of print.

5 Raymond de Becker, *Le livre des vivants et des morts* (Brussels: Toison d'Or, 1942), 1–162; Mounier, *Oeuvres*, vol. 4 (Paris: Seuil, 1963), 538.

6 De Becker, *Livre des vivants*, 90–3.

7 In May 1934, Mounier reflected that his involvement with de Becker was the fruition of a project decided in December 1932.

8 Mounier, "Révolution spirituelle," *Esprit* 11–12 (September 1933), 791–2.

9 Mounier, "Les événements et les hommes," *Esprit* 6 (March 1933), 1027.
10 Interview with Alexandre Marc by John Hellman; on *Esprit*'s relationship with the Desclée De Brouwer publishing house see John Hellman, *Emmanuel Mounier and the New Catholic Left, 1930–1950* (Toronto: University of Toronto Press, 1981), 39, 42, 59, 70, 79, 79, 99.

De Becker wrote to Maritain from Brussels on 2 March 1934 that he had warmly encountered Mounier in person there for the first time and that Marc had already put him in happy contact with the organization of Catholic businessmen backing the young Catholic intelligentsia (in the person of E. Primard). In that letter, de Becker claimed to have grave doubts about on's personalism as potentially leading to "déviations graves." (Christian Roy) De Becker, in this instance, may have been following his friend Mounier's strategy of trying to disingenuously reassure an apprehensive Maritain.

11 Mounier to Georges Izard, 18 November 1933 (unpublished)
12 It won a prize from the Académie française.
13 René Dupuis and Alexandre Marc, *Jeune Europe* (Paris: Plon, 1933). In his interviews, as we have seen, Marc described this publication as one which the pliant Dupuis had co-signed but which Marc had conceived and written. As mentioned in chapter 5, this paid off, according to Marc, when the behind-the-scenes machinations of Dupuis's influential father had much to do with the book's winning the prize from the Académie.
14 Raymond de Becker, *Pour un Ordre nouveau* (Brussels: Editions contemporaines, n.d.), cited in Marc, *Jeune Europe*, 227–8. To learn more about the L'Esprit nouveau movement, Marc suggested *Les jeunes et la transformation du régime* (Brussels: Editions universelles, SA: n.d.), Marcel Laloire, "La jeunesse catholique belge," in *La vie intellectuelle* (Juvisy: Editions du Cerf), and *L'Esprit Nouveau*, the Brussels periodical published by the *Centrale politique* of the Catholic Action movement, ibid., 229.

*L'Esprit nouveau* was an official organ of the Catholic party's Jeunes Gardes Catholiques in the Brussels area. (Christian Roy)

15 Marc, "En Belgique. 'L'Esprit nouveau,'" in *Jeune Europe*, 229–30.
16 De Becker, "Révolution spirituelle d'abord?" *Esprit* 16 (January 1934), 673, 675.
17 Francis Bertin, *L'Europe de Hitler*, vol. 1 (Paris 1976), 142.
18 In the *Sept* of 24 October 1934.
19 "Cahier consacré aux idées de *L'Ordre Nouveau*," *L'Avant-Poste* 5:2 (January–February 1934). This review was directed by Maurice Quoilin, and another Belgian, Armand Bernier, also contributed. on was represented by Aron, Chevalley, Daniel-Rops, Dupuis, Jardin, Marc, and de Rougemont.
20 Maurice Quoilin, "Liminaire," ibid., 2–3.

21 Alexandre Marc and Claude Chevalley, ibid., 26.

22 Alphonse Zimmer de Cunchy, "Rédacteur à *L'Esprit Nouveau* and President général des Equipes Catholiques," "La mission de la France," *Ordre Nouveau* no. 8 (February 1934), 32.

23 For example, it began to provide free advertising for de Becker's review, as did *Esprit.* Cf. *L'Ordre Nouveau*, 22–3, (July–August 1935), back cover.

24 In a letter dated 12 January 1934, Max van Leemputten, of the *Légion nationale Belge*, expressed warm appreciation to Marc for ON's positions. He had received Daniel-Rops's *Elements* as a prize at the end of the school year and his remarks made it clear that he saw ON as a fascist movement.

25 To which his daughter-in-law – the new queen – subscribed. Interviews with Alexandre Marc by John Hellman.

26 Interviews with Alexandre Marc by John Hellman.

27 Dehan, "Jeune Europe," 209.

28 In a brasserie in Paris's Latin Quarter, ostensibly to discuss European unity.

29 De Becker, *Livre des vivants*, 212.

30 Marcel Grégoire, "Au tournant de la politique internationale de la Belgique. Le remarquable discours du Premier Ministre," *La Cité chrétienne*, 20 March 1934, 668–71; Henri Nicaise, "La conférence du désarmement et la paix," *La Cité chrétienne*, 20 September 1934, 181–3.

31 Raymond de Becker, "La lutte de l'église contre l'hitlérisme," *Esprit* 20 (May 1934), 288–9; Mounier, "Entretiens VIII," 9, 31 May 1934, in *Oeuvres*, 4:546–7, 551.

32 In fact a large property, Les Murs Blancs (which had formerly belonged to Chateaubriand), at Chatenay-Malabry, near Paris, was located in 1939 and has served as international headquarters for the Esprit movement to this day.

33 Mounier, "Entretiens VIII," 9 May 1934 (unpublished). (Some of the most important sections of Mounier's diaries dealing with Raymond de Becker, the Hitler Youth, and the Esprit group in Brussels remain unpublished. The editor of Mounier's posthumously published *Oeuvres* was his widow, Paulette Leclercq, a leader of the Brussels Esprit group.)

34 The caller was a Mme Nizota.

35 Mounier, "Entretiens V," 20 February 1932 (unpublished).

36 Mounier, "Entretiens VIII," 25 May 1934 (unpublished).

37 Mounier, "Entretiens VIII," 29 May 1934, in *Oeuvres*, vol. 4 (Paris: Seuil, 1963), 550.

38 Maritain to Mounier, 28 May 1934, in *Maritain/Mounier*, 110–11.

39 On 30 May, Mounier and de Becker had lunch with a number of people including Gosset, Georges Hourdin, Jacques Madaule, Reggui, Pierre-Aimé Touchard, and Paul Vignaux. Mounier, "Entretiens VIII," 31 May

1934 (unpublished). Mounier recorded reservations about de Becker on the part of medievalist and Catholic trade-unionist Paul Vignaux. Six years later, Maritain and Vignaux would again agree in opposing Mounier's collaboration with the Vichy regime.

40 Mounier, "Entretiens VIII," 5 June 1934 (unpublished).

41 Robert Aron to Raymond de Becker, 26 November 1934 (copy in the Marc papers). Aron evaluates a Franco-English meeting and projects a Franco-Belgian meeting. (This letter demonstrates a linkage between German, French and Belgian initiatives.)

42 Mounier to Izard, August (Wednesday) 1934. Mounier spoke with de Becker about the Third Force in Brussels; de Becker would come to Paris to meet with them in the last two weeks of September. De Becker to Mounier, September 1934.

43 De Becker, "Faut-il passer à l'action?" *Esprit* 22 (July 1934), 604.

44 E.g., on 20 September 1934 Henri Nicaise, following the pacifist line of his review since the previous March, argued that Belgian diplomats should restore contacts with Germany. Nicaise, "La conférence du désarmement et la paix."

45 E.g. Robert Aron to P. Fontaine, 21 December 1934, (Marc papers). Aron projects an ON evening in Brussels and envisages eventual contacts with the New Britain movement, and with the "jeunes révolutionnaires belges" and their common review *Le rouge et le noir*.

46 26 October 1934.

47 Dehan, "Jeune Europe," 210.

48 The *L'Avant-Garde* people who began to frequent the Didier salon, besides de Becker, included the Seigneur brothers, Pierre and Albert, Louis Carette, Henri Bauchau, and Robert Triffin. *Robert Triffin, conseiller des princes, témoignage et document* (Brussels: Ciaco, 1990), 17–22.

49 Marcel Grégoire, director of *La Cité chrétienne*, and a notorious pacifist and proponent of cooperation with Germany, also frequented the Didier salon. He had, like Henri Nicaise, strongly supported the line of the Broqueville speech in the review the previous March. Dehan, "Jeune Europe," 213.

50 Jeune Europe had grown from five thousand in June 1933 to six thousand in January 1934. Dehan, "Jeune Europe," 209.

51 Marcel Vercruysse, Jules Parfait, and Alphonse Zimmer de Cunchy were also collaborators of Leclercq's who had joined Jeune Europe at a time when *La Cité chrétienne*'s positions were very similar. Zimmer de Cunchy was also an editor of *L'Esprit nouveau*. Dehan, "Jeune Europe," 208.

52 Henri Nicaise, "Position de Jeune Europe," in *Jeune Europe: Brussels* (February–March 1935), 1, 4. Cited in Dehan, "Jeune Europe," 208–9.

53 Cf. *Esprit*, May 1936.

54 *La Cité chrétienne*, 20 February 1935, cited in Dehan, "Jeune Europe," 213.

55 P. Sauvage, *La Cité chrétienne (1926–1940). Une revue autour de Jacques Leclercq* (Brussels: Académie royale de Belgique, 1987). This study discusses contacts with Jeune Europe but does not pay sufficient attention to contacts with other contemporaries of the review.

56 Maritain to Mounier, "Friday," "very probably 1935" (editor's note), *Maritain/Mounier,* 120–1.

57 Maritain to Mounier, April 1935, and editor's notes, ibid., 102.

58 Mounier, "Entretiens VIII," 26 February 1935 (unpublished). This Juvisy community was a bold precursor for the subsequent worker-priests' experience.

59 Dehan, "Jeune Europe," 217.

60 Mounier, "Entretiens VIII," 26 February 1935 (unpublished).

61 Mounier recorded in his diary that on 15 March 1935 he had lunch with Mme Gez Le Pirries, editor of *L'Europe Nouvelle,* and she had encouraged him to accept "official subsidies." She remarked, when he refused, "That's noble what you are doing, but I couldn't waste my life that way."

62 Schulze-Boysen to Chevalley, 7 March 1935. In a general letter to the ON group on 19 March, Alexandre Marc, mentioning the fact that they were already meeting with Nazis in Paris, suggested a cautious response to Schulze-Boysen's overture, to avoid the appearance of promoting *rapprochement* with the Nazis.

63 Hugo Rheiner, "Das Germanentum und der Untergang des Abendlandes," *Sohlbergkreis* 7 (April 1935), 208–9. This *Sohlbergkreis* writer pointed out the worthwhile points in the fascist tract *Demain la France* by Thierry Maulnier, Robert Francis, and Jean-Pierre Maxence, but faulted Maxence in particular for envisaging a future Europe excluding the Germans and Slavs rather than in a dynamic German-Latin intermixing.

64 In April, on the eve of the Rome congress, a number of French young people – led by Bertrand de Jouvenel – met with a delegation of the Hitler Youth in Paris.

65 "Un programme de Revendications des Jeunes dans l'Ordre International," *Sohlbergkreis* 7 (April 1935), 213.

66 Mounier, "Entretiens VIII," 23 April 1935 (unpublished).

67 In May Mounier announced in *Esprit* his intention of creating a "Centre de liaison des mouvements pour la révolution personnaliste" which would federate Communauté with the group of people associated with *Esprit* co-founder L.-E. Galey (which was to be called Croisade) and the various groups of the Amis d'*Esprit,* which continued to multiply across France.

68 Marc to the ON, 19 March 1935. Marc notes that the ON has a meeting planned in Brussels, to which it proposes to invite a token British representative. Marc to ON consuls (Chevalley), 8 May 1935. Marc asks how

Robert Aron's talk in Brussels was received and suggests that Gibrat and Loustau should also be part of the French delegation which Aron is leading to the Fascist congress in Rome. The July–August 1935 *Ordre Nouveau* advertised de Becker's *L'Esprit Nouveau* as part of the fraternal exchange of free advertising practised by like-minded groups. Marc was at a *Décade* on asceticism in August at which, Raymond de Becker recalled in his memoirs, the two rubbed shoulders with luminaries such as Martin Buber.

69 Jacques Lefranc.

70 Henri Nicaise, "Jeunes catholiques en action," *La Cité chrétienne*, 5 September 1935, 607–11.

71 Nicaise, "Le manifeste des jeunes," *Bulletin de l'union belge pour la S.D.N.* 1 (January 1936), 16–17.

72 This would finally become public in 1937–38.

73 There is a copy of the resolutions from that ON meeting in Brussels in the Marc correspondence dated 18–19 January.

74 This included Hubert Lagardelle and F. de Pierrefeu, of *Plans*, who were now interested in the spiritualist socialism of Henri de Man and worked on the plan of the CGT trade union.

75 "Une conférence d'E. Mounier," *Le Soir* (Brussels), 30 January 1936. Raymond Millet had already pointed out in the leading Parisian daily *Le Temps* (30 June 1935) the cooperation of people from *L'homme réel*, a review directed by Pierre Ganivet (pseudonym for A. Dauphin-Meunier), and a "revue du syndicalisme et de l'humanisme" (which included Lagardelle and de Pierrefeu), in helping Robert Aron organize the French delegation to the upcoming Fascist congress in Rome. Among the Belgians, Raymond de Becker was particularly friendly to the groups he called the French "young socialists," meaning the people at Paul Marion's neo-socialist *L'homme nouveau*, at the syndicalists' *L'homme réel*, and, of course, at the French reviews with which he was personally involved – *Ordre Nouveau* and *Esprit*. Cf. Raymond de Becker, "Les tendances des jeunes intellectuels français," *La Cité chrétienne* (20 November 1936). Millet had noted in *Le Temps* that it was precisely these people who had attended the Italian corporatism congress together. Raymond Millet, "Jeunes Français et jeunes Italiens," *Le Temps*, 30 June 1935.

76 *Esprit* 41 (February 1936).

77 J. Parfait, "Troisième force et jeunesse belge," ibid., 785–92.

78 Raymond de Becker, *Livre des vivants*, 175.

79 Marcel Grégoire, "Au tournant de la politique internationale de la Belgique. Le remarquable discours du Premier Ministre," *La Cité chrétienne*, 20 March 1934, 668–71; Nicaise, "La conférence du désarmement et la paix."

80 Max Liebe, "Hendrik de Man's 'Arbeitsplan'"; H.N., "Die Presse in Bel-

gien," in the special issue on Belgium of *Deutsch-Französische Monatshefte/Cahiers Franco-Allemands* 4–5 (April–May 1936), 161–4, 165–7.

81 Undated 1935 notice, Communauté to ON. They work together toward organizing a Brussels conference in April 1936; 20 March 1936, Communauté (R. Piron) to R. Aron. (They are preparing the Belgian conference in April.) There is the possibility of a common Franco-Belgian declaration, and they are assured of the support of Communauté, of vos (Vlaamse Ou de Stridjers, Flemish veterans), and of the LIGA; Communauté to Aron, 22 April 1936. We have noted that there were plans for a Franco-Belgian meeting and a newspaper project. On the French side this was to involve the Société de Saint-Louis and Esprit.

82 Henri Nicaise, "Jeunesse allemande," *La Cité chrétienne*, 20 November 1936, 53ff.

83 *L'Avant-Garde* reported.

84 F.M., "Le Groupe Esprit de Bruxelles et la politique internationale," *L'Avant-Garde*, 6 May 1936. Cf. Hellman, *Emmanuel Mounier*, 289.

85 *Le Nouvelliste de Bretagne* (Rennes) (6 April 1936); *Croix du Nord* (Lille) (8 April 1936); *Croix du l'[illegible]* (19 April 1936). These clippings remain in the files of Emmanuel Mounier.

86 Mounier to Maritain, 29 April 1936 (*Maritain/Mounier*). Mounier complained that de Brouwer had informed him that they were withdrawing their (last) subsidy to *Esprit* (an annual F10,000 in advertising).

87 Mounier to Maritain, 5 May 1936 (*Maritain/Mounier*). Mounier had written to ask Maritain to visit when Maritain was passing through Brussels, as this was now Mounier's base "for work, friendship, relaxation." But Maritain, who had met Mlle Leclercq, Mounier's fiancée, only once, took his distance. Mme Mounier later recalled that when the Mouniers became engaged her fiancé had rushed to introduce her to Maritain but after they were married in 1935 she only saw Maritain again on about four occasions for the rest of her life. Interview with Mme Mounier by John Hellman.

88 C. 10 June 1936; cf. Hellman, *Emmanuel Mounier*, 114.

89 Denis de Rougemont, "Journal d'Allemagne," edited and reprinted in Denis de Rougemont, *Journal d'une époque, 1926–1946* (Paris: Gallimard, 1968), 320. Rougemont's analyses of Nazism as a religion are unique and eloquent but this particular one was written, as Bruno Ackermann has shown, two years after the event and so should not be taken as a first-hand, contemporary description of how Mounier and de Rougemont felt during the Nazi rally, as the *Journal* might lead one to believe. Mounier's diary account of this visit has disappeared since his death (see note 92 below). This is unfortunate, since Mounier always kept vivid descriptive records of his trips and there seem to be no other published allusions to

this trip to Germany. His contacts with representatives of the French Left were, in contrast, always highly publicized. A photo of Mounier and de Rougemont on this trip was published after Mounier's death in 1950, but the swastika on a flag in the background was blacked out.

90  In early June a brief notice appeared in the confidential Esprit network information sheet (June/July 1936 issue) that the Brussels Esprit group and Monnier [*sic*] with a few others would go to a meeting with English, German, and other youth at Zontéavec on 11–12 July. "Bruxelles," *Journal Intérieur des groupes d'amis d'Esprit* 8–9 (June–July 1936), 6. To describe this as a meeting with "German youth" was misleading: the only young Germans allowed to travel abroad in this period were Nazis.

91  For more on the Didier salon and Jeune Europe see J. Gérard-Libois and José Gotovich, *L'An 40: La Belgique occupée* (Brussels: Centre de recherche et d'information socio-politiques, 1971), 44–7; Dehan, "Jeune Europe."

92  "Un programme de Revendications des Jeunes dans l'Ordre international," *Sohlbergkreis* 7 (April 1935); *Esprit* 41 (February 1936), 791; "Tentation," *Jeune Europe* 3 (1936). This article is not included in the complete bibliography of Mounier's writings in his *Oeuvres*, vol. 4 (Paris: Seuil, 1963), but was found in the folder "Documents sur *Esprit* (1936)" in the Bibliothèque E. Mounier. The documents which were left out of Mounier's "complete bibliography" by his literary heirs often referred to contacts with the Young Nazis or ON. As noted above, the late Mme Mounier told me that Mounier's diary on the period covering the Popular Front and this meeting with the Hitler Youth was lost.

93  "Rencontre de la Jeunesse," *Esprit* 46 (July 1936), 631.

94  The June *Esprit* reported that "The Belgians of 'Jeune Europe' expect to meet English students, a group of Hitler Youth, and young French from various movements there." "Réunion internationale de jeunesse sur la côte Belge," *Esprit* 45 (June 1936), 479. The July issue briefly noted that "The Belgian Esprit groups would participate in the conversations near the seacoast village of Zoute." "Rencontre de la Jeunesse."

95  The issues of the *Journal Intérieur* of the Esprit movement for this period made no mention of this meeting.

96  A few young Englishmen also attended.

97  "Le camp international de Zoute," *L'Avant-Garde*, 16 July 1936; Caret and Moulin are cited in Dehan, "Jeune Europe.".

98  After the Zoute camp meeting during July of the following summer, young people got together at the Didiers' to meet Abetz, who had been prevented from attending the camp. Dehan, "Jeune Europe," 220.

99  De Becker had a complex, from which he much suffered, about his mean and illegitimate origins.

100  De Becker, *Livre des vivants*, 197, 199; "Die Entwicklung des Nationalen

Bewusstseins in Belgien," *Deutsch-Französische Monatshefte/Cahiers Franco/Allemands* 8–9 (1936), 311–7.

101 Mounier, "Was ist der Personalismus?" *Deutsch-Französische Monatshefte* 1: 11 (1936). This is another German-related essay absent from the "complete" bibliography of Mounier's writings in his *Oeuvres*, vol. 4. De Becker's talk was given on 12 November.

102 De Becker, "Les tendances des jeunes intellectuels français"; see also "Une conférence d'E. Mounier." As was noted, these people had attended the Italian corporatism congress together. Millet, "Jeunes Français et jeunes Italiens."

103 Young people from Belgium and other countries exchanged documentation on their respective homelands in Germany at this time. Cf. Dehan, "Jeune Europe," 220.

104 André Falk, "Un camp des jeunes à Winkelmoos," *Monatshefte* 1 (1937), 26.

105 *Monatshefte* 2 (1937), 78–9; "Henri Nicaise," *Esprit* 86 (November–December 1939), 109. Nicaise, who might have been expected to have a high profile in Belgium during the war, died in 1939.

106 De Becker, "Manifeste au service du personnalisme," *L'Indépendance Belge*, 21 January 1937.

107 Martin Hieronimi and Hugo Reiner, "Der Personalismus, eine geistige Erneuerungsbewegung in Frankreich," *Monatshefte* 2 (1937), 58–63.

108 Raymond Millet, *Le Communisme ou quoi?* (brochure, n.d. [c. February 1937]), 101.

109 François Berge, "Les Germains en France," *Monatshefte* 6 (1937), 199.

110 Paul Distelbarth, a writer who had earlier met Mounier in Paris.

111 Distelbarth, *Neues Werden in Frankreich* (Stuttgart: E. Klett, 1938), 180–3; "Massstab unseres Handelns," ibid., 183–90; Distelbarth to Mounier, 8 November 1947 (unpublished).

112 "Plus de querelle d'Allemand," *Monätshefte* 2 (1937), 79.

113 Cf. "Auberges de la jeunesse"; Yves Arvestour, "Qu'est-ce que la centralisation hitlérienne," *A nous la liberté*, 1,2,3 (March 1937).

114 Alphonse de Chateaubriant, "Nouvelle Allemagne," *Monatshefte* 3–4 (March–April 1937), 81–90.

115 De Rougemont commented: "Unser Hauptunterschied beruht auf dem Begriff der Person: für Sie wird er von der nationalen Gemeinschaft abgeleitet, während er für uns sie begründet, so weit diese Gemeinschaft wirklich ist und nicht mythisch oder blass gewollt. Aber was ich vor allem aus dieser Zwiesprache festhalten will, das ist, dass zwischen den verschiedenen europäischen Jugenden ein gemeinsamer Bereich besteht, der mir mindestens ebenso bedeutend erscheint wie unsere Verschiedenheiten." Ibid., 120.

116 Emmanuel Mounier, "Revues des revues: Les *Cahiers Franco-Allemands* (March)," *Esprit* 56 (May 1937), 300.

117 Denis de Rougemont, "Retour à Nietzsche," *Esprit* 56 (May 1937), 313–15.

118 Cf. René Dupuis, "Les gouvernements totalitaires," *Ordre Nouveau* 40 (1 May 1937), 1–22.

119 This was a very different evolution from, for example, their friend Schulze-Boysen's growing determination to defend the Soviet workers' state.

120 Denis de Rougemont, "Ballet de la non-intervention," *Ordre Nouveau* 39 (April 1937), 44.

121 Cf. Etienne Fouilloux's juxtaposition of the papal analyses of the pernicious political culture of Communism in *Divini Redemptoris* and of the troubling situation of the Catholic church in Germany in *Mit brennender sorge*. Etienne Fouilloux, *Les chrétiens entre crise et libération* (Paris: Seuil, 1996).

122 R. Piron, "L'élection du 11 avril à Bruxelles," *Esprit* 56 (May 1937), 340–3; Hellman, *Emmanuel Mounier*, 123.

123 Max Liebe, "Belgischer Sozialismus?" *Monatshefte* 5 (1937), 152–4.

124 "Chronique des amis d'*Esprit*," *Esprit* 58 (July 1937), 654.

125 *Journal intérieur* 20 (November 1937), 9.

126 "Nouvelles autour d'*Esprit*," *Esprit* 58 (July 1937), 654.

127 Interviews with Alexandre Marc. For example, in a letter in the Marc archives, a professor at the Polytechnic School of Dantzig wrote Marc for a summary of ON ideas for his students. Dr. Hans Espe to Marc, 19 October 1937.

128 For example, as we have noted earlier, Hans Geschke in "Geist der Zeit" claimed to admire Denis de Rougemont's conception of man while faulting the personalist's understanding of the German *Blutverwandtschaften* and *Schicksalgemeinschaften*. This was reported in "Revue des revues," *Esprit* 76 (January 1939). Cf. Hellman, *Emmanuel Mounier*, 307n61.

129 For example, François Berge, director of the personalists' ethnic study group, whom we cited earlier, strongly criticized the anti-Semitism of *Mein Kampf*. François Berge, "Bilan de l'ethnologie: Le problème des races," *Esprit* 64 (January 1938), 536.

130 *Journal intérieur* 24 (March 1938), 5.

131 This phrase characterized non-conformist aspirations for Galey, and also for the Esprit group's P.-A. Touchard, editor of the new *Le Voltigeur* pamplets.

132 Their activities were reported in the explicitly "private and confidential" *Journal Intérieur* of the *Esprit* groups (rather than the public "Chronique" of activities of the personalists regularly published in

*Esprit*). The former remains an excellent source for understanding the dissimulated private, as opposed to public, non-conformist agenda.

133 Roger Gal, "L'évolution syndicale," *Esprit* 65 (February 1938), 788.

134 Cf. Hellman, *Emmanuel Mounier*, 123; *Journal intérieur, Mensuel des Groupes Esprit de Belgique* 1 (December 1937) (mimeographed); *Journal Intérieur* [France] 21 (December 1937), 11.

135 Two and a half years later, when Abetz was trying to reshape the political situation in occupied Belgium, Bauchau would administer youth movements for the collaborationist government. Dehan, "Jeune Europe," 220–1.

136 Otto Abetz, *Histoire d'une politique franco-allemande, 1930–1950: Mémoires d'un Ambassadeur* (Paris: Librairie Stock, 1953), 43–4.

137 In the form of spokesperson R. Piron, who had been the Communauté organizer to establish the links with Robert Aron and ON in March 1936.

138 R. Piron, "Lettre de Belgique," *Esprit* 64 (January 1938), 641–5.

139 *Journal intérieur belge* 3 (February 1938) (mimeographed); "Revue des revues," *Esprit* 65 (February 1938), 745–6.

140 *Journal Intérieur, Mensuel des Groupes Esprit de Belgique* 5–6 (April–May 1938); Gérard-Libois and Gotovich, *L'An 40*, 474.

141 *Journal intérieur belge* 3 (February 1938); "Revue des revues," *Esprit* 65 (February 1938).

142 *Journal intérieur belge* 4 (March 1938)

143 Elie Baussart of *Terre Wallonne* and novelist Charles Plisnier began demanding reaffirmation of Belgium's alliance with France. Mounier to Mme Hélin, "January 1938," "January 1939" (unpublished); *Journal intérieur belge* 5 (April–May 1938); Gérard-Libois and Gotovich, *L'An 40*, 65; de Becker, *Livre des vivants*, 229. Baussart decided to marry his (officially) Catholic review *Terre Wallonne* with *Esprit* that spring; he sent the review's subscription lists to Mounier (cf. Hellman, *Emmanuel Mounier*, 125).

144 Ivo Rens and Michel Brelaz, Preface to Henri de Man, *Au-delà au Marxisme* (Paris: Seuil, 1974), 14.

145 For more details on the audience of *Ordre Nouveau*, see Edmond Lipiansky, *Ordre et démocratie. Deux sociétés de pensée: De l'Ordre Nouveau au Club Jean-Moulin* (Paris: Presses Universitaires de France, 1967), 89–91; Jean-Louis Loubet del Bayle, *Les non-conformistes des années 30. Une tentative de renouvellement de la politique française* (Paris: Seuil, 1969), 440.

146 Marc's contribution was a column on Soviet affairs he had written for the *Dossiers de l'Action Populaire* (review of the Jesuits of the Vanves community). Marc to Christian Roy, 24 October 1985. Mounier wrote a very positive review of the book in *Esprit* 56 (May 1937), 306–8.

147   Cf. Aline Coutrot, *Un courant de la pensée catholique: l'hebdomadaire "Sept"* *(mars 1934–août 1937)* (Paris: Cerf, 1961), 103. Hereafter cited as Coutrot, *Sept.*

148   Ibid., 142–3.

149   This is one of the reasons usually given for the silencing of *Sept* a few months later.

150   A follow-up to that of 28 December 1934.

151   *Sept*, 26 February 1937, cited in Coutrot, *Sept*, 168.

152   *Sept*, 12 March 1937. Cf. Coutrot, *Sept*, 170–1.

153   Primard to Marc, 7 April 1937. There was tension between Robert Aron and René Dupuis on the one hand, and the communitarian Catholic activist Eugène Primard of the order of the Société de Saint-Louis on the other, over Primard's pious editorial line. The ON people claimed to envisage France as an essentially revolutionary culture, while Primard was patronized for seeing the country as essentially Christian. Marc, performing his usual role in such confrontations, sought to smooth over antagonism in the name of the great struggle against the atheistic Bolsheviks and depersonalizing capitalism.

154   These reservations were more "understood" than public. Marc's archives contain references to Marc's friend Etienne Gilson's annoyance at being criticized by *Sept* for endorsing Mussolini's expedition.

155   On 8 July the review *La France réelle* huffily berated *Sept* for its prudish attitude toward the invasion of Ethiopia. It pointed out that the Italian episcopacy had provided chaplains for the troops, and the pope had addressed the queen of Italy as "Queen and Empress" and offered a "Golden Rose," a symbol of imperial hegemony. Cf. Coutrot, *Sept*, 180.

156   The Marc correspondence reveals the creative energy of the review until it was slapped down. Even Aline Coutrot, as quasi-official historian blessed by René Rémond and the French Dominicans, observed that the official explanation for its demise – "financial difficulties" – was preposterous to those who knew anything about the facts. Ibid., 75.

157   Cf. ibid., 302.

158   Marc to P. Louvel, 6 September 1937. Marc wrote that his "family situation has become desperate with the disappearance of *Sept*. We are in anguish about this but P. Boisselot has not responded to my letter."

159   Marc (to ON office?), 10 September 1937. This was interfering with his plans to go to Paris (a trip being arranged by Robert Aron, Jean Jardin, and Mme Coutrot).

160   Marc to Boisselot, 10 September 1937. "The problem with *Sept* was its reliance on a religious order. That's why I founded the Amis de *Sept*, but the project was nipped in the bud. I told Gilson several times, at Juvisy, that *Sept* should be run by laymen but was ignored. A new *Sept* should be looked after by laymen, watched over by the Amis de *Sept*

and a group of theologians (including some Latour-Maubourg "bolshe-viks"). The abrupt disappearance of *Sept*, pure and simple, would leave French Catholicism in a quagmire from which it could emerge covered with mud and blood."

161   Boisselot to Marc, 12 September 1937; Marc to Boisselot, 14 September 1937. Marc wrote to Gadoffre, as advised, but wanted to be involved with the founding of the new *Sept*, if there was to be one, as soon as possible.

162   In 1940, after the fall of France, Marc would be invited to lecture in the Vichy National Revolution's national leadership school at Uriage, where Dominican Father Maydieu would be chaplain, and Gadoffre one of the directors. This letter shows that Dominicans were involved in planning special elite schools in the high mountains as early as 1937. As mentioned in note 32, above, by 1939 Mounier and his Esprit inner circle had located a site for a communal residence – built around a small school to provide avant-garde training for adolescents – on an estate at Chatenay-Malabry, on the outskirts of Paris.

163   Paul Flamand to Alexandre Marc, 25 October and 6 November 1937.

164   Boisselot to Marc, 20 October 1937. In two days we will announce the publication of *Temps Présent* as the successor to *Sept*. Needless to say your old position is waiting for you as the review will now function under the *effective* responsibility of laymen. Think about returning.

165   Marc, 31 January 1938 (ferme du Val-des-Pins, Aix-en-Provence) to ON(?). Marc went to Aix because Jardin promised to approach a "Mme D." but he was still waiting for a response. Marc was frustrated because he was obliged to make a living as a freelance journalist composing arti-cles in which he could not say what was really on his mind, and yet he still could not be certain of making enough to live on: what he called the "minimum vital."

166   E.g. Marc to Bergery, 2 April 1938. Marc assured Bergery that he found the issues supported by *La Flèche* interesting and was showing this by cit-ing it in his page of *Temps Présent*.

167   As we have seen, Marc's special, quasi-clandestine, highly unusual convent marriage was to a Protestant from the New Britain movement with a guarded attitude toward Catholicism in general, and toward the Dominicans in particular, not to a strict Catholic like Abella Caprile.

168   Marc to Chevalley, 7 March 1938. Marc, writing on the stationery of the Dominicans' publishing house, Editions du Cerf, described a visit to Paris – where he had seen the influential Ella Sauvageot, among others. He was trying to stay in the middle of Catholic publishing projects and wanted to serve as a conduit to ON ideas there.

169   *Journal Intérieur* 11 (December 1936), 2–3.

170  Suggested reading for the Amis d'*Esprit* in May 1937 includes the books of Aron, Dandieu, and Rougemont. *Journal Intérieur* 2 (May 1937).

171  Philippe Burrin, *La dérive fasciste: Doriot, Déat, et Bergery* (Paris: Seuil, 1986), 224; Claude Estier, *La gauche hebdomadaire, 1914–1962* (Paris: A. Colin, 1962), 262.

172  *Esprit* noted the existence of a hundred Clubs de Presse, but Alexandre Marc told Christian Roy that this project never really got off the ground.

173  It published only ten issues.

174  *Esprit* 297 (May 1937) described *A nous la liberté* as an ON initiative. In fact it was short-lived. Cf. note 13 above and Christian Roy, "Alexandre Marc and the Personalism of L'Ordre Nouveau (1920–1940)" (MA thesis: McGill University, Montreal, 1986), 183.

175  There was, for example, a notably sympathetic note about ON in the March 1937 *Esprit*.

176  Ellul would publish the best-selling *The Technological Society* (New York: Knopf, 1964) after the war.

177  This was the title of a 1937 manifesto by Bernard Charbonneau.

178  Christian Roy, "Aux sources de l'écologie politique: Le personnalisme gascon de Bernard Charbonneau et Jacques Ellul," *Canadian Journal of History/Annales canadiennes d'histoire* 27 (April 1992), 67–100 (1991 Graduate Essay Competition Award).

179  She had spent the years 1934–35 working in factories in the Paris region. In September 1937 she wrote an article called "La Condition ouvrière" which was published after her death in her book *La condition ouvrière* (Paris: Gallimard, 1951), 233–9. Cf. Simone Pétrement, *Simone Weil: A Life* (New York: Pantheon, 1976), 317.

180  *Journal Intérieur* 18 (July 1937), 2.

181  *Journal Intérieur* 21 (December 1937), 4, 6.

182  Jacques Ellul to John Hellman, 30 January 1976.

183  Jacques Ellul to John Hellman, 30 January 1976; recollections of Alexandre Marc (7 August 1973); "Chronique des amis d'*Esprit*," *Esprit* 55 (April 1937), 216.

184  André Sarrail (Bayonne) to Marc.

185  "Le Congrés Esprit 1937," *Esprit* 69 (December 1937), 824; *Journal Intérieur* 22 (January 1938), 1–3, 6.

186  *Journal Intérieur* 24 (March 1938), 6. Ellul had decided that Mounier had intolerable fascist tendencies and, particularly after World War II, would write some acerbic attacks on what he saw as the pernicious influence of Mounier's personalism on Christian spirituality. Charbonneau kept up some contact and, on the eve of the war, would contribute to *Esprit*. After the war, however, Charbonneau would attack the

totalitarian tendencies in communitarian personalism reflected in the fashionable evolutionary theology of Teilhard de Chardin. See Hellman, *Emmanuel Mounier*, 129–30.

187  *Journal Intérieur* 18 (August–September 1937), 5.

188  Prévost to Marc (on ON stationery), 3 August 1937.

189  Interview with Alexandre Marc by John Hellman (Cogne, 1985).

190  It is amply documented by stacks of correspondence among Marc's papers of that period.

191  *Journal Intérieur* 24 (March 1938), 5.

192  As we noted earlier (note 132), their activities were reported in the private *Journal Intérieur* and not among personalists' activities regularly and proudly described in *Esprit*.

193  Roger Gal, "L'évolution syndicale," *Esprit* 65 (February 1938), 788.

194  Mounier to Izard, 3 February 1938 (unpublished).

195  This was edited by Pierre Ganivet (pseudonym for A. Dauphin-Meunier).

196  Also Paul-Ludwig Landsberg, Marcel Moré, Paul Vignaux, Jean Gosset, Julien Reinach, and Henri Chatreix.

197  *Journal Intérieur* 22 (January 1938), 5.

198  See Weil's *The Need for Roots* (*L'enracinement*) with its admiring preface by Christian communitarian T.S. Eliot (New York: G.P. Putnam, 1952).

199  The novelist François's son, future de Gaulle aide.

200  Roy, "Alexandre Marc," 160; Burrin, *Dérive*, 229.

201  *Journal Intérieur* 23 (February 1938), 1.

202  E.g., Belgian *Esprit* circles were going to study de Rougemont's *Penser avec les mains. Journal Intérieur Belge* 3 (February 1938).

203  Cf. the report of the group in Grasse in ibid.

204  Marc to Chevalley, 11 February 1938; Prévost to Marc, 13 February 1938. In fact, Marc would create a European College of Federalist Studies in the early 1960s in the Aosta valley of Italy with the support of local political authorities, and, until recently, he lectured there each summer.

205  C. Chevalley to Marc, 21 March 1938. (Summary: Last night there was a meeting on relaunching the review, at least six issues. We need Marc's plan for reorganization and suggestions. All agree that the review is to be more topical and less doctrinal and utopian. Charbonneau is being considered for an article in the first issue. De Lignac must have told you of the project for a series of articles in *La Flèche* against "l'Union sacrée." Aron will be speaking to Bergery.)

206  As well as with the people of Valois's *Nouvel Age*.

207  Marc to Chevalley, 22 March 1938. (Marc is privately contemptuous of many in the ON group: "une fameuse collection de couillons ... Quelle sinistre bande d'intellectuels mal dessalés!" – especially de Rougemont,

as a typical "gens de lettres." He complains that Aron is the only one to send him some vague news from time to time, and the only one committed to working in *La Flèche, La République*, etc. Marc wonders what Chevalley thinks about emigrating to Canada: "Pays sympathique, hospitalier, de la neige, de l'espace, des familles de vingt-cinq enfants.")

208  Marc to Chevalley, 22 March 1938 (letter 2).

209  Mounier, "Et maintenant?" *Esprit* 66 (March 1938), 803–4.

210  Mounier, "Bilan spirituel: Court traité de la mythique de Gauche," ibid., 873–920; also in *Oeuvres*, 4: 40–75.

211  Noel Régis, "Bilan économique du Front Populaire," *Esprit* 66 (March 1938), 827; Jacques Madaule, "Bilan et avenir politique et parlementaire," ibid., 855; Bernard Serampuy, "Vers de nouvelles valeurs françaises?" ibid., 921–37.

212  Marc to Bergery, 2 April 1938; Vigeoz (Marseilles) to Marc, 6 April 1938; B. Ady Brill (on Parti Frontiste stationery) to Marc, 6 April 1938.

213  Marc to Vigeoz, 8 April 1938.

214  Marc to M. Antonin Fabre (Aix), 8 April 1938. In interviews with Christian Roy, Marc claimed to have taken his distance from Bergery after a joint common lecture tour the previous summer.

215  Marc to Prévost, 14 April 1938.

216  Prévost to Marc, 17 April 1938.

217  Marc to Prévost, 19 April 1938. (Marc charged that the reason that ON had not accomplished more was that the movement harboured too many "discutailleurs, rouspéteurs, critiques, hésitants, sceptiques," but "since it is unfortunately impossible for me to act alone, I have preferred to not insist, rather than to spend my time fighting misunderstandings.")

218  Club des Amis de *La Flèche*. Statuts (c. April 1938) The association was under the moral control of a Comité d'honneur which included Honegger, Milhaud, and Gide, and several well-known Belgians. The complete list was: Mme Marcelle Capy, and MM. Marcel Achard, André Boll, Jean Carlu, Félicien Challaye, Paul Colin, Francis Delaisi, Charles Dullin, Jean Duvivier, Galtier-Boissière, Gide, Honegger, Henri Jeanson, Louis Jouvet, Serge Lifar, Salvador Madariaga, Victor Margueritte, Milhaud, Steve Passeur, Georges Pioch, and Armand Salacrou. The association was administered by a Conseil presided over by Gaston Bergery with Jean Maze as his lieutenant, seconded by Gaston Cohen, Ady Brill, Pierre Foucaud, André Bétron, and André Hunebelle.

219  Prévost to Marc, 30 April 1938. Prévost notes that Robert Aron was going to explain this agenda to the Conseil National of the ON.

220  Pierre Prévost to Marc, 6 June 1938. Prévost refers to the "troubling" differences between Marc – a pillar of the movement, who "formed us" – and de Rougemont, and the other ON people. He wondered if it was

not because religion served as a "comfortable refuge" for the latter.

221 Marc to Chevalley, 7 May 1938. (Marc urged Chevalley to prevent Aron, Albert Ollivier, and Pierre Prévost from leading the ON movement in a "dangerous" direction. Besides infiltrating *Recherches philosophiques*, he suggested contacting Paul Chanson, contributor to *Temps Présent* while also involved in *L'Ordre Réel*, to strengthen the ties between ON and *L'Ordre Réel*. He also suggested strengthening the ON position in the Amis de *La Flèche* by bypassing Aron.)

222 Marc to Pierre Vigeoz, 13 May 1938. (There will be an important meeting of the Marseille group of Nouvel Age. Contact Martintabouret and perhaps Queirel and try, during the meeting, to raise the question of a Ligue fédérale des non-conformistes. "That means, in fact, from your first involvement with the 'Amis de LF': I permit myself to count on you in the name of revolutionary discipline.")

223 Mounier, "Chronique des groupes français," *Esprit* 67 (April 1938), 158–60.

224 *Journal Intérieur* 26 (June 1938), 1–3.

225 Marc to Prévost, 4 May 1938. Besides Bataille, Marc mentioned the "Free University" project as likely to involve Bachelard, Wahl, H. Dubreuil, Chanson, etc. There seems to have been a certain overlap between Marc's ON think-tank and Bataille's circle.

226 André Boutier (Lyon) to Marc, 7 May 1938.

227 "A nos abonnés, à nos lecteurs," *L'Ordre Nouveau* 42 (15 June 1938), inside front cover.

228 Prévost to Marc, 29 June 1938. Prévost counted on Marc to network in Lyon and a few neighbouring places. But the operation "had to be kept rather secret."

229 Marc to Prévost, 1 July 1938. (Marc gave advice to his ON comrades on how to act in a concerted way with regard to Bergery by setting up the Clubs de Presse to bring people together: "The *centres fédérateurs*, made up of all the groups of personalities opposed to the present disorder, to plutocratic democracy, to Stalinism and to fascism, and partisans of a new order at the service of man ... conscious of the fact that the Revolution of Order cannot take place as long as the press continues to poison minds ... are deciding to support the *clubs de presse* initiative ... of ON, *Esprit*, and *frontisme*, an initiative which will thus furnish to the *centres fédérateurs* a concrete and precise opportunity to demonstrate their existence.")

230 This is one of the quotations inscribed on the new Franklin Delano Roosevelt monument in Washington, DC.

231 Marc to Prévost, 1 July 1938.

232 "Remerciements," *L'Ordre Nouveau* 42 (15 June 1938), inside front cover.

233 "Les responsables," ibid., 1.
234 Marc often used this analogy in interviews years later.
235 Joseph Voyant (circular letter), 6 July 1938.
236 B. Serampuy (F. Goguel), "*La Flèche.* Le frontisme," *Esprit* 72 (September 1938), 735–46. P. Burrin cites the critical elements in Goguel's article on "le frontisme" as evidence that the cooperation between Esprit and Bergery's people went downhill after that. Burrin, *Dérive,* 229. This is in line with the Esprit/Editions du Seuil orthodox history of Esprit-Bergery relations, but it ignores the networking that continued to go on behind the scenes and, above all, the way the Munich agreements would bring these people together. See Hellman, *Emmanuel Mounier.*
237 "Notre action: clubs de presse," *Esprit* 53 (February 1937), 798; Note from the Prefecture of Police, 25 February 1937, F7 12966 (AN) (cited in Burrin, *Dérive,* 478n28).
238 Mounier, "Les deux sources du préfascisme," *Esprit* 75 (December 1938), 324.
239 "Esprit en temps de guerre," *Journal Intérieur* 27 (July 1938), 1–7.
240 His essays in *Esprit* in this period demonstrate this.
241 Mounier to Marc, 1 August 1938.
242 Marc to Mounier, 3 August 1938.
243 X. de Lignac to Christian Roy, 26 April 1986.

CHAPTER SEVEN

1 Marc to Jean Maze, 3 October 1938.
2 Mounier, "'Esprit' et l'Action Politique," *Esprit* 73 (October 1938), 54, 58–9.
3 Mounier to Marc, 5 October 1938.
4 Marc to Mounier, 7 October 1938.
5 Mounier to Guy Malengrau, 14 November 1938 (unpublished).
6 Raymond de Becker, *Le livre des vivants et des morts* (Brussels: Toison d'Or, 1942), 161.
7 Interview with Alexandre Marc by John Hellman (7 August 1973).
8 "Où va la Belgique?" *Esprit* 75 (December 1938), 471–6.
9 De Becker, *Livre des vivants,* 229.
10 Even years afterwards, Mounier blamed the *embourgeoisement* of the Catholic church, rather than Nazi agents or de Becker himself, for his Belgian comrade's spinning off into Hitlerite sympathies and collaborationist activities. See John Hellman, *Emmanuel Mounier and the New Catholic Left, 1930–1950* (Toronto and London: University of Toronto Press, 1981), 200–1.
11 Cf. Philippe Burrin, *La dérive fasciste. Doriot, Déat, Bergery, 1933–1945* (Paris: Seuil, 1986), 229, 237. Burrin accepts the orthodox *Esprit* view

that Mounier, Bergery's movement, and ON drifted apart in the later
1930s when – as we see – the contrary was the case.

12 Prévost to Marc, 30 October 1938.

13 *Journal Intérieur* 29 (November 1938), 2–5; Jean Maze, "Autour de la
Flèche," *Esprit* 74 (November 1938), 311–19. (Letter from Jean Maze to
Mounier and Mounier's response). In an example of shaping historical
memory through editing, none of Mounier's writings from the period
1938–40 were included among the multitude in his *Oeuvres*, vols. 1–4
(Paris: Seuil, 1961–63).

14 Voyant would come to represent the Rhône Department for decades as
senator, and his party under the Fourth Republic, the Mouvement
Républicain Populaire (MRP), would draw elements of its program from
a Resistance charter co-written with Marc during the war.

15 Later long-time secretary general of the Commission of European Communities, and rector of the European University in Florence. In the annual meeting of the Réseau International des Historiens du Fédéralisme-
Personnalisme founded by Marc, hosted by Noël at his European University Institute, Florence, on 14 December 1992, M. Noël made his admiration for Marc, and his suspicions about my approach to Marc and his
comrades, very clear to me.

16 Later well-known journalist, militant in the federalist movement, and historian of the European idea.

17 Interview with Alexandre Marc by Gilbert Ganne, "Qu'as-tu fait de ta
jeunesse? III: L'Ordre Nouveau," *Arts* 562 (4–10 April 1956), 7.

18 Claude Chevalley (Fine Hall, Princeton University) to Marc, 6 November
1938. ON stalwart Chevalley became a mathematician at Princeton after
narrowly escaping being drafted into the army, but even in the United
States he continued to harbour traditional ON feelings: he found the
Americans, despite the academic freedom enjoyed in their universities,
vulgar and conformist, not as given to taking independent initiatives as
had been their reputation.

19 Marc to Chevalley, 26 November 1938.

20 "Chronique des groupes Esprit," *Esprit* 77 (February 1939), 780.

21 Luccioni to Marc, c. November 1938.

22 E.g., they planned, with the Amis de *Temps Présent* or Auguste Quirel's
Clairière group, to host Pierre-Henri Simon.

23 *Groupe Esprit de Toulon: Compte-Rendu de la Deuxième Réunion Mensuelle*, 25
November 1938 (forwarded to Marc on 3 December 1938).

24 Ninette Luccioni to Marc, fall 1938.

25 Minutes of the Groupe "Esprit" de Toulon (mimeographed, January 1939).

26 Marc to Georges Izard, 29 November 1938.

27 Cf. Mounier's review of *Bataille de la France*, *Esprit* 76 (January 1939),
621–2.

28 Marc to Izard, 21 January 1939.
29 Marc to Chevalley, 4 January 1939.
30 Prévost to Marc, 17 December 1938.
31 See Bernard Voyenne, "Alexandre Marc: 'homme debout,'" *Le fédéralisme et Alexandre Marc* (Lausanne: Centre de recherches européennes, 1974), 33.
32 Particularly for a supportive article about the project in the December *Esprit.*
33 Marc to Mounier, 21 January 1939.
34 Minutes of the Groupe "Esprit" de Toulon (mimeographed, January 1939) with the personal notes of Luccioni attached to them. This third monthly meeting began with only eleven people present.
35 *Esprit* 77 (February 1939).
36 L. Maggiani (in Toulon) to Marc, 5 February 1939; Marc to M. and Mme Luccioni, 7 February 1939; Robert Aron on NRF stationery to Marc, 7 March 1939. Aron complained that the writing in *Agir* was not sufficiently concrete or topical, or up to journalistic standards. The old *Bulletin de liaison ON* had been better. Marc's mystical Catholic friend Primard "is not our Lenin."
37 Maggiani to Marc, 5 February 1939.
38 Marc to M. and Mme Luccioni, 7 February 1939.
39 Marc to Mounier, 20 February 1939.
40 Valois to Marc (at Val des Pins), 6 March 1939. Valois wrote in his capacity as "Administrateur délégué" of the "Société coopérative des Amis de *Nouvel Age* (Scana)" which had its offices in the "Société d'economie distributive et Compagnie d'organisation rationnellee."
41 Marc to Valois, 12 March 1939.
42 Joseph Voyant to Marc, 14 March 1939. The Comité Ville-Campagne of the CEPH (Coutrot) invited Voyant to their meeting in Paris.
43 Jean Coutrot to Marc, 10 March 1939.
44 Marc to Robert Aron, 12 March 1939.
45 Marc to Coutrot, 12 March 1939.
46 Marc to G. Vandorpe (Nancy), 2 April 1939.
47 Jean de Fabrègues to Marc, c. April 1939.
48 E.g., six *fédérés* delegates from Lyon went to Paris for the congress of the Amis de *Temps Présent.*
49 E.g., Hyacinthe Dubreuil, author of *Standards.* Marc to Hyacinthe Dubreuil, 12 March 1939.
50 Marc to Voyant (Lyon), 2 April 1939.
51 Cf. Voyant to Marc, 14 March 1939; Marc to Moosmann, 12 March 1939; Marc to Robert Aron, 12 March 1939; A. Boutier (Lyon) to Marc, 5 April 1939; Marc to L. Maggiani, 17 April 1939.

52  In this period Jean Maze, writing on old *Sept* stationery and apparently in his role as a high-profile Catholic at *La Flèche*, wanted to see Marc on a visit to Marseille and, if Marc came to Paris, for Marc to visit him there. Jean Maze to Marc, c. March 1939. This sort of ecumenical facility would serve Maze well the next year when he became a central figure in the Vichy regime's efforts to draw the young people of France's different spiritual families into common communitarian activities.

53  Such as André Moosmann. See chapter 1, note 36.

54  P.-H. Simon, for example, lectured to the Social Catholics (Catholic laypersons active in social work) at Marseille on 18 March, to the Amis de *Temps Présent* at Aix on 19 March, to the Clairière community in Marseille on 20 March. P.-H. Simon to Marc, 8 March 1939; Auguste Queirel (Marseille) to Marc, 10 March 1939.

55  I took a course on European literature from Noth at Marquette University in the 1960s where he was then professor of German. He was a modest and self-deprecating man, with a fine sense of irony, who seemed to maintain a sympathetic distance from the right-wing Jesuits who ran Marquette (as did his faculty colleague, novelist J.F. Powers) but he would warmly reminisce about his cordial relationships with the French nonconformists.

56  Marc's comrade Queirel invited people for the lectures in Aix in concert with Marc, as per his letter to Marc of 10 March 1939; brochure for the series of talks of the Amis de *Temps Présent* (Aix-en-Provence).

57  Cf. *L'Aube*, 24 April 1939.

58  E.g., "Revue des revues," *Esprit* 76 (January 1939), where an article by Hans Geschke in *Geist der Zeit* (December 1937) is noted.

59  We have already noted that while Hans Geschke admired Denis de Rougemont's conception of man, he faulted the mainstream personalists' understandings of race and community.

60  Cf. Burrin, *Dérive*, 90.

61  In the *Nouveaux Cahiers* in April.

62  E.g., R.-P. Millet's analysis of the political situation in France, and Bernard Charbonneau's prescription for true political militancy.

63  He had first published it in *Politique* the previous April.

64  "Revue des revues," *Esprit* 80 (May 1939), 302–3.

65  Cf. Burrin, *Dérive*, 275–6.

66  Otto Abetz, *Histoire d'une politique franco-allemande, 1930–1950: Mémoires d'un ambassadeur* (Paris: Librairie Stock, 1953), 105; Francis Bertin, *L'Europe de Hitler* (Paris: Librairie française, 1976), 153; Léon Degrelle, *La Cohue de 1940* (Lausanne: R. Crausaz, 1949), 176; Fred Kupferman, "Diplomatie parallèle et guerre psychologique: le role de la 'Ribbentrop-Dienststelle' dans les tentatives d'action sur l'opinion française: 1934–1939,"

*Relations internationales* 3 (1975), 79–95, and "Le bureau Ribbentrop et les campagnes pour le rapprochement franco-allemand," *Les relations franco-allemandes, 1933–1939* (Paris: Editions du CNRS, 1976), 88–98.

67 S.H., "La propagande nazie en Belgique," *Le Soir*, 16 July 1939, 1; S.H., "Gare aux pièges," *Le Soir*, 18 July 1939, 1; "A propos d'une rencontre d'intellectuels belges et hitlériens," *Le Soir*, 19 July 1939, 1; "Le cas Abetz," *Le Soir*, 20 July 1939, 1; "La mauvaise humeur de la presse nazie," *Le Soir*, 21 July 1939, 1. In fact, "S.H." was Charles Breisdorf and Désiré Denuit, respectively the editor-in-chief and the journalist who would be editor-in-chief of *Le Soir* after the war. Cf. *Le Soir. Un siècle d'histoire*, 65. (Raymond de Becker, named by Abetz during the German occupation, would serve in the interim.) After the war, "S.H." would return to denounce certain post-war activities of the Didier salon, remarking: "The Germans ... were all authentic Nazis ... I was particularly struck by their interest in a Belgian foreign policy which might be independent from that of France and the insistence of the Germans on the differences between the Belgians and the French." S.H., "Abetz parle de ses activités en France et en Belgique," *Le Soir*, 11 December 1945, 1.

68 De Man was given no portfolio and, feeling isolated, would resign after a few months. During the occupation his role would also be short-lived.

69 Bertin, *L'Europe*, 154; J. Gérard-Libois and José Gotovich, *L'An 40: La Belgique occupée* (Brussels: Centre de recherche et d'information sociopolitiques, 1971), 48.

70 Marc had published the article in *Vendémaire*.

71 Interview with Alexandre Marc by John Hellman (Vence, 1984).

72 Jean Coutrot, now "Vice-Président du Centre National d'Organisation Scientifique du Travail," wrote to Marc that he had interceded with the Conseil supérieur de la Défense Nationale on a case of interest to Marc. Jean Coutrot to Marc, 14 February 1940.

73 Minutes of the meeting of the "Groupements Non Conformistes," December 1939 (Marc archives). Pelorson's ideas for orienting French young people would soon be demonstrated in the youth ministry of the Vichy regime.

74 Marc remembered being harassed by the French army for his interest in de Gaulle at the peak of the German invasion of France in the spring of 1940, and spending a week in jail in Marseille for possessing "defeatist propaganda": according to him they were books by Charles de Gaulle.

75 *Esprit* 92 (June 1940), 213, 215–17, 225–34.

76 Among the figures we have just discussed there were people in journalism (Marc, Mounier, et al.), publishing (Flamand, later Beuve-Mery, the Dominicans), planning (Coutrot, the *Nouveaux Cahiers* group, Gibrat and Loustau, Georges Lefranc at the CGT, Henri de Man, André Philip), theology (Congar, de Lubac, Teilhard, Plaquevent), philosophy

(Maritain, Berdyaev), the military (de Gaulle), youth organizations (Père Carré and the *Revue des jeunes*, the *Nouvelles équipes*), "extra-parliamentary" political movements (Aron, Maze, Izard, and Bergery in the Parti Fron-tiste), government service (Bergery, Jardin, Flamand, Schaeffer), speech-writing (Gillouin, Bergery, Perroux), film (Galey), radio and TV (Ollivier, de Lignac), poetry (P. Emmanuel, Loys Masson), cultural formation and education (Pelorson, Lacroix, various experimenters in the orbit of Jeune France, the Ecole Nationale des Cadres d'Uriage).

77 Edouard and Lucienne Didier, Henri de Man, Léon Degrelle.

78 William Irvine, *French Conservatism in Crisis* (Baton Rouge and London: Louisiana State University Press, 1979), 208.

79 "Par la jeunesse, la culture se répandra dans tous les milieux et tous les métiers, par elle se reforgera une communauté nationale." Archives départmentales de la Gironde, Directives générales du Secrétariat général à la Jeunesse transmises aux préfets de la zone occupée. This directive is cited at greater length in Michel Bergès, *Vichy contre Mounier* (Paris: Economica, 1997), 46.

80 Cf. Roger Leenhardt, *Les yeux ouverts. Entretiens avec Jean Lacouture* (Paris: Le Seuil, 1979).

81 E.g., a key July 1941 Jeune France declaration was ornamented with pre-war Mounierist texts on culture. *Jeune France, Principes, Directions, Esprit*, official statement of Jeune France, given to Michel Bergès by the head of Jeune France in Bordeaux. Cited in Bergès, *Vichy*, 52; Mounier, 'Entre-tiens' (28 July 1941), in *Oeuvres*, vol. 4 (Paris: Seuil, 1963), 711. I am grateful to Professors Bergès and Jean-Louis Loubet del Bayle for their sharing of information on this subject.

82 On the importance of Jeune France for the notion of French state cul-ture see Marc Fumaroli, *L'état culturel. Essai sur une religion moderne* (Paris: De Fallois, 1991).

83 These 1934 citations from Mounier are reprinted in Bergès, *Vichy*, 56, 81–93; recollections of Alexandre Marc.

84 See John Hellman, "Les intellectuels catholiques et les origines idéologiques de la Révolution nationale de Vichy," in *L'engagement des intellectuels dans la France des années trente*, edited by Regine Robin and Maryse Souchard (Montreal: UQAM, 1990), 69–80.

85 Notably André Déléage and the Third Force of the Esprit group.

86 Alexandre Marc had "revue internationale" appended to the title of Mounier's review *Esprit* because when it appeared they envisaged it as the French variant, or a distinctive French expression, of a youth revolution which was most advanced in Germany. He correctly anticipated that, like *Plans*, it would be supported by organized circles of "friends," both in France and abroad.

87 Like Schulze-Boysen or Otto Strasser. The Manifesto of Strasser's Black

Front was published in *Plans* (10 December 1931), and a long exposition of his positions was published in early 1933 in three successive issues of *Esprit.*

88 Cf. Schulze-Boysen to Claude Chevalley, 7 March 1935 (Marc archives).

89 As we have seen, Robert Loustau and Robert Gibrat, young engineers in the ON and X-Crise groups, tried to work out a social doctrine for Colonel de la Rocque's Croix de Feu.

90 Notably Georges Lefranc.

91 The (unpublished) Marc correspondence with Jean Coutrot, leader of the X-Crise group, reveals this pattern. We have seen how Robert Gibrat and Robert Loustau had approached Mounier in their effort to facilitate communications between the French youth movements. Both men would hold important positions in the Vichy regime.

   Members of ON also introduced de Gaulle's radically authoritarian and elitist ideas into the best Parisian salons, arranged (in the person of Henri Daniel-Rops) to publish his writings, and gave lectures about them to various groups. Interviews with Alexandre Marc by John Hellman.

92 See Gilbert Gadoffre, *Vers le style du XXe siècle* (Paris: Seuil, 1945).

93 The personalism of Uriage school training is recorded in the dossiers in the school archives relating to school doctrine. (Archives départementales de l'Isère, 102 J 12–13.

   The archives do not reveal the fact that the Vichy government seems to have confiscated the *château* from its hereditary proprietors in a rather impersonal, even brutal, way.

   Personalism continued to be taught at Uriage until the school provoked the jealous hostility of Pierre Laval, who closed the original school at the end of 1942 as a result of a power struggle for control over youth institutions among members of the Vichy government, allowing the castle's transformation into a leadership school for the notorious Militia.

94 The key men who were on, or worked with, the Uriage Study Bureau had been associated with Esprit before the war. Besides Hubert Beuve-Méry, there were the philosophers Mounier and Jean Lacroix, essayist Bertrand d'Astorg, and the school's chaplain, the Abbé René de Naurois. Father Henri de Lubac gave lectures at the school from time to time and influenced the bureau's thinking on religious issues. The bureau also maintained ties with *Esprit* veterans who were serving as advisors at Vichy, such as corporatist economist François Perroux.

95 See Beuve-Méry's book *Vers la plus grande Allemagne* (Paris: P. Hartmann, 1939), and his favourable descriptions of Portuguese youth movements in the Uriage publication *Jeunesse France!* "Jeunesse Portugaise," *Jeunesse ... France!* no. 25 (1 December 1941), 6-7. *Le Monde* journalist Laurent Greilshamer in his *Hubert Beuve-Méry* (Paris: Fayard, 1990) is frank about his subject's admiration for Salazar's Portugal.

96  Beuve-Méry's father had left his mother when he was quite young; the
Dominicans had discovered the boy's precocity and mystical bent and
supported his studies. He always remained quite close to that order,
and its most innovative intellectual activities. At Uriage he circulated
mimeographed texts of one of his major theological interests – the evolutionary speculations of the Jesuit paleontologist Pierre Teilhard de
Chardin, as well as the ideas on work of his friend, and Dominican,
Marie-Dominique Chenu.

97  Examples abound: one which has recently been documented is that of
the devout Catholic Jean Jardin of ON, who became Pierre Laval's right-
hand man. See the biography of Jardin by Pierre Assouline, *Une éminence grise. Jean Jardin (1904–1976)* (Paris: Baland, 1986).

98  Most of them were in agencies concerned with the training of youth, as
is demonstrated by the addresses of the alumni in the Uriage archives.

99  Archives départementales de l'Isère (102 J 142–6: Ecoles régionales de
cadres).

100  Ibid. (102 J 14–22: Ecole nationale des cadres: doctrine; 102 J 23–5:
Ecole nationale des cadres: bibliothèque et documentation).

101  Over against the leading schools of pre-war France this new system was
heavily Catholic: 10 per cent of one of the cohorts of around two hundred early trainees in the Uriage castle were seminarians. France's leading younger theologians, like Chenu and Jesuit Henri (later Cardinal)
de Lubac made important contributions.

102  An excellent synthesis may be found in the seventeen volume collection
*Le Chef et ses jeunes*, Archives départementales de l'Isère (22 J 28 – 22 J
33).

103  While personalism became quite popular in Vichy France, several of
the founders of the personalist movement were not comfortable there.
Jacques Maritain became critical of his French personalist friends and
was one of the leading figures of the French Resistance in North
America by 1942. By the end of that year Alexandre Marc, having
refused an invitation to Uriage and engaged in Resistance activities,
narrowly escaped arrest in France by fleeing to Switzerland. Harro
Schulze-Boysen, at that same time, was discovered to be a key figure in
the *Rote Kapelle* resistance group (engaged in passing secret information on to the Soviet Union). Hitler had him decapitated with an axe
and he was, until recently, considered an important Resistance hero in
the DDR.

104  For more details see the important thesis of Michel Bergès, *Vichy*,
112–13.

105  One of the sceptics was Hubert Beuve-Méry, imposing director of studies at the Uriage school, post-war founder of *Le Monde*. Interview with
John Hellman.

106  Vincent had been one of the most original inter-war non-conformists and personalists as co-founder, with Fabrègues, of the student review *Reaction* in 1929, and contributor to *Combat* (1934–39).

107  On Vincent's role in employing propaganda to create a totalitarian France see Denis Pechanski's excellent *Vichy, 1940–1944. Controle et exclusion* (Brussels: Editions Complexe, 1997), 45.

108  In a 1965 interview with Jean Louis Loubet del Bayle, the contents of which we have only recently learned (from Michel Bergès, *Vichy*), Fabrègues recalled that Mitterrand had zealously distributed *Combat* in the Latin Quarter from 1937 to 1939 from the Marists' student residence at 104 rue de Vaugirard. Since Mitterrand provided Resistance credentials for Fabrègues after the war, the latter had no reason to undermine the former's reputation.

109  The SOL would be transformed into the *Milice* in January 1943. One of Mitterrand's heroes, the romantic mystical Catholic Antoine Mauduit, founded *La Chaine* in the castle at Montmaur with Vichy subsidies – as an Order with a special devotion to French interests and the "true" Pétain. Mauduit volunteered to fight the British and Free French "invasion" of Syria. The Uriage group, linked to *La Chaine*, also accused the Free French fighting alongside the allies of "treason" then.

110  Mitterrand letter (22 April 1942), cited in Pierre Péan, *Une jeunesse française* (Paris: Fayard, 1994), 187.

111  For examples recently come to light see John Hellman, "Vichy France/Québec, 1940–1950: Monasteries, *Miliciens*, War Criminals," *Journal of Contemporary History* 32:4 (Fall 1997), 539–54.

112  Henri Azeau and André Ulmann, *La synarchie* (Paris: Julliard, 1968), 106–7; Bergès, *Vichy*, 330–1. Alexandre Marc recalled several anecdotes from Robert Aron's wartime *sejours* in Jean Jardin's residence on the outskirts of Vichy (e.g., Aron, who had pronounced Jewish features, wandering in absent-mindedly on a meeting between Jardin and German occupation officials). With the blessing of Pierre Laval, Jardin left for Switzerland when the war began to turn against the Axis powers and lived in comfortable exile there looking after Vichy government interests (which are left to our imagination).

113  Archival sources cited in Bergès, *Vichy*, 360.

114  The Archives départementales de l'Isère contains a dossier on the Uriage Order which includes provisional constitutions, annexes, and directives (102 J 150).

Up until very recently, members of the Uriage Order denied its very existence, arguing that it was only a dream, a project which never came to fruition. I am indebted to Antoine Delestre, author of the excellent study *Uriage* (Nancy: Presses Universitaires de Nancy, 1989), whose uncle was secretary to Dunoyer de Segonzac, for the information on the exclusionary provisions of the Uriage Order constitution. This definitive constitution seems to be absent from the above-mentioned dossier in the Uriage archives in Grenoble, but Professor Delestre retains a copy.

Members took an oath of total obedience to Dunoyer de Segonzac and his lieutenant, and in the former's (frequent) absences Beuve-Méry exercised authority. Total "transparency," or frankness, was expected of the members in their comportment toward the leaders (according to handwritten notes by Beuve-Méry in the Uriage archives).

115  It seems plausible, as Jean Moulin's former secretary Daniel Cordier has claimed, that Henri Frenay, the head of *Combat,* had gone so far as to propose his old friend Dunoyer de Segonzac to succeed the betrayed and assassinated Moulin as head of the National Council of the Resistance.

Frenay seems to have been favourable to the early program of the National Revolution – which represented, in his eyes, a national and patriotic anti-Germanic revolution, a Pétainist resistance.

Cf. Pierre Assouline, "Interview: Daniel Cordier," *Lire* 169 (October 1989), 43.

116  Interview with Beuve-Méry by John Hellman.

Among the prominent members of this Uriage network was Roger Bonamy, head of the Comité départemental de Libération de l'Isère and one of the several members of the Uriage Order to infiltrate the French Communist party, and M. Lafleur, the mayor of Grenoble.

117  For the story of the Left-Catholic contribution to the Socialist party see Jean-François Kesler, *De la gauche dissidente au nouveau parti socialiste* (Toulouse: Privat, 1990). Mitterrand himself has praised Mounier's historical role in this regard.

118  Alexandre Marc and Denis de Rougemont became the most prominent figures in a European federalist movement which, by the 1990s, was feeling vindicated.

119  E.g., Jacques Delors, when leader of the European Community, spoke at length of his debt to Mounier on the occasion of a meeting celebrating the fortieth anniversary of Mounier's death at the Lycée Emmanuel Mounier in Châtenay-Malabry, France (30 November 1990). In answer to a question from the author as to the suitability of identifying with a tradition so hostile to American liberal democracy, Delors responded that Europeans were happy to let North Americans go their own way and only wanted to be themselves.

120  See chapter 1, note 42.

121  See chapter 1, note 39.

122  See chapter 1, note 40.

CHAPTER EIGHT

1 For example, his memory of his associations with Otto Abetz, Jean Luchaire, Hubert Lagardelle, and Raymond de Becker.

2 E.g., Emile Noël, M. and Mme Denis de Rougemont, Paul and Simone Fraisse, François and Renée Bedarida.

3 Michel Tournier's *L'Ogre* comes to mind, or the writings of Ernst Junger. Pierre Drieu la Rochelle and Robert Brasillach were more forthright in their admiration for the spirit of original national socialism.

4 A number of examples come to mind: François Mitterrand, François Perroux, Bertrand de Jouvenel, Jean de Fabrègues, and Léon Degrelle are all more easily understood in the context of these original ideals.

5 For example, only in a relatively recent conversation did Marc reveal that Harro Schulze-Boysen, then a pretender to leadership of the entire German youth movement, had taken him to visit the famous Brown Hall Nazi headquarters in Munich and that Hitler seems to have been there at the time.

6 I am indebted to my McGill colleague Peter C. Hoffmann for his knowledge of the Stefan Georg Kreis.

7 E.g., Jean Jardin, Robert Loustau, Robert Gibrat, the Ollivier brothers, François Perroux, and Xavier de Lignac assisted Pétain, Pierre Laval, and Charles de Gaulle.

8 The extermination of European Jews was never discussed in our conversations with Marc, and hardly, if ever, discussed in interviews with the ON people; the role of their group in that tragedy seems to be a taboo subject, as is the Holocaust itself. Robert Aron set the tone immediately after the war in his role as the first prominent historian of the Vichy period.

9 Christopher Hitchens, "Against Sinister Perfectionism: Robert Conquest in Retrospect," *Times Literary Supplement*, 26 November 1999, 5.

10 See, for example, P.C. Hoffmann's recent book, *Stauffenberg: A Family History, 1905–1944* (Cambridge: Cambridge University Press, 1995).

11 E.g., Maulnier and Dandieu.

12 E.g., Sartre, Maurice Merleau-Ponty, and Mounier.

13 E.g., Drieu la Rochelle.

14 See the recent monographs by Stephen Ascheim and Albrecht Betz on the evolution of German and French Nietzscheans: Albrecht Betz, *Exil et engagement: les intellectuels allemands et la France, 1930–1940* (Paris: Gallimard, 1991), Steven Ascheim, *The Nietzsche Legacy in Germany, 1890–1990* (Berkeley: University of California Press, 1992). Hitler visited the Nietzsche archives and attended the funeral of Elizabeth Forster-Nietzsche; Nietzsche was held up as an inspiration for Nazism.

15 E.g., he was friendly with the aggressively anti-American, anti-bourgeois

Abbé Pierre, over the objections of Mme Marc. Interview with Suzanne Marc by John Hellman.

16  E.g., Daniel-Rops and Robert Aron.

17  Hence the warnings of Denis de Rougemont to his comrade Marc about the dangers of my research. Interviews with Alexandre Marc by John Hellman.

18  For example, Marc scrutinized Husserl, Scheler, Heidegger, Dandieu, and Blondel.

19  E.g., Péguy, Bergson, Nietzsche, and Heidegger.

20  E.g., Daniel-Rops, de Rougemont, and Mounier.

21  E.g., Dries, Chagall, and some surrealism.

22  When Marc was young it was expected of converts like him to keep auto-biographical journals. People visited the Benedictines' chapel on the rue Monsieur to observe literary converts, like Joris-Karl Huysmans, in a state of ardent prayer or contemplation.

23  E.g., Cité Universitaire graduate student personality "Richard the Red Guard": Dick Howard, militant anti-Stalinist Marxist with no Catholic background but sympathetic to the Chinese Cultural Revolution and hostile to the American involvement in Vietnam, was the best known American in the *Esprit* circle, publishing articles in *Esprit* and books on the USA in *Esprit*-related publishing houses. He went on to become a well-known professor of political science in the United States.

24  Pierre de Senarclens, a Swiss graduate student who worked for a time at Chatenay-Malabry, kindly warned me of Murs Blancs hostility to historians who took a sceptical attitude toward their orthodox history of their movement.

25  For example, when Mme Mounier allowed me to read Mounier's important wartime diaries, she had closed off sections with paper-clips, explaining that people like economist François Perroux were sensitive about their being published. The clips were removed for Esprit group historian Michel Winock and Uriage school historian Bernard Comte (currently a member of the board of the Amis d'Mounier organization). Neither Winock nor Comte, to this day, has acknowledged any connection between the German youth movements, much less German national socialists, and their subjects. In such ways memory is managed in France.

26  The degree to which a French academic historian, dealing with sensitive subjects, is subject to *de facto* censorship is surprising to a North American. French scholars have belonged to "chapels" or spiritual families, and someone who breaks with his own can find his career in jeopardy. The Communists and the Catholics are the most vindictive, and treat their heretics worse than their public enemies.

27  As Isaiah Berlin has done in a famous essay, "Joseph de Maistre and

the Origins of Fascism," *The Crooked Timber of Humanity* (London: John Murray, 1990), 91–174.

28  Alain de Benoist, "L'ennemi principal," *Elements* 41 (March–April 1982), 48.

29  E.g., editors of the post-war, rejuvenated *Esprit*, originally co-founded by Marc but considered, after World War II, France's leading progressive, Left-wing Catholic theoretical review, identified with the Resistance and the non-conformist tradition.

30  Former *Esprit* editor Olivier Mongin engaged in friendly dialogue with GRECE; after that the late Jean-Marie Domenach, a veteran *Esprit* editor, spokesman for the Uriage group, and Emmanuel Mounier's best-known protege, claimed to speak with a refreshing feeling of liberty when addressing an annual GRECE congress, which I attended. Domenach prefaced his remarks by saying that, finally, he was in a milieu were he could speak freely.

31  For example, Canadian philosopher Charles Taylor has recently described the "Sources of the Self" for modern men and women as rooted in Western Europe. Taylor's mentor at Oxford, Isaiah Berlin, famously denounced the ravages of nationalism, while legitimizing Herder as a serious thinker, and secretly passing on intelligence information to Israel while in British government service. Non-conformists can promote de Benoist's "Europe of a hundred flags" ... but not a Europe inundated with Turkish, North African, or Palestinian immigrants.

32  Alain de Benoist, "An Interview with Alain de Benoist," *Right Now!* (1997), 2.

33  This is the well-argued thesis of Tamir Bar-On's "The Ambiguities of the Intellectual European New Right, 1968–1999" (Ph.D. thesis, Political Science, McGill University, Montréal, Canada, 2000).

34  At the meeting of GRECE which I attended, I was impressed by the prominence of solstice candles on sale, the absence of Christian literature (apart from Bernanos), and the detailed instructions on how the solstice could be observed *en famille*. Unlike those sold at Lourdes, these sacred objects seemed to be manufactured and sold by zealots with non-profit zeal.

35  "An Interview with Alain de Benoist," 3.

36  Bar-On, "The Ambiguities of the Intellectual European New Right," 127, 130–1.

37  The devout always seemed trailing behind, and, in the end, Marc's greatest bond was not with them but with ON comrades.

38  "An interview with Alain de Benoist," 2. The ENR under de Benoist devoted an entire issue of their own journal in France to the thought of North American communitarian thinkers: particularly Alasdair McIntyre, Christopher Lasch, Amitai Etzioni, and Charles Taylor.

39  Cited in Bar-On, "The Ambiguities of the Intellectual European New
    Right," 134–5.

40  Quebec's most prominent demographer addressed a meeting of the
    review *Cité Libre*, founded by Pierre Trudeau, with similar advice for
    Canadians.

41  Alain de Benoist, *Europe, tiers monde – meme combat* (Paris: Robert Laffont,
    1986), 219.

42  For example, Marc often employed his friend Dandieu's notion of the
    "intelligence-sword" as a worthy Christian quality, although it was, like
    many early ON ideas, Nietzschean in inspiration.

43  For ON the New Left was Bergery, Déat, de Man, the "neos." In 1968, for
    ENR and the remaining non-conformists like Marc, there was the spiritual
    and creative and imaginative revolutionary Left as opposed to the dull
    and plodding communists and trade unionists.

44  Ironically, a North American attending a GRECE congress – friskings at
    the door by humourless bodyguards with metal detectors, an attendance
    of sombre, conventionally dressed middle-aged white males, no questions
    allowed from the audience – might be struck by the robotization of de
    Benoist's organization.

45  For example, as mentioned earlier, Marc wanted Jacques-Yvan Morin,
    high-profile *Parti Quebecois* leader and historian of federalism, to succeed
    him as head of his CIFE in Nice. The best-known ENR contact in Quebec
    seems to be Université de Montréal historian Pierre Trepanier, expert on
    the 1930s Canadian Christian Nazi party of Adrien Arcand as well as on
    the Abbé Lionel Groulx, founder of the Université de Montréal History
    department and myth-constructing ideological father of Quebec nation-
    alism (after whom the Social Sciences building in which the History
    department is housed is named).

46  In answer to my question why he identified with a Mounierist political
    culture which was hostile to the United States, Jacques Delors, an ascetic,
    progressive Catholic communitarian, who discreetly supported Marc's
    projects when he was head of the European community, responded as a
    good European: "We are not hostile to Americans. We just want to be
    who we are." Delors is not exceptional: this is a common European
    progressive Catholic perspective, from Pope John Paul II on down.

# Index

*A nous la liberté* 142, 148, 215n13, 249n196, 262n174

Abella Caprile, Margarita 67, 82, 225n79

Abetz, Otto 14, 25–31, 37–8, 40, 46, 98, 102, 104, 129, 133–4, 136–41, 144, 148, 168, 185, 198, 159n135; and Belgium 259n135; Marc breaks with 216n55

*L'Abondance*, 166

Académie française 15–16, 75, 192; politics of 228n19

Academy of Sciences (Soviet) 11

Achenbach, Ernst 103, 237n46

Action Catholique de la Jeunesse française (Action Catholique: ACJF) 101, 112, 114–15, 118, 126, 146

Action Française 4, 5, 14, 24, 27, 41, 60, 84, 99–100, 104, 108, 112, 113–14, 117–18, 147, 172, 175, 180

Adam, Karl 69

*Agir* 164–5, 170, 268n36

Air Academy 111, 247n185

Air France (origins) 247n185

Air Ministry (German) 98, 103

Aix-en-Provence 15, 150, 153

Albert I, King (Belgium) 14, 129; and Ordre Nouveau 203n3, 251n25

Alleman (family) 142

alpinism 11

Amis d'Emmanuel Mounier 277nn25–6

*Anschluss*, the 145, 152

anti-modernism 10, 187

Aosta (valley) 194

appeasement (of Nazi Germany) 133–4, 144, 153, 168

Aragon, Louis 131

*Arbeitdienst* (labour service) 75, 86, 103

*Arbeitsfront* 74

architects, architecture 11, 20, 33, 36, 60–1, 92, 100, 151, 174, 186–9, 197

Aron, Raymond 157, 197

Aron, Robert 15–16, 30–4, 38–9, 42, 64, 75–6, 79, 82–4, 86–7, 101, 107, 109, 122, 124, 135, 150–1, 153, 157, 159–61, 167, 170, 186; archives of 236n39; as historian of Vichy 276n8; patronizes de la Rocque 240n78; on race 220n97; visits to Vichy 274n112

art, artists 20, 33–4, 36, 40, 60, 136, 173–4, 178, 187–9

Artaud, Antoine 42

Association catholique de la jeunesse (ACJF) 6,7, 126, 129

Association des Ecrivains et Artistes Révolutionnaires 131

Astorg, Bertrand d'
272n94
Auberges de la jeunesse,
"ajistes" 43, 99, 124,
136, 142
Augustine, St 6, 188
Autant-Lara, Claude 34
autarchy, autarchians 58,
93
autobiographical journals
277n22
*Avant-Garde, L'* 128–30,
132–4, 136–7, 141, 171;
at the Didier salon
252n48
*Avant-Poste, L'* 128–9,
250n19
aviation, pilots 11

Bakunin, M.A. 84
Bar-On, Tamir 278n33
Barrès, Maurice 190
Barth, Karl 32–3, 70
Bataille, Georges 31, 154,
196
Bauchau, Henri 126–8,
133, 144
Baudoin, Paul 172
Baussart, Elie 259n143
Beauvoir, Simone de
81
Becker, Raymond de 19,
68, 102, 116, 126–34,
137–9, 141, 145, 148,
159–60, 168, 171, 176;
as collaborationist
editor of *Le Soir*, 205n1;
meets Mounier 250n10,
251n39; personality
quirks 254n99
Bédarida, François 276n2
Bédarida, Renée 276n2
Belgium 12, 15, 17, 21,
85, 102, 125–61, 187
Belin, René 156
Benda, Julian 31–2
Benjamin, René 177
Benoist, Alain de 5, 9,
186, 192–200; and
immigrants 278n31;
and the new communi-
tarian philosophers

278n38; and Schulze-
Boysen 233n2
Berchtesgarden confer-
ence 145
Berdyaev, Nicholas 6, 13,
22–3, 27, 32, 60–2,
68–9, 99, 110, 120, 133,
135, 145, 157; shaping
personalism 209n45
Berge, François 142,
258n129
Bergery, Gaston 18, 21,
66, 84–5, 101–3, 106,
111, 116, 118–23, 135,
144, 148, 150–2, 155,
157, 159, 161, 168,
171–2, 184; and Esprit
group 266n236
Bergès, Michel 271n81
Bergson, Henri 32, 79,
178
Berlin, 22–3
Berlin, Isaiah 277n27; and
Charles Taylor 278n31
Berlin, University of, 23,
141
Bernadot, OP, Vincent
112–13
Bernanos, Georges: and
GRECE 278n34; and the
Young Right 212n58
*Bête Noire, La* (Moré),
152
Beuve-Méry, Hubert 8, 9,
168, 176–7, 182, 190,
273n105; and Domini-
cans 273n96; and the
Uriage school 272n94
Bibliothèque Nationale 6,
31, 62, 188; intellectu-
als working there
214n16
"Black Front," the
(Kampfgemeinschaft
revolutionarer National-
sozialisten/Struggle
Community of Revolu-
tionary National Social-
ists) 18, 40, 42, 45, 52,
59–60, 65, 74; Burg
Lauenstein Manifesto
42, 216n49, 271n87

Blanchot, Maurice, 9, 165,
172
Blondel, Maurice 30, 69,
150
Bloy, Léon 167
Blum, Léon 105, 138,
140, 146
Boisselot, OP, Pierre 113,
147; censors Marc
243n134
Bolsheviks, Bolshevism
13, 19, 34, 41, 78, 83,
113, 166
Bonaparte, Napoléon
85
Bordeaux (personalists of)
148–9
Borne, Etienne 113
Boulogne-Billancourt
(congress) 159, 162
Bran, Friedrich 104
Brasillach, Robert 180,
276n3
Brémond, Abbé Henri
214n18
Briand (Aristide), Brian-
dists 38, 87, 122,
214n8
Broqueville, Prime Minis-
ter 129, 137, 252n49
"Brown Hall," the
(Munich) 6, 95
Bulgakoff, Sergei 27
Bureau d'Etudes
Economiques, Sociales
et Humaines (Coutrot)
166

Cagoule 5, 21, 180
*Cahiers Politiques* 145
*Camelots du Roi* ("news
vendors of the King")
114
Camus, Albert 105, 174
Canada 12, 119, 123,
125, 181, 196, 199,
201n2, 208n41;
Trudeau and Lévesque
202n8; publishers
linked 245n154; Marc's
vision of 264n207
Cardijn 146

Carette, Louis 139
Carrel, Alexis 123,
249n196
Catholic Social Doctrine
107
Catholic Worker Move-
ment 190, 218n77
Catholicism, progressive
190, 193, 226n83,
278n29
Centre des Fédérateurs
165
Chagall, Marc 277n21
"(la)Chaine" (community)
180–1, against the Free
French 274n109
Challaye, Félicien
264n218
Chamber of Deputies 157
Chamberlain, Neville
145, 159, 169
Chanson, Paul (*Ordre
Réel,L'*) 115, 160,
265nn221, 225
Chantiers de la Jeunesse
7, 180
Charbonneau, Bernard 9,
10, 120, 148, 150, 165,
196; and *Esprit*
262n186, 269n62
Chateaubriant, Alphonse
de 142
Chavant, Eugene 206
*Chef Compagnon, Le* 134
Chenu, OP, Marie-
Dominique 113,
241n99, 273nn96, 101
Chesterton, G.K. 70
Chevalier, Jacques
241n102
Chevalley, Claude 85, 101,
121, 128, 154, 156,
161–2, 165; background,
214n18; at Princeton
267n18; and Schulze-
Boysen 234n4,
235nn26–8, 237n49;
visits to Germany 237n48
Chevallier, Jean-Jacques
176
Chombart de Lauwe, Paul-
Henri 177

Christian Democrats
(*Aube*) 161, 180
CIFE (Centre International
de Formation
Européenne) 12, 16,
194; Marc's succession
208n41
*Cité chrétienne, La* 125–6,
129, 132–4, 136–7
*Cité radieuse, La* 34
*Civilization* 166
Clair, René 34, 215n32
Claudel, Paul 147, 177
Club de Février 109
Clubs de presse 148,
154–5, 157, 161, 164
Cocteau, Jean 189,
230n40
Colette 102
collaborationists 10, 186
Collège d'altitude 147
Collège de sociologie 154
Collège universitaire d'é-
tudes fédéralistes (Valle
d'Aosta) 16
*Combat* (review, 1930s)
21, 123, 156, 162,
164–6, 178, 180, 190
Combat (Resistance
group) 9, 181–2
Comité du Plan 166
Comité de vigilance des
intellectuels antifascistes
246n169
Commission of European
Communities 267n15
Common Front against
fascism (Front
commun) 18, 84,
118–22, 156
Communauté 120,
134–7, 139, 143, 145,
176, 245n160, 253n67
Commune (Paris) 84
Communism: *see* Commu-
nists
Communists: the French
or Belgian 3, 9, 19, 42,
64, 66, 77, 84, 98, 102,
109–10, 112, 115, 117,
119, 122, 131, 146,
160, 162, 172, 175,

178, 190; the German,
60, 72, 74–5, 77, 83;
the soviet, 17, 22, 55–6,
62, 92, 190; threat to
Catholics 242n110
communitarianism ("pris-
oner") 21, 180, 190
"compagnons" 161–5,
170
Compagnons de France
7, 177, 180
Compagnons de la
Grande Route (collec-
tion) 341
Comte, Bernard
277nn25–6
Confédération Française
des Travailleurs Chré-
tiens (CFTC) 150, 162
Confédération Générale
du Travail (CGT) 19,
100, 121, 144, 150, 156
Congar, OP, Yves 9, 27,
104, 113; at Vatican II
202n71; ties to Marc
242n105
conversion experience
29, 38, 60, 67, 76, 80,
87, 106, 112, 140,
146–7, 149, 163, 170,
185–6, 188–9, 191; and
autobiography, 277n22;
Jacques Maritain's
241n101
Corbusier, Le (Charles
Edouard Jeanneret) 9,
18, 33–8, 112, 198;
background 241n97;
L'Abresle 230n41; Ron-
champs 230n41
Cordier, Daniel 275n115
corporatists, corporatism
5, 6, 37, 59, 105,
115–16, 130, 169
Corradini 48
Courier Royal 108, 123,
166
Coutrot, Jean 98, 107,
151, 161, 165–7,
169–70, 272n91; rela-
tionship with Marc
238–9nn65–6, 270n72

Croix de Feu 5, 101, 106, 108–12, 146, 175

Cultural Revolution (Chinese) 277n23

culture, state 11, 172–3

Daladier, Premier Edouard 159, 169

Dami, Aldo 36, 216n46

Dandieu, Arnaud 15, 30–2, 38, 42, 62–4, 67, 72, 75–6, 79–80, 82–3, 85–7, 94, 109–10, 127, 152, 154, 186; admired for his *Proust*, 214n18; and Bataille 233n92; deathbed conversion 233n92

Daniélou, Charles 61

Daniélou, Cardinal Jean 27, 61, 202n7

Daniélou, Catherine (Izard) 66

Daniélou, Madeleine 61

Daniel-Rops, Henri (Henri Petiot) 16, 30–2, 54, 63, 65, 76, 79, 81, 83, 87, 93, 95, 108, 111, 113–16, 128, 146–7; and de Gaulle 206n15, 272n9; Marc's opinion of 233n98

Dautry, Raoul 103–4, 151

Day, Dorothy 190, 218n77

Daye, Pierre 168

Déat, Marcel 35, 110, 141–2, 163, 168–9

Degrelle, Léon 126, 128–9, 133, 137–8, 140, 143

Déléage, André 63, 109, 144, 150, 163, 271n85

Delestre, Antoine 274n14

Delors, Jacques 9; hommage to Mounier 205n11, 208n41, 275n119

Democracy (liberal) 6, 11, 20, 35, 75, 77, 88, 106–8, 120–1, 123, 138, 151, 157–8, 163, 165–6, 171, 174, 178, 180, 183, 187, 193–4, 196, 200; Delors on 275n119

Depression, the Great 46

Derrida, Jacques 94; and Heidegger 232–3nn92–4

Desclée de Brouwer 61, 127, 131, 138; provide Mounier's office 213n6; withdraw support 255n86

Desjardin, Paul 67; "Decades" colloquia 234n15

Detœuf, Auguste 151

*Deutsche Rundschau* 45

*Deutsche Studentenschaft* 103

*Deutsch-Franzosische Monatsheft/Cahiers Franco-Allemands* 103, 137–9, 141–3

Didier, Edouard and Lucienne (the "Didier salon") 129–33, 135–6, 138, 140, 144–5; and the Zoute meeting 265n98

Distelbarth, Paul 257n110

Domenach, Jean-Marie 9, 190–1; and GRECE 278n30

Dominican fathers 17, 19, 27, 69, 80–2, 104–5, 107, 109, 111–19, 128, 134, 147, 168, 172, 176, 192; elite schools 261n161; internal politics of 230n41; under police surveillance 243n125

Dominicé, Max 27

Dominique, Pierre 123

Doriot, Jacques 5, 35, 57, 102, 106, 111–12, 123, 145, 151, 155

Dossiers de l'Action Populaire 119

Dostoevsky, Fiodor 152

Dreyfus case 35

Dries, Jean 186, 277n21

Drieu la Rochelle, Pierre 10, 64, 75, 78, 112, 131, 141, 267n3

Du Bos, Charles 26, 29, 32; and origins of personalism 205n12

Ducatillon, OP, Father 146

Du Moulin de Labarthète, Henri 179

Dunoyer de Segonzac, Pierre 9, 175, 177, 181–2

Dupuis, René 41, 64, 75, 77, 83–4, 87, 101; Marc's relationship with 227n10, 228n19, 250n13

Dupuy, Jean 236n34

Duveau, Georges 66, 116, 163

Ecole Centrale 114

Ecole des Mines 108

Ecole des Roches (Verneuil) 174

Ecole Nationale d'Administration (ENA) 182

Ecole Normale Supérieure 113, 119

Ecole Polytechnique 107–8, 151, 173, 175, 198

ecological movement (the "greens") 10–11, 107, 120, 148–50

ecumenism 27, 213n65

Editions du Cerf 113, 241n100, 261n168

Editions du Seuil 82, 118, 147, 161, 172–3, 182, 190–1

Eglise Catholique Orthodoxe de France 27

Eliot, T.S. 263n198

Ellul, Jacques 9–10, 120, 124, 148–50; and Mounier's "fascism" 186n262, 249n200; and technological society 262n176

Emmanuel, Pierre 174
engineers 11, 107, 151,
166, 188
Equipes sociales 95, 172
Escriva de Balaguer, Mon-
signor Josemaria 192
*Esprit* 8–9, 14–15, 18, 21,
26, 42, 53–4, 56, 60–3,
65, 67–70, 73, 75, 79,
81, 91, 96–9, 101–2,
109, 113–16, 118–19,
121–2, 125–8, 132–4,
136–9, 141–4, 149, 151,
158–68, 170, 174–5,
177, 179–80, 190–1,
196; circulation growth
(1936), 249n201;
founding of 203n5; and
"frontisme" 266n236;
and GRECE 278n30;
*Journal Intérieur* 207n29,
258n132; post-war trans-
formation 278n29; spu-
rious split with ON
240n78, 246n166,
247n177
*Esprit Nouveau, L'* (de
Becker) 128–30, 144,
250n14
*Esprit Nouveau, L'* (Le Corbusier) 34, 68, 126
Estebe (group) 166, 169
Ethiopia (Italian invasion
of) 107, 143, 146; pre-
vents meeting with Mus-
solini 236n36
Etzioni, Amitai 278n38
Eurasian party (Prague)
43
European College of Fed-
eralist Studies 204n263
*Europe en formation, L'* 16
Europe, eastern 16
European New Right, the
185–200
*Europe nouvelle, L'* 253n61
European University (Flo-
rence) 9, 267n15
Europeanist movement
125–6, 132, 134–5, 140,
150, 161, 168, 182,
192–3

existentialism (*Existenzphilosophie*) 6, 13, 20,
29, 33, 104–6, 162,
182–3, 187; origins of
term 213n2

Fabrègues, Jean de 8,
20–1, 24–5, 101–2, 121,
123, 162–6, 178–80,
191, 274n106; and Mit-
terrand 274n108
Faisceau, Le 34, 36, 65
Faisceau universitaire
36
Fascism: "anti-fascist" 18,
122, 157; French 11,
33–8, 84, 110, 168, 195;
Italian 17, 36, 63, 69,
76, 83, 92, 101–2, 105,
115, 137, 142, 146,
177, 180, 188–9, 191–2;
"white" 10, 14, 22, 181,
189–90, 195, 199
Fascist Congress on Cor-
porations 121, 135–6;
Marc's view of 237n44,
254n75
fascist socialism (Drieu la
Rochelle) 141
Faulconnière, Château de
la (school) 175
February 6, 1934 (riots
of) 18, 92, 97–9,
106–7, 108–10, 118,
128, 174
federalism, federalists 11,
16, 37, 39, 46, 59, 64,
80, 101, 113, 125, 135,
138, 142, 153, 155–6,
182, 186, 189, 193–4,
198–9; post–World War
II 217n58; triumph of
275n18
*fédérateurs, fédérés*, 19, 150,
162, 164, 166–7,
169–70; origins of,
265nn222, 229, 268n48
"Fédération des groupe-
ments non-conform-
istes," 154–5
Fédération du port de
Calais 115

Fernandez, Ramon 112,
131, 234n15
*Feuilles Libres* 165
film (cinema) 10–11,
33–4, 61, 112, 170,
174, 180; René Clair
(role of) 215n32
Flamand, Paul 10,
116–20, 160–1, 164,
169–70, 172–3, 190;
early publishing initia-
tives 244nn137, 142;
and *La Flèche* 244n38;
urges spirituality on ON
245n147
La Flèche 106, 111,
122–3, 151–9, 161, 165,
167, 169–70; Amis de
*La Flèche* 264n218
Folliet, Joseph 113, 160,
167, 241n103, 242n108
Fouilloux, Etienne
258n121
Fraisse, Paul 276n2
*France Catholique, La* 8
*France vivante* 166
Francis, Robert 100, 135
Frankfurt European Youth
Congress 43–50, 63
Frankfurt, University of
104, 137–8, 142
Free French, the 177,
181, 246n163
Frégault, Guy 123,
248n192
Freiburg-im-Breisgau, Uni-
versity of 23, 65, 86, 150
Freikorps 74
Frenay, Captain Henri 9,
182, 275n115
French National Radio
System 8
Frick, Wilhelm (German
minister of the interior)
142
Fried, Ferdinand 54–5,
222n19
Front national syndicaliste
109, 239n75
Front Social ("Frontisme")
101, 111, 118, 122,
152–3, 157, 180

Front unique de la jeunesse européenne 38, 40
*Führerprinzip* 79, 99, 155, 187–8, 199
Fumaroli, Marc 271n82
Fumet, Stanislas 147, 167

Gadoffre, Gilbert 147, 261n161, 272n92
Gait, Maurice 172, 179
Galéjade, La ("Free University") 153–5
Galey, Louis-Emile 61, 101, 111, 116, 122, 144, 150, 163, 172, 180
Gandillac, Maurice de 237n42
Gap (non-conformist meetings) 158–9
Garric, Robert 95, 172
Garrigou-Lagrange, OP, Reginald 192
Garrone, Louis 174
Gaucher, François 172
Gaulle, Charles de 4, 7–9, 15, 57, 81, 102, 108, 110–11, 114, 145, 169, 191, 193, 195; and *Sept* 240n81; and Marc 270n74, 272n91
Gegner 18, 41, 44, 46, 47, 49–50, 60, 65–6, 72–6, 88, 92, 103, 156; context of 221n103
*Gemeinschaft* 134, 142
Georg, Stefan (Kreis) 186–7, 276n10
German Catholic Centre party 55
German New Right 196–7
German Student Exchanges Office 130
German Youth Movements 6, 11, 13, 30, 33, 43, 49–50, 52, 56, 70, 76, 83, 97, 115, 156, 183, 188–9, 191; new scholarship on 203n6
Geschke, Hans 269n59
Gibrat, Robert 98, 108,

111, 122; in Vichy government 239n69
Gide, André 64, 154, 189, 264n218
Gillet, Father Lev 27
Gillouin, René 177
Gilson, Etienne 113–14, 120; faulted for endorsing invasion of Ethiopia 260n154
Giraudoux, Jean 176
Glachant, Charles-Edouard 25, 212n57
Goebbels, Josef 51, 57, 65
Goering, Herman 57, 98, 103
Gray Corps 45, 49; speaks through *Gegner* 229n37
GRECE: *see* Groupement de recherche et d'étude pour la civilisation européenne
Grégoire, Marcel (*La Cité chrétienne*) 129; at Didier salon 252n49
Grenier, Jean 157, 174
Grenoble 20, 175–6, 182, 275n116
*Gringoire* 169
Gropius, Walter 36
Groupement de recherche et d'étude pour la civilisation européenne (GRECE) 9, 191, 193–5; meeting of 278n34
"Groupements Non-Conformistes" (1939) 270n73
Groupement Universitaire Franco-Allemand (GUFA) 26
Guerry, Monsignor Emile 114; and Mounier 242n115
Guevara, Ernesto ("Ché") 198
Guillemin, Henri 113, 157
Guitton, Jean 180

Hachette (publishing house) 25, 41

Halévy, Daniel 64, 110
Hambresin, Emile 130, 141
Hamburg International Congress on Workers' Vacations 139
Hayon, Albert (syndicalist) 119
hébértisme 176
Heidegger, Martin 13, 23, 31, 33, 60, 65, 82, 86–7, 94, 104–5, 150, 156, 161, 187, 198; and Dandieu 231n64; Marc's memory of 211n53
Hélisse, Eugenia 81
Herder, Johann Gottfried von 196; Charles Taylor and Isaiah Berlin on 278n31
Hervé, Gustave 35
Hitchens, Christopher 276n9
Hitler, Adolf 4, 5, 15–18, 22–4, 36, 39, 41, 43, 48, 51–2, 54, 56, 71, 73–6, 83, 88, 93, 99, 116, 122, 124, 126–7, 132–3, 137–8, 140–1, 144, 153, 156, 183, 187, 193, 199
Hitlerjugend 6, 74, 99, 101, 105, 126, 131, 139, 141, 177; contact with the non-conformists (1936) 256nn90,94,95, 98
Hoffmann, Peter C. 276n10
Hoffmann, Stanley 205n11
Holocaust, the 186, 197, 276n8
Hourdin, Georges 65, 115, 256n112, 268n111
Homer 52
*Homme Nouveau, L'* (Paul Marion, neo-socialist) 100–1, 136, 141; and de Becker 254n75
*Homme Réel, L'* (syndicalist) 121, 136, 141, 151

homosexuals, homosexuality 44, 89, 192
Honegger, Arthur 34, 154, 264n218
Hourdin, Georges 167
Hours, Joseph 177
Howard, Dick 277n23
Humeau, Edmond 131
Hurtubise, Claude 245n154
Husserl, Edmund 13, 23, 31, 33, 83, 150; Marc's memory of 209n46, 210n47
Huysmans, Joris-Karl 80

Idées (review) 179–81
Indépendance Belge, L' (Spaak) 14
Information Sociale, L' 121
Institut Européen des Hautes Etudes Internationales (Nice) 16
Institute for Advanced Study (Princeton) 161
International Summer University (Marc) 152
Islam 8, 9, 194; GRECE and the non-conformists and 278n31
Iswolsky, Hélène 218n77
Izard, Georges 61, 64, 66, 98, 106, 118–19, 122, 124, 132, 144, 150–1, 163–4; and Marc 247n187

Jardin, Jean 10, 15, 41, 76, 79, 84, 103, 107–8, 123, 151, 181, 186; at Vichy 205n12, 274n112; as executive assistant 217n69, 237n46
Jaspers, Karl 47, 104; and Marc 213n7, 231n64
Jesuit fathers 17, 53, 80, 85–6, 119, 134, 176; reticence about personalism 245n158; and Marc 259n146
Jesus Christ 146, 188

Jeune Europe, le front européen pour les Etats-Unis d'Europe 132–2, 136–9, 144, 161; growth of 252n50
Jeune France 8, 10, 118, 172–3, 176, 179, 190; uses Mounier's ideas on culture 271nn81–3
Jeune République 166
Jeunes 151
Jeunes Groupes Duboin 150
Jeunesse agricole chrétienne 117
Jeunesse ... France! 177
Jeunesse et socialisme 150
Jeunesse ouvrière chrétienne (JOC: jocistes) 117, 146
Jeunesses patriotes 101
Jews: attitudes toward, 3, 4, 19, 35, 53, 58, 87, 103, 113, 129–30, 144, 146–7, 162, 172–3, 178, 186, 188; Esprit opposition to anti-Semitism 258n129; Uriage exclusion of 274n114
Joan of Arc, St 6, 132, 177
John-Paul II, Pope (Karol Wojtyla) 9, 14, 22, 183, 192; and Scheler 211n55; personalism of 209n42
Journal intérieur des groupes d'amis d'Esprit 150
Jouvenel, Bertrand de 37, 100–2, 112; meets Hitler Youth 253n64
Jouy-en-Josas (Esprit congresses) 149, 157
Juin 1936 166
Jungdeutscher Orden 47
Junger, Ernst 47, 49, 74, 276n3
Juvisy community (Dominicans) 27, 81–2, 112, 120, 134

Kant, Kantianism 6
Karlsruhe 25, 99, 137
Keller, Thomas 12
Kerensky 59
Kessler, Nicolas 201n1
Kierkegaard, Søren 29, 32; and existentialism 213n3
Klemperer, Klemens von 52
Kolbe, Maximilien 192
Komsomol 41
Kovaleski, Father Eugraphe 27
Kraft durch Freude (organization) 74

Labriolo, Arturo 35
Lacroix, Jean 8, 9, 132, 157, 176, 242n177, 272n94
Lagardelle, Hubert 39, 121, 151, 254n75; and Plans 33–7
Lamirand, Georges 20, 172
Lamour, Philippe 16, 33–8, 40, 43, 45–6, 49, 64–5; and Pax-Press 212n57; as orator 216n52
Landsberg, Paul-Ludwig 23, 119, 152, 157; Paul Ricœur and 211n55
La Noue du Vair, Chef de 182
Lapie, Pierre-Olivier 54, 110
Lasch, Christopher 196
Latour-Maubourg (Dominicans of) 147
Laval, Pierre 15, 47, 103, 179, 181, 274n112; hostile to Uriage, 272n93
League of Nations 87
Leclercq, Abbé Jacques 125–30, 132–3
Leenhardt, Roger 173
Lefebvre, Henri 64
Lefranc, Georges 169
Léger, Fernand 34, 36

Légion nationale Belge 251n24
*Le Monde* 9, 16
Lenin (Leninism) 13, 34, 41, 132
Leopold III (King) 169
Le Pen, Jean-Marie (Le Penists) 196
Lévinas, Emmanuel 235n21
Ley, Robert 74
*Libération* 108
Librarie Nationale 36
Liebe, Dr Max 133, 137, 141, 143, 168, 171
Liège, University of 134
Lignac, Xavier de (Jean Chauveau) 8, 108, 119, 145, 152, 154; and Air France 247n185; and de Gaulle 206n15; and Marc 239n71
Ligue d'Action 98
Lippens, Count 139
Lipiansky, Mark (father of Alexandre) 22, 209n44
Lohest, Albert 145
Loubet del Bayle, Jean-Louis 201n1, 217n73, 271n81, 274n108
Loustau, Robert 84, 98, 108, 110–12, 122–3, 145, 151, 155, 172, 178; in the Vichy government 239n69; as "personalist fascist" 240n90
Louvain University 128–30, 132
Lubac, SJ, (Cardinal) Henri de 9, 177; at Vatican II 202n7; at Uriage 272n94
Luchaire, Jean 10, 26, 30–1, 37; and *Pax-Press* 212n57
Lufthansa 40, 46
Lustiger, (Cardinal) Archbishop Jean-Marie 205n11
Lycée Condorcet 31

Lycée français (Brussels) 135
Lycée Saint-Louis 22, 24

Madaule, Jacques 151
Maggiani, L. 162
Maistre, (Count) Joseph de 191
Malraux, André 123, 152
Man, Henri de 23, 35, 116, 121, 125, 137, 140–1, 144–5, 149, 152, 159, 167–9, 171; political career 270n69
Man, Paul de 9, 205n13
Marc, Alexandre: in Aix, 261n165; attitude toward ON group 263n207, 264n217, 278n37; Bergery 261n166, 264n214; Federalist movement 206n16; flees to Switzerland 273n103; Hitler remembered 211n56; infiltrating Amis d'*Esprit* 271n86; infiltrating Amis de *La Flèche* 264n218; "Letter to Hitler" 231–2n71, 248n188; marriage 261n167; memory 276n1; and Mounier 223n46; personalism 217n60; post-war publications, 206n18; Schulze-Boysen remembered 211n56, 217n60; and *Sept* 229n40; and sex 229n40; and Uriage 224n72
Marc, (Mme) Suzanne (Jean) 15, 67, 81, 147, 188, 277n15; and her Lipiansky in-laws 209n43; marriage, 261n167
Marcel, Gabriel 16, 26, 29, 31–3, 60–1, 64, 78–9, 95, 105, 154, 157, 174; and *Esprit* origins 213n6

Mariaux, Franz 44–5
Marion, Paul (neo-socialist) 21, 100–1, 111, 136, 141, 179, 180–1
Maritain, Jacques 4, 6, 24, 60–4, 67–8, 99, 113–14, 116, 119, 121, 125–31, 133–5, 138–9, 145, 147, 154, 157, 189, 201n4; break with the personalists 255n87, 273n103; marriage 225n78
Maritain, Raissa 130, 201n4; *mariage blanc* 225n78
Marrou, Henri-Irénée 25, 174
Marxism, Marx 3, 10–11, 16, 30, 35, 42, 55–6, 59, 63, 69, 71, 78, 84, 105, 112, 120, 129, 149, 152, 189
Masons (franc-maçons) 3, 19, 129, 172–3
Masreel, Franz 34
Massis, Henri 100, 135, 178
mathematicians 188, 198, 267n18
Matignon agreements 123–4, 138
Mauduit, Antoine 274n109
Maulnier, Thierry 8, 64, 78, 85, 100, 102, 123, 135, 156, 165, 168, 196; avoided by ON 248n195
Mauriac, Claude 151
Mauriac, François 79, 114, 146–7
Maurras, Charles 24, 31, 60–1, 114, 117, 119, 135, 147, 178
Maury, Pierre 27
Maxence, Jean-Pierre (*Gringoire*) 65, 100, 169
Maximisme 166
May 1968 197
Maydieu, OP, Jean 105, 113–15, 119, 238n53; directing *Sept* 243n120;

at Uriage 246n163, 261n162; on deportation memorial 242n109

Mayet-de-Montagne ("Ecole Nationale des Cadres civiques") 179

Maze, Jean (*La Flèche*) 148, 156–7, 159, 161, 169–70, 172, 180; Amis de *La Flèche* 218n264; interacting with Marc 269n52; at Vichy 269n52

Mazowiecki, Tadeusz 22, 183; and "Polish *Esprit*" 209n42

McGill University 12

McIntyre, Alasdair 196, 278n38

Médecin, Jacques 16, 194, 199

Merleau-Ponty, Maurice 124, 149, 249n200

Mèves, Eugene 98

Milhaud, Darius 154

*Milice*, the 8, 11, 180, 182

Millet, Raymond 142, 148, 246n165

Millet, R.-P. 109, 119

Mitrinovic, Dimitrije 67, 225n80, 226n81

Mitterrand, François 3, 7–10, 21, 156, 165, 182, 190–1, 195; and *Combat* 274n108; and Fabrègues 274n108; and Mounier 275n117

Mocidade portuguesa (Portuguese Youth Movement) 176–7, 272n95

Mohler, Armin 58

*Monde, Le* 182, 190–1

*Le monde à l'envers* 166

Montmaur, Château de 274n109

Moosmann, André 26, 44, 208n36

Moré, Marcel 152

Morin, Jacques-Yvan 208n41

Moulin, Jean 275n115

Moulin, Leo 133, 139

Moulin-Vert, Club du 17, 77

Mounier, Emmanuel 9, 10, 15–16, 20, 31, 42, 60–4, 68–70, 79, 82–3, 97, 101–2, 104–5, 119–20, 123, 126–32, 134–5, 138–9, 141–4, 148–53, 157–8, 160–2, 167, 170, 173, 176, 189–90; confronts Marc and ON 223n55, 226n87; edited diaries 251n33, 256n92; and Hitler Youth 238n58–9; managing his memory 257n101, 267n13; as originator of personalism 205n11; remembering de Becker 266n10; romanticizing background 241n102; and Otto Strasser 234n8; and Georges Valois 234n9

Mounier, Paulette (Leclercq) 131, 135, 190–1, 277n24; managing historical memory 277nn24–5

Mouvement Travailliste Français (Gibrat-Loustau) 111

*Mouvements* 54, 63

Mumford, Lewis 225n80

Munich agreements 36, 107, 145, 160, 167, 266n236

Munich (city) 23

"Murs Blancs," Les (community: Chatenay-Malabry) 160, 190–1, 224, 251n32, 253n83, 261n162, 264n63, 275n119; managing historical memory 277nn25–6

Musée de l'Homme 174

music (composition, composers) 33–4, 60, 174, 188

Mussolini, Benito 5, 35–7, 48, 76, 78, 88–9, 91, 102, 132, 135, 146

Mystical Body of Christ (doctrine of) 69

*Nación, La* 67; Marc's essays in 231n49

National-Bolsheviks 14, 48, 52, 58, 73

National-Communism 54–6, 192

National Revolution (of Vichy): *see* revolution

National Revolutionaries 74

Naurois, (abbé) René de 105, 120, 246n163, 272n94

Nazis (Nazism, national socialism): Belgian 160, 167, 183; French 18, 65–6, 122, 151, 156, 159, 171; German 5, 7–8, 11, 21, 38, 41, 52, 82, 88, 124, 129, 131, 135–6, 138, 142, 146, 155, 160, 173, 178; "left-wing," 14, 40–1, 48–9, 51–70, 76; original ("pure") 143, 167, 183–4, 186–8, 193–5, 197, 199

Nef, La 166

neo-radicals 18

neo-socialists 18, 20, 84, 110, 132, 136, 144, 167

Neumann, Otto 60–3, 67–70, 79, 105, 127, 133, 140, 188; fictitous obituary 226n95

New Britain 65, 67, 82, 85, 245n155, 252n45

New Left 195–7

"new man," the 72–3, 75, 86–7, 96, 106, 141, 156, 173–4, 178–9, 181, 183–4, 189

"New Middle Ages" 3, 8, 13–14, 22, 25, 62, 69, 120, 126, 189; Berdyaev's book 208n39

"New Order" 5, 8, 10, 14, 18, 23, 25, 27, 38, 40, 42, 63, 73, 76, 88, 90–3, 97–8, 106–8, 110, 116–17, 127, 136, 140, 142–3, 145, 152, 156–8, 161, 163, 166, 168, 170–1, 178, 192–3
New Right 5, 7, 9, 11, 16, 25, 66, 69, 100, 102–3, 106, 135, 156, 165
Nicaise, Henri 126, 129, 133, 136–7, 141, 252n44, 257n105
Nice 12, 16, 194
Niekisch, Ernst 49, 52, 60, 74, 219n95; agreement with Mussolini 227n14; edited by Alain de Benoist 220n98; opposes the Yankee spirit 220n100
Nietzsche, Friedrich (Nietzschean) 6, 10, 14, 21, 29–32, 35, 39, 62–3, 68–9, 75, 78–81, 90, 106, 128, 143, 152, 186–8, 194–5, 199; and Hitler 276n14
"Night of the Long Knives" 58, 98
Nizan, Paul 64–6, 70, 123, 145; and de Rougemont 224n65
Noël, Emile 9, 161, 276n2
"non-conformistes," non-conformism 9, 10, 14, 16, 28, 31, 34, 40, 42–3, 48, 56, 58–9, 72, 74, 75–6, 79, 95, 98, 100, 102, 104–6, 109, 112, 115, 118–19, 123–4, 136, 141–2, 144–6, 148–9, 151, 154, 156–9, 162–3, 165, 167, 169, 172, 178–80, 183, 186–9, 191–200
Northern League (Umberto Bossi) 218n81

Noth, Ernst Erich 167, 269n55
Notre Temps: la revue des nouvelles générations 26, 30
Nouveaux Cahiers (Detœuf) 151, 159, 162, 164–5
Nouveau Siècle (of Valois) 38
Nouvel Age (Valois) 123, 150, 154–4, 162, 164, 166, 265n222, 268n40
Nouvelle Revue Française (NRF) 16, 33, 63–6, 84, 91
Nouvelles Equipes Françaises (syndicalist) 109, 162, 165, 239n75

Ollivier, Albert 8, 109, 119; and the RPF 206n15
Ollivier, Louis 119
Opus Dei 192
Order of the Companions of Péguy 176
Ordre Nouveau (movement) 7, 17, 29, 38, 42, 51, 54, 56, 62, 64, 72, 85, 97, 146, 151, 153, 159, 162–4, 167, 169–70, 177, 186; contact with Esprit 248n195; infiltrating groups 249n195; interest in extra-parliamentary movements 240n88; meeting Nazis in Paris 253n62; Nazi interest in 258nn127–8
Ordre Nouveau, L' (review) 14, 26, 75–8, 81, 84, 95, 103, 107, 109–10, 114, 121–2, 125, 127–9, 132, 136, 141–2, 150, 152, 155–6, 158, 162, 164–5, 174–5; German interest in 236n40; growth 243n127
Ordre Réel, L' (Paul Chanson) 154, 162, 164, 265nn221,225

Ortega y Gasset, José 32
Orwell, George 149, 151
Ouest (Poulet, Daye) 168

Pacelli, Cardinal 117
pacifism 38, 99, 126, 133, 136, 150, 168, 252nn44,49; La Flèche, 262n205
Paris, Henri (comte de) 108, 123
parliamentarianism 152–3, 156–7, 178
Parti fasciste révolutionnaire 34
Parti Frontiste (Bergery) 19, 106, 135, 144, 150, 152–3, 155, 162, 166
Parti Ouvrier Belge (Belgian Workers' Party) 132, 135, 138, 167
Parti populaire français 57, 106, 112, 123, 151, 180
Parti social français (PSF) 5, 108
Pau (convent) 15, 115, 117, 149–50, 243n121
Paulhan, Jean 64
Pax-Press 24–5, 31
peasants 11, 115–17, 173, 176
Pechel, Rudolf 45, 219nn86–7
Péguy, Charles 61, 69, 110, 115, 167, 173, 176, 187
Pélorson, Georges 169, 172, 270n73
Perret, Jacques 162
Perroux, François 105, 116, 124, 145, 149, 151–2, 157, 167, 179; and memory 277n56
personalism, personalist, 5, 9, 12, 14–15, 24, 31, 40, 42–3, 49, 60, 62–6, 70, 75–6, 80, 82–3, 89–90, 92, 94, 96, 103, 105, 111, 119, 122, 126–8, 138–43, 151,

157, 159, 163, 170,
173–4, 178, 182–3, 190,
199; definition of
204n7; origins of
212n62, 213n2
Personalist Manifesto
(1936) 124, 137, 141,
148
Pétain, Marshal Philippe
57, 106, 110, 171, 175,
177, 179; regime of 7,
10,15, 20, 56, 121
Petitjean, Armand 172
Peuple, Le 132
phenomenology 13, 20,
31, 33, 149, 183
Philip, André 132
Pierre, Abbé 277n15
Pierrefeu, François de
151, 246n164, 254n75
Pillias, Emile 98, 143
Pineau, Christian (syndi-
calist) 109
Pius IX, Pope 191
Pius XI, Pope 60, 70
Pius XII, Pope 117, 143,
147
"Plan du Travail" (of
Henri de Man) 132,
137–8
planists, the 101, 109,
141, 173, 175
Plans 14, 26, 33–40,
42–3, 47–9, 53–4, 56,
60–1, 63, 81, 87, 109,
112, 114, 121, 271n86;
Amis de Plans 40; and
Schulze-Boysen 216n50;
publishes Black Front
manifesto 272n87
Plaquevent, Père Jean 80,
82, 150; houses Marc in
Pau 243n121; reports
Marc's conversion
228n34; visits non-
conformist communi-
ties, 245n160
Poland 22, 182, 192;
Esprit links with 209n42
Pontigny (Abbey of)
(Décades) 67, 246n171
Popular Front 11, 18, 97,

104–7, 117, 119, 121,
124, 136, 138, 140, 152
Portugal 175–6
Poulet, Robert 168
Préludes (successor to
Plans) 109
Prévost, Pierre 66,
118–19, 154, 160–1,
165, 169–70
Prezzolini 48
Primard, Eugène 98, 116;
backs Esprit, 245n159,
250n10; and ON
260n153, 268n36
Primo de Rivera, José
Antonio 14, 85, 181;
and Marc's ON 203n4
proletariat 35
propaganda 21
Protestants, Protestantism
80, 120
Proudhon, Pierre-Joseph
66, 151
Proust, Marcel 144
Psichari, Ernest 189
Pucheu, Pierre 179
Pury, Roland de 27

Quadragesimo Anno
(encyclical) 70

racism, racialism 10, 39,
43, 58, 92, 105, 139,
141–4, 161, 181,
183, 193–5, 198–9
Radical party 84
Radio Brussels 171
Radio Jeunesse 170, 172–3
Rassemblement du Peuple
français (RPF) 8, 15,
109, 193, 195
Rathenau, Walther 75
Réaction pour l'ordre 24,
274n106
Recherches philosophiques
265n221
Red Orchestra: see Die
Rote Kapelle
regionalism 42–3, 73, 77,
121
Reichstag fire 53, 72,
74–5, 90

Relève, La (Canadian
journal) 245n154
Rémond, René 189, 195,
260n156
Réseau International des Historiens du Fédéralisme et
du personnalisme (1992-)
267n15
Resistance (the French)
7–8, 16, 190, 273n103;
of Catholic hierarchy
246n162; "Pétainist"
resistance 275n115; of
progressive Catholics
278n29
Rethel (youth meeting)
38
Revah, I.S. 119
revolution: the Christian
(de Becker) 134; the
French (1789) 3, 34,
64, 66, 84, 92, 196; the
French National (1940)
12, 20, 34, 64, 83–4,
106, 109, 121, 124,
156, 162, 172, 176,
179, 181, 186, 191,
195; the German Con-
servative 3, 16, 21, 43,
45, 47, 63, 117, 183,
194, 199; the German
National Socialist 117;
the national Catholic
(de Becker) 129; the
Russian 22, 196; "of the
twentieth century" 135,
143, 163, 175
Révolution prolétarienne, La
166
Revue d'Allemagne 54
Revue des jeunes 95
Revue du Siècle 24, 109
Rex (originally Christus
Rex) 126, 137–40,
143
Reynaud, Paul 110
Rhineland, remilitariza-
tion of 122, 129,
137
Ribbentrop, Joachim von
14, 98, 103, 129, 139,
144, 168; coins the

term "New Order"
202n2
Ricœur, Paul 9; and
Landsberg 211n55
Riefenstahl, Leni 181
Rocque, Colonel François
de la 57, 106, 108–10,
114–15, 146; and ON
239n78
Rohn, Erich 89
Romier, Lucien 123,
249n196
Ronchamps (church) 9
Roosevelt, Franklin
Delano 83, 156,
265n230
Rossoni 102
Rote Kapelle, Die (Red
Orchestra) 219n95,
273n103
Rotoir, Le (commune)
118, 120, 245n160
rouge et noir, Le ("jeunes
révolutionnaires
belges") 252n45
Rougemont, Denis de
8–9, 14, 27, 32, 44,
63–4, 66, 68, 76, 80–1,
84, 103, 105, 119,
121–2, 124, 137–8,
141–3, 146, 148, 150,
154, 157, 167; differ-
ences with Marc
264n220; and ecumeni-
cal movement 204n10;
family background
214–15n21; as historian
of sexuality 204n10,
247n175; as libertine
228n36; memory
276n2, 277n17; and
Nazis 255n89, 257n115,
269n59; as theologian
204n8
Roy, Christian 11–12, 148
royalists 5, 21, 103, 108,
178, 182, 190, 195
Russia 11, 49, 51, 76, 94,
186
Russians, "white" 5, 60

Saint-Cyr 11

Salazar, Antonio 176,
181, 272n95
Saliège, Monsignor Jules
Géraud 120, 246n162
Salomon, Ernst von 74
Sangnier, Marc 99
Sarre, German annexation
of 134
Sartre, Jean-Paul 33, 105,
156, 162, 187
Saulchoir, Le (convent)
27
Sauvageot, Ella 261n168
Schaeffer, Pierre 172–3
Scheler, Max 13, 23,
29–31, 33, 113, 119;
discovered Husserl
210n50; Marc's
encounter with 210n51,
211n54
Schirach, Baldur von 74,
100–1
Schleicher, General Kurt
von 53, 57–8
Schmid, Fred 45, 49, 72
Schmitt, Carl 187
Schultze, M. (Hitler Youth
leader) 139
Schulze-Boysen, Harro 6,
17–18, 37, 40–1, 44,
46–7, 49, 51, 56, 66,
72–5, 91, 97–8, 100,
103, 135, 185, 199; dis-
covers Plans 216n50;
and Gegner 217n66; and
Mannerbund 229n37;
and the Nazi party,
235n28; Die Rote Kapelle
and execution 273n103;
and Soviet Union,
233n2; visits Geneva
237n49; and von
Ribbentrop 237n47
Schumann, Maurice 113
"Sciences Po" (Ecole libre
des sciences politiques )
13, 24, 41, 92, 108, 191
Scouts 7, 101, 172–3, 177
Second Vatican Council
9, 82, 190, 192; and
theologians, 202n7
Section Française de

l'Internationale
Ouvrière (SFIO) 144,
163, 168; see also socialists, socialism
self, sense of (Western)
10, 278n3
Senarclens, Pierre de
277n24
Sept 19, 27, 81, 106,
109–18, 120, 123, 128,
132, 145–8, 158–9,
166–7, 170, 196; Amis
de Sept 242n110,
260n160; circulation
growth 244n140,
248n194; and Ethiopian
invasion 260n155;
profile of supporters
244n139, 248n193;
silencing of 260n149
Serruys, Yvonne 81
Sertillanges, Père Antonin
Gilbert 113
service civil (Ordre
Nouveau's) 86–7,
246n168
Service d'Ordre Légion-
naire (SOL) 21, 180,
274n109
sexuality 81, 189, 198,
204n10, 229n40,
247n175
Shutz, Brother Roger
(Taizé community) 176
Shutzstaffel (SS) 58
Simon, Pierre-Henri 8,
113, 116, 147, 167,
169, 191; lectures for
fédérés 267n22,
269n54
Simon, Yves R. 157,
201n3
SNCF (French National
Railways System) 5, 151
socialism 59, 73, 116,
121, 136, 139, 190;
"national anti-Marxist"
(Perroux) 145
Socialist Revolutionaries
(SR) (Russian) 39
socialists (French) 5, 10,
19, 35, 102, 106, 117,

122, 146, 151, 173, 182, 195

Société de Saint-Louis, La 82, 116–20, 123, 131, 147, 176; and ON 260n53

Sohlbergkreis 19–20, 25–8, 43–4, 99, 102, 104–5, 135–8, 148, 167, 171, 181–3, 185; French involved with 236nn33,35; praises the Young Right 253n63; the review *Sohlbergkreis* 234n13

*Soir, Le* 136, 168, 171; portrayal of the "spiritual revolution" 247n182; under the German occupation 205n13

Sombart, Nicolaus 229n37

Sorel, Georges 30, 34–5, 37, 151

Soviet Union 64, 77, 92, 98, 116, 146, 172

Spaak, Paul-Henri 133, 141, 143, 145, 159–60, 167–8

Spanish Civil War 107, 143

Spengler, Oswald 47

Spiritu, Ugo 101–2, 236n37

Stalin, Joseph (Stalinism) 56, 63, 76, 78, 85, 95, 104, 112–13, 116, 143, 194, 197

Sternhell, Zeev 232n71

Strasser, OSB, Father Bernhard 53, 58

Strasser, Gregor 51–60, 75, 98, 101, 143, 192; support for 223n36

Strasser, Dr Otto 18, 40, 42, 48, 51–60, 65, 71, 75, 90, 92, 97–8, 101, 143; evaluation of 222n30

Sturm-Abteilung (SA) 102

Switzerland 15, 181

syndicalists, syndicalism 35, 45, 48, 109, 119, 144, 151

Syria (Battle, June 1941) 177, 274n109

Taizé (community) 176

Tamié (Cistercian abbey of) 126

*Tat, Die*, the *Tat*-Kreis 18, 45, 52, 53–8, 60, 65–6, 92

Teilhard de Chardin, SJ, Pierre 176, 263n186, 261nn25,28

*Telos* 196

*Témoignage Chrétien* 190

*Temps, Le* 121, 168, 182

*Temps présent* 19, 27, 117, 147, 153, 155, 158, 160, 170; Amis de *Temps Présent* 267n22, 268n48; origins 248n194, 261n164

*Terre Wallonnne* 137

theatre 42, 100, 174, 178

theologians, theology 11, 17, 178, 188, 190, 192

"Third Front" 53, 58, 116

"Third Reich" 51, 54, 77, 93, 95, 102, 105, 142, 171

Third Republic, the 170–1, 173–4, 178

Third Way, the 7, 19, 66, 106, 112, 114, 116–22, 124, 128, 133, 140, 147, 166, 174–5, 178, 190, 192, 195

Thomists, Thomism 21, 60, 179, 182, 192

Thule-Seminar 196

*tiers-mondisme* 182, 197–8

Tirpitz, Admiral von 40

Tolkein, J.R.R. 198

Tonnies, Ferdinand 40

totalitarianism 11

Touchard, Pierre-Aimé 152, 157, 162

Tournier, Michel 276n3

Touvier, Paul 213n3, 243n125

trade unions 40, 53, 58, 66, 112, 121, 123, 136, 142, 162, 166, 169–70, 175

*Travail et liberté* 165

Troisième Force ("Third Force") 18, 61, 66–7, 73, 85, 98, 109, 116, 121–2, 132, 135–7, 152, 164, 180; in Brussels, 252n42, 271n85; Manifesto of 227n8; Maritain reservations about 234n12; membership 239n73, 244n144

Trotskyists, Trotsky 45

Turel, Adrien 72

Trudeau, Pierre Elliott 273n46

Ulmann, André 101

Union Nationale des Etudiants 101

Union Sacrée 152

United States, the Americans 3, 8–9, 20, 32, 38–9, 49, 76, 89, 94, 162, 166, 186, 190–1, 193–4, 198–9

Uriage, Château d' ("Château Bayard") 175, 182

Uriage, Ecole Nationale Supérieure des Cadres 8–10, 15, 20, 105, 114, 120, 142, 147, 174–83, 190; memories of 202n5; network 275n116; Order 274n114; personalism of 272n93–4; training youth 273n98

Vallat, Xavier 179

Valle d'Aosta 194, 218n81, 263n204

Valois, Georges 34, 65, 123, 155, 165, 268n40

Van der Bruck, Moeller 51

Van Zeeland, Prime Minister 168

Van Roey, Cardinal Josef Ernest 143
Vatican 147
Vercruysse, Marcel 141, 252n51
Verdier, Cardinal Jean: defends ON to Cardinal Pacelli 244n143
Verne, Jules 111
Versailles, Treaty of 39, 46, 77, 129, 137–8
*Vie Intellectuelle, La* 27, 112
*Vie Spirituelle, La* 112
Vignaux, Paul 252n39
Vincent, René 179, 274n106–7
*Volksgemeinschaft* 75
Volontaires Nationaux 102, 108, 110–11, 122; Izard's interest in 241n91
*Voltigeur français, Le* 157–60, 165, 170
*Vossische Zeitung* 53
Voyant, Joseph 161, 267n14

Voyenne, Bernard 161, 164, 267n16, 268n31
Vuillemin, Roger 176

Walesa, Lech 209n42
Walter, Jeanne 34, 38
*Wandervögel* 26, 43, 148
Weil, Simone 11, 149, 151, 157, 166, 263n198; and Marc 229n39; factory work 262n179; death 246n163
Weimar Republic 30, 41, 45, 51, 57, 86
Westphal, (Pastor) Charles 27
*Widerstand, Der* 48, 60, 74
*Wiez* 209n42
*Wille zum Reich* 103
Winkelmoos camp (with Hitlerjugend) 141
Winock, Michel (as official *Esprit* historian) 277nn25–6

Winter, Pierre, Dr 34
women 187, 192–4, 198
worker-priests 11

X-Crise (Centre polytechnicien d'études économiques) 107–8, 148, 151, 161, 173, 175, 198

Young Right ("Jeune Droite") 21, 24, 49, 78, 101, 109, 121, 169, 190–1

Zehrer, Hans 45, 53, 55–60, 222n27
Zimmer de Cunchy, Alphonse (*L'Esprit Nouveau*) 128, 251n22
*Znak* 182
Zoute camp (with the Hitlerjugend) 139, 144, 183, 256nn90, 94–5, 98